Revolutionary Patriots

of

Anne Arundel County

Maryland

Henry C. Peden, Jr.

HERITAGE BOOKS
2006

HERITAGE BOOKS
AN IMPRINT OF HERITAGE BOOKS, INC.

Books, CDs, and more—Worldwide

For our listing of thousands of titles see our website
at
www.HeritageBooks.com

Published 2006 by
HERITAGE BOOKS, INC.
Publishing Division
65 East Main Street
Westminster, Maryland 21157-5026

Copyright © 1992 Henry C. Peden, Jr.

All rights reserved. No part of this book may be reproduced or transmitted in any form or by any means, electronic or mechanical, including photocopying, recording or by any information storage and retrieval system without written permission from the author, except for the inclusion of brief quotations in a review.

International Standard Book Number: 978-1-58549-204-3

INTRODUCTION

This book has been compiled primarily for the purpose of serving as a "one volume research tool" for identifying the patriots, soldiers, seamen, and civil officers from Anne Arundel County, Maryland who served in the American Revolution between 1775 and 1783, and thereby enabling descendants to join patriotic organizations such as the DAR, SAR, and SR. However, this book is much more than a mere listing of names because many persons named herein also have dates of birth, death, marriage and other genealogical and historical information included within their respective sketches.

Many primary and secondary sources have been researched and information gleaned for this book. The compiler wishes to express his gratitude for the assistance of the staff and librarians at the Maryland State Archives in Annapolis and the Maryland Historical Society in Baltimore. Contributions and advice from Robert W. Barnes and F. Edward Wright are also appreciated.

It is extremely important to mention that many errors were found in the names of those who took the Oaths of Allegiance and Fidelity to the State of Maryland in 1778, as published in the Calendar of Maryland State Papers, Red Book series. With all due respect to that important publication, a check of the original lists uncovered many misspellings and omissions which have been corrected herein (as have other errors found in other published references).

Anne Arundel County can well be proud of the many men and women who rendered material aid, took the Oath of Allegiance, and went forth to serve in the Revolutionary War in the 7th (or Severn), the 22nd (or Elk Ridge) and the 31st (South and West River) Battalions of Militia. It is, indeed, most unfortunate that most militia lists for Anne Arundel County do not exist today. There are, however, a number of lists for those who served from Anne Arundel County in the various companies of the 1st, 3rd, 4th and 6th Maryland Continental Lines. These regimental companies also included men who served from other counties. In 1776 the First Maryland Line consisted of men from Anne Arundel County and Baltimore County. In 1777 the Third Maryland Line consisted of men from Anne Arundel County, Prince George's County, Talbot County, Somerset County, and Harford County. In 1777 the Fourth Maryland Line consisted of men from Baltimore County, Anne Arundel County, Somerset County, and Harford County. The Sixth Maryland Line also consisted of men from Anne Arundel County, Prince George's County, Frederick County, Cecil County, Harford County, and Queen Anne's County. It is suggested, therefore, that if you do not find your ancestor in this book and he served in the regular Army, then consult the Archives of Maryland, Vol. 18, for additional information, as most company rosters do not indicate which county a soldier came from, and although the company captain may have been from Anne Arundel County (and that is a good indication that his men were also from Anne Arundel

County) such is not always the case due to constant change and reorganization during the war.

To assist the researcher, there are also group entries in this book under the headings of Valley Forge, Camp Colonel Scirvin's, First Maryland Regiment, Third and Fourth Maryland Regiments, and Privateers, in which an attempt was made to identify those soldiers and seamen who were from Anne Arundel County. Again, keep in mind that some of these soldiers may not have been from Anne Arundel County, while others who were from Anne Arundel County could have possibly served in any one of the eight Maryland regiments organized and then reorganized during the war between 1776 and 1783. These lists are by no means complete. If a name is not found, consult Archives of Maryland, Volume 18. In addition to the many hundreds of people individually arranged in alphabetical order in this book, there are also separate group lists under the headings of Militia Officer Commissions, and Justices of the Anne Arundel County Court.

Each entry in this book has been documented with primary and secondary sources, and a key to that documentation has been implemented within the text. A letter followed by a number is the code used for a source and the page within that source. For example, "Ref: H-41" indicates that the source or reference is "Archives of Maryland, Volume 18, page 41." There are also additional sources not listed below which have been incorporated into the text itself. The key to the coded sources and documents is as follows:

A = Calendar of Maryland State Papers, The Red Books, No. 4, Part 2 (Annapolis: Hall of Records Commission, 1953).

B = Calendar of Maryland State Papers, The Red Books, No. 4, Part 3 (Annapolis: Hall of Records Commission, 1955).

C = Hodges, Margaret R. Unpublished Revolutionary Records of Maryland, Volume 2 (Baltimore: Privately printed by the Author, 1941).

D = Anne Arundel County Orphans Court Proceedings, 1782-1784 (Original records accessioned at the Maryland State Archives under MdHR4843-1).

E = Original applications approved by the Maryland Society of the Sons of the American Revolution between 1889 and 1990.

F = Warfield, J. D. The Founders of Anne Arundel and Howard Counties (Baltimore: Kohn and Pollock, 1905).

G = Newman, Harry Wright. Maryland Revolutionary Records (Baltimore: Genealogical Publishing Co., 1980, reprint).

H = Archives of Maryland, Vol. 18, "Muster Rolls of Maryland Troops in the American Revolution, 1775-1783" (Baltimore: Maryland Historical Society, 1900).

HCP = Peden, Henry C. Jr. Marylanders to Kentucky, 1775-1825 (Westminster, Maryland: Family Line Publications, 1991).

I = Clements, S. Eugene and Wright, F. Edward. Maryland Militia in the Revolutionary War (Silver Spring, MD: Family Line Publications, 1987).

J = Calendar of Maryland State Papers, The Red Books, No. 4, Part 1 (Annapolis: Hall of Records Commission, 1950).

K = Brumbaugh, Gaius M. Maryland Records: Colonial, Revolutionary, County and Church (Baltimore: Genealogical Publishing Company, 1967, reprint).

L = Burns, Annie W. Maryland Soldiers of the Revolutionary War Who Settled in Kentucky (Baltimore: Unpublished manuscript, 1939).

LU = Lu, Helen M. and Neumann, Gwen B. Revolutionary War Period Bible, Family and Marriage Records, 8 vols. (Dallas: Privately printed, 1980-1988).

M = McGhee, Lucy K. Maryland Pension Abstracts of the Revolution, War of 1812 and Indians Wars (Washington, D.C.: Privately printed, 1966).

MdHR = Maryland Hall of Records (Code to accession numbers to the original manuscripts at the Maryland State Archives).

MS = Maryland Historical Society (Code to the original manuscript).

N = Archives of Maryland, Vol. 11, "Journal of the Convention, July 26 to August 14, 1775, and Journal and Correspondence of the Council of Safety, August 29, 1775 to July 6, 1776" (Baltimore: Maryland Historical Society, 1892).

O = Archives of Maryland, Vol. 21, "Journal and Correspondence of the Council of Maryland, 1778-1779" (Baltimore: Maryland Historical Society, 1901).

P = Papenfuse, Edward C. et al. A Biographical Dictionary of the Maryland Legislature, 1635-1789, 2 vols. (Baltimore: The Johns Hopkins University Press, 1979 and 1985).

Q = Newman, Harry W. Anne Arundel Gentry, Vol. I (Annapolis: Published by the Author in 1970).

R = Newman, Harry W. Anne Arundel Gentry, Vol. II (Annapolis: Published by the Author in 1971).

S = Newman, Harry W. Anne Arundel Gentry, Vol. III (Annapolis: Published by the Author in 1979).

T = Directory of the Maryland State Society, Daughters of the American Revolution and Their Revolutionary Ancestors, 1892-1965 (Maryland State Society, DAR: 1966).

U = Arps, Walter E. Jr. Heirs and Orphans: Anne Arundel County, Maryland Distributions, 1788-1838 (Silver Spring, Maryland: Family Line Publications, 1985).

V = Archives of Maryland, Vol. 16, "Journal and Correspondence of the Council of Safety, January 1 to March 20, 1777," and "Journal and Correspondence of the State Council, March 20, 1777 to March 28, 1778" (Baltimore: Maryland Historical Society, 1897).

W = Archives of Maryland, Vol. 45, "Journal and Correspondence of the State Council of Maryland, 1780 to 1781" (Baltimore: Maryland Historical Society, 1927).

X = Anne Arundel County Certificates of Discharge, 1777-1788 (Original records at the Maryland State Archives accessioned under MdHR9514).

Y = "Revolutionary Doctors of Anne Arundel County," by Dr. Henry J. Berkley in the "Maryland Genealogical Society Bulletin," Vol. 19, No. 4, Fall, 1978, pp. 303-307, and part of an article originally published in the "Maryland Historical Magazine" in March, 1929, Vol. 24, No. 1).

Z = "Maryland Pension Rolls of 1835: Report from the Secretary of War in Relation to the Pension Establishment of the United States." (Baltimore: Genealogical Publishing Company, 1968, reprint of 1835 government report).

Henry C. Peden, Jr., M.A.
Bel Air, Maryland
October 4, 1991

REVOLUTIONARY PATRIOTS OF ANNE ARUNDEL COUNTY, MARYLAND
1775-1783

ADAMS, DANIEL JENIFER. Rezin Beall of Annapolis recommended to the Council of Safety, on August 27, 1776, that "Major Adams be made an officer when the independent companies are incorporated into a battalion" (Ref: A-83).

ADAMS, JOSHUA. Took the Oath of Allegiance before Hon. Nicholas Worthington in March, 1778 (Ref: Maryland State Papers, Red Book No. 21, p. 8D. Note: His name was mistakenly left off the published list found in Ref: B-27).

AKERLY, JOHN. Private in Captain Richard Dorsey's Company of Artillery on November 17, 1777 (Ref: H-574).

ALCOCK, ROBERT. Pensioned on March 4 1831, at age 75, as a Private in the Maryland Militia (Ref: Z-45).

ALDRICH, NATHANIEL. Enlisted in the First Company of Matrosses under Capt. Nathaniel Smith on January 24, 1776; age 21; born in Elk Ridge, Maryland; height: 5' 8 1/4"; occupation not stated. "Nathan Aldridge" was present at Fort Whetstone Point in Baltimore on September 7, 1776 (Ref: H-563, 569).

ALDRIDGE, NICHOLAS. Took Oath of Allegiance before Hon. Thomas Worthington on February 28, 1778 (Ref: B-21). He was commissioned an Ensign in Capt. Basil Burgess' Company in the Elk Ridge Battalion in March, 1779 (Ref: O-333).

ALDRIDGE, ZACHARIAH. He took the Oath of Allegiance before Honorable Thomas Worthington on February 28, 1778 (Ref: B-21).

ALEXANDER, CHARLES. He was recruited in Anne Arundel County in October, 1780 to serve in the Maryland Line for three years (Ref: H-368).

ALLEN (ALLEIN), ADAM. Resident of Herring Creek Church who was among those who petitioned to form a militia company on March 6, 1776 (Ref: I-143). He took the Oath of Allegiance before Hon. Thomas Harwood in February of 1778 (Ref: B-22). Adam was drafted in Anne Arundel County in October, 1780, to serve in the Maryland Line until December 10, 1780 (Ref: H-369).

ALLEN, JOHN. He was enlisted by Capt. Harwood for the 1st Battalion on June 11, 1777, but being "so greatly intoxicated at the time so as to be almost in a senseless condition," he was discharged from serving (Ref: V-283).

ALLEN, JOHN. Private in Captain Gilbert Middleton's Independent Company of Militia of Annapolis on March 20, 1779 (Ref: (I-144, O-325). Deceased by April 2, 1805 when final distribution was made to his widow Susanna Allen and halves of the remaining to Ruth Allen and Azel Allen (Ref: U-29).

ALLINGHAM (ALLENGEM), JOSEPH. Resident of Herring Creek Church who was among those who petitioned to form a militia company on March 6, 1776, and became a Second Lieutenant in Capt. Richard Weems' Company on April 17, 1776 (Ref: F-223, I-143, N-336).

ALLINGHAM (ALLENJEM), STEPHEN. Enlisted by Captain Edward Tillard in July, 1776 for the Maryland Line; born in Maryland; 5' 11" tall (Ref: H-39).

ALTON, JONATHAN. Took the Oath of Allegiance before Hon. Thomas Worthington on February 28, 1778 (Ref: B-21).

ANDERSON, ABSALOM (1731-1787). Married Anne Waters and had eleven children: William Clarke Anderson, Susanna Anderson Silence, Ann Anderson Hall, Robert Anderson, Absalom Anderson, Richard Anderson, James Anderson, Thomas Anderson, Samuel Anderson, Elizabeth Anderson Bealmear and Joshua Anderson (Ref: T-121). Was appointed an Ensign in Capt. Thomas Mullikin's Company on February 22, 1776 (Ref: N-178). First Lieutenant in Capt. Vachel Gaither's Company in the Severn Battalion on June 17, 1776 (Ref: A-176, F-224, N-495; Reference C-202 mistakenly gives his name as "Abraham" in 1778). Took Oath of Allegiance before Hon. Thomas Worthington on Feb. 28, 1778 (Ref: B-21). When final distribution of his estate was made on October 1, 1807, only 8 of his children were mentioned: Robert Anderson, Absalom Anderson, James Anderson, Thomas Anderson, Samuel Anderson, Elizabeth Anderson Bealmear, Joshua Anderson and Ann Anderson Hall (Ref: U-33).

ANDERSON, ANDREW. Took Oath of Allegiance before Hon. Nicholas Worthington in March, 1778 (Ref: B-27).

ANDERSON, JAMES. Took the Oath of Allegiance before Hon. Richard Harwood, Jr. on March 1, 1778 (Ref: B-22).

ANDERSON, JAMES JR. Took Oath of Allegiance before Hon. Nicholas Worthington in March, 1778 (Ref: B-27).

ANDERSON, WILLIAM (c1720 - 1805) His second wife was Sarah Edwards and their son Edward Edwards Anderson (c1776-1836) married Susan Cheney (c1781-1858) in 1797. William Anderson was a Private in 3rd Maryland Regiment in April, 1778 (Ref: E-2946, H-79). Took the Oath of Allegiance before Hon. Nicholas Worthington in March, 1778 (Ref: B-27). When the final distribution of his estate was administered on January 27, 1807, his legacies were the heirs of Mary Williams, Dennis O'Connor, Elizabeth Cheney and O'Neal O'Connor, with fourths of the remaining balance to William Anderson, Samuel Anderson, James Anderson and Edward E. Anderson (Ref: U-31).

ANDRIS, WILLIAM. Took the Oath of Allegiance before Hon. Nicholas Worthington in March, 1778 (Ref: Maryland State Papers, Red Book 21, p. 8D. Note: His name was mistakenly left off the published list found in Reference B-27).

ANGUS, JOHN. Master of the Brig "Delaware" on March 28, 1778 (Ref: V-556).

ANKERS, EDWARD. Took the Oath of Allegiance before Hon. Reuben Meriweather on March 2, 1778 (Ref: B-24).

ANKERS (ANCKERS), SNOWDEN. Took the Oath of Allegiance before Hon. Reuben Meriweather on March 2, 1778 (Ref: B-24). He was the administrator with will annexed of Joseph Deaver in 1806 (Ref: U-31).

ANLEY, JOSEPH. Took the Oath of Allegiance before Hon. Reuben Meriweather on March 2, 1778 (Ref: B-24).

ANNAN (ANNIM), WILLIAM (of Annapolis). He was a physician who was appointed Surgeon's Mate to Col. Hall's Regiment in 1776 (Ref: Y-303).

ANTHONY, NEGRO. Substitute supplied by Thomas Johnson, Jr. on April 30, 1778 to serve for the duration of the war (Ref: C-205).

APPINGSTALL, WILLIAM. Recruited by Capt. Alexander Truman in October, 1780 to serve in the Maryland Line for three years (Ref: H-369).

APPLEBY, BIGNEL. Took the Oath of Allegiance before Hon. Nicholas Worthington in March, 1778 (Ref: Maryland State Papers, Red Book 21, p. 8D. Reference B-27 incorrectly spelled his name "Bigner" Appleby).

ARCHIBALD, ROBERT. Enlisted by John W. Dorsey on July 22, 1776 (Ref: H-39).

ARMIGER, JOHN. He took the Oath of Allegiance before Hon. Samuel Harrison in March, 1778 (Ref: A-244). He was deceased by January 31, 1818, when final distribution of his estate was made to his widow Mary Armiger, with tenths of the remaining balance going to Samuel Armiger, Benjamin Armiger, Thomas Armiger, William Armiger, Richard Armiger, Mary Armiger Carr, Sarah Ann Armiger, Susannah Armiger, John F. Armiger and Rachel Armiger (Ref: U-52).

ARMIGER, WILLIAM. Oath of Allegiance before Hon. Samuel Harrison in March, 1778 (Ref: A-244). Deceased by August 13, 1800 when final distribution of his estate was made to John Armiger, Mary Whittington, William Armiger, Jesse Armiger, Leonard Armiger and Benjamin Armiger (Ref: U-23).

ARNOLD, WILLIAM. Resident of Herring Creek who was among those who petitioned to form a militia company on March 6, 1776, and he subsequently served in Capt. Richard Weems' Company (I-143, MS.1814). Took the Oath of Allegiance before Hon. Samuel Harrison in March, 1778 (Ref: A-244).

ASHEN, MICHAEL. Took the Oath of Allegiance before Hon. Richard Harwood, Jr. on March 1, 1778 (Ref: B-22).

ASHMEAD, JOSEPH (of Annapolis). Took the Oath of Allegiance before Honorable Richard Harwood, Jr. on March 1, 1778 (Ref: B-22).

ASHMORE, CHARLES. Enlisted by Edward Spurrier in July, 1776 (Ref: H-41).

ATKINSON, JOHN. Took the Oath of Allegiance before Hon. John Dorsey on March 12, 1778 (Ref: B-26).

ATKINSON, THOMAS. He was drafted in October, 1780 to serve in the Army until December 10, 1780 (Ref: H-369). James Collins was administrator de bonis non of a Thomas Atkinson and he made final distribution (sixths) on January 29, 1796 to Nathan Atkinson, Rachel Atkinson, Catharine Atkinson, Elizabeth Atkinson, Thomas Atkinson and Francis Atkinson (Ref: U-9).

ATWELL, BENJAMIN. Two men with this name took the Oath of Allegiance: one before Hon. Samuel Harrison in March, 1778 (Ref: A-244), and another before Hon. Thomas Harwood in February, 1778 (Ref: B-22). Benjamin Atwell, Jr. was one of the Herring Creek petitioners to form a militia company on March 6, 1776 and subsequently served in Capt. Richard Weems' Company (Ref: I-143). One Benjamin Atwell was deceased by June 15, 1797 when final distribution of his estate was administered by his widow, Rachel Atwell (thirds), with sixths of the remaining balance to Joseph Atwell, William Atwell, Margaret Atwell, John Atwell, Benjamin Atwell and Sarah Atwell (Ref: U-16).

ATWELL, DANIEL. Took the Oath of Allegiance before Hon. Samuel Harrison, Jr. in March, 1778 (Ref: B-28). William Attwell was administrator de bonis non with will annexed of Daniel Attwell and made final distribution, March 26, 1811, to widow Mary Attwell and these legatees: William Attwell, Robert Attwell's daughter Catherine Attwell; representatives of Benjamin Attwell; Elizabeth Paisley; representatives of Joseph Attwell; the grandchildren of Mary Lavey; and representatives of Samuel Attwell (Ref: U-39).

ATWELL, JOHN. Took the Oath of Allegiance before Honorable Thomas Harwood in February, 1778 (Ref: B-22).

ATWELL, JOSEPH. Took the Oath of Allegiance before Hon. Samuel Harrison, Jr. in March, 1778 (Ref: B-28). One Joseph Atwell was executor of one Joseph Atwell who died by October 27, 1835, when final distribution of his estate was made to widow Elizabeth Atwell, with thirds of the remaining balance to Benjamin Atwell, Elizabeth Atwell and Priscilla Robinson (Ref: U-91).

ATWELL, ROBERT. Resident of Herring Creek who was among those who petitioned to form a militia company on March 6, 1776 and subsequently served in Capt. Richard Weems' Company (Ref: I-143, MS.1814). Robert also took the Oath of Allegiance before Hon. Samuel Harrison in March, 1778 (Ref: A-244).

ATWELL, SAMUEL. Resident of Herring Creek who was among those who petitioned to form a militia company on March 6, 1776 and subsequently served in Capt. Richard Weems' Company (Ref: I-143, MS.1814). Samuel also took the Oath of Allegiance before Hon. Samuel Lane on March 1, 1778 (Ref: B-23).

ATWELL, WILLIAM. Took the Oath of Allegiance before Hon. Samuel Harrison in March, 1778 (Ref: A-244).

AUBER, JOHN. Served as a Male Attendant in Annapolis hospital (Ref: Y-307).

AVERY, JOHN. Took the Oath of Allegiance before Hon. John Dorsey on March 12, 1778 (Ref: B-26).

AYTON, HENRY. One of the petitioners to the Convention of Maryland to form an independent rifle company in July, 1776 (Ref: B-3). He also took the Oath of Allegiance before Hon. Reuben Meriweather on March 2, 1778 (Ref: B-24). Henry Ayton was commissioned a First Lieutenant in Capt. Benjamin Warfield's Company on March 1, 1778 (Ref: C-201).

BABBER, JAMES. He took the Oath of Allegiance before Hon. Elijah Robosson in March, 1778 (Ref: B-28).

BACON, WILLIAM. Took the Oath of Allegiance on July 1, 1777 (Ref: V-303).

BAGNALL, THOMAS. Enrolled by Capt. Watkins in Anne Arundel County on October 21, 1776 for service to the State (Ref: I-144, MS.1814).

BAGNESS (BAQUES?), JACQUES. Was a Cadet in 1777 and 1st Lieutenant in Capt. William Campbell's Matross Company on June 18, 1779 (Ref: V-308, O-458).

BAKER, ABEDNEGO. Took the Oath of Allegiance before Hon. Reuben Meriweather on March 2, 1778 (Ref: B-25).

BAKER, THOMAS. Took the Oath of Allegiance before Hon. Thomas Worthington on February 28, 1778 (Ref: B-21).

BAKER, ZEBEDIAH. Took the Oath of Allegiance before Honorable John Dorsey on March 12, 1778 (Ref: B-26).

BALDERSON, BARTHOLOMEW. Took the Oath of Allegiance before Hon. John Dorsey on March 12, 1778 (Ref: B-26).

BALDWIN, HENRY. Lieutenant in Maryland Line. He was deceased by March 29, 1797 when Maria Baldwin (now Gambrill) administered the final distribution of his estate (her thirds), and thirds of the remainder to Sarah Baldwin, Elizabeth Baldwin and William Baldwin (Ref: U-15). On February 18, 1830, it was ordered that the Treasurer "pay to Maria Gambrill, widow of Henry Baldwin, an officer of the Revolution, during her widowhood, quarterly, half pay of Lieutenant in consideration for the services of said husband." Also, on January 3, 1835, it was ordered that the Treasurer "pay to William H. Baldwin, of Anne Arundel County, two months pay, due his mother, Maria Gambrill, deceased, upon the pension list of this State." (Ref: K-317).

BALDWIN, JAMES. Took the Oath of Allegiance before Hon. Nicholas Worthington in March, 1778 (Ref: B-27).

BALDWIN, THOMAS. Enrolled by Captain James Disney, Jr. and passed by Colonel Richard Harwood on July 13, 1776 (Ref: H-41). Thomas was probably a son of Samuel Baldwin who died intestate prior to September 10, 1799 (Ref: U-25).

BALL, ALLEN. Took the Oath of Allegiance before Hon. Samuel Harrison, Jr. in March, 1778 (Ref: B-28).

BALL, JOHN JR. 4th Corporal in Capt. Gilbert Middleton's Independent Company of Militia of Annapolis on March 20, 1779 (Ref: I-144, O-325).

BALLOD, RICHARD. His name appeared on a list of defectives from the Maryland Line in August, 1780 (Ref: H-414).

BANNON, JOHN. Born in Scotland. On May 4, 1778, he served as a Substitute, furnished by Vachel Stevens, for the war's duration (Ref: C-205, H-317).

BARBER (BARBOR), CHARLES. Private in Capt. Gilbert Middleton's Independent Company of Militia of Annapolis on March 20, 1779 (Ref: I-144, O-325).

BARBER, GEORGE. Pensioned on March 4, 1831, at age 70, as a Seaman in the United States Navy (Ref: Z-45).

BARBER, JOHN. His name appeared on the rolls of Captain William Marbury's Company of Artillery in November, 1777 (Ref: H-575).

BARBER, SAMUEL. Adjutant of the Severn Battalion of Militia. He was paid 20 pounds for 4 months service in 1776 (Ref: F-223).

BARITT, RALPH. Took the Oath of Allegiance before Hon. Richard Harwood, Jr. on March 1, 1778 (Ref: B-22).

BARLOW, JOHN. Took the Oath of Allegiance before Hon. Reuben Meriweather on March 2, 1778 (B-24).

BARLOW, ZACHARIAS. Took the Oath of Allegiance before Hon. Reuben Meriweather on March 2, 1778 (Ref: B-24).

BARNES FAMILY. For additional biographical data, see Robert Barnes' article "Descendants of James Barnes and Ketura Shipley" (Bulletin of the Maryland Genealogical Society, Vol. 31, No. 4, pp. 369-381, and the information contained in the individual entries that follow herein).

BARNES, ADAM (died circa 1779). Son of James Barnes and Ketura Shipley. Adam married Honor Dorsey (Ref: "Ancestry of Robert

William Barnes," in Maryland Genealogical Society Bulletin, Vol. 32, No. 2, p. 200). Took the Oath of Allegiance before Hon. Reuben Meriweather on March 2, 1778 (Ref: B-25).

BARNES, ANTHONY. His name appeared on the rolls of Captain Richard Dorsey's Company of Artillery on November 17, 1777 (Ref: H-574).

BARNES, AQUILA. Enlisted by Michael Burgess and passed by Col. Hyde in Anne Arundel County on July 20, 1776 (Ref: H-41).

BARNES, DORSEY. Probably a son of John Barnes and Hammutal -----. Took Oath of Allegiance before Hon. Reuben Meriweather on March 2, 1778 (Ref: B-24).

BARNES, ELIJAH (c1755 - August 13, 1840). Probably a son of Nathan Barnes and Ellis -----. He married Catherine Shipley. Elijah was enlisted by Joseph Burgess for the Flying Camp on July 20, 1776 (Ref: H-40).

BARNES, ELY. Enlisted by Joseph Burgess for the Flying Camp on July 20, 1776 (Ref: H-40).

BARNES, JAMES (died after 1792). Son of Adam Barnes and Hannah Dorsey. He was one of the petitioners to the Convention of Maryland to form an independent rifle company in July, 1776 (Ref: B-3). He took the Oath of Allegiance before Hon. Reuben Meriweather on March 2, 1778 (Ref: B-25).

BARNES, JAMES (of Baltimore County). Took the Oath of Allegiance before Hon. Reuben Meriweather on March 2, 1778 (Ref: B-25).

BARNES, JAMES (OF JAMES). Took the Oath of Allegiance before Honorable Reuben Meriweather on March 2, 1778 (Ref: B-25).

BARNES, JAMES. Son of Peter Barnes and Rachel -----. He was one of the petitioners to the Convention of Maryland to form an independent rifle company in July, 1776 (Ref: B-3).

BARNES, JOHN (died c1800). Son of Adam Barnes and Hannah Dorsey. He married Hammutal -----. Took the Oath of Allegiance before Hon. Reuben Meriweather on March 2, 1778 (Ref: B-25).

BARNES, JOHN (OF NATHANIEL), of Baltimore County. Took the Oath of Allegiance before Hon. Reuben Meriweather on March 2, 1778 (Ref: B-25).

BARNES, MICHAEL (died by 1799). Son of Adam Barnes and Hannah Dorsey. He married Patience Shipley, a daughter of William Shipley and Rebecca Ogg, and their son William Barnes was born September 9, 1771 (Ref: "Ancestry of Robert W. Barnes," Maryland Genealogical Society Bulletin, Vol. 32, No. 2, p. 199, Spring, 1991). Michael was one of the petitioners to form an independent rifle company in July, 1776 (Ref: B-3). He took the Oath of Allegiance before Hon. Reuben Meriweather on March 2, 1778 (Ref: B-25).

BARNES, NATHAN. One of the peititioners to the Convention of Maryland to form an independent rifle company in July, 1776 (Ref: B-3). He was commissioned 2nd Lieutenant in Capt. Vachel Stevens' Company in the Elk Ridge Battalion of Militia in March, 1779 (Ref: O-333).

BARNES, NATHAN. Son of Nathan Barnes and Ellis -----. He was one of the petitioners to the Convention of Maryland to form an independent rifle company in July, 1776 (Ref: B-3). Took the Oath of Allegiance before Hon. Reuben Meriweather on March 2, 1778 (Ref: B-24).

BARNES, PETER. Probably a son of Peter Barnes and Rachel-----. Took the Oath of Allegiance before Hon. Reuben Meriweather on March 2, 1778 (Ref: B-24).

BARNES, PHILIMON (of Baltimore County). Took Oath of Allegiance before Hon. Reuben Meriweather on March 2, 1778 (Ref: B-25).

BARNES, PHILIP. Enlisted by Joseph Burgess for the Flying Camp on July 20, 1776 (Ref: H-40).

BARNES, RICHARD. Enlisted by Joseph Burgess for the Flying Camp on July 20, 1776 (Ref: H-40).

BARNES, RICHARD (of Baltimore County). Took the Oath of Allegiance before Hon. Reuben Meriweather on March 2, 1778 (Ref: B-25).

BARNES, ROBERT. Probably a son of Peter Barnes and Rachel -----. Took Oath of Allegiance before Hon. Reuben Meriweather on March 2, 1778 (Ref: B-24).

BARNES, THOMAS. Took the Oath of Allegiance before Hon. Reuben Meriweather on March 2, 1778 (Ref: B-25).

BARNES, VACHEL. One of the petitioners to the Convention of Maryland to form an independent rifle company in July, 1776 (Ref: B-3).

BARNETT, ROBERT. Soldier in the Invalids Regiment who was discharged because of rheumatism on September 15, 1782 (Ref: X-1).

BARNSBY, WILLIAM. Took the Oath of Allegiance before Hon. Thomas Harwood in February, 1778 (Ref: B-22).

BARRETT, THOMAS. Took the Oath of Allegiance before Hon. Samuel Lane on March 1, 1778 (Ref: B-23).

BARRY, BAZIL (BASIL). Enrolled by Capt. James Disney, Jr. and passed by Col. Richard Harwood on July 13, 1776 (Ref: H-41). Took the Oath of Allegiance before Hon. Thomas Worthington on February 28, 1778 (Ref: B-21).

BARRY (BAREY), CORNELIUS. Took the Oath of Allegiance before Hon. Nicholas Worthington in March, 1778 (Ref: B-27).

BARRY, EDWARD. His name appeared on the rolls of Captain Richard Dorsey's Company of Artillery on November 17, 1777 (Ref: H-574).

BARRY, JACOB. Enrolled by Capt. James Disney, Jr. and passed by Col. Richard Harwood on July 13, 1776 (Ref: H-41). He took the Oath of Allegiance before Hon. Richard Harwood, Jr. on March 1, 1778 (Ref: B-22).

BARRY, JAMES. His name appears on the rolls of Capt. Richard Dorsey's Company of Artillery on November 17, 1777 (Ref: H-574).

BARRY, MORDECAI. Took the Oath of Allegiance before Hon. Richard Harwood, Jr. on March 1, 1778 (Ref: B-22).

BARRY, WILLIAM. Drafted in October, 1780 for service until December 10, 1780 (Ref: H-368). Took the Oath of Allegiance before Hon. Nicholas Worthington in March, 1778 (Ref: Maryland State Papers, Red Book No. 21, p. 8D. Source B-27 mistakenly omitted this name from its published list).

BARTLEY, JAMES. Took the Oath of Allegiance before Hon. John Dorsey on March 12, 1778 (Ref: B-26).

BARTON, ISAAC. Enrolled by Capt. Watkins in Anne Arundel County on October 21, 1776 for the service of the State (Ref: I-144, MS.1814).

BARTON, JOHN. Took the Oath of Allegiance before Hon. Nicholas Worthington in March, 1778 (Ref: B-27). Another John Barton took the Oath in 1780. (Ref: Richard B. Miller's "Some Little Known Data Regarding the Maryland Signers of the Oath of Fidelity," Maryland Genealogical Society Bulletin, Vol. 27, No. 1, Winter, 1986 p. 105).

BARTON, MARK. Took Oath of Allegiance before Hon. Elijah Robosson in March, 1778 (Ref: B-28).

BASFORD, BENJAMIN. Took the Oath of Allegiance before Hon. Richard Harwood, Jr. on March 1, 1778 (Ref: B-22).

BASFORD, JOHN. Took the Oath of Allegiance before Hon. Richard Harwood, Jr. on March 1, 1778 (Ref: B-22).

BASFORD, STEPHEN. Second Lieutenant in Capt. Vachel Gaither's Company in the Severn Battalion of Militia, 1776-1778 (Ref: A-176, C-202, F-224, N-495 and Source F-224 incorrectly spells his name "Bosford").

BASFORD, STEPHEN BELL. Took the Oath of Allegiance before Hon. Nicholas Worthington in March, 1778 (Ref: B-27).

BASFORD, THOMAS. Took the Oath of Allegiance before Hon. Richard Harwood, Jr. on March 1, 1778 (Ref: B-22). He died by March 6, 1789 when John Basford administered the final distribution of his estate (eighths): John Basford, Thomas Basford, Richard Basford, Frederick Basford, Zachariah Basford, Benjamin Basford, Jemima Basford, and Rachel Basford Nichols (Ref: U-3).

BASFORD, THOMAS FOWLER. Ensign in Capt. Vachel Gaither's Company in the Severn Battalion of Militia, 1776-1778 (Ref: A-176, C-202, F-224, N-495, and Source F-224 incorrectly spells his name "Bosford").

BATEMAN, HENRY JR. Took Oath of Allegiance before Hon. Nicholas Worthington in March, 1778 (Ref: B-27). Henry became a 1st Lieutenant in Capt. Nicholas Worthington's Company in the Severn Battalion on March 1, 1778 (Ref: C-203) and subsequently Captain of his own company on August 15, 1778 (Ref: O-208. Note: Sources I-144 and J-113 erroneously spell his name "Henry Ballman"). He was deceased by May 25, 1802 when the final distribution of his estate (sixths) was administered to Amzi Bateman, Benjamin Bateman, Elizabeth Bateman, Ann Bateman, Rachel Bateman, and Lemuel Bateman (Ref: U-19).

BATEMAN, HENRY SR. Took Oath of Allegiance before Hon. Nicholas Worthington in March, 1778 (Ref: B-27).

BATEMAN, WILLIAM. Took the Oath of Allegiance before Hon. John Dorsey on March 12, 1778 (Ref: B-26).

BATES, RALER. Born in Scotland. He was a Substitute furnished by John Howard (of Ephraim) on May 14, 1778, for the war's duration (Ref: C-212, H-318).

BATTEE, FERDINANDO. A resident of Herring Creek, "Fardenando Battee, Sr." was among the petitioners to form a militia company on March 6, 1776, and he was elected one of the Corporals in Capt. Richard Weems' Company (Ref: I-143, MS.1814). Two men by this name took the Oath of Allegiance in 1778: one before Hon. Samuel Harrison, and one before Hon. Richard Harwood, Jr. (Ref: A-244, B-22). "Fardinan Battee" (born in Maryland) was enrolled by Capt. Edward Tillard on July 10, 1776. Height: 5' 5" (Ref: H-39). He was deceased by April 3, 1818, when Thomas Franklin was administrator de bonis non and made final distribution on his estate with half to Elizabeth Battee and fourths of the remainder to Samuel Franklin, Ann Franklin, Benjamin Franklin, and Thomas Franklin (Ref: U-52).

BATTEE, FERDINANDO JR. A resident of Herring Creek, "Fardenando Battee, Jr." who was among the petitioners to form a militia company on March 6, 1776 (Ref: I-143). His name also appears on a 1780 list of Substitutes in Anne Arundel County, serving in the Army until December 10, 1780 (Ref: H-370).

BATTEE, JOHN. Born in Maryland. Enrolled by Capt. Edward Tillard on July 10, 1776. Height: 5' 4" (Ref: H-39). He was also one of the residents of Herring Creek who petitioned to form a militia company on March 6, 1776 and subsequently served in Capt. Richard Weems' Company (Ref: I-143, MS.1814).

BATTERSON, THOMAS (negro). His name appeared on a 1780 list of Substitutes in Anne Arundel County, who served until December 10, 1780 (Ref: H-369).

BAXTER, JOHN. Born in Ireland. Enlisted in Anne Arundel County on February 28, 1778 by Daniel Monroe (Ref: C-216, H-313).

BEACHMAN, WILLIAM. Drafted in October, 1780 in Anne Arundel County to serve until December 10, 1780 (Ref: H-369).

BEACHUM, WILLIAM. Took the Oath of Allegiance before Hon. Thomas Dorsey on March 2, 1778 (Ref: B-23).

BEALL, CHRISTOPHER (died August 20, 1831). Pensioned in Anne Arundel County on May 5, 1818 at age 79, as a Private in the Maryland Line (Ref: Z-27).

BEALL, RUSSELL. Took the Oath of Allegiance before Hon. Thomas Worthington on February 28, 1778 (Ref: B-21).

BEALMEAR, FRANCIS. Took Oath of Allegiance before Hon. Nicholas Worthington in March, 1778 (Ref: Maryland State Papers, Red Book No. 21, p. 8D. Note: His name is spelled "Bealmere" in the published list found in Ref: B-27).

BEARD, JOHN. Took the Oath of Allegiance before Hon. Richard Harwood, Jr. on March 1, 1778 (Ref: B-22).

BEARD, MATTHEW. Took the Oath of Allegiance before Hon. Richard Harwood, Jr. on March 1, 1778 (Ref: B-22).

BEARD, RICHARD. Took the Oath of Allegiance before Hon. Richard Harwood, Jr. on March 1, 1778 (Ref: B-22). He was deeeceased by December 11, 1790 when his executors made final distribution of his estate to his widow Mary Beard (her third) and one shilling each to Richard Beard, Stephen Beard, Jonathan Beard, Thomas Beard, Rebecca Watts and Ruth Watkins, with half of remaining balance to Elizabeth Beard and the other half to Luranah Beard (Ref: U-5).

BEARD, RICHARD JR. Took the Oath of Allegiance before Hon. Richard Harwood, Jr. on March 1, 1778 (Ref: B-22).

BEARD, ROBERT. Born in Scotland. On April 28, 1778, he was a Substitute, furnished by Abraham Claude, to serve a 3 year term (Ref: C-204, H-317).

BEARD, STEPHEN. Took the Oath of Allegiance before Hon. Richard Harwood, Jr. on March 1, 1778 (Ref: B-22). Deceased by May 8, 1818, when his executors made final distribution of his estate to Susanna Beard (widow's third) and sevenths of remaining balance to Stephen Beard, John Beard, Susanna Beard Hulms?, Elizabeth Beard Linthicum, Mary Beard Davis, Rebecca Beard Lusby, and John Stockett Beard? (Ref: U-52, U-53).

BEARD, THOMAS. Listed as a Substitute on October 30, 1781 (Ref: W-657).

BEARD, WILLIAM. He was a physician who practiced in Annapolis and moved to Baltimore in 1776. He became Assistant Surgeon to Dr. Charles Wiesenthal on the State Ship "Defence" in 1776 (Ref: Y-303).

BEAVER, JOHN. Took Oath of Allegiance before Hon. Elijah Robosson in March, 1778 (Ref: B-28).

BECRAFT, ABRAHAM. Took the Oath of Allegiance before Hon. Thomas Worthington on February 28, 1778 (Ref: B-21).

BEECHGOOD, JAMES. Took the Oath of Allegiance before Hon. Reuben Meriweather on March 2, 1778 (Ref: B-24).

BEHOO, MOSES. Took the Oath of Allegiance before Hon. Reuben Meriweather on March 2, 1778 (Ref: B-25).

BELLISON, WILLIAM. Born in Scotland. On May 5, 1778, he was a Substitute, furnished by Richard Stringer, for the war's duration (Ref: C-207, H-318). He took the Oath of Allegiance before Hon. Thomas Dorsey on March 2, 1778. (Ref: B-23).

BELT, JOHN SPRIGG. Second Lieutenant in Capt. Edward Tillard's Company in Anne Arundel County in June, 1776 (Ref: H-38, H-40, N-534). Pensioned at age 71 on April 19, 1818 as a Captain in the Maryland Line (Ref: Z-27).

BENNETT, JOEL. Private in Captain Richard Dorsey's Company of Artillery on the rolls of November 17, 1777 (Ref: H-574).

BENNETT, JOSEPH. Enrolled by Henry Ridgely, Jr. and passed by Col. Josias C. Hall on August 26, 1776 (Ref: H-41).

BENNETT, SAYERS JAMES. Took Oath of Allegiance before Hon. Samuel Harrison in March, 1778 (Ref: A-244).

BENNETTE, EDWARD. Enlisted by Richard Talbot and passed by John Dorsey in Anne Arundel County on July 22, 1776 (Ref: H-39).

BENNETTE, GEORGE. Enlisted by John Worthington Dorsey and passed by John Dorsey on July 22, 1776 (Ref: H-39).

BENNINGTON, THOMAS. Born in Scotland. On May 15, 1778, he was a Substitute, furnished by Nicholas Maccubbin (of John) for the duration of the war (Ref: C-205, H-317).

BENSON, JOHN. Enlisted by Edward Spurrier and passed by Thomas Dorsey on July 20, 1776 (Ref: H-41). Took the Oath of Allegiance before Hon. Nicholas Worthington in March, 1778 (Ref: Maryland State Papers, Red Book 21. Note: His name is mistakenly left out of the published list in Reference B-27).

BENSON, THOMAS. Two men with this name took the Oath of Allegiance before Hon. Nicholas Worthington in March, 1778: one signed his name and one made his mark (Ref: The original list in Maryland State Papers, Red Book No. 21, p. 8D, indicates two Thomas Bensons took the Oath; however, just one Thomas Benson is contained in the published list found in Ref: B-27). One Thomas Benson was deceased by April 7, 1796 when final distribution to his estate was made by his executor, John Cheney, to Richard Benson, Thomas Benson, John Benson, Elizabeth Benson, Sarah Benson, John Miller, Ann Warfield, and halves of the remainder to William Benson and Rachel Benson (Ref: U-14).

BERRY, ROBERT. Private in Capt. Gilbert Middleton's Independent Company of Militia of Annapolis on March 20, 1779 (Ref: I-144, O-325).

BERRY, WILLIAM. Born in England. On April 16, 1778, he was a Substitute, furnished by Joseph Eastman and delivered to Lt. Col. Stone, for a 3 year term in the American Army (Ref: C-204, H-317).

BERTHAUD, ADAM. Commissioned 3rd Lieutenant in Capt. John Fulford's Company of Matrosses on July 17, 1776, and stationed at Annapolis (Ref: H-570). He was commissioned 2nd Lieutenant on January 1, 1777 (Ref: V-1).

BETHARD, JERMAN. On March 13, 1777 he petitioned the Council of Safety to inform them that he was wrongfully imprisoned, that he was not an enemy of this country, and that he would take the Oath of Allegiance (Ref: V-171).

BIDDLE, RICHARD. Enlisted by Edward Spurrier and passed by Thomas Dorsey on July 20, 1776 (Ref: H-41).

BIRCKHEAD (BURKHEAD), ABRAHAM. Resident of Herring Creek who was among the petitioners to form a militia company on March 6, 1776 (Ref: I-143).

BIRCKHEAD, FRANCIS. Private in Capt. Richard Chew's Company of Col. John Weems' Battalion on October 5, 1776 (Ref: A-95, I-143). Took the Oath of Allegiance before Hon. Samuel Harrison, Jr. in March, 1778 (Ref: B-29).

BIRCKHEAD, FRANCIS JR. Private in Capt. Richard Chew's Company of Col. John Weems' Battalion on October 5, 1776 (Ref: A-95, I-143). Took the Oath of Allegiance before Hon. Samuel Harrison, Jr. in March, 1778 (Ref: B-29).

BIRCKHEAD (BIRKHEAD), JNO. His name appeared on a 1780 list of Draughts in Anne Arundel County, who served until December 10, 1780 (Ref: H-370).

BIRCKHEAD, JOHN. Private in Capt. Richard Chew's Company of Col. John Weems' Battalion on October 5, 1776 (Ref: A-95, I-143). Took Oath of Allegiance before Hon. Samuel Harrison, Jr. in March, 1778 (Ref: B-29).

BIRCKHEAD, JOHN JR. Private in Captain Richard Chew's Company of Col. John Weems' Battalion on October 5, 1776 (Ref: A-95, I-143).

BIRCKHEAD, JOSEPH. Private in Captain Richard Chew's Company of Col. John Weems' Battalion on October 5, 1776 (Ref: A-95, I-143). Took the Oath of Allegiance before Hon. Samuel Harrison, Jr. in March, 1778 (Ref: B-29).

BIRCKHEAD, MATTHEW. Private in Captain Richard Chew's Company of Col. John Weems' Battalion on October 5, 1776 (Ref: A-95, I-143). Took the Oath of Allegiance before Hon. Samuel Harrison, Jr. in March, 1778 (Ref: B-29).

BIRCKHEAD, NEHEMIAH. Private in Captain Richard Chew's Company of Col. John Weems' Battalion on October 5, 1776 (Ref: A-95, I-143). Took the Oath of Allegiance before Hon. Samuel Harrison, Jr. in March, 1778 (Ref: B-29). He was deceased by August 5, 1811, when final distribution of his estate was made by his executor, Nehemiah Birkhead, to Sarah Birkhead (widow's third) and fourths of the remainder to Mary Birkhead Brewer, Elizabeth Birkhead, Sarah Birkhead, and Nehemiah Birkhead (Ref: U-40).

BIRCKHEAD, NEHEMIAH (OF SAMUEL). Private in Capt. Richard Chew's Company of Col. John Weems' Battalion on October 5, 1776 (Ref: A-95, I-143). Oath of Allegiance before Hon. Samuel Harrison, Jr. in March, 1778 (Ref: B-29).

BIRCKHEAD (BIRKHEAD), SEABORN. Took the Oath of Allegiance before Hon. Samuel Harrison, Jr., in March, 1778 (Ref: B-28).

BIRCKHEAD (BIRKHEAD), THOMAS. Took the Oath of Allegiance before Hon. Thomas Harwood in February, 1778 (Ref: B-21).

BISETT, THOMAS. Took the Oath of Allegiance before Hon. Reuben Meriweather on March 2, 1778 (Ref: B-24).

BISHOP, GREENBURY. Took the Oath of Allegiance before Hon. Reuben Meriweather on March 2, 1778 (Ref: B-24).

BISHOP, JOHN. Took the Oath of Allegiance before Hon. Richard Harwood, Jr. on March 1, 1778 (Ref: B-22).

BISHOP, SOLOMON. Took the Oath of Allegiance before Hon. Reuben Meriweather on March 2, 1778 (Ref: B-24).

BISHOP, WILLIAM. Ensign in Capt. Charles Boone's Company on March 1, 1778 in the Severn Battalion of Militia (Ref: C-203).

BLACK, RUDOLPH (March 14, 1762 - died after 1833, Bracken County, Kentucky). Applied for pension S30774 in 1833 in Kentucky, stating he was born in Anne Arundel County and enlisted in Baltimore County in 1778, and after the war he was in Frederick County before migrating to Bracken County (Ref: L-14).

BLAIR, JOHN. Disabled soldier who was paid on February 11, 1783 (Ref: D-4).

BLAKE, ALEX. His name appears on the rolls of Capt. Richard Dorsey's Company of Artillery on November 17, 1777 (Ref: H-574).

BLAND, GILBERT. Took the Oath of Allegiance before Hon. Reuben Meriweather on March 2, 1778 (Ref: B-24).

BLAND, THOMAS. Enlisted by Richard Talbot and passed by John Dorsey in Anne Arundel County on July 22, 1776 (Ref: H-39).

BLEWER, JAMES. Disabled soldier of the 3rd Maryland Line who was wounded by a ball in his hip and discharged from service on March 1, 1782 (Ref: X-2). Paid on January 13, 1784, April 13, 1784, September 3, 1784, October 26, 1784 and December 17, 1784 (Ref: D-11, 13, 21, 23, 25, in MdHR 4843-1-1).

BLOOM (?), JOHN. Took the Oath of Allegiance before Hon. Reuben Meriweather on March 2, 1778 (Ref: B-24).

BLOUNT, EDWARD. Took the Oath of Allegiance before Hon. Samuel Harrison in March, 1778 (Ref: A-244).

BOND, JOHN. His name appears on the rolls of Capt. William Marbury's Company of Artillery in November, 1777 (Ref: H-575).

BONEY, PHILIP. Took the Oath of Allegiance before Hon. Samuel Harrison in March, 1778 (Ref: A-244).

BOONE (BOON), CHARLES. Ensign in Capt. Joseph Merriken's Company in Severn Battalion on June 19, 1777 and Captain under Col. Elijah Robosson on March 1, 1778 (Ref: A-176, C-202).

BOONE (BOON), JOHN. Captain in the Severn Battalion of Militia commanded by Col. John Weems' in 1776 and Col. Elijah Robosson in June, 1777 and March, 1778 and August, 1778 (Ref: A-176, C-202, F-223, I-144, J-113, O-208).

BOONE, JOHN SR. Took the Oath of Allegiance before Hon. Elijah Robosson in March, 1778 (Ref: B-28).

BOONE, STEPHEN. Second Lieutenant in Capt. Joseph Merriken's Company in the Severn Battalion on June 19, 1777 (Ref: A-176), and 1st Lieutenant in Capt. Charles Boone's Company on March 1, 1778, serving at least to July 30, 1781 (Ref: C-202, W-527). One Stephen Boone was appointed Justice of the Orphans Court and also a Justice of the Peace on November 19, 1778 (Ref: O-241).

BORDLEY, WILLIAM. Served on the Committee of Observation in 1776. He was a physician and paid by the Council for his services in 1777 (Ref: Y-303).

BOSTICK, BARTON. Took the Oath of Allegiance before Hon. Elijah Robosson in March, 1778 (Ref: B-28).

BOSTICK, WILLIAM. Took the Oath of Allegiance before Hon. Elijah Robosson in March, 1778 (Ref: B-28).

BOTTS, JOSEPH. Disabled soldier who was discharged at Frederick Town on November 29, 1783 (Ref: X-3). He was paid on January 13, 1784, April 13, 1784, September 3, 1784, October 26, 1784 and December 17, 1784 in Anne Arundel County (Ref: D-11, D-13, D-21, D-22, D-25, in MdHR 4843-1-1).

BOWEN, SUTLIFF. Took the Oath of Allegiance before Hon. Elijah Robosson in March, 1778 (Ref: B-28).

BOWIE, JAMES. Born in Maryland. Enrolled by Samuel Chew on July 25, 1776 in Anne Arundel County (Ref: H-40).

BOWIE, JOHN. Took the Oath of Allegiance before Hon. Samuel Harrison in March, 1778 (Ref: A-244).

BOWLING, JOHN. Took the Oath of Allegiance before Hon. Reuben Meriweather on March 2, 1778 (Ref: B-24).

BOYLE, JOHN. He was a member of Captain John Fulford's Company of Matrosses stationed at Annapolis on December 12, 1776 (Ref: H-572).

BOYS, MATHEW. Enlisted by John Worthington Dorsey and passed by John Dorsey on July 22, 1776 in Anne Arundel County (Ref: H-39).

BRADLEY, JAMES. His name appeared on the rolls of Captain Richard Dorsey's Company of Artillery on November 17, 1777, noting that he was "in gaol for house breaking." (Ref: H-574).

BRADY, JOHN. Private in Captain Richard Dorsey's Company of Artillery on the rolls of November 17, 1777 (Ref: H-574).

BRADY, WILLIAM. He was a member of Capt. John Fulford's Company of Matrosses stationed at Annapolis on December 12, 1776 (Ref: H-572).

BRAITHWAITE, JOHN. Born in Scotland. On May 4, 1778, he was a Substitute, furnished by John Thomas, for the war's duration (Ref: C-205, H-317).

BRANNON, OWEN. Born in Scotland. He was a Substitute, furnished by John Muir and William Hyde, for a three year term in the American Army on May 3, 1778 (Ref: C-205, H-317).

BRANNUM, RICHARD. Born in Ireland. Enlisted by Thomas Gordon in Anne Arundel County on February 28, 1778 (Ref: C-216, H-313).

BRANON, RICHARD. Took the Oath of Allegiance before Hon. Nicholas Worthington in March, 1778 (Ref: B-27).

BRASHEARS, BENJAMIN. Took the Oath of Allegiance before Hon. Samuel Lane on March 1, 1778 (Ref: B-23).

BRASHEARS, CHARLES. Took the Oath of Allegiance before Hon. Samuel Lane on March 1, 1778 (Ref: B-23).

BRASHEARS, DOWELL. Took the Oath of Allegiance before Hon. Samuel Lane on March 1, 1778 (Ref: B-23).

BRASHEARS, JONATHAN. Took the Oath of Allegiance before Hon. Samuel Lane on March 1, 1778 (Ref: B-23). "Jono. Brashears" was drafted in October, 1780 to serve until December 10, 1780 (Ref: H-370).

BRASHEARS, NATHAN. Took the Oath of Allegiance before Hon. Thomas Harwood in February, 1778 (Ref: B-22).

BRASHEARS, WAYMACK. Took the Oath of Allegiance before Hon. Samuel Lane on March 1, 1778 (Ref: B-23). He was deceased by November 13, 1794 when the final distribution of his estate (sixths) was made to Margery Brashears, Judson Brashears, Jesse Brashears, Levi Brashears, Lilburn Brashears, and Nancy Brashears (Ref: U-12).

BRASHEARS, WILKERSON. Took the Oath of Allegiance before Hon. Samuel Lane on March 1, 1778 (Ref: B-23).

BRASHEARS, WILLIAM. Born in Maryland. Enrolled by Capt. Edward Tillard on July 10, 1776. Height: 5' 5" (Ref: H-38).

BRASHEARS, ZADOCK. Born in Maryland. Enrolled by John Belt in 1776. Height: 5' 8 1/2" (Ref: H-40). He took the Oath of Allegiance before Hon. Thomas Harwood in February, 1778 (Ref: B-22).

BRAY, JOHN. Took the Oath of Allegiance before Hon. Elijah Robosson in March, 1778 (Ref: B-28).

BREWER, JOHN. Enrolled by Captain Thomas Watkins on October 21, 1776 for service to the State (Ref: I-144, MS.1814). Two men with this name took the Oath of Allegiance in March, 1778: one before Hon. Richard Harwood, Jr. and one before Hon. Elijah Robosson (Ref: B-22, B-28).

BREWER, JOHN (OF JOHN). Took Oath of Allegiance before Hon. Richard Harwood, Jr. on March 1, 1778 (Ref: B-22).

BREWER, JOHN SR. Took the Oath of Allegiance before Hon. Thomas Worthington on February 28, 1778 (Ref: B-21).

BREWER, JOSEPH JR. Took the Oath of Allegiance before Hon. Richard Harwood, Jr. on March 1, 1778 (Ref: B-22).

BREWER, JOSEPH SR. Took the Oath of Allegiance before Hon. Richard Harwood, Jr. on March 1, 1778 (Ref: B-22).

BREWER, NICHOLAS. Enlisted by Thomas Mayo on July 20, 1776 (Ref: H-41).

BREWER, NICHOLAS (of Annapolis). Took the Oath of Allegiance before the Hon. Richard Harwood, Jr. on March 1, 1778 (Ref: B-22). Private in Capt. Gilbert Middleton's Independent Company of Militia of Annapolis on March 20, 1779. (Ref: I-144, O-325).

BREWER, NICHOLAS JR. Took the Oath of Allegiance before Hon. Elijah Robosson in March, 1778 (Ref: B-28).

BREWER, NICHOLAS SR. Took the Oath of Allegiance before Hon. Elijah Robosson in March, 1778 (Ref: B-28). Deceased by October 5, 1784, when the final estate distribution was made by his administratrix, Mrs. Rachel Brown, (widow's third) with remaining balance (eighths) to: Nicholas Brewer; John Brewer; Ann Brewer; Elizabeth Brewer; heirs of Sarah Joyce (Sarah Joyce and Caroline Joyce); Joseph Brewer; Lot Brewer; and, Roady Brewer (Ref: U-3).

BREWER, THOMAS STOCKETT (February 6, 1753 - April 1, 1823). Married Susanna Lampley on August 22, 1780 or 1782 in Annapolis and they had 8 children: Sarah Stockett Brewer, Ennas Brewer, John Mercer Brewer, Mary Ann Brewer, Brice Beal Brewer, Allen Thomas Brewer, Eliza Brewer, and Susanna Brewer. Thomas Brewer's widow received pension W9369 (Ref: E-1, E-2, G-111, T-174, LU-4:85). The Treasurer was directed in November, 1812, to "pay to Thomas S. Brewer, of Annapolis, late Sergeant in the Revolutionary War, so long as he may live, half pay of a Sergeant." (Ref: K-323). On February 24, 1824, the Treasurer was directed to "pay to Susanna Brewer, of Annapolis, during her life, quarterly, half pay of a Sergeant, as further remuneration for her husband Thomas' services in the Revolutionary War." (Ref: K-323, Z-27).

BREWER, WILLIAM SR. Took the Oath of Allegiance before Hon. Richard Harwood, Jr. on March 1, 1778 (Ref: B-22).

BRIAN, WILLIAM. Took the Oath of Allegiance before Hon. Nicholas Worthington in March, 1778 (Ref: B-27).

BRICE, JAMES (August 26, 1746 - July 11, 1801). Son of John Brice and Sarah Frisby. Married Julianna Jennings in 1781 and had 6 children: James Frisby Brice, Thomas Jennings Brice, John Brice, Julianna Brice Stephen, Sarah Ann Brice, and Anne Carroll Brice. He was very prominent during and after the war, and served in many offices, including: Executive Council, 1777-1799; Acting Governor, 1792; County Lieutenant, 1777-1780; Alderman of Annapolis, 1780-1792; Mayor of Annapolis, 1782-1783, 1788-1789; Councilman, 1793-1801. On March 6, 1776, he was Captain of an independent Annapolis company, and became Colonel in 1779 (Ref: P-164, N-203, C-208, V-303).

BRICE, JOHN (September 22, 1738 - July 20, 1820). Son of John Brice and Sarah Frisby. Married Mary Clare Maccubbin in 1766 and had 5 children: Nicholas Brice, Edmund Brice, Henry Brice, John Brice, and Margaretta Clare Brice Smith. John was active in the Revolutionary War and served in many offices: Justice in the Anne Arundel County Court, 1777-1778, 1782-1805; member of the Lower House in 1777 and 1778; member of the Committee of Observation, 1774-1775; County Clerk, 1765-1777; Alderman, 1780-1792; Annapolis Mayor,

1780-1781 (Ref: O-241, P-165, T-175; and Anne Arundel County Orphans Court Proceedings, 1777-1779, p. 1, in the Maryland State Archives MdHR9524).

BRIGHT, JAMES. His name appeared on the rolls of Captain William Marbury's Company of Artillery in November, 1777 (Ref: H-575).

BRISSINGTON, ABRAM (a free negro). On May 18, 1778, he became a Substitute, furnished by Isaac Harde and James Collahan and delivered to Col. Stone for a two year term in the American Army (Ref: C-205, H-317).

BRITT, ROBERT. Private in Captain Richard Dorsey's Company of Artillery on November 17, 1777 (Ref: H-574).

BRITTAIN, JAMES. He took the Oath of Allegiance before Hon. John Dorsey on March 12, 1778 (Ref: B-26).

BRITTON, JOHN. Recruited in October, 1780 for a 3 year term (Ref: H-369).

BROGDEN, JOHN. Took the Oath of Allegiance before Hon. Richard Harwood, Jr. on March 1, 1778 (Ref: B-22).

BROGDEN, SAMUEL. Enrolled by Capt. Watkins in Anne Arundel County on October 21, 1776 for service to the State (Ref: I-144, MS.1814); and became a First Lieutenant in Capt. Thomas Watkins' Company in the West River Battalion in 1778 (Ref: C-199). He also took the Oath of Allegiance before Hon. Richard Harwood, Jr. on March 1, 1778 (Ref: B-22).

BROGDEN, WILLIAM (March 8, 1742/43 - September 12, 1824). Son of Rev. William Brogden and ELizabeth Chapman. Married Margaret McCullock in 1795 and had four children: William Brogden, James Brogden, David M. Brogden, and Mary Brogden (and Source T-177 indicates he also had son named Jonathan Sellman Brogden). He was a Captain in the West River (or 31st) Battalion under Col. John Weems on March 9, 1776, commanding 49 privates (Ref: N-232), and rose to the rank of Major by 1780. William took the Oath of Allegiance before Hon. Thomas Harwood in February, 1778, and held several offices during the revolution, including member of the Lower House, 1780-1783, County Justice, 1773-1777, and County Purchasing Agent in 1779 (Ref: B-21, O-333, P-166). One William Brogden was a physician in lower A. A. county (Ref: Y-303).

BROOKES, WALTER. Discharged by Dr. Murray on October 27, 1781 (Ref: W-654).

BROWN, DANIEL. Enlisted by Michael Burgess and passed by Col. Hyde on July 20, 1776 (Ref: H-41).

BROWN, ELY. Took the Oath of Allegiance before Hon. John Dorsey on March 12, 1778 (Ref: B-26).

BROWN, JAMES. Took the Oath of Allegiance before Hon. John Dorsey on March 12, 1778 (Ref: B-26).

BROWN, JOHN. Three men with this name took the Oath of Allegiance in March, 1778: one before Hon. Samuel Harrison, one before Hon. Samuel Lane, and one before Hon. Nicholas Worthington (Ref: A-244, B-23, B-27). One John Brown was enlisted by Thomas Mayo on July 20, 1776 (Ref: H-41), and another John Brown (shoemaker) was drafted in October, 1780, to serve in the Army until December 10, 1780 (Ref: H-369). One John Brown was deceased by October 14, 1795 when the final distribution of his estate was made by his executors, Richard Brown and John Brown, to these legatees: John Brown, Rebecca Lane, Richard Brown (of Richard), Ann Brown (of Richard), Rachel Brown (of Richard), Alley Brown (of Richard), John Brown (of son John), Jennett Brown (of John), Harriet Brown (of John), and John Lane (Ref: U-13). Another John Brown was a Sergeant in 6th Maryland Line in 1777, was wounded (details not stated), and discharged at Frederick Town on November 29, 1783 (Ref: X-4).

BROWN, JOHN (OF JOHN). Two men by this name took the Oath of Allegiance: one before Hon. Thomas Worthington on February 28, 1778 and another before Hon. John Dorsey on March 12, 1778 (Ref: B-21, B-26).

BROWN, JOSHUA. One of the petitioners to the Convention of Maryland to form an independent rifle company in July, 1776 (Ref: B-3). He took the Oath of Allegiance before Hon. Reuben Meriweather on March 2, 1778 (Ref: B-24).

BROWN, RICHARD. Took the Oath of Allegiance before Hon. Samuel Harrison, Jr. in March, 1778 (Ref: B-28).

BROWN, ROBERT. Took the Oath of Allegiance before Hon. Reuben Meriweather on March 2, 1778 (Ref: B-24).

BROWN, SAMUEL (January 9, 1747 - October 6, 1833). Son of Benjamin Brown and Susannah -----. Married Achsah Riggs and had at least one son, John Riggs Brown. He was commissioned 2nd Lieutenant in Capt. John Dorsey's Company in the Elk Ridge Battalion of Militia on March 2, 1777 (Ref: E-248A, C-201).

BROWN, SAMUEL (OF BENJAMIN). Took the Oath of Allegiance before Hon. Reuben Meriweather on March 2, 1778 (Ref: B-24).

BROWN, THOMAS. Took the Oath of Allegiance on March 25, 1778 (Ref: V-550).

BROWN, VALENTINE. Took the Oath of Allegiance before Hon. John Dorsey on March 12, 1778 (Ref: B-26).

BROWN, WILLIAM. Attended to the records of the Committee of Observation in 1776 at his home in London Town (Ref: F-223, N-163). He took the Oath of Allegiance before Hon. Richard Harwood, Jr. on March 1, 1778 (Ref: B-22).

BROWN, WILLIAM. Commissioned a Captain of an artillery company in Annapolis on January 1, 1777 (Ref: V-1).

BROWN, ZECHARIA. Took the Oath of Allegiance before Honorable John Dorsey on March 12, 1778 (Ref: B-26). One "Zachariah Brown" was deceased by April 22, 1835 when final distribution of his estate was made by administrator George Bradford to Sarah A. Brown (widow's third) and fourths of balance to Joshua D. Brown, Bernard McGinn, Lloyd Brown and Zachariag Brown (Ref: U-90).

BRYAN, DANIEL. Master of Galley "Conqueror" on June 16, 1777 (Ref: V-290).

BRYAN, JOSEPH. His name appears as a member of Capt. John Fulford's Company of Matrosses stationed at Annapolis on December 12, 1776 (Ref: H-572).

BRYAN, THOMAS. He was a Substitute, furnished by Philip Hammond (of Nathaniel), on May 7, 1778 to serve until war's end (Ref: C-212, H-319).

BRYANT, GEORGE. Took the Oath of Allegiance before Hon. Thomas Worthington on February 28, 1778 (Ref: B-21).

BRYANT, RICHARD. Took the Oath of Allegiance before Hon. Samuel Harrison in March, 1778 (Ref: A-244).

BUCK, JAMES. Disabled soldier who received pay on January 13, 1784 in Anne Arundel County, but "now living in Frederick." (Ref: D-11, MdHR 4843-1-1).

BULLEN, JOHN. Captain of an independent company of Anne Arundel militia in 1776 (Ref: F-224, V-78). On April 6, 1776, the Treasurer was directed to pay him for the hire of his teams for six days (Ref: N-314, N-400).

BURGESS, BASIL. Son of Col. John Burgess and Sarah Dorsey. On April 4, 1776 he was commissioned a Second Lieutenant of Militia and on August 28, 1777 became a First Lieutenant. On March 30, 1779 he was promoted to Captain in the Elk Ridge Battalion, and subsequently accepted a commission in 1780 in the Maryland Continental Line as an Ensign. He became a Second Lieutenant in 1781 and in 1783 he was assigned to the First Maryland Regiment with the rank of First Lieutenant. In 1785 he married his cousin Eleanor Dorsey and they had 4 children: John Dorsey Burgess, Osgood Burgess, Cynthia Burgess, and Eleanor Burgess. By 1800 he and his family had moved to Mason County, Kentucky (Ref: Q-36, Q-37, O-333). He was still living in 1828 when he received half pay for his Revolutionary War services (Ref: K-324). He took Oath of Allegiance before Hon. John Dorsey on March 12, 1778 (Ref: B-26).

BURGESS, BENJAMIN. Took the Oath of Allegiance before Hon. Samuel Harrison in March, 1778 (Ref: A-244).

BURGESS, CALEB (September 30, 1739-1791). Son of John Burgess and Matilda Sparrow. He 1st married Deborah Warfield, daughter of Alexander Warfield and Thomasine Worthington, prior to 1760. Their children: John Burgess, Caleb Burgess, Samuel Burgess, Alexander Burgess, and Phoebe Burgess Spurrier. He married Susanna Mercer, widow of John Mercer, in 1787 (Ref: Q-32, Q-33). Final distribution of his estate was made January 21, 1807 by the administrator, Rezin Spurrier to widow Susanna Burgess and children, Deborah Burgess Spurrier, Caleb Burgess, John Burgess, Matilda Burgess Simpson, and Samuel Burgess (Ref: U-31). Caleb took the Oath of Allegiance before Hon. Nicholas Worthington in March, 1778 (Ref: B-27).

BURGESS, CALEB (died 1817). Son of Caleb Burgess and Deborah Warfield. Ensign in Capt. Nicholas Worthington's Company in the Severn Battalion in 1778 (Ref: C-203). After the war he moved to Frederick County; he married Ann Warfield in 1802 and they had 4 children: Alexander Burgess, Susan Burgess, Catherine Burgess Warfield, and Elizer Ann Burgess (Ref: Q-47, Q-48).

BURGESS, EDWARD (circa 1733 - December 5, 1809). Son of John Burgess and Jane Mackelfresh, and grandson of Edward Burgess and Sarah Chew. He married Mary Davis, daughter of Thomas Davis and Elizabeth Gaither, and moved to lower Frederick County before 1773. They had 10 children: John Burgess, Elizabeth Burgess, Anne Burgess, Edward Burgess, Margaret Burgess Clagett, Ephraim Burgess, Jane Burgess, Thomas Burgess, Mary Burgess Shekell, and Sarah Burgess. Edward was a Captain early in 1776 and served until his company of the Flying Camp disbanded near Philadelphia at Christmas time that year. His company muster roll can be found in the Archives of Maryland, Vol. 18, pp. 42-43. Edward was one of the Justices who administered the Oath of Allegiance in 1778 in Montgomery County, served as a Justice until 1784, tax commissioner from 1779 to 1795, and served in the legislature (Lower House, Montgomery County) from 1777 to 1779 (Ref: P-181, Q-26, 27, 28).

BURGESS, JOHN (June 8, 1725 - circa 1793). Second son of John Burgess and Jane Mackelfresh. He married Sarah Dorsey in 1755 and had four children: Achsah Burgess, Sarah Burgess, Basil Burgess, and John Burgess (Ref: Q-22, Q-23, Q-24). Served on the Committee of Observation in 1775 (Ref: F-222). Court Justice of Anne Arundel County on June 10, 1777 (Ref: Anne Arundel County Orphans Court Proceedings, 1777-1779, page 1; MdHR 9524). Organized a company in 1776 and became a Captain in the Elk Ridge Battalion under Col. Thomas Dorsey (Ref: C-201). He took the Oath of Allegiance before Hon. Nicholas Worthington in March, 1778 (Ref: B-27). On November 2, 1778 he was a Lieutenant Colonel of militia and later became a Colonel (Ref: O-229).

BURGESS, JOHN. His name appears as a member of Capt. John Fulford's Company of Matrosses stationed at Annapolis on December 12, 1776 (Ref: H-572).

BURGESS, JOSEPH (January 20, 1753 - November 17, 1778). Son of Joseph Burgess and Elizabeth Dorsey. He was commissioned an Ensign in William Smallwood's Regiment on January 14, 1776, and then promoted to 2nd Lieutenant and 1st Lieutenant in Capt. Daniel Dorsey's Company (Ref: Q-25, A-82, H-38, N-534). He was also a First Lieutenant in Captain Brice Howard's Company of Militia in 1776 (Ref: F-223). He enlisted 20 men for the Flying Camp in July, 1776 (Ref: H-40). Joseph saw active service in New York and on December 16, 1776 he was commissioned a Captain in the Fourth Maryland Regiment. He died in battle on November 17, 1778 (Ref: Q-25).

BURGESS, JOSEPH SR. (June 27, 1727 - February 17, 1806). Son of John Burgess and Jane Mackelfresh. Married Elizabeth Dorsey, daughter of Michael Dorsey and Ruth Todd, on January 13, 1751, and they had 18 children: John Burgess, Joseph Burgess, Michael Burgess, Vachel Burgess, Richard Burgess, Ruth Burgess, Joshua Burgess, Philemon Burgess, Ruth Burgess Warfield, Elizabeth Burgess Israel, Jane Burgess Simpson, Sarah Burgess, William Burgess, Honor Burgess, Honor Burgess Hobbs, Nancy Burgess, Lidey Burgess Baxter Maxwell, and Joseph Burgess (Ref:Q-24, Q-25). He took the Oath of Allegiance before Hon. John Dorsey on March 12, 1778 (Ref: B-26).

BURGESS, JOSHUA (1760, Anne Arundel County - October 15, 1831, Mason County, Kentucky). Son of Joseph Burgess and Elizabeth Dorsey. He enlisted in the Flying Camp on July 20, 1776, served until its disbandment at Christmas in 1776. In March, 1779 he was commissioned an Ensign in Capt. Vachel Steven's Company in the Elk Ridge Battalion of Militia, and became a Lieutenant in the Maryland Line on March 14, 1780. He was assigned to the First Maryland Line in 1781 and was subsequently captured by the British. He was listed as a prisoner of war on January 1, 1783. Joshua was an Original Member of the Society of the Cincinnati in Maryland in 1783. He married his cousin Sarah Burgess in 1790 and had eleven children: Achsah Burgess, Mordecai Burgess, Upton Burgess, Sheridan Burgess, Ruth Burgess, Eleanor Burgess Burgess, John Burgess, James Burgess, Michael D. Burgess, Sally Burgess, and Joseph V. Burgess. Joshua and his family moved to Mason County, Kentucky in 1802 (Ref: Q-42, Q-43, H-40, K-324, O-333, HCP-22).

BURGESS, MICHAEL (1754-1817). Son of Joseph Burgess and Elizabeth Dorsey. He married Sarah Warfield, a daughter of Davidge Warfield, in 1783 and had 11 children: Elizabeth Burgess Black, Roderick Burgess, Basil Burgess, Nancy Burgess, Thomas Burgess, Michael Burgess, Joseph Burgess, Rebecca Burgess Oram, Joshua Burgess, Absolom Burgess, and William Burgess (Ref: E-334, E-376, Q-39). He was a Corporal in the Second Company of the militia on February 3, 1776, and by June 29, 1776 he was an Ensign in Captain Daniel Dorsey's Company of the Flying Camp (N-534. Note: Source T-188 erroneously states that he served in Capt. Daniel Dulaney's Company). After the company disbandment in 1776, he returned to the militia and served as an Ensign in Captain Nicholas Ridgely Warfield's Company in the Elk Ridge Battalion in March, 1779 (Ref: Q-39, H-38, H-41, O-333). Took Oath of Allegiance before Hon. Thomas Worthington on February 28, 1778 (Ref: B-21). On April 20, 1819 the final distribution of his estate was made to Sarah Burgess (her widow's third) with elevenths of the remainder to Roderick Burgess, Basil Burgess, Mary Burgess Carr, Thomas Burgess, Michael

Burgess, Joseph Burgess, Rebecca Burgess, Absalom Burgess, Joshua Burgess and William Burgess (Ref: U-55).

BURGESS, RICHARD. Born in South River Hundred, a son of Samuel Burgess and Elizabeth Fowler. He married Mary ---- circa 1757 and they had 10 children: Samuel Burgess, Anne Burgess, Richard Burgess, Charles Burgess, Elizabeth Burgess, George Burgess, Sarah Burgess, Mordecai Burgess, Edward Burgess, and Mary Burgess (Ref: Q-34, Q-35). Richard took the Oath of Allegiance before Hon. John Dorsey on March 12, 1778 (Ref: B-26).

BURGESS, SAMUEL. Took the Oath of Allegiance before Hon. Richard Harwood, Jr. on March 1, 1778 (Ref: B-22).

BURGESS, THOMAS. Took the Oath of Allegiance before Hon. Nicholas Worthington in March, 1778 (Ref: B-27).

BURGESS, VACHEL (1756 - March 30, 1824). Son of Joseph Burgess and Elizabeth Dorsey. He was a Corporal in the militia by February 29, 1776. On April 17, 1777 he became Ensign in the 1st Maryland Line, and by 1779 he was Captain, serving to at least May 25, 1782. Married Rebecca Dorsey in 1782 and had 9 children: Anne Dorsey Burgess, Peregrine Burgess, Juliet Burgess, Elizabeth Burgess Hines, Harriet Burgess Watkins Howard, Thomas D. Burgess, Rebecca Burgess Warfield, Hetty W. Burgess, and Vachel Burgess (Ref: Q-40, H-81). Final distrubution of his estate was made by administrators, Basil Burgess and Thomas D. Burgess, on March 16, 1830 to Mrs. Rebecca Burgess (third), with remaining tenths to Ann D. Burgess, Peregrine Burgess, Juliet Burgess, Elizabeth Hines, Harriet Watkins, Mary V. Burgess, Thomas D. Burgess, Rebecca O. Burgess, Hetty W. Burgess, and Vachel Burgess (Ref: U-80).

BURGOE (BURGOON), JACOB. Took the Oath of Allegiance before Hon. Reuben Meriweather on March 2, 1778 (Ref: B-24).

BURGOE (BURGOON), JOHN. Took the Oath of Allegiance before Hon. Reuben Meriweather on March 2, 1778 (Ref: B-24).

BURGOON (BURGOE), JACOB JR. Took the Oath of Allegiance before Hon. Reuben Meriweather on March 2, 1778 (Ref: B-24).

BURGOON (BURGOONE, BURGOE), ROBERT. Enlisted by John Worthington Dorsey and passed by John Dorsey on July 22, 1776 in Anne Arundel County (Ref: H-39). Took the Oath of Allegiance before Hon. Reuben Meriweather on March 2, 1778 (Ref: B-24).

BURHILL, JOHN. Took the Oath of Allegiance before Hon. Thomas Harwood in February, 1778 (Ref: B-22).

BURKE, PATRICK. Born in Scotland. Enrolled by Henry Ridgely, Jr. and passed by Col. J. Carvil Hall on August 26, 1776 (Ref: H-41). On May 9, 1778, he was a Substitute, furnished by Leonard Selman, for the war's duration (Ref: C-205, H-317).

BURKE, RICHARD. His name appears on the rolls of Capt. Richard Dorsey's Company of Artillery on November 17, 1777 (Ref: H-574).

BURN, MICHAEL. There were two men with this name who served. One was born in England. On May 13, 1778, he was a Substitute, furnished by David Bass, and delivered to Col. Stone for a 3 year term in the American Army (C-204, H-317). The other was born in Scotland. On April 26, 1778, he was also a Substitute, furnished by Ely Dorsey, Jr., to serve for the duration of the war (Ref: C-211, H-318).

BURNS (BURNES), LUKE. Disabled soldier who sustained "a rupture and a wound" and was discharged from the Invalids Regiment on September 15, 1782 (Ref: X-5). He was paid on September 3, 1784 (Ref: D-21 and MdHR 4843-1-1).

BURR, LUKE. Born in Scotland. On May 6, 1778, he was a Substitute, furnished by Henry Hall, for a 3 year term in the American Army (Ref: C-205, H-317).

BURTON, EDWARD. Took the Oath of Allegiance before Hon. Nicholas Worthington in March, 1778 (Ref: B-27).

BURTON, FRANCIS. Born in Scotland. On May 19, 1778, he was a Substitute, furnished by Thomas Harwood and Osbern Harwood, to serve for a 3 year term or the end of the war (Ref: C-210, H-318).

BURTON, JAMES. Took the Oath of Allegiance before Hon. Nicholas Worthington in March, 1778 (Ref: B-27).

BURTON, THOMAS. Enrolled by Capt. Watkins in Anne Arundel County on October 21, 1776 for service to the State (Ref: I-144, MS.1814).

BURTON, WILLIAM. Took the Oath of Allegiance before Hon. Elijah Robosson in March, 1778 (Ref: B-28). He was deceased by December 24, 1804 when final distribution (fifths) was made by his administrator, John Burton, to: John Burton, Mary Burton (wife of Paul Richards), Sarah Burton (wife of Charles Poulton), Nancy Burton (wife of Lancelot Johnson), and the heirs of Edward Burton, namely Elizabeth Burton and Charles Burton (Ref: U-28).

BUTCHER, JOHN. Disabled soldier who was paid on January 13, 1784 and April 13, 1784 and September 3, 1784 and October 26, 1784 and December 17, 1784 in Anne Arundel County (Ref: D-11, D-13, D-21, D-23, D-25, MdHR 4843-1-1).

BUTLER, JAMES. Took the Oath of Allegiance before Hon. Thomas Harwood in February, 1778 (Ref: B-22).

BUTLER, JOSEPH. Born in Scotland. On May 5, 1778, he was a Substitute, furnished by Joseph White, Jr., for a 3 year term in the American Army (ref: C-207, H-318).

BUTLER, NOBLE. Pensioned on March 4, 1831, at age 74, as a Private in the Maryland Militia (Ref: Z-45).

BUTLER, VACEY. Enrolled by Capt. Watkins in Anne Arundel County on October 21, 1776 for service to the State (Ref: I-144, MS.1814).

BUTLER, WILLIAM. Took the Oath of Allegiance before Hon. Reuben Meriweather on March 2, 1778 (Ref: B-24).

BYFIELD, THOMAS. Born in England. On April 22, 1778, he was a Substitute, furnished by Joseph Ringgold and delivered to Col. Stone, to serve for the duration of the war in the American Army (Ref: C-204, H-317).

CADLE, BENJAMIN. Took the Oath of Allegiance before Hon. Nicholas Worthington in 1778 (Ref: Maryland State Papers, Red Book 21, p. 8D). Benjamin married Sarah Tucker on December 13, 1782 in Anne Arundel County; their son, Horace Cadle, married Anna Williams in Baltimore County on September 9, 1819 (Ref: K-423, E-2332T. Note: Original list in Maryland State Papers, Red Book 21, p. 8D contains this name, but it was mistakenly omitted from Source B-27).

CADLE, JAMES. Took the Oath of Allegiance before Hon. Nicholas Worthington in 1778 (Ref: Original list in Maryland State Papers, Red Book 21, p. 8D. Note: This name was incorrectly spelled "James Castle" in Source B-27).

CADLE, SAMUEL. Took the Oath of Allegiance before Hon. Nicholas Worthington in 1778 (Ref: Original list in Maryland State Papers, Red Book 21, p. 8D. Note: This name was mistakenly omitted from Source B-27). Deceased by May 10, 1811, when final distribution of his estate was made by Mrs. Elizabeth Cadle, executrix (widow's third), with fourths of the remainder to Thomas Cadle, Eleanor Cadle, William Cadle, and Priscilla Cadle (Ref: U-40).

CAIN (CANE), HUGH. Born in England. Enlisted by John Hobbs in Anne Arundel County on March 24, 1778 (Ref: C-216, H-313). Pensioned on April 7, 1818, at age 78, as a Private in the Maryland Line (Ref: Z-27).

CALDWELL, WILLIAM. Private in Capt. Gilbert Middleton's Independent Company of Annapolis on March 20, 1779 (Ref: I-144, O-325).

CALE, JOHN. Took the Oath of Allegiance before Hon. Richard Harwood, Jr. on March 1, 1778 (Ref: B-22).

CALHOON, ALEXANDER. Took the Oath of Allegiance before Hon. John Dorsey on March 12, 1778 (Ref: B-26).

CALLAHAN, JOHN. Third Lieutenant in Captain Charles Wallace's Company on October 6, 1777 (Ref: V-392). First Lieutenant in Capt. Gilbert Middleton's Independent Company of Annapolis on March 20, 1779 (Ref: I-144, O-325).

CAMDEN (CAMBDEN), RICHARD. Born in Maryland. Enrolled by Samuel Chew on July 10, 1776. Height: 5' 8" (Ref: H-40).

CAMP COL. SCIRVIN'S. Some men from Anne Arundel County served in Captain Richard Dorsey's Company of Artillery and the following list is of those who were at Camp Col. Scirvin's on January 28, 1782. Although not all of these men were from Anne Arundel County, they all are included here so as not to omit any of those who did serve: Capt. Richard Dorsey, Capt.-Lt. James Smith, Capt.-Lt. Ebenezer Finley, First Lt. Robert Wilmott, First Lt. James Bacques, Second Lt. Nicholas Ricketts, Second Lt. Young Wilkinson, Second Lt. Isac Rawlins, and Second Lt. John Cheever. Sergeants: Jesse Thompson, William Rawlins, James Hatton, William Cornwall, Samuel Carter, Richard Lewis, and William Morgan. Corporals: James Hammond, William Hutton, and Rawleight Spinks. Bombardiers: Dennis McCormack, William Hillen, William Dixon, and John Clark, Gunner. Drummers and Fifers: Thomas Williams, Elisha Redman, Thomas Patten, and Peter Davis. Matrosses: Michael Connor, Peregrine Askew, Thomas Gleeson, Cornelius Harling, John Ireland, Philip Masterson, James Neale, Michael O'Farrell, John Payne, Thomas Bowler, John Compton, Philip Jones, John Clark, John Prout, Thomas Redman, Thomas Randall, Bennet Rayley, Andrew Shrink, John Sandall, Edward Berry, John Stanley, Benedict Johnson, John Smith, Daniel Redden, Hugh McDowell, and John Owens (Ref: W. T. R. Saffell's "Records of the Revolutionary War," New York: Pudney & Russell, Publishers, 1858, pp. 231-232).

CAMP, JOHN. Took the Oath of Allegiance before Hon. Thomas Worthington on February 28, 1778 (Ref: B-21).

CAMPBELL, DANIEL. Took Oath of Allegiance on March 19, 1778 (Ref: V-541).

CAMPBELL, WILLIAM. 3rd Lieutenant in Capt. John Fulford's Matross Company stationed at Annapolis on March 23, 1776, 2nd Lieutenant on July 15, 1776, and 1st Lieutenant on January 1, 1777 (Ref: H-570, V-1). Commissioned a Captain on May 31, 1777 when Fulford became a Major (Ref: V-268, N-458).

CANN, GEORGE. Took the Oath of Allegiance before Hon. John Dorsey on March 12, 1778 (Ref: B-26).

CANN (CAN), JAMES. Took Oath of Allegiance before Hon. Nicholas Worthington in March, 1778 (Ref: Maryland State Papers, Red Book 21, p. 8D. Note: His name is mistakenly left off of the published list in Source B-27).

CANNOR, FRANCIS. He took the Oath of Allegiance before Hon. John Dorsey on March 12, 1778 (Ref: B-26).

CANNOR, WILLIAM. He took the Oath of Allegiance before Hon. John Dorsey on March 12, 1778 (Ref: B-26).

CAPPOCK (COPPUCK), SAMUEL. He took the Oath of Allegiance before Hon. John Dorsey on March 12, 1778 (Ref: B-26).

CAPPOCK, SIMON. Born in Scotland. Named as a Substitute supplied by Joshua Brown, Jr. on May 18, 1778 for the war's duration (Ref: C-213, H-319).

CARBURY, PETER. Disabled "soldier in the State Regiment who was wounded in a barge explosion" and medically discharged on November 13, 1783 (Ref: X-6).

CAREY, WILLIAM. Took the Oath of Allegiance before Hon. Thomas Harwood in February, 1778 (Ref: B-22).

CARR, BENJAMIN JR. Took the Oath of Allegiance before Hon. Thomas Harwood in February, 1778 (Ref: B-22).

CARR, BENJAMIN SR. Took the Oath of Allegiance before Hon. Thomas Harwood in February, 1778 (Ref: B-22).

CARR, DANIEL (of Baltimore County). Took the Oath of Allegiance before Hon. Reuben Meriweather in Anne Arundel County on March 2, 1778 (Ref: B-25).

CARR, JAMES. Took the Oath of Allegiance before Hon. Reuben Meriweather on March 2, 1778 (Ref: B-24).

CARR, JOHN. Took the Oath of Allegiance before Hon. Samuel Lane on March 1, 1778 (Ref: B-23).

CARR, JOHN JR. Took the Oath of Allegiance before Hon. Samuel Lane on March 1, 1778 (Ref: B-23).

CARR, WALTER. Took the Oath of Allegiance before Hon. Samuel Lane on March 1, 1778 (Ref: B-23). On September 17, 1828, Rezin Estep, the administrator of Elizabeth Crosby, deceased, made the final distribution of her estate (ninths) to Benjamin Carr, Walter Carr, William Carr, Jacob Carr's heirs, Jesse Dew's heirs, Thomas Dawkins, Samuel Dew's heirs, Mary Carr's heirs, and John Carr's heirs (Ref: U-77).

CARROLL, BRIAN. Enlisted by John Ijams in Anne Arundel County on March 12, 1778 (Ref: C-216, H-313).

CARROLL, CHARLES (of Annapolis). Physician and ardent patriot, but no known military service. Died in 1775. (Ref: Y-303).

CARROLL, CHARLES (April 1, 1702 - May 30, 1782). Son of Charles Carroll and Mary Darnall. Married Elizabeth Brooke in 1737 and they had a son, Charles Carroll of Carrollton. He took the Oath of Allegiance before Hon. Reuben Meriweather on March 2, 1778 (Ref: B-24, P-194, 195).

CARROLL, CHARLES, BARRISTER (March 22, 1723 - March 23, 1783). Son of Charles Carroll and Dorothy Blake. Married Margaret Tilghman in 1763 and they had twins who died in infancy. He was a Delegate to the Maryland Convention in 1774 and 1775, and President in 1776;

Senator, 1776 to 1781; and, a member of the Council of Safety in 1775 and 1776 (Ref: F-222, P-195, 196).

CARROLL, CHARLES, OF CARROLLTON (September 19, 1737 - November 14, 1832). Son of Charles Carroll, Sr. and Elizabeth Brooke. Married Mary Darnall in 1768 and had 7 children: Charles Carroll, Elizabeth Carroll, Mary Carroll Caton, Louisa R. Carroll, Anne B. Carroll, Catherine Carroll Harper, and Elizabeth Carroll. Charles was a very prominent patriot, serving in many offices between 1774 and 1801, including representing the City of Annapolis at the Convention of Maryland from 1774 through 1776; Senator, 1776-1801, including President of the Senate in 1783; and served on the Committees of Safety, Observation, and Correspondence, 1774-1776 (Ref: A-77, F-222, J-1, J-4, P-197). He was also one of the collectors of all gold and silver in Anne Arundel County in exchange for continental money for use of Congress (Ref: N-132). On March 11, 1833 "the General Assembly of Maryland, apprised of the death of the venerated Charles Carroll, of Carrollton, would at the close of a career of such distinguished patriotism and private worth, offer every tribute of reverence for those excellencies which have proved themselves to Maryland, in permanent benefits; strengthened the Councils of the Fathers of our Freedom, and mingled in the lustre of our revolutionary renown. Resolved, That the resolute patriotism of Charles Carroll, when at the hazard of his brilliant private interests he dedicated himself to the cause of American Independence, consecrates his life among the memorials of civil heroism, to adorn and enforce the history of human liberty; this patriotic sacrifice, and the continued and cogent efforts of his mind, and all his earnest labours in advancing the consummation of our Independence, in awakening the people of Maryland to the sense of their rights, and their power, and in sustaining their ardour in their vindication through the crisis of our revolution, command our admiration and our gratitude. A full portrait was directed to be procured and placed in the Senate Chamber, the scene of his legislaive labours; the theatre of that body whose peculiar Constitution he framed, and the site of the sublime surrender of military authority, by the Father of our Country, with whose honor the deserts of Charles Carroll are entwined." (Ref: K-327. One chapter of the Maryland Society, Sons of the American Revolution was named in his honor in 1972).

CARROLL, CHARLES (1751 - October 9, 1836). He married Elizabeth Warfield in 1795 and they had two sons: James Carroll and John David Carroll. He took the Oath of Allegiance in 1778 (Ref: E-1822K, T-199).

CARROLL, DANIEL. On November 12, 1778, he took the Oath of Fidelity as part of his election and qualification as a member of the Council (Ref: J-124).

CARROLL, DENNIS. Born in Scotland. Named as a Substitute supplied by Nicholas Miller on May 20, 1778 for the duration of the war (Ref: C-214, H-319).

CARROLL (CARROL), HENRY. Private in Capt. Richard Dorsey's Artillery Company on November 17, 1777 (Ref: H-574).

CARROLL (CARRALL), JOHN. His name appears on a list of Capt. John Fulford's Artillery Company stationed at Annapolis, December 12, 1776 (Ref: H-572).

CARROLL, NICHOLAS (MACCUBBIN) March 1, 1750/1 - May 22, 1812. Son of Nicholas Maccubbin and Mary Clare Carroll. Married Ann Jennings in 1783 and had 5 children: Nicholas Maccubbin, Thomas H. Maccubbin, John H. Maccubbin, Mary Clare Maccubbin Spence, and Ann Maccubbin Mason. Nicholas changed his name to Nicholas Maccubbin Carroll in accordance with the conditions specified in the will of his uncle, Charles Carroll, Barrister, in 1783. He served in the legislature, 1778-1785, was a Court Justice in 1779-1780, and was Mayor of Annapolis, 1784-1785 and 1790-1791 (Ref: P-201, P-202).

CARTY, TIMOTHY. Took the Oath of Allegiance before Hon. Thomas Worthington on February 28, 1778 (Ref: B-21).

CARVEL, ALEXANDER. Took the Oath of Allegiance before Hon. Richard Harwood, Jr. on March 1, 1778 (Ref: B-22).

CARVELL, JOHN. Took the Oath of Allegiance before Hon. Richard Harwood, Jr. on March 1, 1778 (Ref: B-22).

CARVELL, WILLIAM. Took the Oath of Allegiance before Hon. Richard Harwood, Jr. on March 1, 1778 (Ref: B-22).

CARWIN, JAMES. Enlisted by Michael Burgess and passed by Col. Hyde on July 20, 1776 (Ref: H-41).

CARY, JAMES. Took the Oath of Allegiance before Hon. Elijah Robosson in March, 1778 (Ref: B-28).

CATHEL, JOSIAH. Matross in Capt. Brown's Company who procured two men to enlist and so was given his discharge from further service (Ref: V-410).

CATHERSIDE, ABRAM. Born in Scotland. He was named as a Substitute supplied by Nicholas Worthington on May 7, 1778 for the duration of the war (Ref: C-212, H-318).

CATRELL (QUATRELL), ALEXANDER. Took Oath of Allegiance before Hon. Thomas Worthington on February 28, 1778 (Ref: B-21. Note: His name is illegible. It could be possibly either Catrell or Cantrell or Quatrell or Quantrell).

CAYHILL, DAVID. Named as a Substitute supplied by Thomas Watkins, Jr. on June 10, 1778 for a 3 year term (Ref: C-209, H-320).

CHAFFEY, JOHN. A resident of Herring Creek, he was among the petitioners to form a militia company on March 6, 1776 (Ref: I-143).

CHALMERS (CHALMBNERS), JOHN. Second Sergeant in Capt. Gilbert Middleton's Independent Company of Militia of Annapolis on March 20, 1779 (Ref: I-144, O-325).

CHALMERS, THOMAS. His name appeared on a list of Captain William Marbury's Company of Artillery in November, 1777 (Ref: H-575).

CHAMBERS, EDWARD. Private in the Maryland Line. Pensioned on June 20, 1818, at age 69, as a Private (Ref: Z-27). On February 16, 1820, the Treasurer was ordered "to pay to Edward Chambers, of Anne Arundel County (a man of colour), during life, half pay of a private, as further compensation for those services rendered by him during the Revolutionary War" (Ref: K-327).

CHAPLAIN, JOHN. Took the Oath of Allegiance before Hon. John Dorsey on March 12, 1778 (Ref: B-26).

CHAPLIN, HUGH. Enrolled by Capt. Thomas Watkins on October 21, 1776 for the service of the State (Ref: I-144, MS.1814).

CHAPMAN, ABRAHAM. Born in Maryland. Enrolled by Samuel Chew on July 10, 1776. Height: 5' 4" (Ref: H-40).

CHAPMAN, CHARLES. Enlisted by Richard Talbot and passed by John Dorsey on July 22, 1776 (Ref: H-39).

CHAPMAN, THOMAS. Born in Scotland. Named as a Substitute supplied by Nicholas Worthington on April 6, 1778 for a 3 year term (Ref: C-205, H-317). He took the Oath of Allegiance before Honorable Nicholas Worthington in March, 1778 (Ref: Original list in Maryland State Papers, Red Book No. 21, p. 8D. Note: His name is mistakenly omitted from the list published in Reference B-27).

CHASE, SAMUEL (April 17, 1741 - June 19, 1811). Son of Rev. Thomas Chase and Matilda Walker. He first married Ann Baldwin, daughter of Thomas Baldwin, in 1762 and they had 6 children: Matilda Chase Ridgely, Thomas Chase, Nancy Chase, Fanny Chase, Ann Chase, and Thomas Chase. Ann died in 1776; Samuel married second to Hannah Kitty Giles in 1784 and had 2 children: Elizabeth Chase Dugan Cole and Mary Chase Barney. Samuel was a very prominent patriot during the revolutionary period in Baltimore and Anne Arundel Counties. He was a Delegate to the Maryland Convention, 1774-1776; a member of the Lower House, 1777-1788, the Committee of Correspondence, 1773-1775, the Council of Safety in 1775 and the Committee of Observation for Anne Arundel County, 1774-1775; Commissioner, Baltimore Town, 1788-1796; and, a Delegate to the Continental Congress, 1774-1777; subsequently elected in 1781-1784, but did not attend. He died in Washington, D. C. and was buried at Old St. Paul's Cemetery in Baltimore (Ref: A-77, F-222, J-1, J-4, J-28, N-3, P-214, 215).

CHATLING, WILLIAM. Soldier in the 2nd Maryland Line who was wounded twice, taken prisoner for a year, and served for 6 years and 2 months altogether. He was discharged on June 20, 1783 (Ref: X-7).

CHENEY, ANDREW FRANCIS. Physician in Annapolis who was paid by the Council of Maryland for his medical services on April 1, 1777 (Ref: V-194, Y-303).

CHENEY, BENJAMIN. Two men with this name took the Oath of Allegiance: one before Hon. Thomas Harwood in February, 1778, and one before Hon. Nicholas Worthington in March, 1778 (Ref: B-22, B-27).

CHENEY, ISAIAH. Enrolled by Captain James Disney, Jr. and passed by Colonel Richard Harwood on July 13, 1776 (Ref: H-41).

CHENEY, JOSEPH. Took the Oath of Allegiance before Hon. Nicholas Worthington in March, 1778 (Ref: B-27).

CHENEY, SAMUEL. Took the Oath of Allegiance before Hon. Nicholas Worthington in March, 1778 (Ref: B-27).

CHENEY, ZACHARIAH. Took Oath of Allegiance before Hon. Nicholas Worthington in March, 1778 (Ref: Maryland State Papers, Red Book No. 21, p. 8D. Note: Source B-27 spelled his name "Chaney" instead of "Cheney").

CHENEY, ZEPHENIAH. Took the Oath of Allegiance before Hon. John Dorsey on March 12, 1778 (Ref: B-26).

CHESTER, SAMUEL. Private in Capt. Richard Dorsey's Company of Artillery on November 17, 1777 (Ref: H-574).

CHEW, BENJAMIN. Captain of the ship "Chase" on April 30, 1777 (Ref: V-234).

CHEW, JOHN. Two men with this name took the Oath of Allegiance before Hon. Samuel Harrison, Jr. in March, 1778 (Ref: A-244, B-28). One John Chew was an Ensign in Capt. Richard Weems' Company in the West River Battalion on March 1, 1778 (Ref: C-199). One John Chew was a resident of Herring Creek and was among those who petitioned for a militia company on March 6, 1776. He was also elected Sergeant in Capt. Richard Weems' Company (Ref: I-143).

CHEW, LOCK. Took the Oath of Allegiance before Hon. Samuel Harrison, Jr. in March, 1778 (Ref: B-28).

CHEW, NATHANIEL. Took the Oath of Allegiance before Hon. Samuel Harrison, Jr. in March, 1778 (Ref: B-28). Nathaniel was a resident of Herring Creek and among those who petitioned for a militia company on March 6, 1776. He was subsequently elected Sergeant in Capt. Richard Weems Company (Ref: I-143).

CHEW, RICHARD. Captain of a company in Col. John Weems' West River (or 31st) Battalion in 1776 to 1780 (Ref: A-95, A-140, I-143, C-200, N-232). He took the Oath of Allegiance before Honorable Samuel Harrison, Jr. in March, 1778 (Ref: B-28). Commissioned a Major on April 21, 1781 (Ref: W-409).

CHEW, SAMUEL (circa 1734 - July 29, 1786). Son of Samuel Chew and Henrietta Maria Lloyd. Married Elizabeth Snowden, widow of Richard Snowden, Jr., and they had five children: Samuel Lloyd Chew, Henrietta Maria Chew Galloway, Elizabeth Chew Fitzhugh, Ann Chew, and John Croley Chew. He was a Justice from 1757 to 1777, and he took the Oath of Allegiance before Hon. Samuel Harrison, Jr. in March, 1778 (Ref: B-28, P-218).

CHEW, SAMUEL. Second Lieutenant in Capt. Richard Chew's Company in the West RIver Battalion on March 1, 1778 (Ref: C-200). Took the Oath of Allegiance before Hon. Samuel Harrison, Jr. in March, 1778 (B-28).

CHEW, SAMUEL LLOYD (1756-1796). Son of Samuel Chew and Elizabeth Snowden. He married Dorothy Harrison in 1777. Samuel was a First Lieutenant in Captain Edward Tillard's Company by June 29, 1776 (Ref: H-38, N-534, P-218).

CHEW, WILLIAM. First Lieutenant in Capt. Richard Chew's Company in the West River Battalion on March 1, 1778 (Ref: C-200).

CHILDS (CHILD), BENJAMIN. Born in Maryland. Enrolled by Samuel Chew on July 25, 1776. Height: 5' 6 1/2" (Ref: H-40).

CHILDS (CHILD), CEPHAS. Took Oath of Allegiance before Hon. Samuel Harrison in March, 1778 (Ref: A-244). He was deceased by April 16, 1807, when the final distribution of his estate was made to Martha P. Childs (third) with fifths of the remainder to Henry Childs, John Childs, Benjamin Childs, Samuel Childs, and Ann Childs (Ref: U-32).

CHILDS (CHILD), JOHN. Took Oath of Allegiance before Hon. Samuel Harrison in March, 1778 (Ref: A-244).

CHILDS (CHILD), SAMUEL. Took Oath of Allegiance before Hon. Samuel Harrison, Jr. in March, 1778 (Ref: B-28).

CHILDS (CHILD), WILLIAM. He took the Oath of Allegiance before Hon. Samuel Harrison in March, 1778 (Ref: A-244).

CHILDS (CHILD), ZACHARIAH. He took the Oath of Allegiance before Hon. Samuel Harrison, Jr. in March, 1778 (Ref: B-28). Zachariah Childs administered the final distribution of the estate of Elizabeth Childs on September 4, 1792, with eighths of the estate balance to: Ann Childs (wife of Isaac Simmons), Sarah Childs, Zachariah Childs, Children of Elizabeth Childs (wife of William Fisher), Cephas (or Sephas) Childs, Mary Childs (wife of Lewis Fisher), Nelly Childs, and Barbary Childs (Ref: U-8).

CHISHOLM, ARCHIBALD. Took Oath of Allegiance before Hon. Nicholas Worthington in March, 1778 (Ref: B-27). He was a Private in Capt. Gilbert Middleton's Independent Company of Annapolis on March 20, 1779 (Ref: I-144, O-325). On May 11, 1814, Dr. Wilson Waters, administrator of Archibald Chisholm, made final distribution of his estate to Elizabeth Chisholm (widow's third) with sixths of the remainder to Mary Gibbs, Eliza Coyle, Charlotte Chisholm, Eleanor Fitzhugh, Catharine Chisholm and Emily Chisholm (Ref: U-44).

CLANCEY, DENNIS. Born in Scotland. Named as a Substitute supplied by Dr. Michael Pue on May 4, 1778 for a three year term (Ref: C-211, H-318).

CLANSEY, MICHAEL. His name appears on a list of Capt. John Fulford's Company of Artillery stationed at Annapolis on December 12, 1776 (Ref: H-572).

CLARK, EDWARD. Took the Oath of Allegiance before Hon. Thomas Worthington on February 28, 1778 (Ref: B-21).

CLARK, JAMES. Recruited and passed by James Brice in late 1777 (Ref: H-313).

CLARK, JOHN. Private in Captain Richard Dorsey's Company of Artillery on November 17, 1777 (Ref: H-574).

CLARK, THOMAS. Born in England. Enlisted by Daniel Munro in Anne Arundel County on April 11, 1778 (Ref: C-216, H-314).

CLARK, WILLIAM. Took the Oath of Allegiance before Hon. Richard Harwood, Jr. on March 1, 1778 (Ref: B-22). One William Clark was shown on the rolls of Capt. Richard Dorsey's Artillery Company on November 17, 1777 and reported as being "in gaol for house breaking." (Ref: H-574).

CLARKE, JAMES. His name appears on a list of Capt. John Fulford's Company of Artillery stationed at Annapolis on December 12, 1776 (Ref: H-572).

CLARKE, ROBERT. Private in Capt. Gilbert Middleton's Independent Company of Annapolis on March 20, 1779 (Ref: I-144, O-325).

CLARVO, JOHN. Took the Oath of Allegiance before Hon. Richard Harwood, Jr. on March 1, 1778 (Ref: B-22).

CLEMMENTS, FRANCIS T. His name appears on a list of Capt. William Marbury's Company of Artillery in November, 1777 (Ref: H-575).

CLIVEY, ISAAC. Enrolled by Capt. Thomas Watkins on October 21, 1776 for the service of the State (Ref: I-144, MS.1814).

COALE, FRANCIS. Took the Oath of Allegiance before Hon. John Dorsey on March 12, 1778 (Ref: B-26).

COALE, JOHN. A resident of Herring Creek, he was among those who petitioned to form a militia company on March 6, 1776 (Ref: I-143). He took the Oath of Allegiance before Hon. Thomas Harwood on February 7, 1778 (Ref: B-22).

COALE, JOSEPH. Took the Oath of Allegiance before Hon. Thomas Worthington on February 28, 1778 (Ref: B-21).

COALE, THOMAS. Toook the Oath of Allegiance before Hon. Thomas Worthington on February 28, 1778 (Ref: B-21). He was deceased by September 6, 1803, when final distribution of his estate was made to Sarah Coal (third) with fourths of the remaining balance to Charles Ridgely Coale, Alfred Coale, Harriet Coale, and Anna Maria Coale (Ref: U-18).

COALE, WILLIAM. Took the Oath of Allegiance before Hon. Thomas Worthington on February 28, 1778 (Ref: B-21).

COALTER, DANIEL. Private in Capt. Gilbert Middleton's Independent Company of Annapolis on March 20, 1779 (Ref: I-144, O-325).

COCKBURN, ALEXANDER. Recruited by Capt. Alexander Truman in October, 1780, for a three year term (Ref: H-369).

COCKERTON, JOHN. Private in Capt. Richard Dorsey's Company of Artillery on November 17, 1777 (Ref: H-574).

COE, WILLIAM. On March 20, 1819, he declared he enlisted in May, 1777, under Capt. William Campbell in the 2nd Company of Matross (Artillery) stationed at Annapolis. He served with Henry Litzinger and fought in the battles of Paoli and Germantown (Ref: National Genealogical Society Quarterly, Volume 23, No. 1, p. 5 (1935). On February 16, 1821, the Treasurer was ordered to "pay to William Coe, now of Annapolis (formerly of Baltimore County), half pay of a private of matross for his services rendered during the war." On February 17, 1834, the Treasurer was ordered to "pay to Mary Coe, widow of William Coe, the three months pay due her husband ($12.50) at the time of his death." (Ref: K-330).

COFFIN, ARTHUR. Took the Oath of Allegiance on March 21, 1778 (Ref: V-535).

COLBERT, DANIEL. Born in Ireland. Enlisted by Daniel Munro in Anne Arundel County on February 25, 1778 (Ref: C-215, H-313).

COLE, JAMES. His name appears on a list of Capt. John Fulford's Company of Artillery stationed at Annapolis on December 12, 1776 (Ref: H-572).

COLE, JOSEPH. Born in England. He was a Substitute supplied by William Spurrier on April 16, 1778 for a three year term (Ref: C-204, H-317).

COLE, LEVI. Pensioned on May 20, 1818, at age 70, as a Mariner (Ref: Z-27).

COLE, THOMAS. One of the petitioners to the Convention of Maryland to form an independent rifle company in July, 1776 (Ref: B-3). He was commissioned 1st Lieutenant in Capt. Charles White's Company in the Elk Ridge Battalion of Militia in March, 1779 (Ref: O-333).

COLLENSON, EDWARD. Took the Oath of Allegiance before Hon. Samuel Harrison, Jr. in March, 1778 (Ref: B-28).

COLLINS, GEORGE. Drafted in Anne Arundel County in October, 1780 to serve until December 10, 1780 (Ref: H-370).

COLLINS, JOHN. Drafted in Anne Arundel County in October, 1780 to serve until December 10, 1780 (Ref: H-369).

COLLINS, WILLIAM. Born in Maryland. Enrolled by John S. Belt in July, 1776. Height: 5' 6" (Ref: H-40).

COLLIOR, THOMAS. His name appears on a list of defectives from the Maryland Line on April 25, 1781 (Ref: H-416).

COMBLY, BENJAMIN. Drafted in Anne Arundel County in October, 1780 to serve until December 10, 1780 (Ref: H-369).

CONAWAY, JOHN. Took the Oath of Allegiance before Hon. Richard Harwood, Jr. on March 1, 1778 (Ref: B-22).

CONDON, MARTIN. Private in Capt. Richard Dorsey's Company of Artillery on November 17, 1777 (ref: H-574).

CONDRAM, THOMAS. His name appears as a member of Capt. John Fulford's Artillery Company stationed at Annapolis, December 12, 1776 (Ref: H-572).

CONNALSON, JOSEPH. Took Oath of Allegiance before Hon. Nicholas Worthington in March, 1778 (Ref: B-27).

CONNAR, WILLIAM. Took the Oath of Allegiance before Hon. Thomas Dorsey on March 2, 1778 (Ref: B-23).

CONNER, CALEB. Born in Maryland. Enrolled by Capt. Edward Tillard on July 10, 1776. Height: 5' 9" (Ref: H-39).

CONNER, JAMES (of Baltimore County). Took the Oath of Allegiance before Hon. Reuben Meriweather in Anne Arundel County on March 2, 1778 (Ref: B-25).

CONNER, PATRICK. Disabled soldier who was reported dead by August 16, 1783. (Ref: D-8, MdHR 4843-1-1).

CONNOLLY, JOHN (1762-1849). He enlisted on June 5, 1781 in Prince George's County, Maryland and joined Capt. Williams' Company of Col. Peter Adams' 3rd Maryland Line at Annapolis; was with Col. John Stewart's 2nd Maryland Line at the surrender at Yorktown. He died in Boone County, Missouri. His children were Milly Searcy, Jennie White, Sarah Martin, Benjamin Connolly, Sandford Connolly, John J. Connolly, James Connolly, and Francis Connolly. His brother, Benjamin, was killed in Camden, South Carolina (Ref: National Genealogical Society Quarterly, Vol. 33, No. 2, 1945, p. 60).

CONNOLLY, MICHAEL. His name appears on a list of defectives from the Maryland Line on July 2, 1781 (Ref: H-414).

CONNOR, JAMES. Soldier in the 5th Maryland Line who "lost his leg by a shot on Staten Island." Discharged from the service on November 1, 1783 (Ref: X-8). He received payments in 1784 (ref: D-11, 13, 21 and MdHR 4843-1-1).

CONNOR, JOHN. Two men with this name took the Oath of Allegiance before Hon. Reuben Meriweather on March 2, 1778 (Ref: B-24, B-25).

CONNOR, THOMAS. Private in Capt. Richard Dorsey's Company of Artillery on November 17, 1777 (Ref: H-574).

COOK, HENRY. Enrolled by Capt. Thomas Watkins on October 21, 1776 for the service of the State (Ref: I-144, MS.1814).

COOLEY, THOMAS. Took the Oath of Allegiance before Hon. Thomas Harwood in February, 1778 (Ref: B-22).

COOLEY, WILLIAM. Took the Oath of Allegiance before Hon. Elijah Robosson in March, 1778 (Ref: B-28, V-532).

COOPER, CECIL (of Baltimore County). Took the Oath of Allegiance before Hon. Reuben Meriweather on March 2, 1778 (Ref: B-25).

COOPER, EDWARD. Took the Oath of Allegiance before Hon. Thomas Worthington on February 28, 1778 (Ref: B-21). Born in Scotland. Named as a Substitute supplied by Solomon Bishop in April 21, 1778 for a 3 year term (Ref: C-211, H-318).

COOPER, GEORGE. Private in Capt. Richard Dorsey's Company of Artillery on November 17, 1777 (Ref: H-574).

COOPER, THOMAS. Took the Oath of Allegiance before Hon. John Dorsey on March 12, 1778 (Ref: B-26).

COPE, JOHN. Recruit passed by James Brice in late 1777 (Ref: H-313).

CORD, JAMES. Took the Oath of Allegiance before Hon. Reuben Meriweather on March 2, 1778 (Ref: B-24). He was deceased by October 10, 1792 when final distribution of his estate was made to Sarah Cord (third), with tenths to Rebecca Cord, Sarah Cord, John Cord, Henry Cord, Hellen Cord, Ann Cord, Catherine Cord, Sophia Cord, George Cord, and Jesse Cord (Ref: U-9).

CORNELIUS, JOHN. Took the Oath of Allegiance before Hon. John Dorsey on March 12, 1778 (Ref: B-26).

COSIVE, JOHN. Took the Oath of Allegiance before Hon. Samuel Lane on March 1, 1778 (Ref: B-23).

COUGHLAN, EDWARD. Private in Capt. Richard Dorsey's Company of Artillery on November 17, 1777 (Ref: H-574).

COULSON (COLSON), ROBERT. Took the Oath of Allegiance before Hon. Reuben Meriweather on March 2, 1778 (Ref: B-25).

COULSTON, JOHN. Born in England. Enlisted in Anne Arundel County on January 19, 1778 (Ref: C-215, H-313).

COURSEY, PATRICK. His name appears as a member of Capt. John Fulford's Artillery Company stationed at Annapolis, December 12, 1776 (Ref: H-572).

COWLEY, EDWARD. Born in Maryland. Enrolled by Capt. Edward Tillard on July 10, 1776. Height: 5' 6" (Ref: H-39).

COWLEY, JAMES. Took the Oath of Allegiance before Hon. Samuel Harrison in March, 1778 (Ref: A-244).

COWLEY, WILLIAM. Born in Maryland. Enrolled by Capt. Edward Tillard on July 10, 1776. Height: 5' 6" (Ref: H-39).

COWMAN, JOHN. Drafted in Anne Arundel County in October, 1780 to serve until December 10, 1780 (Ref: H-370).

COWMAN, RICHARD. Paid for contracting wagons and teams in 1780 (Ref: W-241).

COX, JOHN. Took the Oath of Allegiance before Hon. John Dorsey on March 12, 1778 (Ref: B-26).

COX, WILLIAM. Took the Oath of Allegiance before Hon. Thomas Worthington on February 28, 1778 (Ref: B-21).

CRACROFT, JOHN. Took the Oath of Allegiance before Hon. Thomas Worthington on February 28, 1778 (Ref: B-21).

CRAGG, ROBERT. Took the Oath of Allegiance before Hon. Thomas Harwood in February, 1778 (Ref: B-22).

CRAGON, LAWRENCE. Born in Scotland. Named as a Substitute supplied by Basil Fisher on April 26, 1778 for the duration of the war (Ref: C-211, H-318).

CRAIGE, ALEXANDER. Sergeant in Capt. Richard Dorsey's Company of Artillery on November 17, 1777 (Ref: H-573).

CRAMLICK (CRAMBLICK), JACOB. Took the Oath of Allegiance before Hon. Reuben Meriweather on March 2, 1778 (Ref: B-25). On June 13, 1804, administrator de bonis non Stephen Cramlick made final distribution on the estate of John Cramlick (died testate) with legacies to Mary Chambers and Michael Cramlick and eights of the remaining balance to Andrew Cramlick, Elizabeth Cramlick, John Cramlick, Jacob Cramlick, Stephen Cramlick, Frederick Cramlick,

Nancy Howard, and his grandchildren Thomas and Elizabeth Cramlick (Ref: U-27).

CRAMLICK (CRAMBLICK), JACOB JR. Took Oath of Allegiance before Hon. Reuben Meriweather on March 2, 1778 (Ref: B-25).

CRANDALL, FRANCIS. Took the Oath of Allegiance before Hon. Samuel Harrison in March, 1778 (Ref: A-244).

CRANDALL, GEORGE. Took the Oath of Allegiance before Hon. Samuel Harrison in March, 1778 (Ref: A-244).

CRANDALL, JOHN. A resident of Herring Creek, he was among the petitioners to form a militia company on March 6, 1776 (Ref: I-143).

CRANDELL, ADAM. Took the Oath of Allegiance before Hon. Samuel Lane on March 1, 1778 (Ref: B-23).

CRANDELL, JOSEPH. Two men with this name took the Oath of Allegiance: one before Hon. Thomas Harwood in February, 1778, and one before Hon. Samuel Lane on March 1, 1778 (Ref: B-22, B-23). "Joseph Crandle" was enrolled by Samuel Chew on July 25, 1776. Height: 5' 5" (Ref: H-40).

CRANDELL, THOMAS. Took the Oath of Allegiance before Hon. Thomas Harwood in February, 1778 (Ref: B-22). On August 23, 1818, Hester Crandall was the administratrix with will annexed of Thomas Crandall, and she made final distribution of his estate to Hester Crandall (widow's third), with the remainder of the balance to Elizabeth Caroline Crandall (Ref: U-54).

CRANDELL, WILLIAM. Second Lieutenant in Capt. John Deale's Company in the West River Battalion on March 1, 1778 (Ref: C-200).

CRANDELL, WILLIAM (OF FRANCIS). Took Oath of Allegiance before Hon. Thomas Harwood in February, 1778 (Ref: B-22).

CRASBY, JOSEPH. Born in Maryland. Enrolled by John S. Belt in July, 1776. Height: 5' 8 1/2" (Ref: H-40).

CROK, GEORGE. Took the Oath of Allegiance before Hon. Nicholas Worthington in March, 1778 (Ref: B-27).

CROMWELL, FRANCIS (October 2, 1752 - c1813). He married first Elizabeth Gray and second to Patience Stansbury. Their children were: Zachariah Cromwell, William Cromwell, Elizabeth Cromwell Jones, Sarah Cromwell Johnson, John Cromwell, Anne Cromwell Cheney, and Mary Cromwell Boone (Ref: T-246). He was a 1st Lieutenant in Capt.Joseph Maccubbin's Company in Severn Battalion on March 1, 1778 and later became a Captain in 1779 (Ref: C-202, T-246).

CROMWELL, JOSHUA (December 8, 1744 - July, 1793). Son of John Cromwell and Comfort Robosson. Married Hellen Gray in 1767. Joshua was Ensign in Capt. George Watts' Company of Militia in 1776 (Ref:

F-223, N-178), and Second Lieutenant in Capt. Vachel Gaither's Company in the Severn Battalion on June 19, 1777 (Ref: A-176, F-223, E-2697).

CROMWELL, RICHARD. First Lieutenant in Capt. Caleb Owings' Company in Severn Battalion in 1777-1778 (Ref: A-176, C-202).

CROSS, JOHN. Enrolled by Captain Thomas Watkins on October 21, 1776 for the service of the State (Ref: I-144, MS.1814). The final distribution of the estate of John Cross was made by James Iglehart, administrator de bonis non, to Jemima Cross Wiggins (widow's third), and thirds of the remaining balance to Elizabeth Cross, Mary Ann Cross and Rebecca Cross (Ref: U-62).

CROSS, ROBERT. Took the Oath of Allegiance before Hon. Richard Harwood, Jr. on March 1, 1778 (Ref: B-22).

CROW, EDWARD. Born in Scotland. Named as a Substitute supplied by Dr. Mark B. Sappington on May 18, 1778 for a 3 year term (Ref: C-207, H-318).

CROWE, SAMUEL. Enrolled by Capt. Thomas Watkins on October 21, 1776 for the service of the State (Ref: I-144, MS.1814).

CROXALL, CHARLES. Pensioned on December 13, 1828 in Anne Arundel County for service with the Pennsylvania Line during Revolutionary War (Ref: Z-53).

CRUTCHLEY, JOSEPH. Took the Oath of Allegiance before Hon. Samuel Harrison in March, 1778 (Ref: A-244).

CRUTCHLEY (CRUCHLEY), RICHARD. Took the Oath of Allegiance before Hon. Thomas Harwood in February, 1778 (Ref: B-22).

CRUTCHLEY, THOMAS. Took the Oath of Allegiance before Hon. Samuel Harrison in March, 1778 (Ref: A-244). He was a resident of Herring Creek and among those who petitioned for a militia company on March 6, 1776 (Ref: I-143).

CULBERTSON, WILLIAM. Private in Capt. Richard Dorsey's Company of Artillery on November 17, 1777 (Ref: H-574).

CUMMING, DAVID. Took the Oath of Allegiance before Hon. John Dorsey on March 12, 1778 (Ref: B-26).

CUMMING, JAMES. Took the Oath of Allegiance before Hon. Samuel Lane on March 1, 1778 (Ref: B-23).

CURRAY, JAMES. Took the Oath of Allegiance before Hon. Samuel Lane on March 1, 1778 (Ref: B-23).

CURTIS, JOHN. Two men with this name in Captain Richard Dorsey's Company of Artillery on November 17, 1777: one was a Sergeant and one was a Private. (Ref: H-573, H-574).

CURTIS, THOMAS. Took the Oath of Allegiance before Hon. John Dorsey on March 12, 1778 (Ref: B-26).

CUTLER, JACOB. He took the Oath of Allegiance before Hon. Thomas Harwood in February, 1778 (Ref: B-22).

CUTONG, PETER. Recruit passed by James Brice in late 1777 (Ref: H-313).

DABBS, JOHN. Took the Oath of Allegiance before Hon. John Dorsey on March 12, 1778 (Ref: B-26).

DACE, MICHAEL. Born in Scotland. His name appears on a list of Substitutes supplied by John Shipley on April 30, 1778, to serve in the American Army for a 3 year term (Ref: C-211, H-318).

DADS, JOHN. Drafted in October, 1780 to serve until December 10, 1780 (Ref: H-370).

DALEY, MATHEW. Enlisted by Edward Spurrier and passed by Thomas Dorsey on July 20, 1776 (Ref: H-41).

DANIELSON (DONNELSON), MOSES. Took Oath of Allegiance before Hon. Nicholas Worthington in March, 1778 (Ref: B-27). Note: Original list shows he made his mark by his name which someone spelled "Moses Donnelson," but his son signed his own name as "Moses Danielson, Jr." on the same list).

DANIELSON, MOSES JR. Took Oath of Allegiance before Hon. Nicholas Worthington in March, 1778 (Ref: B-27).

DARBY, ASA (April 13, 1756, Anne Arundel County, Maryland - December 30, 1833 in Chester County, South Carolina). Son of George and Anne Darby. Married Dorcas Goore in 1779 in Craven County, South Carolina and had 10 children: Nancy Darby Sealy, George Darby, Anne Darby Sanders, Lydia Darby Sanders, John Darby, Elizabeth Darby Estes, James Darby, Mary Darby Humphries, William Jefferson Darby and Thomas Darby. Asa Darby was a Private in the 6th Company of Montgomery County Militia in the Upper Battalion (Ref: Old Southern Bible Records, by Memory A. Lester, 1974, pp. 97-98; and I-194).

DARE, GIDEON. Resident of Herring Creek and one of the petitioners to form a militia company on March 6, 1776 and subsequently elected Lieutenant (Ref: I-143, N-336). Became a 1st Lieutenant in Capt. Richard Weems' Company in the West River Battalion in 1778 (Ref: C-199, F-223). Took the Oath of Allegiance before Hon. Samuel Harrison, Jr. in March, 1778 (Ref: B-28).

DARE, JOSEPH. Took Oath of Allegiance before Hon. John Dorsey on March 12, 1778 (Ref: B-26).

DARNALL, BENNIT. Took the Oath of Allegiance before Hon. Samuel Lane on March 1, 1778 (Ref: B-23).

DARNALL, HENRY. Took the Oath of Allegiance before Hon. Samuel Harrison in March, 1778 (Ref: A-244).

DARNALL, PHILIP. Took the Oath of Allegiance before Hon. Samuel Harrison in March, 1778 (Ref: A-244).

DARNALL, PHILIP JR. Took the Oath of Allegiance before Hon. Samuel Harrison in March, 1778 (Ref: A-244).

DAVENPORT, WILLIAM. Took the Oath of Allegiance before Hon. Samuel Harrison in March, 1778 (Ref: A-244).

DAVID, JOHN. Commissioned Captain of the Row Galley "Conqueror" on February 27, 1777 (Ref: V-153, V-290).

DAVID, VALENTINE. His name appears on a list of discharged soldiers of the militia, raised to serve in the Continental Army, in 1781 (Ref: H-407).

DAVIDGE, AZEL. Took the Oath of Allegiance before Hon. Nicholas Worthington in March, 1778 (Ref: B-27).

DAVIDGE, ROBERT. Commissioned Ensign in the Severn Battalion of Militia on August 15, 1778 under Capt. Henry Bateman (Ref: I-144, J-113, O-208).

DAVIDSON, JAMES (November 5, 1760 - November 28, 1841). He married Amelia Reed and they had nine children: Priscilla Davidson, James Davidson, Nelson Davidson, John Davidson, Thomas Davidson, Matilda Davidson Iglehart, Pamela Davidson Kepler, Margaret Davidson Brooks, and Eleanor Davidson Tumblert (Ref: T-258). Enlisted by Thomas Mayo in July, 1776. (Ref: H-41). His name also appeared on a list of Substitutes supplied by John Brogden on May 16, 1778 to serve in the American Army for three years or the duration of the war (Ref: C-210, H-318) and on a list of Substitutes in October, 1780 to serve until December 10, 1780 (Ref: H-370), and on a list of discharged soldiers of the militia raised to serve in the Continental Army in 1781 (Ref: H-407, E-84, G-17. Note: Source T-258 states he was captured in New Jersey on January 25, 1780 and was held prisoner for 11 months in New York. After being released, he served for 9 months under Capt. Lilburn Williams in the 3rd Maryland Regiment). Also, a James Davidson married Mary Howard (date not given) in Anne Arundel County, according to Source G-112, and a James Davidson 2nd was pensioned on July 7, 1818, as a Private (Ref: Z-27), while a James Davidson was pensioned on March 4, 1831, age 74 (Ref: Z-27).

DAVIDSON, JOHN (June 21, 1745 - February 2, 1807, Baltimore County; buried in Annapolis with full military honors). Married Anne Marie Lutrell (Luthall) in 1796 and had 3 children: John Thomas Davidson, Pinkney Davidson, and Ann Janette Davidson Waters. He was a Second Lieutenant in Allen's Independent Company in 1776 and a Captain in the 2nd Maryland Line; subsequently became a Major in the 5th Maryland Line, 1781-1783. After the war he was a General in the 8th Brigade, Maryland Militia, 1794-95. He was also appointed Naval

Officer, Third District, in 1777, served on the Executive Council from 1783 to 1801, and was Mayor of Annapolis, 1799-1800 (Ref: P-257, V-392, W-649).

DAVIES, THOMAS. Took the Oath of Allegiance before Hon. Thomas Worthington on February 28, 1778 (Ref: B-21).

DAVINSON, JAMES. Took the Oath of Allegiance before Hon. Elijah Robosson in March, 1778 (Ref: Original list in Maryland State Papers, Red Book No. 21. Note: His name is mistakenly given as "James O'Davinson" in Ref: B-28).

DAVIS, AMOS. One of the petitioners to the Convention of Maryland to form an independent rifle company in July, 1776 (Ref: B-3). Took Oath of Allegiance before Hon. Thomas Worthington on February 28, 1778 (Ref: B-21). Served on the Committee of Observation in 1775 (Ref: F-222).

DAVIS, DANIEL. Took the Oath of Allegiance before Hon. Richard Harwood, Jr. on March 1, 1778 (Ref: B-22).

DAVIS, ICHABOD. Took the Oath of Allegiance before Hon. Thomas Worthington on February 28, 1778 (Ref: B-21).

DAVIS, IGNATIUS. Enlisted by Richard Talbot and passed by John Dorsey on July 22, 1776 (Ref: H-39).

DAVIS, JESSE. On March 13, 1777 he petitioned the Council of Safety to inform them that he had been wrongfully imprisoned, that he was not an enemy of this country, and that he would take the Oath of Allegiance (Ref: V-171).

DAVIS, JOHN. Two men with this name took the Oath of Allegiance: one before Hon. Thomas Worthington on February 28, 1778 and one before Hon. Nicholas Worthington in March, 1778 (Ref: B-21, B-27). One John Davis was recruited in October, 1780 by Capt. Alexander Truman for a 3 year term (Ref: H-369).

DAVIS, JOHN (of Baltimore County). Took Oath of Allegiance before Hon. Reuben Meriweather on March 2, 1778. (Ref: B-25. Note: Source B-25 lists two John Davises of Baltimore County, but only one was found on the original list).

DAVIS, JOSEPH (OF LUKE). Took the Oath of Allegiance before Hon. Thomas Worthington on February 28, 1778 (Ref: B-21).

DAVIS, PHILIP. Born in Maryland. Enrolled by Capt. Edward Tillard on July 10, 1776. Height: 5' 6 1/2" (Ref: H-39).

DAVIS, ROBERT. Two men with this name took the Oath of Allegiance: one before Hon. Thomas Worthington on February 28, 1778, and one before Hon. Richard Harwood, Jr. on March 1, 1778 (Ref: B-21, B-22). One Robert Davis enrolled in military by Capt. James Disney, Jr. on July 13, 1776 (Ref: H-41).

DAVIS, ROBERT JR. Took the Oath of Allegiance before Hon. Reuben Meriweather on March 2, 1778 (Ref: B-24).

DAVIS, ROBERT SR. Took the Oath of Allegiance before Hon. Reuben Meriweather on March 2, 1778 (Ref: B-24).

DAVIS, ROBERT PAIN. Took the Oath of Allegiance before Hon. Richard Harwood, Jr. on March 1, 1778 (Ref: Original Maryland State Papers, Red Book No. 21; Source B-22 mistakenly gives his name as "Robert Pam Davis"). Commissioned an Ensign in Capt. Thomas Watkins Company on August 17, 1779 (Ref: O-496).

DAVIS, WALTER. Took the Oath of Allegiance before Hon. Thomas Worthington on February 28, 1778 (Ref: B-21).

DAVIS, WILLIAM. Enrolled by Captain Thomas Watkins on October 21, 1776 for service of the State, and became an Ensign in the West River Battalion in 1778 (Ref: I-144, C-199). Took the Oath of Allegiance before Hon. Richard Harwood, Jr. on March 1, 1778 (Ref: B-22).

DAVIS, WILLIAM JR. Took the Oath of Allegiance before Hon. Richard Harwood, Jr. on March 1, 1778 (Ref: B-22).

DAVY, WILLIAM. Took the Oath of Allegiance before Hon. Thomas Worthington on February 28, 1778 (Ref: B-21).

DAWES, RICHARD. Private in Capt. William Marbury's Company of Artillery in 1777 (Ref: H-575).

DAWSON, HENRY. Private in Capt. Gilbert Middleton's Independent Company of Militia of Annapolis on March 20, 1779 (Ref: I-144, O-325).

DAY, ROBERT. Born in Maryland. Enrolled by Capt. Edward Tillard on July 10, 1776. Height: 5' 10" (Ref: H-39).

DAY, THOMAS. Took the Oath of Allegiance before Hon. Reuben Meriweather on March 2, 1778 (Ref: B-24).

DEALE, JOHN. Born in Maryland. Enrolled by Capt. Edward Tillard on July 10, 1776. Height: 5' 8" (Ref: H-39). Another John Deale was a Captain in Col. John Weems' West River (31st) Battalion on March 9, 1776, and commanded 34 men (Ref: C-200, N-232). One John Deale took the Oath of Allegiance before Hon. Thomas Harwood in February, 1778 (Ref: B-22).

DEALE, JOSEPH. Resident of Herring Creek and one of the petitioners to form a militia company on Match 6, 1776 (Ref: I-143). His name appears on a list of recruits in Capt. Fulford's Artillery stationed at Annapolis on December 12, 1776 (Ref: H-572). On May 12, 1823, final distribution (sixths) of his estate was made by Richard Weems, executor, to James Deale, John Harrison, Nathan Deale, William Deale, Joseph Cowley and Samuel Deale (Ref: U-64).

DEALE, RICHARD. Took the Oath of Allegiance before Hon. Samuel Lane on March 1, 1778 (Ref: B-23). "Richard Deale, a draught from the militia of Anne Arundel County, having been refused by Col. Adams, commandant in the City Annapolis, and having appeared before this Board, on examination is found to be unfit for the service and is therefore discharged." (Ref: W-443).

DEALE, THOMAS. Resident of Herring Creek and one of the petitioners to form a militia company on March 6, 1776 (Ref: I-143).

DEALE, WILLIAM. Took Oath of Allegiance before Hon. Samuel Harrison in March, 1778 (Ref: A-244). Deceased by August 27, 1816 when final distribution was made by James Tucker and William O'Hara, administrators: equal fourths to Martin Deale, Ann Tucker, Elizabeth Deale, and William Deale (Ref: U-48).

DEARDS, WILLIAM. Paid by the Council of Safety on April 6, 1776 for straw for the use of the troops (Ref: N-314).

DEAVER, JOSEPH. One of the petitioners to the Convention of Maryland to form a rifle company in July of 1776 (Ref: B-3). Two men with this name took the Oath of Allegiance: one before Hon. Thomas Worthington on February 28, 1778 and one before Hon. Reuben Meriweather on March 2, 1778 (Ref: B-21, B-25).

DEAVER, SAMUEL. His name appears on a list of discharged soldiers of the militia, raised to serve in the Continental Army, in 1781 (Ref: H-407).

DEAVER, STEPHEN. Two men with this name took the Oath of Allegiance: one before Hon. Thomas Worthington on February 28, 1778 and one before Hon. Reuben Meriweather on March 2, 1778 (Ref: B-21, B-25).

DEAVOUR, MISAIL. Drafted in October, 1780 to serve until December 10, 1780 (Ref: H-369).

DELANY, WILLIAM. Private in Capt. Richard Dorsey's Artillery Company on November 17, 1777, "in gaol on susspion of house breaking." (Ref: H-574).

DELL, JAMES. Took the Oath of Allegiance before Hon. Thomas Worthington on February 28, 1778 (Ref: B-21).

DEMPSEY, JOHN. Pensioned on August 14, 1818, at age 76, in Anne Arundel County, as a Private in the Virginia Line, and reported dead (Ref: Z-27).

DENISON (DENNISON), RICHARD. Born in Maryland. Enlisted by Capt. Edward Tillard on July 10, 1776. Height: 5' 7 1/2" (Ref: H-39).

DENT, JOHN. Corporal in the Maryland Line; disabled soldier who was paid on January 13, 1784 and April 13, 1784 and September 3, 1784 and October 26, 1784 and December 17, 1784 (Ref: D-11, 13, 21, 22, 25). On April 12, 1809 final distribution of the estate of

John Dent was made by his Mrs. Eleanor Dent, administratrix, to Eleanor Dent (third), and fifths to Erasmus Dent, Walter Dent, John Dent, Richard Dent and Elizabeth Maria Dent (Ref: U-37).

DENT, WALTER. Took the Oath of Allegiance before Hon. John Dorsey on March 12, 1778 (Ref: B-26).

DERLING, ROBERT. Born in Scotland. His name appears on a list of Substitutes supplied by Beale Dorsey on May 18, 1778 to serve in the American Army for the duration of the war (Ref: C-213, H-319).

DIFFEY, ALEXANDER. Took the Oath of Allegiance before Hon. John Dorsey on March 12, 1778 (Ref: B-26).

DIGGONS, SAMUEL. Took the Oath of Allegiance before Hon. Thomas Worthington on February 28, 1778 (Ref: B-21).

DISNEY, EDWARD. Took the Oath of Allegiance before Hon. John Dorsey on March 12, 1778 (Ref: B-26). On May 31, 1822 the final distribution of the estate of Edward Disney was made by Margaret Disney, administratrix, to Margaret Disney (third), with halves to John Disney and Edward Disney (Ref: U-62).

DISNEY, JAMES. Took the Oath of Allegiance before Hon. John Dorsey on March 12, 1778 (Ref: B-25).

DISNEY, JAMES, JR. Captain in the 3rd Maryland Line, July, 1776 (Ref: H-38, H-41, N-534). His deposition was taken on August 27, 1776, regarding a dispute over election results and who was eligible to vote and bear arms, stating that Capt. Thomas Watkin's life was threatened (Ref: A-82).

DISNEY, JAMES (OF WILLIAM). Took the Oath of Allegiance before Hon. Richard Harwood, Jr. on March 1, 1778 (Ref: B-22).

DISNEY, RICHARD. Took the Oath of Allegiance before Hon. Thomas Dorsey on March 2, 1778 (Ref: B-23).

DISNEY, RICHARD JR. Enrolled by Capt. James Disney, Jr. and passed by Col. Richard Harwood on July 13, 1776 (Ref: H-41).

DISNEY, THOMAS. Took the Oath of Allegiance before Hon. Thomas Dorsey on March 2, 1778 (Ref: B-23).

DISNEY, WILLIAM. Took the Oath of Allegiance before Hon. Thomas Dorsey on March 2, 1778 (Ref: B-23).

DITTY, THOMAS. Took the Oath of Allegiance before Hon. Samuel Harrison in March, 1778 (Ref: A-244).

DIXON, JOHN. Took the Oath of Allegiance before Hon. John Dorsey on March 12, 1778 (Ref: B-26).

DIXON, SAMUEL. Took the Oath of Allegiance before Hon. Thomas Dorsey on March 2, 1778 (Ref: B-23). His name appeared on a list of Substitutes supplied by Belt Mulliken on May 18, 1778 to serve to war's end (Ref: C-207, H-318).

DOBSON, JOHN. Matross who was discharged from the service on December 31, 1777 because he was "subject to fits" (Ref: V-450).

DODSON, JOHN. Recruited and passed by James Brice on February 27, 1778 (Ref: C-215, H-313).

DOHERTY, PATRICK. Took Oath of Allegiance before Hon. Nicholas Worthington in March, 1778 (Ref: B-27).

DOLTREY, JESSE. Born in America. His name appears on a list of Substitutes supplied by Luke Bullen on May 11, 1778 for a 3 year term in the American Army (Ref: C-204, H-317).

DONNINGHAM (DONNINGTON), JOHN. Took the Oath of Allegiance before Hon. Thomas Worthington on February 28, 1778 (Ref: B-21).

DONNINGTON (DONNINGHAM), JAMES. Took Oath of Allegiance before Hon. Thomas Worthington on February 28, 1778 (Ref: B-21).

DORAGHY, ARTHUR. Born in Scotland. His name appears on a list of Substitutes supplied by Benjamin Shipley on May 15, 1778 to serve in the American Army for the duration of the war (Ref: C-213, H-319).

DORITY, JESSE. Born in Scotland. His name appears on a list of Substitutes supplied by Richard Odle and Beal Gaither on May 6, 1778 to serve in the American Army for 3 months (Ref: C-212, H-318).

DORSEY, AMOS (died in June, 1793). Son of Ely Dorsey and Deborah Dorsey. Married Mary Dorsey in 1784 and had 4 children: Deborah Dorsey Ridgely, Elizabeth Dorsey Ridgely, Mary Ann Dorsey Worthington, and Amos Dorsey. Amos took the Oath of Allegiance before Hon. Reuben Meriweather on March 2, 1778 (Ref: B-24, R-145).

DORSEY, AQUILA. Enrolled by Capt. Thomas Watkins for the service of the State on October 21, 1776 (Ref: I-144).

DORSEY, BASIL (1745, Anne Arundel County - July, 1799, Frederick County). Son of John and Elizabeth Dorsey. He married Hannah Crockett in 1768. Served as Captain of Militia on December 28, 1776, in the Linganore Hundred Battalion of Frederick County; resigned his commission in 1777 (Ref: R-126, T-276).

DORSEY, BENJAMIN. Took the Oath of Allegiance before Hon. Thomas Dorsey on March 2, 1778 (Ref: B-23. Note: Although he may have been a son of John and Elizabeth Dorsey, Source R-121 does not indicate that he took the Oath).

DORSEY, C. A. (Doctor). First Major in the Elk Ridge Battalion commanded by Col. Thomas Dorsey in 1778 (Ref: F-224).

DORSEY, CALEB (March 13, 1749 - April 14, 1837). Son of Thomas Beale Dorsey and Anne Worthington. Married Elizabeth Worthington in 1773 and they had 13 children: Nancy Dorsey, Susannah Dorsey Brooke, Thomas Beale Dorsey, Sarah Dorsey, Caleb Dorsey, John Dorsey, Charles Worthington Dorsey, Elizabeth Worthington Dorsey Baer, Comfort Worthington Dorsey, John Worthington Dorsey, Sarah Meriweather Dorsey Waring, Reuben Meriweather Dorsey, and Nicholas Dorsey. Caleb took the Oath of Allegiance before Hon. John Dorsey on March 12, 1778 (Ref: B-26, R-194, R-195).

DORSEY, CALEB. Son of Ely Dorsey and Deborah Dorsey. Married Dinah Warfield and they had one son, Caleb Dorsey. Commissioned a Second Lieutenant in the Elk Ridge Battalion of militia on February 28, 1776 (Ref: R-141, N-191).

DORSEY, CALEB (July 8, 1740 - August, 1795). Son of John Dorsey and Elizabeth Dorsey. Married first to Sophia Dorsey in 1759 and they had one daughter, Elizabeth Dorsey. Married second to Rebecca Hammond in 1762 and they had 11 children: Sarah Dorsey Lawrence, George Dorsey, Achsah Dorsey Gwinn, Caleb Dorsey, Sophia Dorsey Owings, Rebecca Dorsey, John Dorsey, William Dorsey, Larkin Dorsey, and Richard Dorsey. He served on the Committee of Observation in 1775, and took the Oath of Allegiance before Hon. Nicholas Worthington in March, 1778 (Ref: B-27, F-222, R-180, R-181).

DORSEY, CHARLES. Enlisted by John Burgess for the Flying Camp and passed on July 20, 1776 (Ref: H-40).

DORSEY, DANIEL. Captain in the 3rd Maryland Line in July, 1776 (Ref: H-38).

DORSEY, EDWARD (OF CALEB). Took Oath of Allegiance before Hon. John Dorsey on March 12, 1778 (Ref: B-26. See notes under "Edward Hill Dorsey, 1758-1799," q.v.). Edward Dorsey of Caleb, was drafted in October, 1780 to serve until December 10, 1780 (Ref: H-369).

DORSEY, EDWARD (OF EDWARD), died by July 6, 1782. Son of Edward Dorsey and Sarah Todd. Married Deborah Maccubbin (?) and had 11 children: Ely Dorsey, Benjamin Dorsey, Rhesaw Dorsey, John Lawrence Dorsey, Sophia Dorsey Dorsey, Elizabeth Dorsey Dorsey, Edward Dorsey, Rachel Dorsey Glover, Sarah Dorsey Talbot, Deborah Dorsey Wilson, and Leaven Dorsey. "Edward Dorsey, Jr." was one of the petitioners to the Convention of Maryland to form an independent rifle company in July, 1776 (Ref: B-3). "Edward Dorsey, of Edward" took the Oath of Allegiance before Hon. John Dorsey in 1778 (Ref: B-3, 26, R-127).

DORSEY, EDWARD (OF JOHN), October, 1728 - after 1790. Son of John and Honor Dorsey. Married Betty Gilliss and had six children: Ezekiel John Dorsey, Joseph Dorsey, Edward Hill Dorsey, Mary Hill Dorsey, Elizabeth Hill Dorsey Van Bebber, and Henry Dorsey. He served on the Committee of Observation in 1775 in Anne Arundel County (Ref: F-222), and he may have taken the Oath of Allegiance in Baltimore County in 1778 (Ref: R-25).

DORSEY, EDWARD HILL (April 8, 1760 - February 15, 1839). Son of Edward Dorsey and Elizabeth Gilliss. Married Deborah Maccubbin in 1781 and they had six children: Edward Hill Dorsey, Rebecca Dorsey, Robert Dorsey, Samuel Dorsey, Elizabeth Hill Dorsey Wilkins, and Ann Dorsey. His death notice states that "Major Edward Dorsey of Edward died at the residence of his son, Edward H. Dorsey..(and)..was a Revolutionary worthy." (Baltimore American, February 19, 1839). Note: It is not clear with so many Dorseys named Edward whether Edward H. and Edward of Edward were the same person. Source R-39 and R-127 has both Edwards with a wife named Deborah Maccubbin--another uncertainty.

DORSEY, EDWARD HILL (September 2, 1758 - March 24, 1799). Son of Edward Dorsey and Priscilla Hill. Married Elizabeth Dorsey in 1786 and they had nine children: Mary Dorsey Murray, Caroline Dorsey Donaldson, Priscilla Dorsey Hanson, Hill Dorsey, Robert Dorsey, Hammond Dorsey, Sarah Dorsey, Elizabeth Dorsey, and an unnamed infant son. Edward may have been the Edward Dorsey of Caleb who was drafted during October, 1780. (Ref: R-191, R-192. See notes on Edward Dorsey of Caleb, q.v.).

DORSEY, ELIAS, of Baltimore County (buried September 20, 1794). Son of Vachel Dorsey and Ruth Dorsey. Married first to Susanna Snowden in 1779 and second to Mary Lawrence in 1788. His children were Mary Dorsey Lawrence and Ruth Dorsey Howard. Elias was commissioned a First Lieutenant in the Soldier's Delight Hundred on September 11, 1777 and rose to the rank of Major in 1781 (Ref: R-37). Took the Oath of Allegiance before Hon. Reuben Meriwether on March 2, 1778 in Anne Arundel County (Ref: B-24).

DORSEY, ELY (1744 - March 14, 1803, Frederick County). Son of Edward Dorsey and Sarah Todd. He married Ruth Dorsey in 1765 and they had six children: Mary Dorsey, Edward Dorsey, Michael Dorsey, Honor Dorsey Poffenberger, Ruth Dorsey Davey, and Allen Dorsey. Ely served on the Committee of Safety in 1775 and was later commissioned a Lieutenant in 1776 in Capt. John Watkins' Company. On December 10, 1776 he became a Captain in the 2nd Maryland Line. He was taken prisoner at the battle of Staten Island on August 22, 1777, later released, and served through March, 1779 (Ref: R-133, R-134, T-277).

DORSEY, ELY (died in February, 1794). Son of John and Elizabeth Dorsey. He married first to Mary Crockett in 1744 and they had children John Crockett Dorsey and Mary Dorsey. He married second to Deborah Dorsey and had seven children: Caleb Dorsey, Ely Dorsey, Amos Dorsey, Elizabeth Dorsey Ridgely and Eleanor Dorsey Dorsey (Ref: R-124). Ely took Oath of Allegiance before Hon. Reuben Meriwether on March 2, 1778, and also served on the Committee of Observation in 1775 (Ref: B-24, F-222).

DORSEY, ELY JR. Took the Oath of Allegiance before Hon. John Dorsey on March 12, 1778 (Ref: B-26).

DORSEY, ELY (OF VACHEL). One of the petitioners to the Convention of Maryland to form an independent rifle company in July, 1776

(Ref: B-3. Note: This information could possibly pertain to "Elias Dorsey, of Vachel," q.v.).

DORSEY, EZEKIEL JOHN (born November 5, 1751). Son of John and Honor Dorsey. Married Amelia Gillis. He took the Oath of Allegiance before Hon. Reuben Meriweather on March 2, 1778 (Ref: B-24, R-25).

DORSEY, GILBERT. Enrolled by Capt. Thomas Watkins for the service of the State on October 21, 1776 (Ref: I-144).

DORSEY, HENRY. His name appears on a list of discharged soldiers of the militia, raised to serve in the Continental Army, in 1781 (Ref: H-407).

DORSEY, HENRY HALL (November 8, 1759 - February, 1819). Son of Joshua Dorsey and Elizabeth Hall. Married Mary Wright in 1795 and had 2 children: Harriet Dorsey Hammond and Mary Dorsey Hall. He took the Oath of Allegiance before Hon. John Dorsey on March 12, 1778, and signed his name "Henry H: Dorsey" (Ref: B-26, R-74).

DORSEY, JOHN (July 3, 1734 - March 9, 1779). Son of Michael Dorsey and Ruth Todd. Married Anne Dorsey and they had 7 children: Philemon Dorsey, Vachel Dorsey, Michael Dorsey, Catherine Dorsey Warfield, Ruth Dorsey Watkins, Eleanor Dorsey Burgess, and Elizabeth Dorsey. John was a prominent figure during the Revolutionary War. He was a Lieutenant Colonel in the Elk Ridge Battalion under Col. Thomas Dorsey in 1778 (Ref: C-201, P-276), and one of the Justices who administered the Oath of Allegiance in 1778 (Ref: B-26). He is probably the John Dorsey who took the Oath of Allegiance before Hon. Reuben Meriweather on March 2, 1778 (Ref: B-24). He served on the Committee of Observation in 1775, and a Delegate to the Maryland Convention in July, 1775 (Ref: F-222, R-27, J-4. See notes on "John Dorsey, 1736-1810," q.v.).

DORSEY, JOHN (1736 - January 2, 1810). Son of Edward Dorsey and Sarah Todd. Married Mary Hammond in 1757 and they had nine children: Robert Dorsey, Larkin Dorsey, Alexander Dorsey, William Hammond Dorsey, Elizabeth Dorsey Dorsey, Sarah M. Dorsey, Walter Dorsey, John E. Dorsey, and Clement Dorsey. He is styled Colonel in Source R-130, but the fact that he was a member of the Maryland Convention in 1775 and a Colonel in the Elk Ridge Battalion from 1776 to 1778 also applies to another John Dorsey (1734-1779), q.v., cited in that same reference (R-27), which also refers to the death notice of a Colonel John Dorsey on January 2, 1810 in his 76th year (see Baltimore Federal Gazette, January 6, 1810). Simple arithmetic shows that this John was born in 1734, not 1736. (It is difficult to ascertain which historical facts pertain to which John. Perhaps there were two Colonel John Dorseys).

DORSEY, JOHN, OF JOHN (March 31, 1751 - January, 1796). Son of John Dorsey and Elizabeth Dorsey. Married Margaret Boone in 1782 and had six children: Humphrey Dorsey, Caleb Dorsey, Charles Boone Dorsey, Stephen Boone Dorsey, Richard Dorsey, and Margaret Anne Dorsey Gaither. John was a Captain in the Elk Ridge Battalion in 1778 under Col. Thomas Dorsey and Lieutenant Colonel John Dorsey (Ref:

C-201, R-184, T-277). He also took the Oath of Allegiance before Hon. John Dorsey on March 12, 1778, according to Source R-184, which cites as its source The Maryland State Papers, Red Book, Part 4, Item 155. However, this published list appears to be in error as the original lists show the name as "John Dorsey of Ml.", which would indicate John Dorsey of Michael, not John. If such is true, then this entry belongs to him, q.v.).

DORSEY, JOHN (OF MICHAEL). He was one of the petitioners to the Convention of Maryland to form an independent rifle company in July, 1776 (Ref: B-3). He served on the Committee of Observation in 1775 (Ref: F-222. Note: See the information contained under John Dorsey, of John, q.v., regarding the Oath of Allegiance in 1778).

DORSEY, JOHN (OF SEVERN JOHN). Was one of the petitioners to the Convention of Maryland to form an independent rifle company in July, 1776 (Ref: B-3). He served on the Committee of Observation in 1775 (Ref: F-222).

DORSEY, JOHN (c1760 - September 30, 1815). Married Mary Cummings and had 8 children: Margaret Dorsey, John Dorsey, Samuel Thomas Dorsey, Basil Dorsey, Elizabeth Dorsey, Mary Dorsey, William Dorsey, and David Alexander Dorsey. He took the Oath of Allegiance in Anne Arundel County on March 12, 1778 and died in Frederick County in 1815 (according to Source T-277).

DORSEY, JOHN WORTHINGTON (October 8, 1751 - May 13, 1823). Son of Thomas Beal Dorsey and Anne Worthington. Married Comfort Worthington in 1778 and they had 7 children: Thomas Beale Dorsey, Samuel Worthington Dorsey, John Tolley Worthington Dorsey, Caleb Dorsey, Mary Tolley Dorsey, Edward Worthington Dorsey, and Charles Samuel Worthington Dorsey. John became a 2nd Lieutenant on June 6, 1776 in the 3rd Maryland Line and participated in the battles of Long Island and White Plains. In 1778 he became a Captain in the Elk Ridge Battalion under Col. Thomas Dorsey (Ref: C-201, R-196, N-534, H-38).

DORSEY, JOSEPH (1753 - circa January, 1837, Washington County, Pennsylvania). Son of Edward Dorsey and Betty Gilliss. Married Amelia Gilliss in 1780 and they had 12 children: Edward Gilliss Dorsey, Henry Dorsey, Ezekiel Dorsey, Mary Hill Dorsey Wilson, Elizabeth Dorsey Workman, James Dorsey, John Dorsey, Matilda Dorsey Blaine, Harriet Dorsey Wilson, Clarissa Dorsey West, Nancy Dorsey Dubois, and Rebecca Dorsey (Ref: R-38, R-39). He took the Oath of Allegiance before Hon. Reuben Meriweather on March 2, 1778 (Ref: B-24).

DORSEY, JOSEPH JR. Took the Oath of Allegiance before Hon. Thomas Dorsey on March 2, 1778 (Ref: B-23).

DORSEY, JOSHUA SR. (July 8, 1736 - 1799). Son of Henry Dorsey and Elizabeth Worthington. Married Elizabeth Hall in 1759 and they had 11 children: Henry Hall Dorsey, William Henry Dorsey, Isaac Dorsey, Elizabeth Dorsey Dorsey, Allen Dorsey, Thomas Hall Dorsey, Margaret Dorsey, John Hall Dorsey, Joshua Dorsey, Mary Dorsey Goldwait, and

William Dorsey. He was a Lieutenant under Capt. Thomas Philips in May 13, 1776 (Ref: R-64, N-422). He took the Oath of Allegiance before Hon. John Dorsey on March 12, 1778 (Ref: B-26).

DORSEY, JOSHUA (born in Anne Arunel County; died November 28, 1818, Frederick County). Son of Philemon Dorsey and Catherine Ridgely. Married Jane Kennedy and had a daughter, Elizabeth Dorsey Johnson. Joshua was elected Clerk of the Senate in 1783 and served until 1789 (Ref: P-277, P-278).

DORSEY, LACON (LEAKIN, LARKIN), born February 15, 1747. Son of Francis Dorsey and Elizabeth Baker. Believed to have taken the Oath of Allegiance in 1778 in Washington County, and married Ann Schmid there in 1783 (Ref: R-108).

DORSEY, LANCELOT (OF EDWARD). Son of Edward Dorsey and Sarah Todd. Married Deborah Ridgely; issue unknown. He took the Oath of Allegiance before Hon. John Dorsey on March 12, 1778 (Ref: B-26, R-130).

DORSEY, LANCELOT (OF JOHN). Took the Oath of Allegiance before Hon. John Dorsey on March 12, 1778 (according to Source B-26, which cites Maryland State Papers, Red Book, Part 4, Item 155. However, this published list is apparently in error as the original list gives the name as "Lancelot Dorsey of Ml.", which would indicate it pertained to Lancelot Dorsey, of Michael, not John. If such is true, then this entry belongs to that person, q.v.).

DORSEY, LANCELOT (OF MICHAEL), July 17, 1747 - March 1, 1829). Son of Michael Dorsey and Ruth Todd. Married Sarah Warfield and had 10 children: Deale Dorsey, Dennis Dorsey, Darius Dorsey, Dathan Dorsey, Philemon Dorsey, Ann Dorsey Elder, Ruth Dorsey Ridgely, Lydia Dorsey, Elizabeth Dorsey and Michael Dorsey. Lancelot furnished a Substitute for the 4th Maryland Line in 1777 (Ref: R-31. Note: See entry under Lancelot Dorsey, of John, q.v., as it pertains to the Oath of Allegiance in 1778).

DORSEY, LARKIN (born 1760 and died in the West Indies without issue). Son of Edward Dorsey and Sarah Todd. Captain during the Revolution (Ref: R-130).

DORSEY, MICHAEL, JR. (October 29, 1745 - February 28, 1812). Son of Michael Dorsey and Ruth Todd. Married Honor Elder and had 8 children: Owen Dorsey, Elizabeth Dorsey Ball, Honor Dorsey, Cecil Dorsey, Michael Dorsey, Jemina Dorsey Warfield, Lloyd Dorsey, and John Dorsey (R-30). Michael was one of the petitioners to the Convention of Maryland to form an independent rifle company in July, 1776 (Ref: B-3). Note: Source R-30 states he took the Oath of Allegiance before Hon. Reuben Meriweather in 1778, but Source B-24 does not include him on the list.

DORSEY, NATHAN, M.D. Son of Nathan Dorsey and Sophia Owings. On March 1, 1776 he was a Junior Mate on the ship "Defense" in the Maryland Navy. He died in 1806 in Philadelphia (Ref: R-43).

DORSEY, NICHOLAS (1713 - May, 1780). Son of Nicholas Dorsey and Frances Hughes. Married Sarah Griffith in 1736 and they had 12 children: Rachel Dorsey Lindsay, Lydia Dorsey Dorsey, Nicholas Dorsey, Charles Dorsey, Catherine Dorsey Wood, Henry Dorsey, Sarah Dorsey, Vachel Dorsey, Lucretia Dorsey Welsh, Frances Dorsey Chapman Warfield, Orlando Dorsey, and Achsah Dorsey Warfield (Ref: R-88, which states that Nicholas was a non-juror in 1779 but may have taken the Oath of Allegiance by 1780 as many non-jurors did to prevent their property from being triple taxed).

DORSEY, NICHOLAS (OF EDWARD). Took the Oath of Allegiance before Hon. John Dorsey on March 12, 1778 (according to Source B-26 which cites Maryland State Papers, Red Book, Part 4, Item 155). However, this published list appears to be in error since the original list gives the name as "Nicholas Dorsey of Josa.", not Edward, and Source B-26 is, therefore, incorrect.

DORSEY, NICHOLAS, OF HENRY (January 8, 1750 - October 7, 1788). Son of Henry Dorsey and Elizabeth Worthington. Married Lucy Sprigg and had 5 children: Fredrick Dorsey, Samuel Dorsey, Dennis Dorsey, Roderick Dorsey, Mary Dorsey and, possibly, John Dorsey (Ref: R-66). Nicholas was one of the petitioners to the Convention of Maryland to form an independent rifle company in July, 1776 (Ref: B-3). Took the Oath of Allegiance before Hon. Reuben Meriweather on March 2, 1778 (Ref: B-24).

DORSEY, NICHOLAS, OF JOSHUA (June 2, 1725 - October 9, 1792). Son of Joshua Dorsey and Anne Ridgely. Married Elizabeth Worthington and had 7 children: Nicholas Worthington Dorsey, Elizabeth Dorsey Warfield, Lloyd Dorsey, Anne Worthington Dorsey Worthington, Mary Dorsey Dorsey, Joshua Dorsey and Sarah Dorsey Ball (Ref: R-62. However, this source does not credit Nicholas with taking the Oath of Allegiance in 1778). He took the Oath of Allegiance on March 12, 1778 before Hon. John Dorsey, but Source B-26 (a published list of those who took the oath) mistakenly gives his name as Nicholas Dorsey of Edward. The original Maryland State Papers, Red Book 22, gives his name as "Nicholas Dorsey, of Josa.", which indicates that Nicholas Dorsey of Joshua took the Oath of Allegiance, and not Nicholas Dorsey of Edward, q.v. Also, Source T-277 states he died in 1780, not in 1792).

DORSEY, NICHOLAS, OF NICHOLAS (November 1, 1759 - October 16, 1821). Son of Nicholas Dorsey and Elizabeth Worthington. Married Rachel Warfield in 1779 and had eleven children: Nicholas Dorsey, Joshua W. Dorsey, Noah Dorsey, Matilda Dorsey Hall, Clarissa Dorsey Waters, Alfred Dorsey, Reuben Dorsey, Ezra Dorsey, Lloyd Dorsey, Evelina Dorsey, and Mortimer Dorsey (Ref: R-70). Nicholas was a Private in 1776 and fought in the battle of White Plains. In December, 1776 he was an Ensign in the 4th Maryland Line. In 1777 he became a Lieutenant and on November 10, 1778 he resigned (Ref: E-2934, and R-70, which cites Revolutionary War pension claim W9411). "Nicholas Dorsey, Jr." was appointed a Justice of the Peace in November, 1778 (Ref: O-241). Source T-277 states he married second to Elizabeth Worthington and died in 1821 in Montgomery County, Maryland (also styled him "Nicholas W. Dorsey, Jr.").

DORSEY, NICHOLAS (OF NICHOLAS), of Baltimore County (1741 - August, 1797). Son of Nicholas Dorsey and Sarah Griffith. Married Ruth Todd in 1765 and had 10 children: Charles Dorsey, Samuel Dorsey, Anne Dorsey, Josiah Dorsey, Samuel Dorsey, Eleanor Dorsey, Elizabeth Dorsey Hawkins Bayley, Jeremiah Dorsey, John Dorsey, and Henry Gough Kennedy Dorsey. Nicholas resided in Baltimore County and in 1775 represented Delaware Hundred on the Committee of Observation (Ref: R-90).

DORSEY, PHILEMON (February 7, 1743 - January, 1807). Son of Philemon Dorsey and Catherine Ridgely. Married Anne Dorsey in 1770 and had seven children: George Dorsey, John Dorsey, Elizabeth Dorsey Stringer, Elenor Dorsey Banks, Mary Dorsey Gardiner, Anne Dorsey Dorsey, and Catherine Dorsey (Ref: R-68). Philemon was one of the petitioners to form an independent rifle company in July, 1776 (Ref: B-3), and took the Oath of Allegiance before Hon. Reuben Meriweather on March 2, 1778 (Ref: B-25).

DORSEY, PHILIP. Served on the Committee of Observation in 1775 (Ref: F-222).

DORSEY, RICHARD (1754, Anne Arundel County - May 16, 1799 in Baltimore Town). Son of Edward Dorsey and Sarah Todd. Married Rebecca Hawkins (the widow Pierpont) circa 1784 and they had 5 children: Edward Dorsey, Sarah Dorsey Suter, Eudocia Dorsey Gird Hills, Mary Dorsey, and Edward John Dorsey. On July 16, 1776 he became 3rd Lieutenant in Capt. Nathaniel Smith's Company of Matrosses and then Captain in the First Continental Artillery Regiment in 1777 (H-573, T-278). He was wounded at the battle of Camden on August 16, 1780 and received pay from the State for his disability in 1791 (Ref: K-337). He was an Original Member of the Society of the Cincinnati in 1783. His widow married Hugh Stewart, and died in 1818 (Ref: R-134, R-135).

DORSEY, RICHARD. Private in Capt. William Marbury's Company of Artillery in 1777 (Ref: H-575).

DORSEY, RICHARD (December 6, 1756 - May 11, 1826). Son of John Dorsey and Elizabeth Dorsey. Married Ann Wayman in 1796 in Montgomery County (lived in Anne Arundel) and had 12 children: Mortimer Dorsey, Eliza Dorsey Norris Hobbs, Caroline Dorsey Wheeler Hood, John Dorsey, Caleb Dorsey, Richard Dorsey, Louisa Dorsey Hood, Mary Dorsey Gist, Hanson Dorsey, Achsah Dorsey Ridgely, Henry Dorsey, and Septimus Dorsey. Richard was a Private in Capt. William Marbury's Company of Artillery in 1777-1778. Served in Col. Moses Rawlings' Regiment, and was wounded and taken prisoner at the battle of Fort Washington in 1780 (Ref: R-186, R-187, R-188, R-189, F-442, T-278).

DORSEY, SAMUEL (December 7, 1741 - September 11, 1777). Son of Caleb Dorsey and Priscilla Hill. Married Margaret Sprigg in 1772 and they had one son, Edward Hill Dorsey. He served on the Committee of Observation in 1775 and manufactured ordnance for the Army at his Elk Ridge iron works. He also furnished tents and bayonets for the militia, He sometimes signed his name "Samuel Dorsey. of Caleb" and sometimes "Samuel Dorsey, of Belmont" (Ref: F-222, N-535, and, R-190 which gives his name as "Samuel Dorsey, Jr.").

DORSEY, SAMUEL, JR. One of the petitioners to the Convention of Maryland to form an independent rifle company in July, 1776 (Ref: B-3. Note: Source R-190 states that he signed his name Samuel Dorsey, Jr., which would imply he was a son of Samuel, but he actually was Samuel Dorsey, son of Caleb).

DORSEY, THOMAS (died in 1790). Son of Basil Dorsey and Sarah Worthington. Married first to Elizabeth Ridgely, daughter of Col. Henry Ridgely, circa 1756, and had a son Daniel Dorsey. Married secondly to Elizabeth Ridgely, daughter of Judge Nicholas Ridgely, in 1761, and had 8 children: Archibald Dorsey, Theodore Dorsey, Nicholas Dorsey, Mary Dorsey Norwood, Elizabeth Dorsey Berry, Juliet Dorsey Hawkins, Harriet Dorsey Berry, and Matilda Dorsey Sullivan (Ref: R-178). Thomas was most prominent in the Revolution. He was one of the Justices to administer the Oath of Allegiance in March, 1778 (Ref: B-23), a Justice of the Peace in November, 1778, and Colonel of the Elk Ridge Battalion in 1778. He was a collector of gold and silver in Anne Arundel County in exchange for continental money for use of Congress (Ref: C-201, F-222, F-223, F-224, N-132, O-241, P-278). He served on the Committee of Observation in 1775, was a Delegate to the Maryland Convention in 1775-1776, and was a Signer of the Association of Freemen of Maryland in 1775 (Ref: F-222, R-179, J-4, J-35, J-55). He was appointed a Purchaser of Provisions for the United States Army on March 25, 1778 (Ref: V-551).

DORSEY, THOMAS (born on March 15, 1737). Son of Henry Dorsey and Elizabeth Worthington. Married Mary Ann Warfield and they had 4 children: Benedict Dorsey, Elizabeth Dorsey Warfield, Rebecca Dorsey Burgess, and Mary Ridgely Dorsey Burgess. He took the Oath of Allegiance before Hon. Thomas Worthington on February 28, 1778 (Ref: B-21, R-65, R-66).

DORSEY, VACHEL (March 15, 1758 - December, 1805). Son of Henry Dorsey and Elizabeth Worthington. He married first to Elizabeth Battee in 1778 and second to Lydia Stringer in 1801; no issue. Took the Oath of Allegiance before Hon. Thomas Worthington on February 28, 1778 (Ref: B-21, R-68).

DORSEY, VACHEL (October 20, 1726 - by March, 1798). Son of John and Honor Dorsey. He married Ruth Dorsey and had 6 children: Johnsa Dorsey, Vachel Dorsey, Edward Dorsey, Ruth Dorsey Owings, Elias Dorsey and Leaven Dorsey. His lands were partly in Anne Arundel County and Baltimore County. He took the Oath of Allegiance before Hon. Edward Cockey on February 28, 1778 in Baltimore County (Ref: R-23).

DORSEY, VACHEL (died by April 24, 1815). Son of Nathan Dorsey and Sophia Owings. He married Clementine Ireland in 1786 and they had 10 children: Elizabeth Dorsey Hall, John Ireland Dorsey, James

Ireland Dorsey, Louisa Dorsey, Andrew Dorsey, Samuel Dorsey, Daniel Horatio Dorsey, Ezekiel Dorsey, Sarah Ann Dorsey, and Rebecca Dorsey Adams. As stated in Source R-41, "according to his grandson, he served in the Revolutionary War, was wounded with the result that one leg was amputated. It has been difficult to place his service, as several Vachel Dorseys, all contemporaries and within the age brackets to serve, participated. Furthermore, the loss of militia muster rolls for Anne Arundel County adds further difficulties in war placement. He was not granted Federal bounty land for his service and he was not a participant of State bounty warrants granted to soldiers of the Continental Establishments, all of which may indicate that his service was with the militia. According to available records searched, he was not pensioned by the State or Federal Government for his disability. Though the absence of a pension and his not applying do not disprove his service." (Ref: R-41, R-42, F-490, U-48. Note: Source T-279 indicates he was born January 27, 1756, died May 14, 1813, and served in the Navy at the time of or during the Revolutionary War (but this is not specified in Ref: R-41).

DORSEY, VACHEL (1760 - October 27, 1814). Son of Vachel Dorsey and Ruth Dorsey. He married first to Sarah Nelson in 1783 and they had 5 children: Maria Cecelia Dorsey, Caroline Dorsey, Mary Dorsey, Rachel Dorsey and Charles Dorsey. Married second to Elizabeth Dorsey in 1798 and had 5 more children: Elizabeth Hall Dorsey, Essex Ridley Dorsey, Evaline Mary Dorsey Comegys, Anne Dorsey and Emma Ridgely Dorsey. Vachel entered the military in 1776, served with the Elk Ridge Battalion and subsequently served with th Flying Camp until it was disbanded at Christmas, 1776. On May 1, 1777 he was commissioned an Ensign in Col. Hartley's Regiment, became a Lieutenant, and served until August 22, 1779 when he resigned (Ref: H-41, R-33, R-34).

DORSEY, WILLIAM HENRY (born May 31, 1761) Son of Joshua Dorsey and Elizabeth Worthington. He died in a British military prison during the Revolutionary War (Ref: R-65).

DOVE, JOHN. Took the Oath of Allegiance before Hon. Samuel Lane on March 1, 1778 (Ref: B-23).

DOVE, MARK. Took the Oath of Allegiance before Hon. Samuel Harrison, Jr. in March, 1778 (Ref: B-28).

DOVE, WILLIAM. He took the Oath of Allegiance before Hon. Thomas Harwood in February, 1778 (Ref: B-22). Deceased by December 19, 1792, when the final distribution of his estate was made to Sarah Dove (third), and sevenths to Elizabeth Dove, Joseph Dove, Thomas Dove, James Steward (husband of Alice Dove), and John Hooper (husband of Mary Dove), and Sarah Dove (Ref: U-9).

DOVE, WILLIAM JR. Born in Maryland. Enlisted by Capt. Edward Tillard on July 10, 1776. Height: 5' 8" (Ref: H-39).

DOWELL, JOHN. Resident of Herring Creek and one of the petitioners to form a militia company on March 6, 1776 and subsequently elected a Corporal (Ref: I-143). He took the Oath of Allegiance before Hon. Samuel Harrison, Jr. in March, 1778 (Ref: B-28).

DOWELL, THOMAS. Took the Oath of Allegiance before Hon. Samuel Harrison, Jr. in March, 1778 (Ref: B-28).

DRAWATER, ROBERT. Took the Oath of Allegiance before Hon. Reuben Meriweather on March 2, 1778 (Ref: B-25).

DRUMMOND, JOHN. Took the Oath of Allegiance before Hon. John Dorsey on March 12, 1778 (Ref: B-26).

DRURY, CHARLES. Took the Oath of Allegiance before Hon. Samuel Lane on March 1, 1778 (Ref: B-23).

DRURY, SAMUEL SR. (1751 or 1759 - 1843). He married Anne Ijams and they had ten children: Henry Childs Drury, Samuel Drury, Jr., Elizabeth Drury, Ruth Drury, Mary Drury, Margaret Drury Hopkins, Ann Drury, Plummer Drury, John Drury, and William Drury (Ref: T-282). He was an Ensign in Captain William Simmons' Company in the West River Battalion in 1778 (Ref: C-200). Took the Oath of Allegiance before Hon. Samuel Lane on March 1, 1778 (Ref: B-23). On October 23, 1817 Samuel Drury, Sr. was administrator de bonis non with will annexed of Plummer Ijams, and made final distribution (thirds) to William Drury, Samuel Drury, and the heirs of Plummer Ijams, Jr. (Ref: U-51).

DRURY, WILLIAM. Took the Oath of Allegiance before Hon. Samuel Harrison in March, 1778 (Ref: A-244).

DUE, RICHARD. Took the Oath of Allegiance before Hon. Thomas Worthington on February 28, 1778 (Ref: B-21).

DUFFIELD, RICHARD. Took the Oath of Allegiance before Hon. John Dorsey on March 12, 1778 (Ref: B-26).

DUFFY, MICHAEL. Disabled soldier, reported out of state when paid August 16, 1783 in Anne Arundel County; also paid on January 13, 1784 and April 13, 1784 and June 9, 1784 and September 3, 1784 and October 26, 1784 and December 17, 1784 (Ref: D-8, 12, 13, 18, 21, 23, 25).

DUNN, PATRICK. Private in Captain William Marbury's Company of Artillery in 1777 (Ref: H-575).

DUNNAVIN, TIMOTHY. Private in Captain Richard Dorsey's Company of Artillery on November 17, 1777 (Ref: H-574).

DUVALL, EMOS (AMOS). Took the Oath of Allegiance before Hon. John Dorsey on March 12, 1778 (Ref: B-26).

DUVALL, GABRIEL. Private in Capt. Gilbert Middleton's Independent Company of Militia of Annapolis on March 20, 1779 (Ref: I-144, O-325).

DUVALL, GABRIEL (December 6, 1752 - March 6, 1844). Born and died in Prince George's County, but resided in Annapolis circa 1777 to circa 1802, during which time he was a prominent patriot. Son of Benjamin Duvall and Susanna Tyler. Married Mary Bryce in 1787 and had a son, Edmund Bryce Duvall, and possibly a daughter, Polly Duvall. A lawyer by profession, Gabriel served as Clerk of the 4th to 9th Maryland Conventions, 1775-1776; Clerk of the Council of Safety in 1776; Clerk of the Lower House in 1777; Clerk of the Commission for the Sale of Confiscated British Property in 1781-1782; and, served on the Executive Council from 1782 to 1786. He was also a Major in the Anne Arundel County Militia in 1794, U.S. Congressman, 1794-1796, first Comptroller of the U.S. Treasury, 1802-1811, and Associate Justice of the U.S. Supreme Court, 1811-1835 (Ref: P-290, P-291).

DUVALL, JOSEPH. His name appears on a list of recruits in Capt. Fulford's Artillery stationed in Annapolis on December 12, 1776 (Ref: H-572).

DUVALL, MILES. Son of Hugh Duvall, a French Huguenot. Miles was a Privateer in the Revolutionary War and afterwards a coast trader supposedly killed in 1787 by pirates. His son Gabriel was born in Annapolis in 1787 and removed to Kentucky with his mother in 1790, where he died August 1, 1827. Gabriel Duvall married Mary Grable and they had five children: Cyrus Duvall, Joseph Duvall, Thomas Duvall, Gabriel Duvall, and Louisiana Duvall (Ref: HCP:44).

DUVALL, THOMAS. Took the Oath of Allegiance before Hon. Thomas Worthington on February 28, 1778 (Ref: B-21).

DUVALL, ZACHARIAH (February 10, 1743, Prince Georges County - April 11, 1806, Anne Arundel County). Married Jemina Selby in 1765. Source T-288 states he married Zemima Selby and had 5 children: Zachariah Duvall, Mary Duvall Merriken, John Duvall, Lewis Duvall, and Henry Duvall. He took the Oath of Allegiance before Hon. Richard Harwood, Jr. on March 1, 1778, and assisted in providing food and horses for the Army in 1781 (Ref: E-2781, B-22).

DYCUS, ISAAC. Enrolled by Capt. Thomas Watkins for the service of the State on October 21, 1776 (Ref: I-144).

DYER, JAMES. Disabled soldier who was paid on December 11, 1783 and January 13, 1784 and April 13, 1784 and June 9, 1784 and September 3, 1784 and October 26, 1784 and December 17, 1784 (Ref: D-10, 11, 14, 18, 23, 25).

EARL, PAUL. Took the Oath of Allegiance before Hon. Reuben Meriweather on March 2, 1778 (Ref: B-24).

EARP, EDWARD. Took the Oath of Allegiance before Hon. Reuben Meriweather on March 2, 1778 (Ref: B-24).

EARP, JOSHUA. Took the Oath of Allegiance before Hon. Reuben Meriweather on March 2, 1778 (Ref: B-24).

EARP, PETTICOAT. Enlisted by John Worthington Dorsey on July 22, 1776 (Ref: H-39). Took the Oath of Allegiance before Hon. Reuben Meriweather on March 2, 1778 (Ref: B-24).

EARP, THOMAS. Took the Oath of Allegiance before Hon. Reuben Meriweather on March 2, 1778 (Ref: B-24).

EARP, WILLIAM. Took the Oath of Allegiance before Hon. Reuben Meriweather on March 2, 1778 (Ref: B-24).

EASSON, JOHN. Born in Scotland. He was a Substitute, furnished by Charles Ridgely on May 12, 1778, for the duration of the war (Ref: C-207, H-318).

EASSON (EASON), WILLIAM. Took Oath of Allegiance before Hon. Thomas Harwood in February, 1778 (Ref: B-22).

EASTON, JOHN. His name appeared on a List of Defectives from the Maryland Line on August 16, 1780 (Ref: H-415).

EASTON, RICHARD. Took the Oath of Allegiance before Hon. John Dorsey on March 12, 1778 (Ref: B-26).

EATON, WILLIAM. Resident of Herring Creek who helped form a militia company there on March 6, 1776 (Ref: I-143).

EDDINGS, JOHN. Took the Oath of Allegiance before Hon. Thomas Harwood in February, 1778 (Ref: B-22).

EDGE, WILLIAM. Enlisted by Joseph Burgess for the Flying Camp on July 16, 1776 (Ref: H-40).

EDMONDSON, POLLARD. Third Lieutenant, 4th Independent Company, commissioned by the Council of Safety in 1776 (Ref: F-222).

EDMONSTON, SAMUEL. Surgeon in the Annapolis hospital in 1776 (Ref: Y-303).

EDWARDS, AQUILA. Son of Edward and Anne Edwards. Took the Oath of Allegiance before Hon. Nicholas Worthington in March, 1778 (Ref: B-27, R-223).

EDWARDS, EDWARD (born June 7, 1711). Son of Cadwallader Edwards and Catherine Bourne, widow of Henry. Edward married Jemima Welsh in 1734/5 and had one son, Edward Edwards (Ref: R-221, R-222). Either he or his son took the Oath of Allegiance before Hon. Nicholas Worthington in 1778 (Ref: B-27).

EDWARDS, EDWARD JR. (died in 1786). Son of Edward Edwards and Jemima Welsh. Married Anne ----- and they had twelve children: Catherine Edwards Lusby, Elizabeth Edwards Anderson, Jemima Edwards Evans, Mary Edwards Waters, Sarah Edwards Anderson, Anne Edwards Linthicum, Margaret Edwards Fonderen, Aquila Edwards, William Edwards, Cadwallader Edwards, Jonathan Edwards and Edward Edwards. He was an Ensign in the 4th Maryland Regiment, resigning his commission on November 1, 1777 (Ref: R-223, R-224). Final distribution of his estate was made by William Edwards, administrator, on September 23, 1793, giving tenths of the balance to: Children of Jemima Evans; children of Catherine Lusby; William Anderson, husband of Elizabeth Edwards; Sarah Edwards; Cephas Waters, husband of Mary Edwards; John Linthicum, husband of Mary Edwards (sic); John Fonerdon, husband of Margaret Edwards; William Edwards; Cadwallader Edwards; and, Jonathan Edwards (Ref: U-10, U-11).

ELISHA, THOMAS. Took the Oath of Allegiance before Hon. John Dorsey on March 12, 1778 (Ref: B-26).

ELLICOTT, ANDREW. Appointed a Justice of the Peace for Anne Arundel County on November 19, 1778 (Ref: O-241).

ELLICOTT, ANDREW JR. Took the Oath of Allegiance before Hon. John Dorsey on March 12, 1778 (Ref: Original list in Maryland State Papers, Red Book 22. Note: Ref. B-26 mistakenly gives his name as Elliott instead of Ellicott). Commissioned a Captain in the Elk Ridge Battalion under Col. Thomas Dorsey on March 1, 1778 and a Major under Col. Edward Gaither on November 2, 1778 (Ref: C-201, O-229).

ELLICOTT, DAVID. Took the Oath of Allegiance before Hon. John Dorsey on March 12, 1778 (Ref: Original list in Maryland State Papers, Red Book 22. Note: Ref. B-26 mistakenly gives his name as Elliott instead of Ellicott).

ELLICOTT, JONATHAN. Took the Oath of Allegiance before Hon. John Dorsey on March 12, 1778 (Ref: Original lists in Maryland State Papers, Red Book 22. Note: Ref. B-26 mistakenly gives his name as Elliott instead of Ellicott). Commissioned a Second Lieutenant in Capt. Charles Fox's Company in the Elk Ridge Battalion of Militia in March, 1779 (Ref: O-333).

ELLICOTT, JOSEPH. Took the Oath of Allegiance before Hon. John Dorsey on March 12, 1778 (Ref: Original list in Maryland State Papers, Red Book 22. Note: Ref. B-26 mistakenly gives his name as Elliott instead of Ellicott).

ELLICOTT, JOSEPH JR. Took the Oath of Allegiance before Hon. John Dorsey on March 12, 1778 (Ref: Original list in Maryland State Papers, Red Book 22. Note: Ref. B-26 mistakenly gives his name as Elliott instead of Ellicott).

ELLIOTT, EDWARD. Born in England. He was a Substitute, furnished by Dennis Stephens, on May 13, 1778 for the duration of the war (Ref: C-204, H-317).

ELLIOTT, JAMES. Took the Oath of Allegiance before Hon. Thomas Harwood in February, 1778 (Ref: B-22).

ELLIOTT, JOHN. Enrolled by Capt. Thomas Watkins on October 21, 1776 for the service to the State (Ref: I-144, MS.1814). He took the Oath of Allegiance before Hon. Richard Harwood, Jr. on March 1,

1778 (Ref: B-22). John Elliott married Sarah Warfield on July 12, 1787 (Ref: G-113).

ELLIOTT, MATTHEW. Enrolled by Capt. Thomas Watkins on October 21, 1776 for service to the State (Ref: I-144, MS.1814). He took the Oath of Allegiance before Hon. Richard Harwood, Jr. on March 1, 1778 (Ref: B-22).

ELLIOTT, RICHARD. Took the Oath of Allegiance before Hon. Richard Harwood, Jr. on March 1, 1778 (Ref: B-22).

ELLIOTT, ROBERT. Took the Oath of Allegiance before Hon. Nicholas Worthington in March, 1778 (Ref: B-27). Deceased by May 11, 1793 when William Elliott, admin., made final distribution by giving halves of balance to John Elliott and Samuel Elliott. Sureties were James Cadle and William Hays (Ref: U-9).

ELLIOTT, ROBERT WELCH. Took the Oath of Allegiance before Hon. Richard Harwood, Jr. on March 1, 1778 (Ref: B-22).

ELLIOTT, THOMAS. Two men with this name took the Oath of Allegiance: one before Hon. Richard Harwood, Jr. on March 1, 1778, and one before Hon. Nicholas Worthington in March, 1778 (Ref: B-22, B-27). One Thomas Elliott was surviving executor of Sarah Elliott and made distribution of her estate on April 15, 1789, by giving sevenths of the balance to Thomas Elliott, Robert Elliott, William Elliott, Ann Elliott, and heirs of James Elliott, heirs of Sarah Elliott, and heirs of Elizabeth Cadle (Ref: U-3). One Thomas Elliott was pensioned on April 25, 1818 and reported dead (Ref: Z-27).

ELLIOTT, WILLIAM. Took Oath of Allegiance before Hon. Nicholas Worthington in March, 1778 (Ref: B-27). He was drafted in October, 1780 to serve until December 10, 1780 (Ref: H-368).

ELTHAM, JOHN. Born in Ireland. Enlisted and passed by James Brice in Anne Arundel County on February 28, 1778 (Ref: C-216, H-313).

ENNIS, LEONARD. Private in the Maryland Line from 1780 through 1783 (Ref: H-443, H-510, H-533). Married Jane Burke in November, 1783 (Ref: G-113).

EVANS, JAMES. Enlisted by Thomas Mayo on July 20, 1776 (Ref: H-41).

EVANS, JOHN. Took the Oath of Allegiance before Hon. John Dorsey on March 12, 1778 (Ref: B-26).

EVANS, JOSEPH. Took the Oath of Allegiance before Hon. John Dorsey on March 12, 1778 (Ref: B-26). First Lieutenant in Capt. Andrew Ellicott's Company in the Elk Ridge Battalion on March 1, 1778 (Ref: C-201).

EVANS, LEWIS. Took the Oath of Allegiance before Hon. John Dorsey on March 12, 1778 (Ref: B-26).

EVANS, WILLIAM. Took the Oath of Allegiance before Hon. Samuel Harrison, Jr. in March, 1778 (Ref: B-28). He was a disabled sodlier who was discharged at Frederick Town on November 29, 1783 (Ref: X-9). He received the half pay of a private on January 13, 1784, April 13, 1784, June 9, 1784, September 3, 1784 and December 17, 1784 (Ref: D-12, 13, 18, 21, 23, 25). He subsequently received a pension of $40 per year from March 4, 1789 (Ref: K-340).

EVERETT (EVERITT), JOHN. Born in Maryland, Enlisted by John Kilty in July, 1776. Neight: 5' 4" (Ref: H-40).

EVERETT, WILLIAM. Born in Maryland. Enlisted by John S. Belt in July, 1776. Height: 5' 4 1/2" (Ref" H-40).

EWING, NATHANIEL. "Ordered that the Treasurer of the Western Shore pay to Lieutenant Nathaniel Ewing six pounds four shillings for expences incurred in guarding a sick prisoner sent from the Colony of North Carolina, from the City of Annapolis to Pennsylvania." (Ref: N-497).

EYER (EYRE), FREDERICK. Maimed soldier who received half pay in Anne Arundel County on May 19, 1783 and April 13, 1784 (Ref: D-6, D-13). He subsequently received a pension under the Act of June 7, 1785 of $40 per year from March 4, 1789 (Ref: K-340, which source incorrectly spelled his name "Eyen").

FAHEY, PATRICK. Took the Oath of Allegiance before Hon. John Dorsey on March 12, 1778 (Ref: B-26).

FAIRBROTHER, FRANCIS. In November, 1806 the Treasurer was ordered to pay him half pay of a private. On March 6, 1832 the Treasurer was ordered to pay to Patience Fairbrother, of Anne Arundel County, widow of Francis, a soldier of the Revolutionary War, half yearly, the half pay of a private, for the service rendered by her husband during said war (Ref: K-340, K-341). He was also a County Coroner from June 3 to August 3, 1778 (Ref: O-121, O-175). He married Patience Reeves in July, 1793, in Anne Arundel County (Ref: G-113). He was deceased by September 25, 1790 when final distribution of his estate was administered by Ann Fairbrother. She received a widow's third and Mrs. John Kerr (Elfrida Fairbrother) received the remaining balance (Ref: U-5).

FAIRBROTHER, THOMAS. Enlisted by Thomas Mayo on July 20, 1776 (Ref: H-41).

FANNING, THOMAS. His name appears on a list of recruits in Capt. Fulford's Company of Artillery in Annapolis on December 12, 1776 (Ref: H-572).

FARIS, WILLIAM. He petitioned the Committee of Observation in 1776, stating he neglected to enroll himself from a dislike for the military officers of Annapolis and not from a dislike of the common cause. On July 3, 1776 his firearms were returned and he was considered as fully enrolled (Ref: J-34, J-35). He took the Oath of Allegiance before Hon. Thomas Worthington on February 28, 1778

(Ref: B-21). He was deceased by April 8, 1808, when final estate distribution was made. Priscilla Faris received her widow's third, and thirds went to William Faris, Ann Pitt, and Abigail Carr (Ref: U-35).

FARRARA (FERRARA), EMANUEL. Enlisted in the summer of 1780 in 1st Maryland Line and was wounded (no date given) in South Carolina (Ref: X-10).

FENNELL, ROBERT. Took the Oath of Allegiance before Hon. Thomas Worthington on February 28, 1778 (Ref: B-21).

FENNELL, STEPHEN. Private in Capt. Richard Dorsey's Company of Artillery and shown as convalescent on November 17, 1777 (Ref: H-574, H-618). On February 13, 1833, the State Treasurer was ordered to "pay Stephen Fennell, of Brown County, Ohio, during life, quarterly, half pay of a private" (Ref: K-341).

FENTON, CHARLES (a Mulatto). He was enlisted by Edward Spurrier and passed by Thomas Dorsey on July 20, 1776 (Ref: H-41). Took the Oath of Allegiance before Hon. Reuben Meriweather on March 2, 1778 (Ref: B-25).

FERGUSON (FURGANSON), DAVID. Born in Maryland. Enlisted by Samuel Chew on July 25, 1776. Height: 5' 11" (Ref: H-40).

FERGUSON, WILLIAM. Recruit passed by James Brice in 1777 (Ref: H-313).

FIELDER (FIELDON), JACOB. Took the Oath of Allegiance before Hon. Elijah Robosson in March, 1778 (Ref: B-28).

FIGENCER, JOHN. Took the Oath of Allegiance before Hon. John Dorsey on March 12, 1778 (Ref: B-26).

FINLEY, EBENEZER. First Lieutenant in Captain Richard Dorsey's Company of Artillery on November 17, 1777 (Ref: H-573).

FINLEYSON (FINLAYSON, FINLISON), GEORGE. Soldier of the 2nd Maryland Line who was wounded and subsequently discharged on June 6, 1783 at Newburgh. His papers were signed by George Washington (Ref: X-12). He received half pay in Anne Arundel County on August 16, 1783, December 11, 1783, January 13, 1784, April 13, 1784, June 9, 1784, September 3, 1784 and December 17, 1784 (Ref: D-8, D-10, D-12, D-14, D-21, D-23, D-25). He later received a pension of $40 a year from March 4, 1789 (Ref: K-341).

FIPPS, ROGER. Took the Oath of Allegiance before Hon. Thomas Harwood in February, 1778 (Ref: B-22).

FIRST MARYLAND REGIMENT. This regiment was organized in 1776 from Baltimore and Anne Arundel County. Which soldier was from which county is not easily determined from the muster rolls themselves, but judging by their surnames and the names of their company captains, the following appear to have been from Anne Arundel

County, although this list is by no means complete: Peter Adams, John Adams, William Allen, John Boon, Ignatius Boon, Christopher Beall, William Basford, John Babbs, Vachel Burgess, William Brown, Philip Brisoce, George Bateman, Thomas Boarman, Joseph Crosbey, Richard Chaney, John Chaney, John Clements, William Courts, James Clements, Henry Clements, John Connelly, John Cheney, John Carroll, William Clements, Jonathan Dyer, Notley Dutton, James Downes, Edward Edwards, Edward Ellicott, Thomas Elliott, Francis Fairbrother, Archibald Ford, Jonathan Fowler, Joseph Ford, Henry Gaither, James Griffith, John Green, William Green, Benjamin Gray, Nicholas Gassaway, Samuel Gosnell, Joseph Gee, Samuel Glasgow, Amos Green, Richard Green, James Greenwalt, John Gardiner, George Gee, Joseph Galloway, Jacob Gray, Jon Gassaway, John Griffin, Nathan Griffin, Mack Griffin, John Giles, Richard Gardiner, Henry Gassaway, Samuel Hanson, Thomas Harwood, Elisha Hall, Leonard Hickey, Lancelot Hutton, Robert Hanson, William Hart, Francis Hickey, Patrick Ivory, William Joyce, Zachariah Jacobs, John Ijams, Isaac Jenkins, Joseph Jenkins, Isaac Jones, Archibald Johnson, Adam King, Thomas King, Philip King, Henry Leeke, John Lanham, William Lucas, Samuel Luckett, Joshua Lamb, Richard Lanham. David Luckett, Archibald McAllister, Daniel Monroe, Frederick Mire, Alexander Murray, Benjamin McNamara, Darby MacNamara, Richard Medcalf, Robert Medcalf, Peter McNaughton, John McCoy, William Nixon, Alexander Naylor, Nicholas Naylor, Patrick Noland, Thomas Neale, John Owings, Joseph Owings, Samuel Owings, Nathan Peake, Ezekiel Pearce, Joshua Pearce, John Pearce, Nicholas Pindall, James Peale, John Penn, Stephen Penn, Benjamin Phelps, John Purdy, Benjamin Price, James Quay, Zachariah Roberts, Vincent Ricketts, Bazil Ridgely, John Ricketts, James Reynolds, Richard Roberts, William Roberts, John Reynolds, Robert Rowe, John Smith, Valentine Smith, John Slack, Thomas Sheridan, Clement Sewall, Elisha Steel, Barton Swann, William Sutherland, Alexander South, John Shrivenor, Roger Skiffington, William Smoot, John Sullivan, Patrick Sim, John Taylor, Ludowick Taylor, William Timmons, William Tucker, Coxon Talbot, Aquila Taylor, John Tucker, William Taylor, Notley Tippet, John Wilson, Leonard Watkins, Jonathan White, Ignatius Ward, William Wood, Hugh Wallace, Igantius Ward, Thomas Wyndham, Richard Waters, Walter Warfield, John Williams, Thomas Ward, John West, Alexander West, and Samuel Willshire (Ref: Archives of Maryland, Vol. 18, pp. 78-180). The following men served under Capt. Jonathan Sellman in the First Company of the First Maryland Regiment in 1782 and 1783: Lt. Nicholas Gassaway, Ensign Henry Baker, and Sgt. Jesse Simms. Corporals: George Childs, John Mills 1st, and William Dillon. Drummers: Thomas Gossage, James Bailey, William Hamilton 1st, and William Swan. Privates: John Carr, Richard Hall, John Adams 1st, John Baley 1st, Peter Bocard, Michael Lollar, Daniel Clancey, John Ferrall, Basil Brown, Andrew Fernen, Thomas Canada, John Brown, Samuel Hamilton, Nehemiah Hadder, William Lilley, Patrick Mollihan, John Goddard, John Williams 1st, Robertson Ross, William Sterling, Barney Lemmon, Thomas Drudge, William Franklin, Thomas Thomas, James Crozier, John B. Haislip (died September 11, 1782), Charles Goldsbury, Benjaim Stuard, Alexander Francis, Peregrine Howard, Richard Procter, Robert Taylor, Samuel Harper, William Gates, Edward Hammond, Barney Wilson, Noah Sears, Thomas Thompson, William Peters, Joseph Thompson, Cornelius McLochlin,

Edward Richardson, William Lynch, Aquilla Diver, Thomas Baley, Jacob Blake 1st, John Hancock, Isaac Henderson, Frederick Wilmott, John Osban, William Butler, Thomas Cardiff, Samuel Trig, James Thomas Jr., James Thomas Sr., Benton Harris, Benjamin Boyd, John Beal, and William Kernal (Ref: Archives of Maryland, Vol. 18, pp. 429-431, and W.T.R. Saffell's Records of the Revolutionary War (New York: Pudney & Russell, Publishers, 1858, pp. 234-235).

FISH, BENJAMIN. Ensign in Capt. John Boone's Company in the Severn Battalion under Col. Nicholas Worthington on June 19, 1777, and Col. Elijah Robosson on March 1, 1778 (Ref: A-176, C-202). Commissioned a Second Lieutenant on August 15, 1778 (Ref: I-144, J-113, O-208). He took the Oath of Allegiance before Hon. Elijah Robosson in March, 1778 (Ref: B-28). He was deceased by November 9, 1791 when the final distribution of his estate was made by his executor, William Fish, to an unnamed widow (third), with the remainder of the estate balance going to Richard Fish and William Fish (Ref: U-7).

FISH, WILLIAM. Took the Oath of Allegiance before Hon. Elijah Robosson in March, 1778 (Ref: B-28).

FISHER, BASIL. One of the petitioners to the Convention of Maryland to form an independent rifle company in July, 1776 (Ref: B-3). He took the Oath of Allegiance before Hon. Reuben Meriweather on March 2, 1778 (Ref: B-25).

FISHER, JOHN. Took the Oath of Allegiance before Hon. Reuben Meriweather on March 2, 1778 (Ref: B-24).

FISHER, JOHN SR. Took the Oath of Allegiance before Hon. Reuben Meriweather on March 2, 1778 (Ref: B-24).

FISHER, SETH. One of the petitioners to the Convention of Maryland to form an independent rifle company in July, 1776 (Ref: B-3).

FISHER, WILLIAM. Private in Captain Richard Chew's Company in Colonel John Weems' Battalion on October 5, 1776 (Ref: A-95, I-143). Took the Oath of Allegiance before Hon. Samuel Harrison in March, 1778 (Ref: A-244). Final distribution of the estate of one William Fisher was made on March 16, 1830 by John Sellman, administrator, to Etta Fisher, now Etta Rogers (widow's third), and fifths of the remaining balance to John H. Fisher, William Fisher, Mary A. Fisher, Hezekih Fisher, and Susanna Fisher (Ref: U-80).

FITGENCY, JOHN. Drafted in October, 1780 to serve until December 10, 1780. (Ref: H-369).

FITZJARROLD, JOHN. His name appeared on a list of recruits in Capt. John Fulford's Company of Artillery in Annapolis on Dec. 12, 1776 (Ref: H-572).

FLANNIGAN, DENNIS. Enlisted on December 24, 1777 in Capt. Dorsey's Matross Company. Wounded at Camden. Discharged on November 15, 1783 (Ref: X-11).

FLATTERY, JOHN. Took the Oath of Allegiance before Hon. John Dorsey on March 12, 1778 (Ref: B-26).

FLOWERS, RALPH. Took the Oath of Allegiance before Hon. Samuel Harrison, Jr. in March, 1778 (Ref: B-28).

FOARD, JOSEPH. Took the Oath of Allegiance on March 23, 1778 (Ref: V-547).

FOGGETT, RICHARD. Took the Oath of Allegiance before Hon. Richard Harwood, Jr. on March 1, 1778 (Ref: B-22). On February 12, 1820 the Treasurer was ordered to pay Richard Foggett, of Anne Arundel County, late a soldier in the Revolutionary War, during life, quarterly, half pay of a private, as a further remuneration for his war services. On March 19, 1835, the Treasurer was ordered to pay to Artridge Foggett, of Anne Arundel County, the amount due her late husband, Richard, upon the pension list of this State, at the time of his death, and half pay of a private during her life. On February 6, 1850 the Treasurer was ordered to pay the arrears of the pension to her legal representative, Gassaway Owens, due to her in May, 1849 (Ref: K-342). "Richard Fogget" was drafted as a substitute by Capt. Mitchell in October, 1780 and served through at least October 30, 1781 (Ref: H-370, W-657). He was given a pension on March 4, 1831, age 74, as a Private (Ref: Z-45).

FOLGER, ROBERT. Recruited by Captain Alexander Truman in October, 1780, to serve in the Army for three years (Ref: H-369).

FOLKS, JOHN. His name appeared on a list of recruits in Capt. John Fulford's Company of Artillery in Annapolis on December 12, 1776 (Ref: H-572).

FOLLITT, JOSEPH. He was a Substitute, furnished by Nicholas Worthington on May 30, 1778, for a three year term in the Army (Ref: C-208, H-319).

FOOKES, JONATHAN. On March 13, 1777 he petitioned the Council of Safety to advise them that he was wrongfully imprisoned, that he was not an enemy of this country, and that he would take the Oath of Allegiance (Ref: V-172).

FORBES, JOHN. Took the Oath of Allegiance before Hon. Samuel Harrison, Jr. in March, 1778 (Ref: B-28).

FORBES, WILL (?). Private in Capt. Richard Dorsey's Artillery Company on November 17, 1777 (Ref: H-574).

FORD, JOSEPH. Recruit passed by James Brice in 1777 (Ref: H-313). Took Oath of Allegiance before Hon. Samuel Harrison, Jr. in March, 1778 (Ref: B-28).

FOREMAN, LEONARD. In his pension application in 1833, Leonard Foreman stated he was born in Anne Arundel County in 1758 and was left an orphan at age 6. He was drafted into the Revolutionary War in 1777, and served under Captain Caleb Owings, in the Maryland Line under Gen. Smallwood, for six months. He resided in Baltimore City at the time of his application. He died in August of 1841 and his widow, Ann Cavy Fowler Foreman applied and received pension W10036 in 1853. She said they were married in October, 1818 in Anne Arundel County (Ref: Copies of Revolutionary War pension applications). Information from a descendant (and subsequent research by this compiler) has determined that Leonard Foreman was born on December 25, 1758, an only child of Philip and Mary Foreman. He married first to Rachael Mattox (1748-1815) in 1782 in Baltimore and had 5 children: Elijah Foreman, Rachel Foreman Moss Williams, Mary Foreman Fowler, Henry Foreman, and Eleanor Foreman Stansbury; secondly he married Ann Cavy Adams (1779-1858), who was a widow of Lemuel Fowler and Ebenezer Thomas. Leonard Foreman died on August 23, 1840. (Ref: U-1, U-60, and information from Charles E. Bouis of Atlanta, Georgia, in 1989).

FORRESTER, ALEX. Born in 1746 in Maryland. Occupation: Labourer. Height: 5' 5". Private in Capt. Nathaniel Smith's Artillery Company stationed at Baltimore on February 19, 1776 (Ref: H-565). Private in Captain Richard Dorsey's Company of Artillery on November 17, 1777, and reported "sick in the country with fevers" (Ref: H-574).

FORRESTER, CORNELIUS. Born in 1755 in Maryland. Occupation: Labourer. Height: 5' 10 3/4". Private in Capt. Nathaniel Smith's Artillery Company stationed in Baltimore on February 19, 1776 (Ref: H-565). Private in Captain Richard Dorsey's Company of Artillery on November 17, 1777 (Ref: H-574), reported suffering from rheumatism at that time (Ref: H-618).

FORRESTER, JOHN. Born in 1748 in Maryland. Occupation: Labourer. Height: 5' 8 1/2". Private in Capt. Nathaniel Smith's Artillery Company stationed in Baltimore on February 19, 1776 (Ref: H-565).

FORRESTER, WILLIAM. Took the Oath of Allegiance before Hon. Elijah Robosson in March, 1778 (Ref: B-28).

FORSTER, NATHANIEL. Took the Oath of Allegiance before Hon. Samuel Harrison, Jr. in March, 1778 (Ref: B-28).

FORSYTH, JOHN. Took the Oath of Allegiance before Hon. Nicholas Worthington in March, 1778 (Ref: Original list in Maryland State Papers, Red Book 21. Note: Reference B-27 mistakenly left his name off their published list).

FOSH, JAMES. Enlisted by Richard Talbot on July 22, 1776 (Ref: H-39).

FOSTER, WILLIAM. Took the Oath of Allegiance before Hon. Nicholas Worthington in March, 1778 (Ref: B-27).

FOURTH MARYLAND REGIMENT. Col. Josias Carvil Hall was Commander of the 4th Maryland Regiment that served with Gen. George Washington in 1779. Captains Jonathan Sellman, John Sprigg Belt, and Edward Spurrier served from Anne Arundel County. The men who served in their companies were as follows: Capt. Jonathan Sellman's Company -- Henry Gassaway, William Peach, Richard Chew, Daniel Shellay, Calib Tidings, Jno. Pike, John Reading, Andrew Hagan, Edward Marshall, Joseph Batchelry, Jarvis Williams, William King, John Lucas, John King, Robert Richardson, John Easton, Conrad Smith, John Barnett, Patrick Birmingham, William Flanagan, James Street, Robert Gray, John Blewer, John Williams, John Bates, Richard Brown, John Murphy, John Rowley, Patrick Murphy, William Bright, Stephen Watkins, Miles Johnson, William How, Thomas Readman, George McIntosh, Brice McHenry, Isaac Holliday, Samuel Elliott, Thomas McCormack, Richard Cantwell, Richard Biddle, Joshua Allender, James Wallingsford, William Allman, James Pike, Martin Allcock, John Cupit?, Thomas Holes?, James Carvar?, Jam: Warrick, John Howell, Nathan Hull, Edward Moriston, Andrew Chivas, Francis James, Richard Tague, Francis James, Reuben Smith, and Peter Spulmire(?). Capt. John Sprigg Belt's Company -- James Clark, William Leammon, Thomas Edwards, Hugh Robinson, Henry Heitland, Robert Harpham, William Dumas, John Hadd, Thomas McAway, Abraham Boyce, Thomas Turner, John Heltenhead, Thomas Davis, Laurance Thompson, Daniel Quinn, William Carty, John Church, John Linch, Nichols Hiner, Peter Fountain, Joseph Butler, Arthur Bowden, John Hodges, William Morris, Joseph Carroll, Isaac Isaacs, John Miles, Hugh Gill, William Wood, Thomas Williams, William Baker, James Jarrott, Matthew Kelly, Samuel Eyles, John Welch, Robert Mallows, William Warrick, William James, Jeremiah Belford, John French, William Hall, Richard Muston, Edward Nichols, Stephen McAwat, Gerold Parker, Richard Frewn, Richard Clark, Michell Rigorey, Anthony Jackson, William Shadwick, John Daily, Samuel Boazer, Richard Harris, Robert Bowen, Richard Cheney, Dennis Swenney, and John Hays. Capt. Edward Spurrier's Company -- John Colin, James Ferrald, Hugh McMillan, James Daffin, Daniel Leary, Charles Dorsey, Samuel Oram, Peter Gummy, Michall Leary, John Lindey, John Craige, Thomas Jessop, John Knox, Michael Dease, George Whelan, George Strutt, Thomas Dwyer, Patrick Glassney, Alexander Montgomery, Joseph Cole, John Goldsborough, Dennis Carroll, Christopher Flannery, William Downs, James Stuart, Cornelius McLaughlin, Robert Lynch, John Suell, Vecheld Morton, William Frazier, Joseph Jenkins, Jacob Lavely, Henry Cooke, Thomas Smith, John Chatterton, John Marks, John Simmons, Jacob Hindes, William Williams, Thomas Enniss, James McKinley, Thomas Murphy, William Hedge, Adam Jameson, Robert Stuart, William Barden, Robert Darling, John Clooney, John Williss, John Johnston, Nicholas Dowan, Richard Fenwick, Thomas Sims, Christ. Brown, and William Leake (Ref: Edward Blair Baker's "Fourth Maryland Regiment, Col. Josias Carvil Hall, Commander, June, 1779 - January, 1780," in Maryland Magazine of Genealogy, Vol. 3, No. 2, Fall, 1980, pp. 77-85).

FOWLER, DANIEL. Private in the Independent Company of Militia of Annapolis of Capt. Gilbert Middleton on March 20, 1779 (Ref: I-144, O-325).

FOWLER, JOSEPH. Born in England. Enlisted and passed by James Brice in Anne Arundel County on January 12, 1778 (Ref: C-215, H-313).

FOWLER, JUBB. Private in the Independent Company of Militia of Annapolis of Capt. Gilbert Middleton on March 20, 1779 (Ref: I-144, O-325). On January 1, 1807, the final distribution of the estate of John Fowler was settled, naming widow Hannah Fowler and Jubb Fowler, deceased's father (Ref: U-31).

FOWLER, SAMUEL. Took the Oath of Allegiance before Hon. Nicholas Worthington in March, 1778 (Ref: B-27). Substitute, furnished by Philemon Warfield on June 2, 1778, for a nine month term in the Army (Ref: C-208, H-319). Also drafted in October, 1780 to serve until December 10, 1780 (Ref: H-368).

FOWLER, SAMUEL (OF JOHN). Took the Oath of Allegiance before Hon. Nicholas Worthington in March, 1778 (Ref: B-27).

FOWLER, THOMAS. Two men with this name took the Oath of Allegiance: one before Hon. Thomas Worthington on February 28, 1778, and one before Hon. Richard Harwood, Jr. on March 1, 1778 (Ref: B-21, B-22).

FOWLER, THOMAS (OF JOHN). Took the Oath of Allegiance before Hon. Nicholas Worthington in March, 1778 (Ref: Original lists in Maryland State Papers, Red Book 21. Note: Ref. B-27 mistakenly lists his name as "Thomas Fou (?) Corsen of John", instead of "Thomas Fowler, son of John"). He was deceased by December 3, 1801 when the final distribution of his estate was handled by Vachel Gaither and Thomas Bicknell, administrators de bonis non, and naming Priscilla Fowler (widow's third), with the remaining balance of the estate going to Achsah Fowler, wife of Ninian Riggs (Ref: U-22).

FOWLER, WILLIAM. Private in the Independent Company of Militia of Annapolis of Capt. Gilbert Middleton on March 20, 1779 (Ref: I-144, O-325).

FOX, ANTHONY. In November, 1806 the Treasurer was ordered to pay to Anthony Fox, of Anne Arundel County, late a soldier in the Revolutionary War, half yearly payments, half pay of a private (Ref: K-343).

FOX, CHARLES. Took the Oath of Allegiance before Hon. Reuben Meriweather on March 2, 1778 (Ref: B-24). In March, 1779, he was commissioned a Captain in the Elk Ridge Battalion of Militia (Ref: O-333).

FOX, EDWARD. Resident of Herring Creek who served as Clerk in Capt. Richard Weems' Company of Militia formed on March 6, 1776 (Ref: I-143, MS.1814).

FOX, JOHN. Born in Scotland. He was a Substitute, furnished by Col. Thomas Dorsey on May 19, 1778, for the duration of the war (Ref: C-207, H-318).

FRANCEWAY, JOHN. Born in France. Enlisted and passed by James Brice in Anne Arundel County on January 12, 1778 (Ref: C-215, H-313).

FRANCIS, LEWIS. Substitute, furnished by Nicholas Maccubbin on June 2, 1778, for a three year term in the Army (Ref: C-208, H-319).

FRANKLIN, JACOB. A resident of Herring Creek who was a petitioner to form a militia company on March 6, 1776, and was subsequently elected Sergeant in Capt. Richard Weems' Company (Ref: I-143, MS.1814). He also took the Oath of Allegiance before Hon. Samuel Harrison on March 2, 1778 (Ref: B-24). He was deceased by February 20, 1821 when the final distribution of his estate was settled by Thomas Franklin, executor, with fifths of the balance going to daughter Ann Franklin, son Benjamin Franklin, son Samuel Franklin, son Thomas Franklin, and heirs of daughter Mary Franklin Deale (Ref: U-58).

FRANKLIN, JOHN. Two men by this name took the Oath of Allegiance: one before Hon. Thomas Harwood in February, 1778, and one before Hon. Samuel Harrison on March 2, 1778 (Ref: B-22, B-24). One was a resident of Herring Creek who petitioned to form a militia company on March 6, 1776, and was subsequently elected a Sergeant in Capt. Richard Weems' Company (Ref: I-143, MS.1814). One John Franklin was deceased by November 30, 1802 wheh final distribution of his estate was settled by Dr. William Murray, administrator, with Mary Franklin receiving her third and the balance to John Franklin (Ref: U-21).

FRANKLIN, THOMAS. Enrolled by Capt. Thomas Watkins on October 21, 1776 for the service of the State (Ref: I-144, MS.1814).

FRANKLIN, WILLIAM. Took the Oath of Allegiance before Hon. Samuel Harrison, Jr. in March, 1778 (Ref: B-28).

FRAZIER (FRASER), JAMES. Born in Maryland. Enlisted by Capt. Edward Tillard on July 10, 1776. Height: 5' 7" (Ref: H-39). One James Frazier was given a pension on March 4, 1831, age 74, as a Mariner in the Navy (Ref: Z-45).

FRAZIER, JOHN. Took the Oath of Allegiance before Hon. Samuel Harrison, Jr. in March, 1778 (Ref: B-28).

FRAZIER, JOSEPH. Took the Oath of Allegiance before Hon. Samuel Harrison, Jr. in March, 1778 (Ref: B-28).

FRAZIER, WILLIAM. Took the Oath of Allegiance before Hon. Samuel Harrison, Jr. in March, 1778 (Ref: B-28).

FREELAND, JAMES. 2nd Corporal in the Independent Company of Militia of Capt. Gilbert Middleton of Annapolis on March 20, 1779 (Ref: I-144, O-325).

FRENCH, BENJAMIN. Private in Captain Richard Chew's Company in Colonel John Weems' Battalion on October 5, 1776 (Ref: A-95, I-143).

FRENCH, OTHO. Took the Oath of Allegiance before Hon. Richard Harwood, Jr. on March 1, 1778 (Ref: B-22).

FRENCH, WILLIAM. He took the Oath of Allegiance before Hon. Richard Harwood, Jr. on March 1, 1778 (Ref: B-22), and was drafted in October, 1780 to serve in the Army until December 10, 1780 (Ref: H-370).

FROST, JAMES. Took the Oath of Allegiance before Hon. John Dorsey on March 12, 1778 (Ref: B-26).

FROST, JOHN. Enlisted by Michael Burgess and passed by Col. Hyde on July 20, 1776 (Ref: H-41). Took Oath of Allegiance before Hon. Reuben Meriweather on March 2, 1778 (Ref: B-24).

FROST, WILLIAM. One of the petitioners to the Convention of Maryland to form an independent rifle company in July, 1776 (Ref: B-3). He took the Oath of Allegiance on March 17, 1778 (Ref: V-539).

FRY, WILLIAM. Took the Oath of Allegiance before Hon. Thomas Dorsey on March 2, 1778 (Ref: B-23).

FULFORD, JOHN. Commissioned Captain of a Company of Matrosses on February 9, 1776; stationed at Annapolis (Ref: H-570, H-572, N-145). Promoted to Major on May 31, 1777, and William Campbell became Company Captain (Ref: V-268).

FULK, WOOLDRICK C. Took the Oath of Allegiance before Hon. Elijah Robosson in March, 1778 (Ref: B-28).

FULTON, WILLIAM. Disabled soldier reported dead in August, 1783 (Ref: D-8).

FUNER (TUNER?), MICHAEL. Soldier in the 1st Maryland Line who was wounded several times and medically discharged at High Hills of the Santee in South Carolina on October 3, 1781 (Ref: X-13).

GAINER, ROBERT. Enlisted by Richard Talbot and passed by John Dorsey on July 22, 1776 (Ref: H-39).

GAITHER, AMOS (c1720 - September, 1790). Son of John Gaither and Elizabeth Duvall. Married (wife unknown) and had daughters Mary Gaither Gambrill and Eleanor Gaither Bicknell. On February 4, 1782, he received money from the State of Maryland for some unrecorded service (Ref: Q-70, Q-71).

GAITHER, BEALE (born on November 14, 1755). Son of Edward Gaither and Sarah Howard (Ref: Q-145). Enrolled by Capt. Thomas Watkins on October 21, 1776, for service to the State (Ref: I-144, MS.1814). In March, 1778 he took the Oath of Allegiance in Anne Arundel

County. By October, 1794, he had moved to Berkeley County, now West Virginia (according to Source Q-145).

GAITHER, BENJAMIN (c1750, Anne Arundel County, Maryland - 1788, Rowan County, North Carolina). Son of John Gaither and Anne Ruley. Married Rachel Jacob and they had 8 children: John Gaither, Jeremiah Gaither, Zachariah Gaither, Basil Gaither, Edward Gaither, Reason Gaither, Anne Gaither, and Rachel Gaither (Ref: Q-76). Benjamin took Oath of Allegiance before Hon. Nicholas Worthington in March, 1778 (Ref: B-27. Source Q-76 states it was taken before Hon. John Dorsey). Sheriff of Anne Arundel County (Ref: K-345).

GAITHER, EDWARD JR. Second Major in the Elk Ridge Battalion from 1776 to at least 1778 (Ref: C-201, F-224). He took the Oath of Allegiance before Hon. Reuben Meriweather on March 2, 1778 (Ref: B-24). He served on the Committee of Observation in 1775 (Ref: F-222). On November 19, 1778 he was appointed a Justice of the Peace (Ref: O-241).

GAITHER, EDWARD (1723-1793). Son of Edward and Rachel Gaither. He married Sarah Howard circa 1744 and had 9 children: Edward Gaither, Joseph Gaither, Sarah Gaither Merriken, Henry Gaither, Ephraim Gaither, Beale Gaither, John Howard Gaither, Elijah Gaither, and Margarey Gaither Brown Warfield (Ref: Q-140). He took the Oath of Allegiance before Hon. Nicholas Worthington in March, 1778 (Ref: B-27, although Source Q-141 indicates Hon. John Dorsey).

GAITHER, ELIJAH (born March 28, 1759, Anne Arundel County, Maryland - circa 1800 in now West Virginia). Son of Edward Gaither and Sarah Howard. By 1786 he was in Washington County, Maryland, and by 1794 he was in Hardy County, Virginia (Ref: Q-146). He took the Oath of Allegiance before Hon. Thomas Dorsey on March 2, 1778 (Ref: B-24, although Ref: Q-145 recognizes the taking of the oath but does not give the name of the magistrate).

GAITHER, HENRY. On March 10, 1780, the Commissary delivered three camp kettles to Capt. Henry Gaither for the use of the recruits in Annapolis. (Ref: Archives of Maryland, Volume 43, page 104).

GAITHER, JOHN (April 24, 1713 - September 6, 1784). Son of Benjamin Gaither and Sarah Burgess. He married Agnes Rogers, widow of John Williams, circa 1744 and they had ten children: John Rogers Gaither, Zachariah Gaither, Vachel Gaither, Samuel Gaither, Anne Gaither, Sarah Gaither, Mary Gaither, Agnes Gaither, Susannah Gaither Waters, and Evan Gaither. He took the Oath of Allegiance before Hon. Thomas Worthington on February 28, 1778. (Ref: B-21, Q-95).

GAITHER, JOHN HOWARD (September 8, 1757, Anne Arundel County - April 24, 1840 in Washington County, Maryland). Son of Edward Gaither and Sarah Howard. He took the Oath of Allegiance before Hon. Nicholas Worthington in March, 1778 (Ref: B-27, although Ref: Q-145 indicates Hon. John Dorsey).

GAITHER, JOHN ROGERS (1752, Anne Arundel County, Maryland - 1825, Harrison County, Indiana). Son of John Gaither and Agnes Rogers. By July 3, 1776, he had been commissioned a First Lieutenant of the Flying Camp, and served until it disbanded in December, 1776. He returned to Montgomery County and married Mary Perry. After 1780 he moved to Jefferson County, Kentucky (now Nelson County) and styled himself "John Gaither, Jr." By 1796 the area he was living in became Bullitt County. He died in Harrison County, Indiana, according to a descendant of John's son James W. Rogers (Ref: Q-103).

GAITHER, JOSEPH. Probably a son of Benjamin Gaither and Sarah Burgess, and if so, then he was born on March 10, 1722/3 (Ref: Q-90). He took the Oath of Allegiance before Hon. Thomas Dorsey on March 2, 1778 (Ref: B-24).

GAITHER, JOSHUA. Two men by this name took the Oath of Allegiance: one before Hon. Thomas Dorsey on March 2, 1778, and the other one before Hon. Nicholas Worthington in March, 1778 (Ref: B-24, B-27). One Joshua Gaither (born n 1726 and died after 1803) was a son of John Gaither and Elizabeth Duvall, and he may have married Sarah Jacob and had children Jeremiah Gaither and Susannah Gaither (Ref: Q-71, Q-72).

GAITHER, REZIN (died in 1807). Son of John Gaither and Elizabeth Duvall. He married Sarah Yieldhall circa 1773 and had 7 children: John Gaither, Sarah Gaither, Rebecca Gaither, Ruth Gaither, Rezin Gaither, Joshua Gaither, and Elizabeth Gaither. On February 22, 1776, the records of Anne Arundel County were removed from Annapolis and committed to his house for safekeeping. He was one of the clerks of Mr. John Brice. Rezin took the Oath of Allegiance before Hon. Nicholas Worthington in March, 1778 (Ref: Q-72, Q-73, B-27).

GAITHER, REZIN (died by 1820). Son of Samuel and Ruth Gaither. He married Sarah Ridgely and they had at least 4 sons: Elijah Gaither, Rezin Gaither, William Gaither, and Greenbury Gaither. Took the Oath of Allegiance before Hon. Thomas Worthington on February 28, 1778 (Ref: Q-78, B-27).

GAITHER, SAMUEL (died in 1783). Son of John Gaither and Elizabeth Duvall. He married Ruth ----- and had two children: Rezin Gaither and Actions (Nackey) Gaither Ridgely (Ref: Q-75). Samuel took the Oath of Allegiance before Hon. Thomas Worthington on February 28, 1778 (Ref: B-21).

GAITHER, SETH. Son of John Gaither and Anne Ruley. Married Rebecca Yieldhall in 1778. He took the Oath of Allegiance before Hon. Nicholas Worthington in March, 1778 (Ref: B-27, although Ref: Q-78 indicates Hon. John Dorsey).

GAITHER, THOMAS. Took the Oath of Allegiance before Hon. Thomas Worthington on February 28, 1778 (Ref: B-21). Enlisted by Michael Burgess and passed by Col. Hyde on July 20, 1776 (Ref: H-41).

GAITHER, VACHEL (c1750 - 1804). Son of John Gaither and Agnes Rogers. He married Ruth Marriott in 1782 and had 10 children: Juliette Gaither Clarke Bicknell, Benjamin Gaither, Elizabeth Gaither Mullikin, Anne R. Gaither, John Marriott Gaither, Agnes Gaither Owens, Ruth Gaither, Evan Gaither, Vachel Marriott Gaither, and Rachel Gaither (Ref: Q-106). He was a First Lieutenant in Capt. Thomas Mullikin's Company in early 1776, resigned but was re-commissioned on June 17, 1776. He became a Captain in the Severn Battalion on June 19, 1777 and served through 1781 (Ref: A-176, C-202).

GAITHER, WILLIAM. Probably a son of Benjamin Gaither and Sarah Burgess. If so, he was born July 11, 1728 and died in 1782, d.s.p. (Ref: Q-90). He took Oath of Allegiance before Hon. Elijah Robosson in March, 1778 (Ref: B-28).

GAITHER, ZACHARIAH (c1750 - December, 1802). Son of John Gaither and Agnes Rogers. He married Sarah Warfield in 1781 and had 8 children: Zachariah Gaither, Lucy Gaither, John Gaither, James Gaither, Edward Gaither, Evan Gaither, Greenbury Gaither, and Rachel Gaither (Ref: Q-104, U-38). He was one of the petitioners to the Convention of Maryland to form an independent rifle company in July, 1776 (Ref: B-3). He took Oath of Allegiance before Hon. Nicholas Worthington in March, 1778 (Ref: B-27, although Source Q-104 indicates it was before Hon. John Dorsey). He was an Ensign in Capt. Basil Burgess Company in the Elk Ridge Battalion on March 30, 1779 (Ref: K-345).

GALE, EDWARD. Enrolled by Captain Thomas Watkins on October 21, 1776, for service to the State (Ref: I-144, MS.1814).

GALLWAY, JOHN. Took the Oath of Allegiance before Hon. Reuben Meriweather on March 2, 1778 (Ref: B-24).

GALLOWAY, BENJAMIN (1752 - August 18, 1831, Hagerstown, Maryland). Son of Samuel Galloway and Anne Chew. He married Henrietta Maria Chew in 1775; died without issue. He was in the Lower House of Anne Arundel County in 1777 and was appointed Attorney General in 1778. He was a Justice of the Orphans Court from 1782 to at least 1785 (Ref: P-338, P-339, V-455).

GALLOWAY, JOSEPH. Commissioned Second Major in the South River Battalion on January 22, 1776 (Ref: A-83, F-222, V-103). Delegate to the Convention of Maryland on November 8, 1776 (Ref: J-55).

GALLOWAY, SAMUEL. Took the Oath of Allegiance before Hon. Reuben Meriweather on March 2, 1778 (Ref: B-24). He was deceased by March 20, 1799 when John Galloway, surviving executor, made the final distribution of his estate to John Galloway and Ann Cheston, each receiving equal halves (Ref: U-24).

GALVIN, JOHN. Born in Ireland. Enlisted and passed by Lieut. James Brice on January 12, 1778 (Ref: C-215, H-313).

GALWITH, JOHN. Born in Maryland. He was enrolled by John S. Belt in July, 1776. Height: 5' 4 1/2" (Ref: H-40).

GALWITH, JONAS. Took the Oath of Allegiance before Hon. Thomas Harwood on February 28, 1778 (Ref: B-22).

GAMBRILL, JOSHUA. Took Oath of Allegiance before Hon. Nicholas Worthington in March, 1778 (Ref: B-27).

GARDNER, GEORGE SR. Took the Oath of Allegiance before Hon. Samuel Lane on March 1, 1778 (Ref: B-23).

GARDNER, JOHN. Three men by this name took the Oath of Allegiance: one before Hon. Samuel Lane on March 1, 1778, one before Hon. John Dorsey on March 12, 1778 and one before Hon. Samuel Harrison in 1778 (Ref: B-23, B-25, A-244). One John Gardner (Gardiner) was enrolled by Samuel Chew on July 25, 1776. Height: 5' 9" (Ref: H-40). One John Gardiner was deceased by November 26, 1787 when final distribution of his estate was made to Sarah Gardiner (her widow's third), with fifths of the remainder to Elizabeth Gardiner, James Gardiner, George Gardiner, William Gardiner, and Mary Gardiner (Ref: U-1).

GARDNER (GARDINER), PETER. Born in Maryland. He was enrolled by Samuel Chew on July 25, 1776. Height: 5' 2" (Ref: H-40).

GARDNER (GARDENER), WILLIAM. Took the Oath of Allegiance before Hon. Thomas Dorsey on March 2, 1778 (Ref: B-24).

GARY, GIDEON. Enrolled by Captain Thomas Watkins on October 21, 1776, for service to the State (Ref:I-144, MS.1814). Two men with this name took the Oath of Allegiance: one before Hon. Thomas Dorsey on March 2, 1778, and one before Honorable Nicholas Worthington in March, 1778 (Ref: B-24, B-27). One Gideon Gary was deceased by April 20, 1790 when the final distribution of his estate was made by Leonard Sellman, executor, to an unnamed widow (one third) with fifths of the remainder to Mary Gary, Lloyd Gary, Leonard Gary, Deborah Gary, and Everard Gary (Ref: U-4).

GASSAWAY, BRICE JOHN (c1755 - c1800). Son of Nicholas Gassaway and Catherine Worthington. A resident of Patuxent Hundred, he married Dinah Griffith and had seven children: George Gassaway, Henry Gassaway, Ann Gassaway Warfield Worthington, Catherine Gassaway Hammond, Sarah Gassaway Brown, Elizabeth Gassaway Porter, and Mary Gassaway Gibbons. He took the Oath of Allegiance before Hon. Thomas Worthington on February 28, 1778. In March, 1779 he was a First Lieutenant in the Elk Ridge Battalion of Militia and by 1782 he was a Captain (Ref: B-21, Q-176, O-233, T-326). His date of death is not known, but he was still alive in 1790 as he was his mother's executor (Ref: U-9).

GASSAWAY, HENRY (May 16, 1758 - February 10, 1818). Son of Henry Gassaway and Dinah Battee. He married first to Margaret Sellman in 1787 and second to Lavena Killman in 1807 (Ref: Q-181). In November, 1804, the Treasurer was directed to "pay to Henry

Gassaway, late a Lieutenant in the Revolutionary War, half pay of a Lieutenant, quarterly payments during life, as a further reward to those meritorious services which he rendered to his country in establishing her liberty and independence." (Ref: K-345, K-346, Q-182).

GASSAWAY, JOHN (June 18, 1754 - June 25, 1820). Son of Henry Gassaway and Dinah Battee. He married twice: first to Mary Quynn, daughter of Allen, in 1788, and they had three children: Elizabeth Gassaway, John Gassaway, and Louisa Gassaway. He married secondly to Elizabeth Price in 1799 and they had 2 children: Thomas Jefferson Gassaway and Louisa Emily Gassaway (Ref: G-23, G-114, H-38, Q-177, Q-178). In 1776 John was commissioned an Ensign in the 2nd Maryland Regiment and became a Lieutenant in 1779 and a Captain in 1780. He became an original member of the Society of the Cincinnati in 1783 (Ref: Q-178). In December, 1815, the Treasurer was directed to "pay to John Gassaway, late a Captain of the Maryland troops in the Revolutionary War, during life, half pay of a Captain." On February 10, 1820 the State Treasurer was directed to "pay to Mrs. Elizabeth L. Gassaway, of Annapolis, during her widowhood, half pay of a Captain, as a further compensation for those services rendered by her late husband, John Gassaway, during the Revolutionary War." On December 19, 1821 the State Treasurer was directed to "pay to Elizabeth L. Gassaway, widow of Gen. John Gassaway of Annapolis, $38 due on his Revolutionary War pension at his death" (Ref: K-346, Z-27).

GASSAWAY, NICHOLAS (June 25, 1738 - 1791). Son of John Gassaway and Sarah Cotter. Married (name unknown) and had three children: John Gassaway, Mary Gassaway Stewart, and Sarah Cotter Gassaway White. Took Oath of Allegiance before Hon. Richard Harwood, Jr. on March 1, 1778 (Ref: B-22, Q-169).

GASSAWAY, NICHOLAS (January 20, 1757 - November, 1806). Son of Henry Gassaway and Dinah Battee. He married Amelia Israel in 1791 and they had 3 children: Hanson Gassaway, John Gassaway, and Berry Gassaway. Nicholas enlisted in the militia on February 25, 1776 under Capt. John Day Scott's Company, and by December 10, 1776 he was a Sergeant in the 1st Maryland Regiment. He was an Ensign in the 3rd Maryland Regiment on April 17, 1777 and by 1779 he was a Lieutenant stationed in New York. He served through 1783, and after the war he was a member of the Society of the Cincinnati (Ref: Q-179, Q-180).

GASSAWAY, THOMAS (June 5, 1747 - October 7, 1787). Son of Henry Gassaway and Rebecca Chapman. He married Elizabeth ----- and they had 3 children: Louis Gassaway, Mary Gassaway Pinkney, and Sophia Gassaway Gardiner. At the time of his death he was Register of Wills for Anne Arundel County (Ref: Q-176, Q-177). He is probably the Thomas Gassaway who took the Oath of Allegiance before Hon. John Dorsey on March 12, 1778 (Ref: B-25, although the taking of the oath is not acknowledged in his biography found in Source Q-177).

GATEWOOD (GALWOOD), JOHN. Took the Oath of Allegiance before Hon. Samuel Harrison in March, 1778 (Ref: A-244).

GATWORTH, GABRIEL. On March 4, 1780, the Commissary delivered to "Gabriel Gatworth, formerly a soldier in the 2nd Maryland Regiment, two coats in lieu of the like number which were left in Annapolis and taken by order of the Governor and Council." (Ref: Archives of Maryland, Vol. 43, p. 102).

GEE, JOSEPH. Drummer in Maryland Line. He married Belinda Vernon in 1781 in Anne Arundel County (Ref: G-23, G-114). "Joseph Jee" was enrolled in July, 1776 by Edward Tillard. Height: 5' 6 1/2". Born in England. (Ref: H-39).

GEOGHEGAN, ANTHONY. Musician in the Maryland Line. He married Anne Lilly in 1792 in Bourbon County, Kentucky (Ref: G-23, G-114).

GEOGHEGAN, ROBERT. Took Oath of Allegiance before Hon. Nicholas Worthington in March, 1778 (Ref: B-27).

GIBBS, THOMAS. Took the Oath of Allegiance before Hon. Richard Harwood, Jr. on March 1, 1778 (Ref: B-22).

GIDDINGS, JOHN. Born in Maryland. He was enrolled by Samuel Chew on July 25, 1776. Height: 5' 8" (Ref: H-40).

GILBERT, JOSEPH. Took the Oath of Allegiance before Hon. Samuel Harrison in March, 1778 (Ref: A-244).

GILLISS, JOHN. He was one of the petitioners to the Convention of Maryland to form an independent rifle company in July, 1776 (Ref: B-3). On March 1, 1778 he took the affirmation of allegiance to the Maryland before Honorable Reuben Meriweather, for Quakers, Mennonists, and Dunkers (Ref: B-239. Note: The original list is missing from the Maryland State Archives, MdHR4584).

GIVENS, JOHN. Took the Oath of Allegiance before Hon. Richard Harwood, Jr. on March 1, 1778 (Ref: B-22).

GLADMAN, MICHAEL. Enlisted by Richard Talbot and passed by John Dorsey on July 22, 1776 (Ref: H-39).

GLOVER, JOHN. Took the Oath of Allegiance before Hon. Richard Harwood, Jr. on March 1, 1778 (Ref: B-22).

GLOVER, RICHARD. Took the Oath of Allegiance before Hon. Thomas Worthington on February 28, 1778 (Ref: B-21).

GLOVER, WILLIAM. Private in Capt. William Marbury's Company of Artillery in 1777 (Ref: H-575).

GODFREY, SAMUEL. Took the Oath of Allegiance before Honorable John Dorsey on March 12, 1778 (Ref: B-25).

GODMAN, FRANCIS. Took the Oath of Allegiance before Honorable John Dorsey on March 12, 1778 (Ref: B-25).

GODMAN, SAMUEL (1740-1796). He married Anne Henderson in 1763, and they had 8 children: Samuel Godman, Robert Godman, Cassius Godman, Brutus Godman, Thomas Jefferson Godman, John Davidson Godman, Stella Godman, and Margaret Godman. Samuel was a 1st Lieutenant in the 3rd Maryland Line under Captain Edward Norwood, and a Captain in the 4th Maryland Line (Ref: T-336, H-38, N-534). On August 27, 1776, in his deposition, he stated that as he was "reading the resolution of the Convention requiring voters to have at least fifty acres of land or property worth forty pounds, he was interrupted by persons who demanded that every free man carrying arms be allowed to vote. In anger, some men had threatened the life of Captain Thomas Watkins over this matter" (Ref: A-82). On March 10, 1856 "the Commissioner of the Land Office issued to the legal representatives of Capt. Samuel Godman, of the Maryland Line in the Revolutionary War, a common warrant for 200 acres of land to the westward of Fort Cumberland in Allegany County (Ref: K-347).

GOLDER, ARCHIBALD. Captain in the Maryland Line. He married Sarah Ashmead in 1782 (Ref: G-23, G-114). He was deceased by April 2, 1812 when his final distribution was made by John Golder, administrator, to Sarah Golder (widow third), with fifths of the remaining balance to John Golder, Robert Golder, Archibald Golder, Henrietta Golder, and George Golder (Ref: U-42).

GOLDSMITH, WILLIAM. 2nd Lieutenant in Capt. Gilbert Middleton's Independent Company of Militia of Annapolis on March 20, 1779 (Ref: I-144, O-325).

GOLLICON, JOHN. Born in Scotland. He was a Substitute, supplied by Henry Ayton on April 26, 1778, to serve until the war's end (Ref: C-211, H-318).

GOOD, JOHN. Soldier in the Light Infantry Company of Smallwood's Battalion, being unable for further duty was discharged on July 8, 1777 (Ref: V-312).

GORDON, FRANCIS. Took the Oath of Allegiance before Hon. Nicholas Worthington in March, 1778 (Ref: B-27).

GORDON, JOHN. He was appointed First Lieutenant of the Row Galley "Johnson" on May 8, 1777, commanded by Capt. James Belt (Ref: V-244).

GORDON, THOMAS. Recruited by Colonel Adams in October, 1780, to serve three years in the army (Ref: H-370).

GORE, GEORGE. Born in New England, but residing in Annapolis at the time of his enlistment on July 26, 1782 for service on the Barge "Fearnought" under Capt. Levin Spedden. Height: 5' 8". Dark complexion. (Ref: H-612).

GOTT, EZEKIEL. A resident of Herring Creek who petitioned the Convention of Maryland to form an independent militia company on March 6, 1776, and was subsequently in Capt. Richard Weems' Company (Ref: I-143, MS.1814). Took Oath of Allegiance before Hon. Samuel Lane on March 1, 1778 (Ref: B-23).

GOTT, JOSEPH. A resident of Herring Creek who petitioned the Convention of Maryland to form an independent militia company on March 6, 1776, and was subsequently in Capt. Richard Weems' Company (Ref: I-143, MS.1814). He was deceased by August 10, 1802 when final distribution of his estate was made by Robert Franklin, administrator, giving sixths (although seven persons are named) to Elizabeth Gott, Rachel Deale, Henrietta Deale, Mary Connor, Priscilla Crandall, Elizabeth Franklin, and Rispa Gott (Ref: U-20).

GOTT, RICHARD. Took the Oath of Allegiance before Hon. Samuel Harrison in March, 1778 (Ref: A-244, which questionably listed the name as "Goll").

GRAHAM, THOMAS. Private in Captain Gilbert Middleton's Independent Company of Militia of Annapolis on March 20, 1779 (Ref: I-144, O-325).

GRAHAME, JAMES. Took the Oath of Allegiance before Hon. Reuben Meriweather on March 2, 1778 (Ref: B-25).

GRAINGER, THOMAS. Private in Capt. Richard Dorsey's Company of Artillery on November 17, 1777 (Ref: H-574).

GRAITWOOD, JOHN. Enrolled by Henry Ridgely, Jr. and passed by Col. J. Carvil Hall on August 26, 1776 (Ref: H-41).

GRAMES, JOHN. Born in Maryland. He was enrolled by Samuel Chew on July 25, 1776. Height: 5' 7" (Ref: H-40).

GRAMLICK, JACOB. Took the Oath of Allegiance before Hon. Reuben Meriweather on March 2, 1778 (Ref: B-25).

GRANT, DANIEL. Furnished rooms for the meetings of the Committee of Safety in Annapolis in 1776 (Ref: Y-303).

GRANT, WILLIAM. Private in Capt. William Marbury's Company of Artillery in 1777 (Ref: H-575).

GRAVELL, BENJAMIN. Took the Oath of Allegiance before Hon. Richard Harwood, Jr. on March 1, 1778 (Ref: B-22). "Benjamin Gravel" was enrolled by Capt. Thomas Watkins on October 21, 1776, for service to the State (Ref: I-144, MS.1814). "Benjamin Gravels" was a Substitute on April 24, 1778, supplied by Thomas Harwood, to serve for three years or to the end of the war. He was born in Scotland (Ref: C-210, H-318).

GRAY, BENJAMIN. A recruit in the First Maryland Regiment in January, 1780. (Ref: Archives of Maryland, Vol. 43, p. 65).

GRAY, JOHN. Took the Oath of Allegiance before Honorable Elijah Robosson in March, 1778 (Ref: B-28).

GRAY, JOHN (OF JOSHUA). First Lieutenant in Capt. John Hammond's Company in the Severn Battalion on June 19, 1777 (Ref: A-176). Commissioned a Captain on September 2, 1777 (Ref: V-359).

GRAY, JOHN NELSON. Took the Oath of Allegiance before Hon. Richard Harwood, Jr. on March 1, 1778 (Ref: B-22).

GRAY, JOSHUA. Second Lieutenant in Capt. John Boone's Company in the Severn Battalion on June 19, 1777 and August 15, 1778 (Ref: A-176, I-144, O-208). He was deceased by June 5, 1824 when final distribution of his estate was made by William Graves, administrator, to Mary Gray (third), with fourths to sons George Gray, Joshua Gray, Joseph Gray and John Gray (Ref: U-66).

GRAY, RICHARD. Took Oath of Allegiance on September 10, 1777 (Ref: V-368).

GRAY, ZACHARIAH. Second Lieutenant in Capt. John Hammond's Company in the Severn Battalion on June 19, 1777 (Ref: A-176). Took the Oath of Allegiance before Hon. Elijah Robosson in March, 1778 (Ref: B-28). He was deceased by March 17, 1821 when final distribution was made by Charles Robinson, admn., to Elizabeth Gray (third) with remainder to his son John Gray (Ref: U-59).

GREEN, ELIJAH. Took the Oath of Allegiance before Hon. Nicholas Worthington in March, 1778 (Ref: B-27). He was deceased by June 27, 1788 when the final distribution of his estate was made to Sarah Green (widow's third) with the remaining fifths to Lancelot Green, Jacob Green, Anne Maccalley, Elizabeth Green, and Sarah Warfield (Ref: U-2).

GREEN, JOHN. Private in Captain Gilbert Middleton's Independent Company of Militia of Annapolis on March 20, 1779 (Ref: I-144, O-325).

GREEN, JOHN (OF RICHARD). He was one of the petitioners to the Convention of Maryland to form an independent rifle company in July, 1776 (Ref: B-3). He took the Oath of Allegiance before Hon. Thomas Worthington on February 28, 1778 (Ref: B-21).

GREEN, MICHAEL. Enrolled by Captain Thomas Watkins on October 21, 1776, for service to the State (Ref: I-144, MS.1814).

GREEN, RICHARD. Took the Oath of Allegiance before Hon. Samuel Lane on March 1, 1778 (Ref: B-23).

GREEN, WILLIAM. Took the Oath of Allegiance before Hon. Thomas Worthington on February 28, 1778 (Ref: B-21).

GREENBURY, RANDALL. Took Oath of Allegiance before Hon. Reuben Meriweather on March 2, 1778 (Ref: B-24).

GREENUP, SAMUEL. Took the Oath of Allegiance before Hon. Thomas Worthington on February 28, 1778 (Ref: B-21).

GREENWELL, JOHN (born 1760). Took the Oath of Allegiance before Hon. Elijah Robosson in March, 1778 (Ref: B-28). Private in the Militia (Ref: G-24).

GREYER, LAWRENCE. Enlisted by John Worthington Dorsey and passed by John Dorsey on July 22, 1776 (Ref: H-39).

GRIEST, ISAAC (of Baltimore). On August 23, 1780, the Council of Maryland directed him to "impress vessels sufficient to transport three hundred troops of the Extra Regiment from Annapolis to the Head of Elk." (Ref: Archives of Maryland, Volume 43, pp. 264-265).

GRIFFIN, FREDERICK. Took the Oath of Allegiance before Hon. Samuel Harrison in March, 1778 (Ref: A-244).

GRIFFIN, HENRY. Took the Oath of Allegiance before Hon. Samuel Harrison in March, 1778 (Ref: A-244).

GRIFFIN, NATHAN. Took the Oath of Allegiance before Hon. Samuel Harrison, Jr. in March, 1778 (Ref: B-28).

GRIFFIS, HUGH. Took the Oath of Allegiance before Hon. Samuel Harrison, Jr. in March, 1778 (Ref: Maryland State Papers, Red Book 22. Note: His name is mistakenly spelled "Hugh Greffis" in the published list in Source B-28).

GRIFFIS, JOHN JR. Took the Oath of Allegiance before Hon. Samuel Harrison, Jr. in March, 1778 (Ref: Maryland State Papers, Red Book 22. Note: His name is mistakenly spelled "John Greffis Jr." in the published list in Ref: B-28). Drafted in October, 1780, to serve until December 10, 1780 (Ref: H-369). A John Griffis was deceased by October 21, 1824 when final distribution was made by Henry Childs, admin., with fifths to John Griffis, Ann Crandel, Elizabeth Griffis, Joseph Griffis and William Griffis (Ref: U-67).

GRIFFIS, LITTLETON. Took the Oath of Allegiance before Hon. Samuel Harrison, Jr. in March, 1778 (Ref: Maryland State Papers, Red Book 22. Note: Name is mistakenly spelled "Littleton Greffis" in the published list in Ref:B-28).

GRIFFITH, CHARLES GREENBURY. Born in Anne Arundel County in 1744, a son of Orlando Griffith and Katherine Howard, he moved to Frederick County by 1770 and was quite prominent during the Revolutionary War. He died in Frederick County in 1792. (For more about his patriotic service, see Source P-377).

GRIFFITH, DENNIS. Took the Oath of Allegiance before Hon. Thomas Worthington on February 28, 1778 (Ref: B-21).

GRIFFITH, HENRY. Born in Anne Arundel County circa 1720, a son of Orlando Griffith and Katherine Howard, he moved to Frederick County by 1770 and was quite prominent during the Revolutionary War. He died in Frederick County in 1794. (For more about his patriotic service, see Source P-377, P-378).

GRIFFITH, JOHN. Private in Capt. Richard Chew's Company of Col. John Weems' Battalion on October 5, 1776 (Ref: A-95, I-143, MS.1814).

GRIFFITH, JOSHUA. Served on Committee of Observation in 1775 (Ref: F-222).

GRIFFITH, W. Took the Oath of Allegiance before Hon. Thomas Dorsey on March 2, 1778 (Ref: B-24).

GRIFFITHS, DAVID. Took the Oath of Allegiance before Hon. Samuel Harrison in March, 1778 (Ref: A-244).

GRIM, FRANCIS. Took the Oath of Allegiance before Hon. Thomas Worthington on March 1, 1778 (Ref: B-22).

GRIMES, NATHANIEL. Enlisted by Thomas Mayo on July 20, 1776 (Ref: H-41).

GRIMES, STEPHEN. Enlisted by Thomas Mayo on July 20, 1776 (Ref: H-41).

GRIMES, WILLIAM. Enlisted by Thomas Mayo on July 20, 1776 (Ref: H-41).

GRINNOL (GRINNEL), THOMAS. Took the Oath of Allegiance before Hon. Nicholas Worthington in March, 1778 (Ref: Maryland State Papers, Red Book 21. Note: His name is spelled "Thomas Grimmel" in the published list in Ref: B-27). "Thomas Grinall" was enrolled by Henry Ridgely, Jr. and passed by Col. J. Carvil Hall on August 26, 1776 (Ref: H-41).

GUESS, BASIL. Private in Capt. Richard Chew's Company of Col. John Weems' Company on October 5, 1776 (Ref: A-95, I-143, MS.1814).

GUNDUN, BENJAMIN. He was a Substitute, supplied by Nicholas Maccubbin on June 2, 1778, to serve for three years (Ref: C-208, H-319).

HACKETT, JOHN. Born in Scotland. Appears as a Substitute on April 26, 1778, supplied by Talbot Shipley and George Shipley (Ref: C-211, H-318).

HADEN, GEORGE. Took the Oath of Allegiance before Hon. Nicholas Worthington in March, 1778 (Ref: B-27).

HAGER (HAGAR), JOHN. Took Oath of Allegiance before Hon. Reuben Meriweather on March 2, 1778 (Ref: B-24).

HAGER, JOHN JR. Took the Oath of Allegiance before Hon. Reuben Meriweather on March 2, 1778 (Ref: B-24).

HAISLUP (HAISLIP), WILLIAM. Took the Oath of Allegiance before Hon. Thomas Dorsey on March 2, 1778 (Ref: B-24).

HALEY, CALEB. Private in 2nd Maryland Line who enlisted July 18, 1780, was wounded, and transferred to Invalids Corps in summer of 1782. Paid full pay until November 15, 1783 when the record indicates he was dead (Ref: X-14). Elizabeth Haley, of Annapolis, wife of Caleb, petitioned the State (no date given) that her husband was on duty, having served in three campaigns. She was very poor and prayed for rations and other necessaries (Ref: Archives of Maryland, Volume 43, page 534).

HALFPENNY, MARK. Enlisted by John Worthington Dorsey and was passed by John Dorsey on July 22, 1776 (Ref: H-39).

HALL, EDWARD. Enrolled by Capt. Watkins on October 21, 1776, for service to the State (Ref: I-144, MS.1814). "Edward Hall, of Henry" took the Oath of Allegiance before Hon. Richard Harwood, Jr. on March 1, 1778 (Ref: B-22).

HALL, ELISHA. Private in Captain Gilbert Middleton's Independent Company of Militia of Annapolis on March 20, 1779 (Ref: I-144, O-325). He was deceased by June 1, 1816 when John Hilton (administrator with will annexed) made the distribution (thirds) to Henry Hall, Eliza Hall and Jane Hall (Ref: U-47).

HALL, HENRY. There were two men with this name who served. One was a Captain of Militia on February 22, 1776, and another enrolled under Henry Ridgely, Jr., and was passed on August 26, 1776 (Ref: H-41, N-178). They also took the Oath of Allegiance in March, 1778: one before Hon. Richard Harwood, Jr. and one before Hon. Samuel Harrison, Jr. (Ref: A-244, B-22). Major Henry Hall (born 1751) was son of Henry Hall and Elizabeth Watkins (Ref: P-385). One Henry Hall was deceased by December 21, 1832 when Richard H. Hall (his administrator de bonis non with will annexed) made final distribution to Rachel S. Hall (widow's third) with sevenths of the remaining balance to the estate of Joseph Hall, Richard G. Stockett, Basil Warren, Thomas W. Hall, Thomas H. Hall, Richard H. Hall, and Osborn S. Hall (Ref: U-85).

HALL, JOHN. Served on the Committee of Observation in 1775 (Ref: F-222). He was a Representative to the Maryland Convention, 1775 and 1776 (Ref: A-77, F-222, J-1, J-4). Colonel of the Severn Battalion of Militia in 1776 (Ref: F-224). He refused the office of Judge of Admiralty in 1776 (Ref: F-223).

HALL, JOHN (OF EDWARD). Took the Oath of Allegiance before the Hon. Nicholas Worthington in March, 1778 (Ref: B-27).

HALL, JOHN (November 23, 1729 - March 8, 1797). Son of Henry Hall and Martha Bateman. Married Eleanor Dorsey in 1767, but died without progeny. Served in numerous positions in both Anne Arundel and St. Mary's Counties from 1762 through 1795, including the Council of Safety in 1776 and 1777, and a Delegate to the Continental Congress in 1774 and 1775 (Ref: P-387).

HALL, JOHN (of West River). Took the Oath of Allegiance before Hon. Thomas Harwood on February 28, 1778 (Ref: B-22).

HALL, JOSIAS CARVIL (1746-1814). Colonel in the 4th Maryland Line. He was actually from the Baltimore-Harford area, but men from Anne Arundel County served in his regiment (Ref: H-41). (Refer to Henry C. Peden's books on the Revolutionary Patriots of Baltimore County, and the Revolutionary Patriots of Harford County, as well as detailed information in source P-388, 389).

HALL, NATHANIEL. Enlisted by Thomas Mayo on July 20, 1776 (Ref: H-41).

HALL, RICHARD. On February 2, 1832, the Treasurer was ordered to pay Richard Hall, of Anne Arundel County, a soldier of the revolution during life, half yearly, half pay of a private, for his services. Then, on January 5, 1841, the Treasurer was ordered to pay to Mrs. Ann Cadle, legal representative of Richard Hall, deceased, a pensioner of Maryland, $17.60 due Richard Hall at the time of his death (Ref: K-350). Two men by this name took the Oath of Allegiance: one before Hon. Thomas Worthington on February 28, 1778 and one before Hon. Samuel Harrison, Jr., in March, 1778 (Ref: A-244, B-21). One Richard Hall was enrolled by Capt. Thomas Watkins on October 21, 1776, for service as a Private in the 2nd Maryland Line (Ref: I-144, MS.1814, Z-53).

HALL, THOMAS HENRY. Took the Oath of Allegiance before Hon. Richard Harwood, Jr. on March 1, 1778 (Ref: B-22). Still alive in April, 1790 (Ref: U-4).

HALL, WILLIAM. His name appears as a Substitute on May 30, 1778, supplied by Capt. John Boone, for a 3 year term (Ref: C-208, H-319).

HALL, WILLIAM 3RD. Took the Oath of Allegiance before Hon. Richard Harwood, Jr. on March 1, 1778 (Ref: B-22).

HAMILTON (HAMELTON), JOHN. Took the Oath of Allegiance before Hon. Samuel Harrison, Jr. in March, 1778 (Ref: A-244).

HAMILTON, JOHN G. Took Oath of Allegiance before Hon. John Dorsey on March 12, 1778 (Ref: B-26).

HAMMOND, ANDREW. Ensign in Capt. James Disney's Company in the 3rd Maryland Line in July, 1776 (Ref: H-39). Still alive in June, 1817 (Ref: U-50).

HAMMOND, BEALE. Took the Oath of Allegiance before Hon. Nicholas Worthington in March, 1778 (Ref: Original list in Maryland State Papers, Red Book 21. Note: Source B-27 gives his name as "Beale Hamman").

HAMMOND, CHARLES SR. (June 4, 1729 - September, 1777). Son of Philip Hammond and Rachel Brice. Married Rebecca Wright and had 6 children: Rezin Hammond, Philip Hammond, John Hammond, Hannah Hammond Hopkins, Charles Hammond, and William Hammond (Ref: Q-256). He was one of the three Commissioners of the Paper Currency in Annapolis on May 30, 1776 (Ref: E-3065 and Maryland State Papers, Black Books No. 1, pp. 199, 219, but not mentioned in Ref: Q-256).

HAMMOND, CHARLES, OF JOHN (died 1796). Son of John Hammond and Anne Dorsey. Married ------ and had 7 children: John Hammond, Sarah Hammond Dorsey, Anne Hammond Wood, Charles Hammond, Elizabeth Hammond, Rezin Hammond, and Mary Hammond Deborough. Charles served on the Committee of Observation in 1775 and 1776 (Ref: Q-260. F-222). Took the Oath of Allegiance before Hon. John Dorsey on March 12, 1778 (Ref: B-26). He was commissioned a 1st Lieutenant in Captain John Dorsey's Company in the Elk Ridge Battalion on August 28, 1777 and a Captain on March 12, 1778 (Ref: C-201, Q-260).

HAMMOND, GEORGE. Was an Ensign in Capt. Caleb Owings' Company of the Severn Battalion in June, 1777 and March, 1778 (Ref: A-176, C-202). He took the Oath of Allegiance before Hon. Elijah Robosson in March, 1778 (Ref: B-28).

HAMMOND, GREENBURY. Took Oath of Allegiance before Hon. Nicholas Worthington in March, 1778 (Ref: B-27).

HAMMOND, JOHN. Two men by this name took the Oath of Allegiance: one before Hon. John Dorsey on March 12, 1778 (Ref: B-26) and one before Hon. Nicholas Worthington in March, 1778 (Ref: Original list in Maryland State Papers Red Book No. 21, p. 8D. Note: His name is mistakenly omitted from Source B-27). John Hammond (1735-1784), son of Philip Hammond and Rachel Brice, married Ann ----- in 1772, and took the Oath noted above (Ref: P-394). Another John Hammond was a Captain in the Severn Battalion in June of 1777, and he was threatened with courtmartial for failing to attend a meeting (Ref: A-176). One John Hammond was deceased by April 10, 1798 when administrator Rezin Hammond made final distribution of his estate (fourths) to Charles Hammond, Philip Hammond, Rezin Hammond, and Hannah Hammond Hopkins (Ref: U-17).

HAMMOND, JOHN, OF NATHAN (1740 - March 25, 1806, Frederick County). Son of Major Nathan Hammond and Ann May Welsh. He arrived Martha Hawkins, daughter of Matthew Hawkins, a wealthy Quaker, prior to 1770 and had three children: Ariana Hammond Walker, Rachel Hammond, and Charles Hammond. He was a Captain in the Militia in 1777 (Ref: E-2670, Q-266). He took the Oath of Allegiance before Hon. Thos. Worthington on February 28, 1778 (Ref: B-21).

HAMMOND, LAWRENCE. Took Oath of Allegiance before Hon. John Dorsey on March 12, 1778 (Ref: B-26).

HAMMOND, MATTHIAS (May 24, 1740 - November 11, 1786). Son of Philip Hammond and Rachel Brice. Never married. He was one of those who burned the ship "Peggy Stewart" in Annapolis in October, 1774 (Ref: P-395). Served on the Committee of Observation in 1775 (Ref: F-222) and was actively involved in the county elections in August, 1776.

Took the Oath of Allegiance before the Hon. Nicholas Worthington in March, 1778 (Ref: A-83, B-27). He was also a Representative to the Maryland Convention in 1775 (Ref: J-1, J-4).

HAMMOND, NEHEMIAH. Took the Oath of Allegiance before Hon. Samuel Harrison, Jr. in March, 1778 (Ref: A-244).

HAMMOND, PHILIP (May 23, 1744 - April 21, 1799). Son of Major Nathan Hammond and Ann Welsh. He married Barbara Raitt circa 1769 and had eight children: Arianna Hammond Mackelfresh, Nathan Hammond, George Hammond, Walter Charles Hammond, Lloyd Thomas Hammond, Mary Hammond, Philip Greenbury Hammond, and Ann Hammond. Took the Oath of Allegiance before Hon. Nicholas Worthington in March, 1778 (Ref: Q-262, B-27, T-361).

HAMMOND, PHILIP. Took the Oath of Allegiance before Hon. Samuel Harrison, Jr. in 1778 (Ref: BA-244).

HAMMOND, PHILIP (1755 - 1822). Son of Charles and Rebecca Hammond. Married Elizabeth Wright in 1784 and had thirteen children: Thomas Hammond, Philip Hammond, Rezin Hammond, John Hammond, Henry Hammond, Matilda Hammond Brown, Harriet Hammond Pue, Charles Hammond, Denton Hammond, Elizabeth Hammond Newburn, Matthias Hammond, Mary Ann Hammond Dorsey, and George Washington Hammond. As "Philip Hammond, Jr." he took Oath of Allegiance before Hon. Reuben Meriweather on March 2, 1778 (Ref: Q-268, Q-269, B-25).

HAMMOND, REZIN (1745 - September 1, 1809). Son of Philip Hammond and Rachel Brice. Never married. He was a Representative to the Maryland Convention in 1776, and active in the county elections in August, 1776 (Ref: A-77, A-82, P-398, 399). Captain in the militia and a Lieutenant Colonel in the Severn Battalion of Militia in 1776 under Col. John Hall (Ref: A-162, F-224).

HAMMOND, THOMAS (1745-1776). Son of Lawrence Hammond and Margaret Hughes. He married Elizabeth Jacob and had a son Thomas Hughes Hammond. Thomas was an officer in the Severn Battalion in 1775 and on August 5, 1776 was a Captain assigned to Colonel Josias C. Hall's Battalion of the Flying Camp, attached to the 3rd Maryland Line (Ref: H-39). Thomas Hammond was one of the several hundred Marylanders who were killed in battle in New York in August, 1776 (Ref: Q-236, Q-237).

HAMMOND, THOMAS. Took the Oath of Allegiance before Hon. Thomas Worthington on February 28, 1778 (Ref: B-21). Private in Capt. Gilbert Middleton's Independent Company of Militia of Annapolis in March, 1779 (Ref: I-144).

HAMMOND, WILLIAM. Served on Committee of Observation in 1775 (Ref: F-222). Took the Oath of Allegiance before Hon. Thomas Worthington on February 28, 1778 (Ref: B-21).

HAMMOND, WORTHINGTON. Quartermaster in Col. John Hall's Severn Battalion of Militia in 1776 (Ref: F-224).

HAMPTON, WILLIAM. Born in Scotland. His name appears as a Substitute on May 9, 1778, supplied by Isaac Harris, for a 3 year term (Ref: C-206, H-317).

HANCOCK, STEPHEN (1745 - October 7, 1809). He married Margaret Anne Cromwell. He was a Private in the 1st and 3rd Maryland Regiments from 1780 to 1783 (Ref: E-265, E-266). Final distribution of his estate was made on January 16, 1812 by Francis Hancock, administrator, to Anne Hancock (widow's third) with sixths to Francis Hancock; the children of Ann Boone, namely Stephen Boone, Robert Boone and Mary Anne Thomas; Ann Williams, daughter of Sally Williams; Rhody Stewart; Stephen Hancock; and Absalom Hancock (Ref: U-41).

HANCOCK, WILLIAM (OF WILLIAM). Commissioned an Ensign in Capt. John Gray's Company in the Severn Battalion on September 2, 1777 (Ref: V-359).

HANDLEN, JOHN. Private in Capt. Richard Dorsey's Company of Artillery on November 17, 1777 (Ref: H-574).

HANNAH, NICHOLAS. Fourth Sergeant in Capt. Gilbert Middleton's Independent Company of Militia of Annapolis on March 20, 1779 (Ref: I-144, O-325).

HANNEN, THOMAS. Recruited in October, 1780 by Lt. James J. Skinner, to serve for 3 years (Ref: H-369).

HANS, WILLIAM. Took the Oath of Allegiance before Hon. Thomas Dorsey on March 2, 1778 (Ref: B-24). "William Hands" was deceased by January 17, 1798 when final distribution of his estate was made by administratrix Catherine Hands to Catherine Hands (widow's third) and with ninths of the remaining balance to William Hands, John Hands, Margaret Hands, Achsah Hands, Sarah Hands, Lancelot Hands, Ephraim Hands, Nicholas Hands, and Mary Hands (Ref: U-16).

HANSLAP, HENRY. Captain in the Severn Battalion in 1776 (Ref: F-222).

HANSON, ALEXANDER CONTEE (October 22, 1749 - January 16, 1806). Son of John Hanson, Jr. and Jane Contee. He was born in Charles County and resided in Frederick County where he served in the Legislature and on the Committee of Observation in 1775, and was Clerk of the Senate in 1777. In Anne Arundel County he was Judge of the General Court, 1778-1779, and was a Delegate to the Constitutional Ratification Convention in 1788 (Ref: P-404).

HANSON, ISAAC. He was a Quartermaster in the Fourth Maryland Line on May 1, 1777, Ensign on November 8, 1779, and Lieutenant on December 15, 1779 (Ref: H-122). The General Assembly granted him half pay as a disabled soldier in Anne Arundel County in 1784/5 (Ref: D-21, D-22, K-351).

HANSPAN, JOHN CODLEP (CUTLIP). In December, 1817, the Treasurer was ordered to pay him quarterly, half pay of private in Rev. War

(Ref: K-351). He was pensioned at age 95 on July 29, 1818, and died July 12, 1824 (Ref: Z-27).

HARDEN, NICHOLAS. Took the Oath of Allegiance before Hon. Thomas Worthington on February 28, 1778 (Ref: B-21).

HARDEN, NICHOLAS JR. Took Oath of Allegiance before Hon. Thomas Worthington on February 28, 1778 (Ref: B-21).

HARDESTY, HENRY. Took the Oath of Allegiance before Hon. Thomas Dorsey on March 2, 1778 (Ref: B-24).

HARDESTY, JOHN. Took the Oath of Allegiance before Hon. Thomas Dorsey on March 2, 1778 (Ref: B-24). He was deceased by October 24, 1806 when the final distribution of his estate was made by administrator Joseph McCeney to Agnes Hardesty, now Agnes Simmons (widow's third) with fifths of the remaining balance to Mary Hardesty, Harriet Hardesty, Richard Hardesty, Elizabeth Hardesty, and Elias Hardesty (Ref: U-30).

HARDING, ROBERT. Enlisted in 1st Maryland Line on May 10, 1777; lost his eyesight circa September 10, 1779; discharged March 18, 1780 (Ref: X-15).

HARLEY, JON. Enrolled by Capt. Watkins on October 21, 1776, for service to the State (Ref: I-144, MS.1814).

HARN, JOHN 3RD. Took the Oath of Allegiance before Hon. John Dorsey on March 12, 1778 (Ref: B-26).

HARNSBURY, NATHANIEL ROBERT. Recruited in October, 1780 by Major Steward, to serve for 3 years (Ref: H-370).

HARPER, JOHN. Took the Oath of Allegiance before Hon. Thomas Worthington on February 28, 1778 (Ref: B-21).

HARPHAM, ROBERT. Born in Scotland. His name appears as a Substitute on May 18, 1778, supplied by Col. John Dorsey, for the duration of the war (Ref: C-213, H-319).

HARRINGTON, WILLIAM. Born in Scotland. His name appears as a Substitute on May 8, 1778, supplied by Benjamin Galloway, for a 3 year term (Ref: C-206, H-317).

HARRIS, ISAAC. On February 6, 1776, he was appointed Armourer to the troops stationed in Annapolis by the Council of Safety (Ref: N-296).

HARRIS, NATHAN. Took the Oath of Allegiance before Hon. Thomas Worthington on February 28, 1778 (Ref: B-21).

HARRIS, RICHARD. Took the Oath of Allegiance before Hon. Thomas Worthington on February 28, 1778 (Ref: B-21).

HARRIS, ROBERT. Enrolled by Capt. Watkins on October 21, 1776, for service to the State (Ref: I-144, MS.1814).

HARRIS, THOMAS. Took the Oath of Allegiance before Hon. Samuel Harrison, Jr. in March, 1778 (Ref: B-28).

HARRIS, WILLIAM. Took the Oath of Allegiance before Hon. Reuben Meriweather on March 2, 1778 (Ref: B-24).

HARRIS, ZEKIEL. His name appeared on a list of recruits for the artillery at Annapolis on December 12, 1776, under Capt. John Fulford (Ref: H-572).

HARRISON, BENJAMIN. Resident of Herring Creek, he was commissioned an Ensign in 1776 and then 2nd Lieutenant in Capt. Richard Weems' Company in the West River Battalion in 1778 (Ref: I-143, C-199, F-223, N-336). He took the Oath of Allegiance before Hon. Samuel Harrison, Jr. in March, 1778 (Ref: B-28). He probably was the son of Richard Harrison and Sarah Hall, and was born circa 1754 and died in 1825 (Ref: See information in source P-416).

HARRISON, CLEMENT. Took the Oath of Allegiance before Hon. Samuel Harrison, Jr. in March, 1778 (Ref: A-244).

HARRISON, GEORGE. He took the Oath of Allegiance before Hon. John Dorsey on March 12, 1778 (Ref: B-26).

HARRISON, HORATIO. Resident of Herring Creek, he was among those who signed to form an independent company on March 6, 1776 and subsequently became a private in Capt. Richard Weems' Company (Ref: I-143, MS.1814).

HARRISON, JOHN. Took the Oath of Allegiance before Hon. Samuel Harrison, Jr. in March, 1778 (Ref: B-28).

HARRISON, KINSEY. In December, 1816, the Treasurer was ordered to pay Kinsey Harrison, of Anne Arundel County, quarterly, half pay of a private during his life, as a further remuneration for his services (Ref: K-352). He was pensioned on May 3, 1818, age 76, as Private in Maryland Line (Ref: Z-27).

HARRISON, RICHARD. Enrolled under Henry Ridgely, Jr. and passed by Colonel Josias Carvil Hall on August 26, 1776 (Ref: H-41). Ensign in Capt. Richard Chew's Company in the West River Battalion in 1778 (Ref: C-200). Took Oath of Allegiance before Hon. Samuel Harrison, Jr. in March, 1778 (Ref: B-28). He was deceased by February 8, 1799 when Mrs. Mary Harrison, administratrix made final distribution of his estate to Mary Harrison (widow's third) and the remainder equally to Eleanor Harrison and Joseph Harrison (Ref: U-24).

HARRISON, SAMUEL JR. He was one of the Justices who administered the Oath of Allegiance in March, 1778, and was subsequently appointed a Justice of the Peace on November 19, 1778 (Ref: A-244, B-24, B-28, B-29, O-241).

HARRISON, SAMUEL (OF RICHARD). Appointed Justice of the Peace on November 19, 1778 (Ref: O-241).

HARRISON, WALTER. Took the Oath of Allegiance before Hon. Samuel Harrison, Jr. in March, 1778 (Ref: B-28).

HARVEY, CARTER. Took the Oath of Allegiance before Hon. Reuben Meriweather on March 2, 1778 (Ref: B-25).

HARVEY, CHARLES. Enlisted by John Worthington Dorsey and passed by John Dorsey on July 22, 1776 (Ref: H-39).

HARWOOD, BENJAMIN. 1st Lieutenant in Capt. John Bullen's Independent Company of Militia in 1776 (Ref: F-224). Captain on October 6, 1777 (Ref: V-392).

HARWOOD, NICHOLAS (March 14, 1747/8 - October 10, 1810). Son of Capt. Richard Harwood and Anne Watkins. Married Anne -----, and they had six children: Nicholas Harwood, James Harwood, Henry Harwood, Anne Harwood, Sarah Ann Harwood Duvall, and Mary Harwood Green. At the beginning of the Revolution Nicholas was the Clerk of the Convention of Maryland, and he was the Clerk of the Court for several years (Ref: S-77, S-78). The final distribution of his estate was made by Lewis Duvall, administrator de bonis non, on May 8, 1824 with sixths going to Nicholas Harwood, James Harwood, Lewis Duvall (in right of his wife, unnamed), Ann Harwood, William Shereen (in right of his wife, unnamed), and Henry S. Harwood (Ref: U-66).

HARWOOD, OSBORN J. Pensioned March 4, 1831, age 74. Private (Ref: Z-45).

HARWOOD, OSBORN SPRIGG (May 2, 1760 - December 21, 1847). Son of Thomas Harwood and Rachel Sprigg. Married Elizabeth Ann Harwood in 1791 and they had 5 children: Maria Harwood, Margaret Harwood Hall, Rachel Ann Harwood Iglehart, Mary Elizabeth Harwood, and Thomas Richard Sprigg Harwood. In the spring of 1777 Osborn enlisted in Capt. William Brogden's Company and subsequently was attached to the 1st Maryland Line. He participated in the battle of Germantown on October 4, 1777. He was commissioned 2nd Lieutenant in Capt. Thomas Watkins' Company on August 17, 1779 (Ref: O-496). In 1832 he filed for and received pension S8677 (Ref: S-61, S-62).

HARWOOD, RICHARD (OF THOMAS). Private in Capt. William Marbury's Company of Artillery in 1777 (Ref: H-575).

HARWOOD, RICHARD. Took the Oath of Allegiance before Hon. Thomas Harwood on February 28, 1778 (Ref: B-22).

HARWOOD, RICHARD JR. (April 20, 1739 - February 21, 1826). Son of Richard Harwood and Anne Watkins. Married Margaret Hall in 1767 and they had 12 children: Ann Elizabeth Harwood Sellman, Elizabeth Ann Harwood, Richard Hall Harwood, Henry Hall Harwood, Joseph Harwood, Thomas Harwood, Mary Harwood, Henrietta Harwood Cowan Hall, Benjamin Harwood, Priscilla Harwood Weems Mills, William

Harwood, and Edward Harwood. He was commissioned a Lieutenant Colonel in Col. John Weems' West River Battalion in 1776, and later became a Colonel, serving through February, 1782 (Ref: S-69, S-70, S-71, H-40, C-199, and F-224 which refers to him as being in the South River Battalion). He was appointed a Justice on June 10, 1777, and he also administered the Oath of Allegiance in March, 1778 (Ref: B-22; Anne Arundel Orphans Court Proc., 1777-79, MdHR 9524, p. 1). Richard was commissioned by the Assembly to receive subscription in 1779 (Ref: O-499. Source P-421 states that he was born December 1, 1738, and that he married secondly to Lucinda Battee (nee Harwood?), widow of John Battee, in 1806).

HARWOOD, THOMAS (April 24, 1743 - September 23, 1804). Son of Capt. Richard Harwood and Anne Watkins. Married Margaret Strachan in 1772 and they had 2 children: William Harwood and Richard Harwood. He was actively involved in the county elections in August, 1776, and was Commissioner of Continental Loan Office. He was also one of the Justices who administered the Oath of Allegiance in February, 1778, and was appointed a Justice of the Orphans Court in November, 1778 (Ref: A-82, A-83, B-22, S-72, S-73, S-74, O-241). He was commissioned County Sheriff on October 12, 1779 (Ref: O-554).

HARWOOD, THOMAS SR. Took the Oath of Allegiance before Hon. Richard Harwood, Jr. on March 1, 1778 (Ref: B-22).

HARWOOD, THOMAS JR. (died on May 15, 1791). Son of Thomas Harwood and Rachel Sprigg. Married Anne Whyte in 1778 and had 2 children: Thomas Harwood and Caroline Harwood Smith. Thomas Harwood, Jr. was a Lieutenant in the 7th Maryland Line in early 1775, and in 1776 he was Captain in the 1st Maryland Line, but resigned his commission on June 10, 1777. As Thomas Harwood 3rd he took the Oath of Allegiance before Hon. Thomas Harwood on February 28, 1778 (Ref: B-22, S-62, S-63).

HARWOOD, WILLIAM (February 3, 1749/50 - July 4, 1804). Son of Capt. Richard Harwood and Anne Watkins. Married Mary Elizabeth Williams in 1774 and they had eleven children: William Harwood; Anne Harwood Watkins; Eleanor Harwood Watkins; Margaret Harwood Watkins; Mary Harwood Sefton; Maria Harwood Stewart; Louisa Harwood Stewart; Frederick Harwood; Richard Harwood; John Thomas Harwood; and, Elizabeth Harwood. William was an Ensign in Captain Thomas Watkins' Company in 1776, and Capt. Thomas Noble Stockett's Company in the South River Battalion in 1778 (Ref: N-158, S-79; F-223; and source C-199 refers to him as being in the West River Militia Company). Took the Oath of Allegiance before Hon. Richard Harwood, Jr. on March 1, 1778 (Ref: B-22). He was High Sheriff of Anne Arundel County for two days in January, 1778. By 1786 he was Clerk of the Lower House (Ref: S-79, S-80, N-158).

HATHERLY, BENJAMIN. Took Oath of Allegiance before Hon. Reuben Meriweather on March 2, 1778 (Ref: B-24).

HATHERLY, JOHN. Took the Oath of Allegiance before Hon. Reuben Meriweather on March 2, 1778 (Ref: B-24). He was deceased by August 25, 1785 when the final distribution of his estate was made by his executors to his widow (unnamed), who received "a third after deduction of a legacy left by the testator to Benjamin Hatherly and Nathan Hatherly, each of whom received a negro and one half of the remainder of the balance." (Ref: U-2).

HATHERLY (HATHARLY), NATHAN. Took the Oath of Allegiance before Hon. Thomas Dorsey on March 2, 1778 (Ref: B-24).

HATTON, WILLIAM. He was a member of the Matross Company of Annapolis and, being an disabled, he procured Abraham Lawell to serve in his stead during the war, and he was subsequently discharged October 13, 1779 (Ref: O-554).

HAVERS, JOHN. Recruited and passed by James Brice on January 12, 1778 (Ref: C-215, H-313).

HAWK, MACHL. Enrolled by Capt. Watkins on October 21, 1776, for service to the State (Ref: I-144, MS.1814).

HAWKER (HAWKES), ROBERT. "Robert Hawker" took the Oath of Allegiance before Hon. Richard Harwood, Jr. on March 1, 1778 (Ref: B-22). "Robert Hawkes" was enrolled by Capt. Watkins on October 21, 1776, for service to the State of Maryland (Ref: I-144, MS.1814).

HAWKINS, JOHN. Took the Oath of Allegiance before Hon. John Dorsey on March 12, 1778 (Ref: B-26). He was deceased by October 28, 1793 when the final distribution of his estate was made by executor Andrew Mercer to his heirs, namely Priscilla Hawkins, John Mercer, Thomas Hawkins, William Hawkins, Rezin Hawkins, Nicholas Hawkins, Charles Hawkins, Caleb Hawkins, Rebecca Hawkins, and Ruth Hawkins (Ref: U-11).

HAWKINS, NICHOLAS. Took Oath of Allegiance before Hon. John Dorsey on March 12, 1778 (Ref: B-26).

HAWKINS, THOMAS. Recruited in October, 1780 by Colonel Adams, to serve for 3 years (Ref: H-370).

HAWKINS, WILLIAM. Took the Oath of Allegiance before Hon. Reuben Meriweather on March 2, 1778 (Ref: B-24).

HAYCROFT, WILLIAM. Took the Oath of Allegiance before Hon. Elijah Robosson in March, 1778 (Ref: B-28).

HAYNES, RICHARD. Took the Oath of Allegiance before Hon. Nicholas Worthington in March, 1778 (Ref: B-27).

HAYWOOD, THOMAS. Took the Oath of Allegiance before Hon. Samuel Harrison, Jr. in March, 1778 (Ref: B-28).

HAZELIP, JOHN. Took the Oath of Allegiance before Hon. John Dorsey on March 12, 1778 (Ref: B-26).

HAZELIP, WILLIAM. Took Oath of Allegiance before Hon. John Dorsey on March 12, 1778 (Ref: B-26).

HAZLE (HAZEL), CALEB. Second Lieutenant in Capt. Joseph Maccubbin's Company in the Severn Battalion on March 1, 1778 (Ref: C-202). Disabled soldier paid in Anne Arundel County on January 13, 1784 (Ref: D-11).

HEADWOOD, JOHN. Born in Ireland. Recruited by Cornelius Mills and passed by James Brice on February 12, 1778 (Ref: C-215, H-313).

HEARN (HERN), CHARLES. Enrolled by Capt. Thomas Watkins on October 21, 1776, for service to the State (Ref: I-144, MS.1814).

HEARN, EDWARD. Enrolled under Henry Ridgely, Jr. and passed by Col. Josias Carvil Hall on August 26, 1776 (Ref: H-41).

HEARN, MICHAL. Took the Oath of Allegiance before Hon. Thomas Dorsey on March 2, 1778 (Ref: B-24).

HEATH, WILLIAM. Commissioned a First Lieutenant in Capt. John Gray's Company in the Severn Battalion on September 2, 1777 (Ref: V-359). He took the Oath of Allegiance before Hon. Elijah Robosson in March, 1778 (Ref: B-28).

HEINS, JACOB (of Montgomery County). Took the Oath of Allegiance before Hon. Reuben Meriweather on March 2, 1778 in Anne Arundel County (Ref: B-25).

HENCOCK, STEPHEN. Took the Oath of Allegiance before Hon. Elijah Robosson in March, 1778 (Ref: B-28).

HENCOCK, WILLIAM. Took the Oath of Allegiance before Hon. Elijah Robosson in March, 1778 (Ref: B-28).

HENDRICKSON, JAMES. Corporal in Capt. Richard Dorsey's Company of Artillery on November 17, 1777 (Ref: H-574).

HENNESSY (HANASY), EDWARD. Born in Ireland. Recruited by Cornelius Mills and passed by James Brice on May 22, 1778 (Ref: C-217, H-314).

HENNESSY, JAMES. Took the Oath of Allegiance before Hon. Samuel Harrison, Jr. in March, 1778 (Ref: B-28).

HENRIGHT, JOHN. Matross who lost the use of his arm "which not likely soon if at all to recover" was discharged on December 31, 1777 (Ref: V-450).

HENRY, ADAM. Born in Scotland. Recruited and passed by James Brice in Anne Arundel County on January 8, 1778 (Ref: C-215, H-313).

HENSLEY, EDWARD. Enrolled by Capt. Thomas Watkins on October 21, 1776, for service to the State (Ref: I-144, MS.1814).

HENSHAW, CHARLES. Took the Oath of Allegiance before Hon. Elijah Robosson in March, 1778 (Ref: B-28).

HENSHAW, CHARLES SR. Took the Oath of Allegiance before Hon. Elijah Robosson in March, 1778 (Ref: B-28).

HENSHAW, JAMES. Took the Oath of Allegiance before Hon. Elijah Robosson in March, 1778 (Ref: B-28).

HENWARD (HENWOOD), CHARLES. Took the Oath of Allegiance before Hon. Elijah Robosson in March, 1778 (Ref: B-28, V-532).

HENWARD (HENWOOD), WILLIAM. Took the Oath of Allegiance before Hon. Elijah Robosson in March, 1778 (Ref: B-28). Deceased by 1797 (Ref: U-15).

HEWITT, THOMAS. Private in Capt. William Marbury's Company of Artillery in 1777 (Ref: H-575).

HICKEY, THOMAS. Born in Scotland. His name appears as a Substitute on April 26, 1778, supplied by Walker Chase, for a 3 year term (Ref: C-211, H-318).

HIGGINS, JAMES. Enlisted by Joseph Burgess for the Flying Camp on July 20, 1776 (Ref: H-40).

HIGGINS, JOHN JR. Took the Oath of Allegiance before Hon. Reuben Meriweather on March 2, 1778 (Ref: B-25).

HIGGINS, JOSEPH. Took the Oath of Allegiance before Hon. Reuben Meriweather on March 2, 1778 (Ref: B-24).

HIGGINS, PATRICK. Took Oath of Allegiance before Hon. John Dorsey on March 12, 1778 (Ref: B-26).

HILL, ABEL. Ensign in Capt. Abraham Simmons' Militia Company in South River Battalion in 1776 (Ref: N-161, F-223, and source C-199 refers to him being in the West River Militia Company in 1778). He took the Oath of Allegiance before Hon. Samuel Lane on March 1, 1778 (Ref: B-23).

HILL, HENRY D. Took the Oath of Allegiance before Hon. Samuel Lane on March 1, 1778 (Ref: B-23).

HILL, JOHN (1746 - February 5, 1828). On March 5, 1828, the Treasurer ordered that George Hill, of Anne Arundel County, lawful heir and representative of John Hill, be paid whatever sum was due from his pension at the time of his death for services as a Private in the Maryland Line (Ref: K-353, Z-27).

HILL, JOSEPH. A resident of Herring Creek and one of the petitioners to form a company of militia on March 6, 1776. He was subsequently elected Corporal in Capt. Richard Weems' Company (Ref: I-143). Joseph Hill, Jr. took Oath of Allegiance before Hon. Samuel Harrison, Jr. in March, 1778 (Ref: A-244).

95

HILL, RICHARD. Took the Oath of Allegiance before Hon. Thomas Worthington on February 28, 1778 (Ref: B-21).

HILL, THOMAS. Took the Oath of Allegiance before Hon. Thomas Dorsey on March 2, 1778 (Ref: B-24).

HILLIARY, THOMAS JR. Took the Oath of Allegiance before Hon. Thomas Harwood on February 28, 1778 (Ref: B-22).

HILLUM, THOMAS. Born in Scotland. His name appears as a Substitute on May 19, 1778, supplied by John W. Dorsey, for the duration of the war (Ref: C-213, H-319).

HIND, ISAAC. Born in Scotland. His name appears as a Substitute on May 18, 1778, supplied by Benjamin Howard, for the duration (Ref: C-207, H-318).

HINKS, EDWARD. His name appeared on a list of defectives from the Maryland Line on August, 1781 (Ref: H-415).

HINTON, LOVELY (LOVEDY). Born in Maryland. Enrolled by Samuel Chew on July 25, 1776. Height: 5' 6" (Ref: H-40).

HIPSLEY, CHARLES. Took the Oath of Allegiance before Hon. Reuben Meriweather on March 2, 1778 (Ref: B-24).

HIPSLEY, JOSHUA. Took the Oath of Allegiance before Hon. Thomas Worthington on February 28, 1778 (Ref: B-21).

HOBBS, HENRY CORNELIUS. He took the Oath of Allegiance before Hon. Reuben Meriweather on March 2, 1778 (Ref: B-25).

HOBBS (HOBS), JOHN. Took the Oath of Allegiance before Hon. Thomas Dorsey on March 2, 1778 (Ref: B-24).

HOBBS, JOHN HENRY. One of the petitioners to the Convention of Maryland to form an independent rifle company in July, 1776 (Ref: B-3).

HOBBS, JOSEPH JR. Took the Oath of Allegiance before Hon. Reuben Meriweather on March 2, 1778 (Ref: B-25). One of the petitioners to the Convention of Maryland to form an independent rifle company, he was enlisted by Joseph Burgess for the Flying Camp on July 20, 1776 (Ref: B-3, H-40).

HOBBS, JOSEPH SR. Took the Oath of Allegiance before Hon. Reuben Meriweather on March 2, 1778 (Ref: B-24).

HOBBS, NICHOLAS. Commissioned an Ensign in Capt. Robert Warfield's Company in the Elk Ridge Battalion of Militia in March, 1779 (Ref: O-333).

HOBBS, NOAH. Took the Oath of Allegiance before Hon. Reuben Meriweather on March 2, 1778 (Ref: B-24). One of the petitioners to the Convention of Maryland to form an independent rifle company in July, 1776 (Ref: B-3).

HOBBS, THOMAS (1741-1824). Married Nancy Baker (Ref: T-392, which includes the same data for a Peter Hobbs, an obvious error). Thomas took the Oath of Allegiance before Hon. Reuben Meriweather on March 2, 1778 (Ref: B-24). He was a petitioner to form an independent rifle company in July of 1776 (Ref: B-3). Served on the Committee of Observation in 1775 (Ref: F-222).

HOBBS, WILLIAM. Two men by this name took the Oath of Allegiance: one before Hon. Thomas Worthington on February 28, 1778, and another before Hon. John Dorsey on March 12, 1778 (Ref: B-21, B-26).

HODGES, WILLIAM. Took the Oath of Allegiance before Hon. Elijah Robosson in March, 1778 (Ref: B-28). Married Mary Holland in 1792 (Ref: G-116).

HOHARO (O'HARO), WILLIAM. His name appeared on a list of recruits for Capt. Fulford's Artillery at Annapolis on December 12, 1776 (Ref: H-572).

HOHNE, CHRISTOPHER. Private in Capt. William Marbury's Company of Artillery in 1777 (Ref: H-575).

HOLLAND, ANTHONY. Took the Oath of Allegiance before Hon. Reuben Meriweather on March 2, 1778 (Ref: B-25).

HOLLAND, EDWARD. Private in Capt. William Marbury's Company of Artillery in 1777 (Ref: H-575). Took Oath of Allegiance before Hon. Nicholas Worthington in March, 1778 (Ref: B-27). He married Mary Simpson in 1793 (Ref: G-116).

HOLLAND, ISAAC. Private in Capt. William Marbury's Artillery in 1777 (Ref: H-575). Pensioned on October 15, 1821, age 68, as a Drummer (Ref: Z-27).

HOLLAND, THOMAS. Took the Oath of Allegiance before Hon. Thomas Worthington on February 28, 1778 (Ref: B-21).

HOLLAND, WILLIAM. Took the Oath of Allegiance before Hon. Thomas Worthington on February 28, 1778 (Ref: B-21).

HOLLIDAY, BENONI. Took the Oath of Allegiance before Hon. Richard Harwood, Jr. on March 1, 1778 (Ref: B-22).

HOLLIDAY, JOHN. Two men by this name took the Oath of Allegiance: one before Hon. Thomas Harwood on February 28, 1778 and another one before Hon. Samuel Harrison, Jr. in March, 1778 (Ref: A-244, B-22).

HOLLIDAY, WILLIAM. Enlisted by Capt. James Disney, Jr. and passed by Colonel Richard Harwood on July 13, 1776 (Ref: H-41). Took the

Oath of Allegiance before Hon. Thomas Harwood on February 28, 1778 (Ref: B-22).

HOLLYDYOAK, JOHN. On March 9, 1827, the Treasurer was ordered to pay to Ann Hollydyoak, of Annapolis, during life, half yearly, half pay of a private, for her husband John's services during the Revolutionary War (Ref: K-355).

HOLMES, B. Took the Oath of Allegiance before Hon. John Dorsey on March 12, 1778 (Ref: B-26).

HOLMES, WILLIAM. Took the Oath of Allegiance before Hon. Thomas Worthington on February 28, 1778 (Ref: B-21).

HOLSON, JOHN. Took the Oath of Allegiance before Hon. John Dorsey on March 12, 1778 (Ref: B-26).

HOOD, BENJAMIN. Took the Oath of Allegiance before Hon. Reuben Meriweather on March 2, 1778 (Ref: B-24).

HOOD, EDWARD. Enlisted in 1777 in 3rd Maryland Line. Disabled by a wagon as he was carried to the hospital. Discharged December 31, 1780 (Ref: X-16). Pensioned on May 30, 1818, age 68, and died April 22, 1825 (Ref: Z-27).

HOOD, HENRY B. Took the Oath of Allegiance before Hon. Nicholas Worthington in March, 1778 (Ref: Original list in Maryland State Papers, Red Book 21. Note: Source B-27 gives his name simply as "Henry Hood").

HOOD, JAMES. In December, 1817, the Treasurer was ordered to "pay James Hood, a soldier of the Revolutionary War, half pay of Asst. Commissary." On March 28, 1832, the Treasurer was ordered to "pay to Kitty Hood, widow of James, during widowhood, half pay of a Lieutenant." (Ref: K-355). Kitty Hood also applied in 1840, age 76, for the pension of her deceased husband who served in the 2nd Maryland Line from 1777 to 1780. She had married James in 1784 in Baltimore and her maiden name was Franklin. They had 6 children: Rachel Hood Wolfe, Leah Hood Barnes, Letitia Hood Wolfe, John Hood, James Hood and Sarah Hood. James Hood died in 1819 and Kitty Franklin Hood died in 1847. (Ref: NGS Quarterly, Vol. 20, No. 4 (1932), pp. 120-121; H-122; E-254).

HOOD, JOHN. Enlisted by John Worthington Dorsey and passed by John Dorsey on July 22, 1776 (Ref: H-39). Took the Oath of Allegiance before Hon. Nicholas Worthington in March, 1778 (Ref: B-27).

HOOD, JOHN JR. Served on the Committee of Observation in 1775 (Ref: F-222). Took the Oath of Allegiance before Hon. Reuben Meriweather on March 2, 1778 (Ref: B-24).

HOOD, JOHN SR. Took the Oath of Allegiance before Hon. Reuben Meriweather on March 2, 1778 (Ref: B-25). Deceased by April 9, 1795 (Ref: U-13).

HOOD, ROBERT. Took the Oath of Allegiance before Hon. Nicholas Worthington in March, 1778 (Ref: B-27).

HOOFMAN (HOOPMAN), ANDREW. Recruited in October, 1780 by Major Steward, to serve for 3 years (Ref: H-370).

HOOPER, ABRAHAM. Pensioned on September 2, 1818, age 78, as a Private in the Maryland Line, and died on September 23, 1822 (Ref: Z-27).

HOPKINS, ELISHA. On September 26, 1781 he petitioned the Council for relief for not attending to the militia, as his family was very ill (Ref: W-627).

HOPKINS, PHILIP. Took the Oath of Allegiance before Hon. Thomas Worthington on February 28, 1778 (Ref: B-21).

HOPKINS, RICHARD (c1760-c1826). Married Hannah Hammond in 1789 (Ref: T-399). Oath of Allegiance before Hon. Samuel Lane on March 1, 1778 (Ref: B-23).

HOPPER, JOHN. Enlisted by Capt. James Disney, Jr. and passed by Col. Richard Harwood on July 13, 1776 (Ref: H-41).

HORN, THOMAS. Recruited in October, 1780 to serve for 3 years (Ref: H-369).

HOUGHTON, JOHN. Took the Oath of Allegiance before Hon. Richard Harwood, Jr. on March 1, 1778 (Ref: B-22).

HOWARD, BENJAMIN (September 4, 1742 - 1780). Son of John Howard and Mary Hughes. Married Mary Govane circa 1772 and had two children: James Govane Howard and Sarah S. Howard Hood. Benjamin was Quartermaster in Col. Thomas Dorsey's Elk Ridge Battalion in 1776 (Ref: F-224, R-257). He took the Oath of Allegiance before Hon. Thomas Dorsey on March 2, 1778 (Ref: B-24).

HOWARD, BRICE (died in July, 1799). Son of Cornelius Howard and Rachel Worthington. He married Anne Ridgely and had 8 children: Harriet Howard Cross, Margaret Howard, George Howard, Thomas Worthington Howard, Jeremiah Brice Howard, Anne Howard Dorsey, Brice Worthington Howard, and William Cornelius Howard (Ref: R-324). He took the Oath of Allegiance before Hon. Thomas Worthington on February 28, 1778 (Ref: The original list in Maryland State Papers, Red Book No. 22. Source B-21 mistakenly gives his first name as "Bruce"). He was commissioned a Captain of Militia in 1776 (Ref: F-223, N-426), and served on the Committee of Observation in 1775 (Ref: F-222).

HOWARD, CHARLES WALLACE. Commissioned a First Lieutenant in Capt. Benjamin Harwood's Independent Company of Annapolis, October 6, 1777 (Ref: V-392).

HOWARD, DENUNE (March 18, 1757 - May, 1842). Son of Vachel Howard and Jeane Denune, relict of John Williams. He married Anne Anderson in 1778 and had 11 children: Vachel Howard, Infant boy Howard, Brice Howard, Mary Howard, John Howard, William Howard, Harvey Howard, Sarah Howard Morris, Cornelius Howard, George Howard, and Absolum Howard. Denune took Oath of Allegiance before Hon. Nicholas Worthington in March, 1778 (Ref: R-286, 287; Original list in Maryland State Papers, Red Book 21. His name is difficult to read, which is why source B-27 questionably states it is "Don (?) Howard").

HOWARD, EPHRAIM, OF HENRY (December 3, 1745 - December, 1788), M.D. Son of Henry Howard and Sarah Dorsey. He married Achsah Dorsey and had 7 children: Henry Howard, Brutus Howard, Cincinnati Howard, Sarah Howard Elder, Ephraim Howard, Elizabeth Howard, and Achsah Howard. Ephraim was one of the early patriots who led a party from Elk Ridge to Annapolis on October 19, 1774, and burned the British vessel "Peggy Stewart." He was a delegate to the First Maryland State Convention, a member of the Association of Freemen, and served on the Committee of Observation in 1775. On September 3, 1777, he was commissioned a Surgeon in Col. Thomas Dorsey's Battalion. He took the Oath of Allegiance before Hon. John Dorsey on March 12, 1778 (Ref: J-4, R-312, R-313, B-26, F-222, P-465, P-466, V-359).

HOWARD, JAMES. Served on the Committee of Observation in 1775 (Ref: F-222). He was appointed 2nd Lieutenant in Capt. Daniel Dorsey's Company in the 3rd Maryland Line on July 24, 1776 (Ref: H-38). He took the Oath of Allegiance before Hon. John Dorsey on March 12, 1778 (Ref: B-26). James was appointed a Purchasing Agent in March, 1779, for Anne Arundel County (Ref: O-333).

HOWARD, JOHN. Married Mary King in 1776 (Ref: G-116). Was a Private in Capt. Richard Dorsey's Artillery Company on November 17, 1777 (Ref: H-574), and First Sergeant in Capt. Gilbert Middleton's Independent Company of Militia of Annapolis, March 20, 1779 (Ref: I-144, O-325). He was paid as a disabled soldier in Anne Arundel County on August 16, 1783, and was noted as being "on order Baltimore" (Ref: D-8). On March 28, 1805, his nephew James Govane Howard, as heir at law, was assigned lot 351 in Allegany Co. (Ref: R-259).

HOWARD, JOHN BEALE (November 30, 1748 - 1788). Son of Henry Howard and Sarah Dorsey. Married Rebecca Boone circa 1770 and had 5 children: Henry Howard, Anne Slade Howard Mockabee, John Beale Howard, Rebecca Boone Howard Riggs, and Margaret Howard (Ref: R-315). John was one of the petitioners to the Convention of Maryland to form an independent rifle company in July, 1776 (Ref: B-3). On March 2, 1778, "J. B. Howard" took the Oath of Allegiance before Hon. Reuben Meriweather (Ref: B-25).

HOWARD, JOSEPH (November 17, 1763 - 1805). Son of Cornelius and Elizabeth Howard. Married Dorcas Howard in 1787 and had 8 children: Rebecca Dorcas Howard Ayres, Elisha Howard, Elizabeth Howard Meixsel, George Howard, Mary Howard Hebb, Joseph Howard, Dorcas Howard Haller, and Anne Howard Hughes. On May 9, 1777, Joseph enlisted in the First Maryland Line and was on the rolls on November 1, 1780 (Ref: R-284, R-285, H-116).

HOWARD, JOSEPH (March 13, 1749 - April, 1791). Son of Joseph Howard and Margaret Williams. He married Martha Hall in 1771 and had eight children: Henry Hall Howard, Joseph Howard, Eleanor Howard, Martha Howard, Margaret Howard Duckett Clarke, Kitty Howard, Margarey Howard, and Elizabeth Howard Duckett (Ref: R-328). He took the Oath of Allegiance before Hon. Nicholas Worthington in March, 1778 (Ref: B-27).

HOWARD, JOSEPH JR. (c1720 - 1784). Son of Joseph Howard and Margarey Keith. He married Margaret Williams and had 4 children: Margaret Howard Rutland, Joseph Howard, Margarey Howard Hall, and Benjamin Howard (Ref: R-310). Took the Oath of Allegiance before Hon. Nicholas Worthington or Hon. John Dorsey in March, 1778 (Ref: R-310, R-311, B-27).

HOWARD, JOSHUA (November 28, 1752 - after 1803). Son of Henry Howard and Sarah Dorsey. Married first to Rebecca Owings and had 9 children: Sarah Howard Winchester, Mary Howard Thomas, Rachel Howard Robertson, Samuel Howard, Joseph Howard, Beale Howard, Deborah Howard Worthington, Joshua Howard, and Henry Howard. Married second to Elizabeth Warfield in 1792 and had a son, John Howard (Ref: R-317). He took the Oath of Allegiance before Hon. John Dorsey on March 12, 1778 (Ref: B-26). Joshua was also one of the petitioners to the Convention of Maryland to form an independent rifle company in July, 1776 (Ref: B-3).

HOWARD, PHILIP. Took the Oath of Allegiance before Hon. Reuben Meriweather on March 2, 1778 (Ref: B-24).

HOWARD, SAMUEL (January 6, 1745/6 - August, 1787). Son of Samuel Howard and Patience Dorsey. Married Jemina Elder in 1770 and had 9 children: William Howard, Patience Howard Norwood, Anna M. Howard Shipley, Elizabeth Howard, Jemina Howard Norwood, Ruth Howard, Honor Howard, Samuel Howard, and John Howard. He was one of the petitioners to the Convention of Maryland to form an independent rifle company in July, 1776, and served as a Captain through 1781. He was appointed Commissary in May, 1782 (Ref: R-245, B-3, N-233).

HOWARD, SAMUEL HARVEY (August 23, 1750 - April 24, 1807). Son of Samuel Howard and Anne Harvey. Married first to Susan -----, and had 4 children: Anne Howard Moale, Susanna Howard Edmondson, Louisa Harvey Howard Tilden, and Elizabeth Howard Golder; married second to Mary Higginbotham and had 2 children: Samuel Harvey Howard and Anne Howard. Samuel was a Captain in the Militia, but was commissioned a First Lieutenant in an Independent Company of Annapolis in 1777. He replaced Francis Fairbrother as County Coroner in 1778, and was Captain of the Independent Company from 1780 to 1782. After the war he was the Registrar of the Court of Chancery (Ref: R-246, O-175, V-392). Appointed a Purchaser of Clothing on June 5, 1781 (Ref: W-462).

HOWARD, THOMAS CORNELIUS (c1745 - January 24, 1801). Son of Cornelius Howard and Rachel Worthington. Married Eleanor Ridgely and had 9 children: Thomas Worthington Howard, Henry Howard, Charles Howard, Brice Howard, Rachel Howard Duvall, Mary Howard Howard, Elizabeth Howard Rowan, Rebecca Howard Young, and Anna Howard Ayton (Ref: R-321, T-406). Commissioned an Ensign in 1776 in Capt. Brice Howard's Company (Ref: F-223). Took Oath of Allegiance before Hon. Thomas Worthington on February 28, 1778 (Ref: B-21).

HOWARD, THOMAS HENRY. He was a spectator at Anne Arundel County election on August 1, 1776 and heard Rezin Hammond advise the people to lay down their arms, for it was their right to vote (Ref: A-82).

HOWARD, VACHEL. Married Jeane Denune circa 1756 and had 8 children: Denune Howard, Kindsey Howard, Selby Howard, Joseph Howard, Cornelius Howard, Nancy Howard Wade, Mary Howard, and Cornelia V. Howard Lansdale. Took the Oath of Allegiance before Hon. Nicholas Worthington in March, 1778 (Ref: B-27, R-277). Served on the Committee of Observation in 1775 (Ref: F-222).

HOWARD, VACHEL DENTON. One of the petitioners to the Convention of Maryland to form an independent rifle company in July, 1776 (Ref: B-3).

HOWARD, WILLIAM. Third Corporal in Capt. Gilbert Middleton's Independent Company of Militia of Annapolis on March 20, 1779 (Ref: I-144, O-325).

HUDSON, EDWARD. Took the Oath of Allegiance before Hon. John Dorsey on March 12, 1778 (Ref: B-26).

HUDSON, ROBERT. Commissioned an Ensign in Capt. Hammond's Company in the Elk Ridge Battalion on October 3, 1777 (Ref: V-387). He took Oath of Allegiance before Hon. John Dorsey on March 12, 1778 (Ref: B-26).

HUGHES, JAMES. Took the Oath of Allegiance before Hon. Samuel Lane on March 1, 1778 (Ref: B-23).

HUGHS, JOHN. He was recruited by Daniel Monroe and passed by James Brice on February 9, 1778 (Ref: C-215, H-313).

HUGHS, MICHAEL. Enrolled by Capt. Watkins on October 21, 1776, for service to the State (Ref: I-144, MS.1814).

HUMPHRIES, JAMES. Recruited in October, 1780 by Capt. Alexander Truman, to serve for 3 years (Ref: H-369).

HUMPHREYS, WILLIAM. Enlisted by Thomas Mayo on July 20, 1776 (Ref: H-41).

HUNT, CHARLES. Enlisted by Edward Spurrier and passed by Thomas Dorsey on July 20, 1776 (Ref: H-41).

HUNTER, JAMES. Took the Oath of Allegiance before Hon. Richard Harwood, Jr. on March 1, 1778 (Ref: B-22). Deceased by April 20, 1814 (Ref: U-43).

HUSE, SAMUEL. His name appears on a list of Capt. Richard Chew's Company of Col. John Weems' Battalion on October 5, 1776 (Ref: A-95).

HUTTON, HENRY. Took the Oath of Allegiance before Hon. Samuel Lane on March 1, 1778 (Ref: B-23).

HUTTON, JAMES. A resident of Herring Creek and one of the petitiones to form a company of militia on March 6, 1776. He subsequently became a Private in Capt. Richard Weems' Company (Ref: I-143, MS.1814). James took the Oath of Allegiance before Hon. Samuel Harrison, Jr. in March, 1778 (Ref: A-244).

HUTTON, JOSEPH. Took the Oath of Allegiance before Hon. Samuel Harrison, Jr. in March, 1778 (Ref: A-244).

HYATT, ELY. One of the petitioners to the Convention of Maryland to form an independent rifle company in July, 1776 (Ref: B-3, H-39). He took the Oath of Allegiance before Hon. Reuben Meriwether on March 2, 1778 (Ref: B-25).

HYDE, THOMAS (1725-1795). Son of John and Elizabeth Hyde of England. He was an Attorney, Colonel and Supervisor of Maryland Bills of Credit in 1775 and Supplier of War Materials during the Revolutionary War. In 1749 he married Elizabeth Bishop and had 3 sons: William Hyde, John Hyde, and Thomas Hyde (Ref: E-2802, and Robert McIntire's "Annapolis Families," p. 353 (1980).

HYDE, WILLIAM (born May 4, 1750). Son of Thomas Hyde and Elizabeth Bishop. On March 9, 1776, the Council of Safety ordered that the public service requiring that the Regular Troops now in Annapolis be armed as quickly as possible, it ordered that Captain William Hyde deliver up to Major Thomas Price the 80 stand of public arms now in the possession of the said Captain Hyde or of his Company of Militia together with all the things belonging to said eighty stand of arms and that a receipt be given by said Major Price for the same, or such part thereof as may be delivered, and that said Major Thomas Price return a list to the Council of whatever arms he may receive. (Ref: N-203). William Hyde subsequently became a Lieutenant Colonel in the Flying Camp (Ref: Robert McIntire's "Annapolis Families," p. 353 (1980).

HYNES, JACOB. Born in Scotland. His name appears as a Substitute on April 28, 1778, supplied by John Dorsey of Severn John Dorsey, for a 3 year term (Ref: C-211, H-318).

IGLEHEART, JAMES. Took the Oath of Allegiance before Hon. Richard Harwood, Jr. on March 1, 1778 (Ref: B-22).

IJAMS, JACOB. Son of George and Elizabeth Ijams. He married (wife unknown) and had a son William Ijams. Jacob took the Oath of Allegiance before Hon. Richard Harwood, Jr., on March 1, 1778 (Ref: Q-334, B-22).

IJAMS (IIAMS), JOHN (1712-1783). Son of William Ijams and Elizabeth Plummer. He married Rebecca Jones and they had 8 children: Elizabeth Ijams Fenley, Anne Ijams Stockett, Mary Ijams Ijams, William Ijams, Isaac Ijams, Thomas Plummer Ijams, John Ijams, and Rebecca Ijams Sunderland. John, a wealthy merchant and member of the Old South River Club, was styled Captain because of service in the colonial militia (Ref: Q-297, T-417). Took the Oath of Allegiance before Hon. Richard Harwood, Jr. on March 1, 1778 (Ref: B-22).

IJAMS, JOHN JR. (c1755-1823). Son of John Ijams and Rebecca Jones. Married Mary Waters in 1782 in Frederick County and they had seven children: Jacob Ijams, John Waters Ijams, Plummer Ijams, Anne Ijams McLaughlin, Jane Ijams Burgee, Elizabeth Ijams Duvall, and Mary Ijams Montgomery. Recommended by the Council of Safety to be an Ensign on September 16, 1776 in Anne Arundel County (Ref: Q-311, Q-312, A-88, T-417). He was a 2nd Lieutenant in Capt. Thomas Watkins' Company in the West River Battalion in 1778 (Ref: C-199). He also took the Oath of Allegiance before Hon. Richard Harwood, Jr. on March 1, 1778 (Ref: B-22). John Ijams became a Captain and was involved in recruiting services in 1780-1781, and was paid accordingly (Ref: Q-311).

IJAMS, JOHN (November 18, 1725 - 1789). Son of George and Elizabeth Ijams. Married Ariana Worthington (widow of Nicholas Watkins) in 1758 and had six children: Vachel Ijams, Brice Ijams, Ariana Ijams Hendren, Beale Ijams, Denton Ijams, and Nicholas W. Ijams. John took the Oath of Allegiance in 1778 and subsequently moved to Prince George's County (Ref: Q-337, Q-338).

IJAMS, JOHN (October 20, 1747 - June 2, 1785). Son of Thomas and Artridge Ijams. Married Susanna Taylor (possibly born Watkins and a widow of Joseph Taylor) in 1778; children unknown. John took Oath of Allegiance before Hon. Richard Harwood, Jr. on March 1, 1778 (Ref: Q-304, B-22).

IJAMS, JOHN (June 5, 1756 - d.s.p. in 1791). Son of Plummer Ijams and Ruth Childs, daughter of Henry Childs. John took the Oath of Allegiance before Hon. Richard Harwood, Jr. on March 1, 1778 (Ref: Q-301, B-22).

IJAMS, JOHN. He resigned his commission as Third Lieutenant of an Artillery Company in the service of the State on May 31, 1777 (Ref: V-268).

IJAMS, JOHN FREDERICK (1765, Maryland - January 24, 1839, Tennessee). He was a resident of Prince George's County at the time of his enlistment in 1780 in Annapolis. He served under Col. Peter Adams in the 1st Maryland Regiment and was at Yorktown in 1781, and subsequently served until 1783 when he was discharged. After the war he moved to Virginia and then to Georgia where he married Mary Johnson circa 1789 in Wilkes County. He applied for a pension for his service in 1833 in Grainger County, Tennessee (Ref: Q-343, Q-344).

IJAMS (IIAMS), PLUMMER (1716 - November 26, 1792). Son of William Ijams and Elizabeth Plummer. Married Ruth Childs circa 1747 and they had 5 children: Plummer Ijams, Elizabeth Ijams Drury, Margaret Ijams Selby, John Ijams, and Ann Ijams Drury. Plummer took the Oath of Allegiance before Hon. Richard Harwood, Jr. on March 1, 1778 (Ref: Q-300, Q-301, B-22, U-51, T-418).

IJAMS, PLUMMER JR. (October 29, 1748 - February, 1795). Son of Plummer Ijams and Ruth Childs. Married Jemima Welsh in 1760 and they had five children: Anne Ijams Sanks, Plummer Ijams, Ruth Ijams Mussetter, Rebecca Ijams Duvall and John Ijams. He took Oath of Allegiance before Hon. Nicholas Worthington in March, 1778 (Ref:Q-312, Q-313, B-27, T-418).

IJAMS, THOMAS (December 26, 1754 - June 24, 1834). Son of John Ijams, son of Richard. He served about three months as a private under Col. Thomas Dorsey in the State Militia. He married Catherine G. Hampton in 1785 in Baltimore County. By 1793 they had moved to Washington County, Pennsylvania, and in 1834 Thomas applied for a pension in Belmont County, Ohio. He and his wife are buried in Old Cemetery near Glencoe, Ohio (Ref: Q-328, Q-329).

IJAMS (IIAMS), THOMAS. Two men with this name took the Oath of Allegiance in March, 1778: one before Hon. Nicholas Worthington, and another before Hon. Thomas Dorsey (Ref: B-24, B-27). One Thomas Ijams (1745-1806) married Mary Ijams (Ref: T-418).

IJAMS, VACHEL (January, 1759, Maryland - January 20, 1833, Alabama). Son of John Ijams and Ariana Worthington. He enlisted in Capt. Watkins' Company in September, 1776, and was discharged December 18, 1776. In August, 1777, he enlisted in the Maryland Line and served in Capt. Brogden's Company at the battle of Germantown. He was discharged in October, 1777. Subsequently, he moved to Prince George's County and served again in the militia in 1781, receiving a discharge on December 11, 1781. Shortly thereafter he moved to Rowan County, North Carolina where he again served as a Sergeant in Captain Sharpe's Company in 1782-1783. He married Lilah Gaither in 1789, but she died and he married Martha Cunningham in 1791. They had 8 children: Joseph Ijams, Basil Gaither Ijams, Burgess Ijams, Wilson Ijams, Pearson Ijams, Nancy Ijams Bolton McClamrock (or McClannaugh), Elizabeth Ijams Hernden, and Margaret Ijams Edwards. Vachel died in Lauderdale County, Alabama and is buried in a private cemetery near Florence (Ref: Q-339, Q-340, I-144).

IJAMS (IIAMS), WILLIAM. Took the Oath of Allegiance before Hon. Thomas Dorsey on March 2, 1778 (Ref: B-24).

IJAMS, WILLIAM (born November 26, 1755). Son of Thomas and Artridge Ijams. Married Charity Ryan in 1782. William took the Oath of Allegiance before Hon. Thomas Worthington on February 28, 1778 (Ref: Q-304, B-21).

IJAMS, WILLIAM (December 22, 1723 - November, 1780). Son of George Ijams and Elizabeth Basford. Married first to Elizabeth ----- in 1764 and second to Anne Ijams (widow of Richard Williams, Jr.) in 1770. He apparently had no issue from either marriage (Ref: Q-334, Q-335, Q-336). He took the Oath of Allegiance before Hon. Richard Harwood, Jr. on March 1, 1778 (Ref: B-23).

IJAMS, WILLIAM (OF JOHN). Son of John Ijams and Rebecca Jones. He married Elizabeth Howard and had eleven children: Richard D. Ijams, William Howard Ijams, Rebecca Ijams, Rachel Ijams, Mary Ijams, Comfort Ijams, Sarah Ijams, John Ijams, Joseph Howard Ijams, Frederick Ijams, and Isaac Ijams. He took the Oath of Allegiance before Hon. Richard Harwood, Jr. on March 1, 1778 in Anne Arundel County, Maryland, and by 1806 he was in Fairfield County, Ohio where he died testate in 1816 (Ref: Q-306, Q-307, B-23).

INMON, JOSHUA. Took the Oath of Allegiance before Hon. Thomas Worthington on February 28, 1778 (Ref: B-21).

IRE, FREDERICK. He was listed as a maimed soldier in Anne Arundel County on August 16, 1783, at which time he was paid and listed as "gone away," but was subsequently paid on December 11, 1783 (Ref: D-8, D-10).

IRELAND, HENRY. Enlisted by Michael Burgess and passed by Col. Hyde on July 20, 1776 (Ref: H-41).

ISAACS, JAMES. He was listed as a maimed soldier in Anne Arundel County and paid on December 11, 1783, January 13, 1784, April 13, 1784, September 3, 1784, October 26, 1784, December 17, 1784 (Ref: D-10, 12, 13, 21, 23, 25). He served in the 2nd Maryland Line from July 22, 1780 to September 30, 1782 and was medically discharged due to a "paralytic affliction" (Ref: X-17).

ISLECK, PASCHO (PASCO). His name appeared as a Subtitute in October, 1780 to serve until December 10, 1780. He subsequently served in the Continental Army in 1781 (Ref: H-369, H-409).

ISRAEL, BASIL. Took the Oath of Allegiance before Hon. Thomas Worthington on February 28, 1778 (Ref: B-21). He was commissioned 1st Lieutenant in Capt. Nicholas Ridgely Warfield's Company in the Elk Ridge Battalion of Militia in March, 1779 (Ref: O-496).

ISRAEL, BELA. Took the Oath of Allegiance before Hon. Thomas Worthington on February 28, 1778 (Ref: B-21).

ISRAEL, ROBERT. Took the Oath of Allegiance before Hon. Thomas Worthington on February 28, 1778 (Ref: B-21).

IVORY (IVERY), CHARLES. "Charles Ivery" took the Oath of Allegiance before Hon. Richard Harwood, Jr. on March 1, 1778 (Ref: B-23). "Charles Ivory" was born in Scotland, and was a Substitute, furnished by Stephen Watkins on May 2, 1778, for a 3 year term or the duration of the war (Ref: C-210, H-318).

JACKSON, ANTHONY. He served in the 4th Maryland Line and was wounded on July 6, 1779 (no details given). He was transferred to the Invalids Regiment and subsequently discharged on April 25, 1781 (Ref: X-18).

JACKSON, RENGARD. Born in Ireland in 1755. Enlisted in Annapolis on July 7, 1776, by Capt. James Young for Col. Thomas Ewing's Battalion of the Flying Camp. Height: 5' 3" with black hair (Ref: H-55).

JACKSON, ANN. On February 20, 1822, it was ordered that the Treasurer pay to Ann Jackson, of Annapolis, half pay of a private for her husband's services during the Revolutionary War (Ref: K-358. Note: Husband's name not given).

JACKSON, ROBERT. Took the Oath of Allegiance before Hon. Samuel Harrison, Jr. in March, 1778 (Ref: B-28).

JACOB, DORSEY (born May 19, 1746). Son of Richard Jacob and Hannah Dorsey Howard. Married Ruth Merriken (Ref: T-420). Took the Oath of Allegiance before Hon. Elijah Robosson in March, 1778 (Ref: B-28).

JACOB, EZEKIEL. Took the Oath of Allegiance before Hon. Richard Harwood, Jr. on March 1, 1778 (Ref: B-23). He was deceased by August 6, 1808 when the final distribution of his estate was made by Anne Jacob, administratrix, to Anne Jacob (widow's third), with fourths of the remainder to Priscilla Jacob, Anne Jacob, David Love Jacob, and Elizabeth Jacob (Ref: U-30).

JACOB, JOHN. Took the Oath of Allegiance before Hon. Richard Harwood, Jr. on March 1, 1778 (Ref: B-23).

JACOB, JOHN SR. Took the Oath of Allegiance before Hon. Richard Harwood, Jr. on March 1, 1778 (Ref: B-23).

JACOB, JOSEPH. The Council of Maryland recorded the fact that he took the Oath of Fidelity and Support to the State on April 9, 1778 (Ref: O-22). He was deceased by July 8, 1800 when the final distribution of his estate was made by Mrs. Patience Gaither, administratrix, with sevenths of the balance going to Patience Gaither, Dorsey Jacob, John Hall, Daniel Hall, Richard Hall, Elizabeth Hall and Sarah Hall (Ref: U-23. See "Joseph Jacobs" q.v.).

JACOB, RICHARD. Took the Oath of Allegiance before Hon. Richard Harwood, Jr. on March 1, 1778 (Ref: B-23).

JACOB, RICHARD SR. (January 30, 1697/98 - June 25, 1779). Resided in South River Hundred and married Hannah Dorsey Howard in 1719. Their 12 children were: Joseph Jacob, Sarah Jacob Robinson, Hannah Jacob Hall, Richard Jacob, Samuel Jacob, Susanah Jacob Bone Pumphrey, Anne Jacob, Rachel Jacob Fish, John Jacob, Zachary Jacob, Elizabeth Jacob, and Dorsey Jacob. Took Oath of Allegiance before Hon. Elijah Robosson in March, 1778 (Ref: B-28, T-420).

JACOB, RICHARD (OF JOSEPH). Took the Oath of Allegiance before Hon. Elijah Robosson in March, 1778 (Ref: B-28).

JACOB, RICHARD (born August 22, 1730). Son of Richard Jacob and Hannah Dorsey Howard. Married Hannah Asburnham (Ref: T-420). Took the Oath of Allegiance before Hon. Elijah Robosson in March, 1778 (Ref: B-28).

JACOB, SAMUEL (April 11, 1734 - after 1790). Married Bethiah Owley and they had 7 children: Joseph jacob, Hannah Jacob Brewer, Lum Jacob, Sarah Jacob Merriken, Elizabeth Jacob Roles Cromwell, and Shadrach Jacob. Lieutenant in Capt. John Boone's Company in the 7th Battalion of Militia in 1777 (Ref: T-421). Two men with this name took the Oath of Allegiance in March, 1778: one before Hon. Richard Harwood, Jr., and the other one before Hon. Elijah Robosson (Ref: B-23, B-28. Note: Data under "Samuel Jacobs" may apply).

JACOB, WILLIAM. Took the Oath of Allegiance before Hon. Richard Harwood, Jr. on March 1, 1778 (Ref: B-23).

JACOB, ZACHARIAH. Took the Oath of Allegiance before Hon. Elijah Robosson in March, 1778 (Ref: B-28. Note: Data under "Zachariah Jacobs" may apply).

JACOBS, JOSEPH. Enlisted by Thomas Mayo on July 20, 1776 (Ref: H-41).

JACOBS, SAMUEL. First Lieutenant in Captain Joseph Merriken's Company in the Severn Battalion on June 19, 1777 (Ref: A-176). He was appointed a Justice of the Peace in Anne Arundel County on November 19, 1778 (Ref: O-241).

JACOBS, ZACHARIAH. Private in the Severn Battalion on August 15, 1778 (Ref: I-144, J-113, O-207). Commissioned Ensign in Capt. John Boone's Company in the Severn Battalion on August 15, 1778 (Ref: I-144, J-113, O-208, W-411).

JAMES, WILLIAM. Enlisted by Michael Burgess and passed by Col. Hyde on July 20, 1776 (Ref: H-41). Private in Capt. William Marbury's Artillery Company in 1777 (Ref: H-575).

JANQUARY, ABRAHAM. Private in Captain Richard Chew's Company in Colonel John Weems' Battalion on October 5, 1776 (Ref: A-95, I-143).

JARVIS, JACOB. Enlisted by Joseph Burgess for the Flying Camp and passed on July 20, 1776 (Ref: H-40).

JARVIS, JOHN. Private in Capt. Richard Dorsey's Company of Artillery on Nov. 17, 1777 (Ref: H-574). He married Anne Richards in 1779 (Ref: G-116).

JEAN, THOMAS. Took the Oath of Allegiance before Hon. Thomas Worthington on February 28, 1778 (Ref: B-21).

JEAN, WILLIAM. Took the Oath of Allegiance before Hon. Thomas Worthington on February 28, 1778 (Ref: B-21).

JEE, JOSEPH. Born in England. Enrolled by Capt. Edward Tillard on July 10, 1776. Height: 5' 6 1/2" (Ref: H-39).

JEFFERSON, EDWARD. Enlisted by Thomas Mayo on July 20, 1776 (Ref: H-41).

JENKINS, JOHN. Born in Wales. He was a Substitute, furnished by John Henry Maccubbin on April 25, 1778, for a three year term (Ref: C-204, H-318).

JENKINS, RICHARD. Born in Scotland. He was a Substitute, furnished by Ely Elder on May 15, 1778, for the duration of the war (Ref: C-213, H-319).

JENKINS, THOMAS (of Baltimore County). He took the Oath of Allegiance before Hon. Reuben Meriweather on March 2, 1778 (Ref: B-25).

JENKINS, WILLIAM. Born in France. Recruited and passed by Daniel Munro on September 30, 1778 in Anne Arundel County (Ref: C-217, H-314).

JENNINGS, EDMOND. Took Oath of Allegiance before Hon. Nicholas Worthington in March, 1778 (Ref: B-27).

JENNINGS, THOMAS (c1736, England - December 10, 1796, Maryland). He married Juliana ----- and had ten children: Thomas Jennings, George Jennings, Anne Jennings Carroll, William Jennings, John Jennings, Daniel Jennings, Horner Jennings, Horatio Jennings, Juliana Jennings Brice, and Elizabeth Jennings Hodges. Thomas was a lawyer and served in many offices, including Common Councilman of Annapolis (1767-1779), Attorney General (1770), Annapolis Mayor (1772), Committee of Observation (1775), Senate (1776-1779), and a Justice of the Orphans' Court in 1791 (Ref: P-488, P-489, F-222).

JENNINGS, WILLIAM. Born in England. He was recruited and passed by Daniel Munro on April 9, 1778 (Ref: C-216, H-314).

JERVIS, JOHN. Enrolled by Captain Thomas Watkins on October 21, 1776, for service to the State (Ref: I-144, MS.1814).

JESUP, THOMAS. Born in Scotland. He was a Substitute, furnished by Charles Worthington on May 5, 1778, for a two year term (Ref: C-212, H-318).

JIMSON (JENISON), JOHN. Enlisted by Michael Burgess and passed by Col. Hyde on July 20, 1776 (Ref: H-41).

JOHNS, JOHN. Took the Oath of Allegiance before Hon. Samuel Harrison, Jr. in March, 1778 (Ref: B-28).

JOHNS, KINSEY. Resident of Herring Creek and one of the petitioners to form a company of militia on March 6, 1776 (Ref: I-143). He took the Oath of Allegiance before Hon. Samuel Harrison, Jr. in March, 1778 (Ref: B-28).

JOHNSON, BENEDICT. He was a maimed soldier in Anne Arundel County and paid on April 13, 1784 and September 3, 1784 and October 26, 1784 and December 17, 1784 (Ref: D-13, D-21, D-23, D-25).

JOHNSON, ELIJAH. Took the Oath of Allegiance before Hon. Thomas Worthington on February 28, 1778 (Ref: B-21).

JOHNSON, GEORGE. Took the Oath of Allegiance before Hon. Elijah Robosson in March, 1778 (Ref: B-28).

JOHNSON, HENRY. Private in Capt. William Marbury's Company of Artillery in 1777 (Ref: H-575). He also took the Oath of Allegiance before Hon. Reuben Meriweather on March 2, 1778 (Ref: B-24).

JOHNSON, HORATIO (c1757 - 1840). Son of Thomas Johnson and Ann Riston. He married first Sarah Norwood and second Elizabeth Warfield. Horatio was a tobacco inspector at Elk Ridge Landing. He was commissioned Ensign in Capt. Edward Norwood's Militia Company on February 7, 1776 (Ref: N-139, P-493).

JOHNSON, JAMES. Born in Scotland. He was enrolled by John S. Belt in July, 1776 (Ref: H-39).

JOHNSON, JOHN. Born in Scotland. He was a Substitute, furnished by Stephen Mockeyby on May 16, 1778, for the duration of the war (Ref: C-207, H-318).

JOHNSON, JONATHAN. Took Oath of Allegiance on March 20, 1778 (Ref: V-543).

JOHNSON, JOSEPH. Took the Oath of Allegiance before Hon. John Dorsey on March 12, 1778 (Ref: B-26).

JOHNSON, O'NEAL. Took the Oath of Allegiance on March 19, 1778 (Ref: V-541).

JOHNSON, RICHARD. Enlisted by Michael Burgess and passed by Col. Hyde on July 20, 1776 (Ref: H-41).

JOHNSON, ROBERT. Private in the Severn Battalion on August 15, 1778 (Ref: I-144, J-113, O-207). He took the Oath of Allegiance before Hon. Nicholas Worthington in March, 1778 (Ref: B-27).

JOHNSON, THOMAS (November 4, 1732 - October 26, 1819). Son of Thomas Johnson and Dorcas Sedgwick, he was born in Calvert County, resided in Anne Arundel County, and died in Frederick County. He married Anne Jennings in 1766 and had seven children: Thomas Jennings Johnson, James Johnson, Joshua Johnson, Elizabeth Johnson, Rebecca Johnson Johnson, and Dorcas Johnson. Thomas was a very prominent attorney, patriot and political leader. He was a Delegate to the Maryland Convention on July 26, 1775, and served on the Committee of Correspondence and the Council of Safety, as well as in the Lower House in Anne Arundel and Frederick Counties. He attended the Maryland Conventions from 1774 through 1776, and was the first Governor of Maryland from 1777 to 1779. He was a Delegate to the Continental Congress from 1774 through 1776 and was subsequently elected a Delegate but declined to serve from 1779 to 1784. He was also Senior Brigadier General in the Militia in 1776 and 1777. After the war Thomas was a Justice of the Orphans' Court and Chief Judge of the General Court, and although he was selected to serve as U. S. District Judge, Secretary of State, Chief Judge of the Circuit Court of the District of Columbia, and again as Governor of Maryland (in 1788), he declined to serve in any of those offices (Ref: P-495, 496, F-222, J-1, 4, 28, N-3).

JOHNSON, WILLIAM. Private in Capt. William Marbury's Company of Artillery in 1777 (Ref: H-575).

JOICE (JOYCE), JAMES. He took the Oath of Allegiance before Hon. Samuel Harrison, Jr. in March, 1778 (Ref: B-28).

JOICE (JOYCE), RICHARD. Private in Captain Richard Chew's Company of Col. John Weems' Battalion, October 5, 1776 (Ref: A-95, I-143). Took the Oath of Allegiance before Hon. Samuel Harrison, Jr. in March, 1778 (Ref: B-28). He was deceased by April 28, 1788 when the final distribution of his estate was made by Henry Ashbaw, executor, to his widow (unnamed) with thirds of the remainder to Richard Joyce, William Joyce and Elijah Joyce (Ref: U-1).

JOICE (JOYCE), WILLIAM. He was a Substitute, furnished by Richard Weems on June 10, 1778, for a 9 month term (Ref: C-208, H-319).

JONES, BENJAMIN. Enrolled by Captain James Disney, Jr. and passed by Colonel Richard Harwood, Jr. on July 13, 1776 (Ref: H-41) and was Sergeant in Capt. Richard Dorsey's Company of Artillery on November 17, 1777 (Ref: H-574).

JONES, DAVID. Born in England. He was recruited and passed on by John Hobbs on March 24, 1778 (Ref: C-216, H-313). Took the Oath of Allegiance before Hon. Richard Harwood, Jr. on March 1, 1778 (Ref: B-23).

JONES, DAVID. The Council of Maryland recorded the fact that he took the Oath of Fidelity and Support to the State on April 9, 1778 (Ref: O-22).

JONES, HANBURY. Enlisted by Richard Talbot and passed by John Dorsey on July 22, 1778 (Ref: H-39).

JONES, HENRY. Took the Oath of Allegiance before Hon. Richard Harwood, Jr. on March 1, 1778 (Ref: B-23).

JONES, HUGH. Took the Oath of Allegiance before Hon. Nicholas Worthington in March, 1778 (Ref: B-27).

JONES, ISAAC. Born in Maryland. Enrolled by Capt. Edward Tillard on July 10, 1776. Height: 5' 9" (Ref: H-39, H-40). Isaac took the Oath of Allegiance before Hon. Richard Harwood, Jr. on March 1, 1778 (Ref: B-23). Either this or another Isaac Jones was drafted in October, 1780 to serve until December 10, 1780 (Ref: H-369. Note: See the next entry regarding Isaac Jones).

JONES, ISAAC JR. Took the Oath of Allegiance before Hon. Richard Harwood, Jr. on March 1, 1778 (Ref: B-23). He was probably the Isaac Jones enrolled by Capt. James Disney, Jr. and passed by Col. Richard Harwood, Jr. on July 13, 1776 (Ref: H-41. Note: See the preceding entry for Isaac Jones also).

JONES, JACOB. Took the Oath of Allegiance before Hon. John Dorsey on March 12, 1778 (Ref: B-26).

JONES, JACOB (OF WILLIAM). Took the Oath of Allegiance before Hon. Reuben Meriweather on March 2, 1778 (Ref: B-24).

JONES, JASON. Pensioned on March 4, 1831, at age 77, as a Private in the Maryland Line (Ref: Z-45), and his marriage to Elizabeth Thompson (widow) in Anne Arundel County on November 25, 1799, was proven (Ref: G-116, U-19). "Jarson Jones" took the Oath of Allegiance on March 2, 1778 (Ref: V-525).

JONES, JEREMIAH. Two men by this name took the Oath of Allegiance: one before Hon. Reuben Meriweather on March 2, 1778 and one before Hon. John Dorsey on March 12, 1778 (Ref: B-24, B-26).

JONES, JOHN. Took the Oath of Allegiance before Hon. John Dorsey on March 12, 1778 (Ref: B-26).

JONES, JOHN PAUL. A Frenchman by birth and an American by choice, John Paul Jones is regarded as the "Father of the American Navy." His heroism in fighting against larger and better equipped ships in the Revolutionary War established a tradition that has never been forgotten. Jones' reply to a British demand to surrender was "I have not yet begun to fight," and it has become the United States Navy slogan. John Paul Jones lies entombed at the U. S. Naval Academy in Annapolis, Maryland. The 6th chapter of the Maryland Society of the Sons of the American Revolution was named in his honor in 1971 and it conducts patriotic observances throughout Anne Arundel County. (Ref: Henry C. Peden, Jr.'s "Centennial History of the Maryland Society of the Sons of the American Revolution, 1889-1989," p. 27. Note: Obviously, additional information is available in most American History textbooks).

JONES, JONATHAN. A resident of Herring Creek and one of the petitioners to form a company of militia on March 6, 1776. He was subsequently elected a Corporal (Ref: I-143, MS.1814). He also took the Oath of Allegiance before Hon. Samuel Harrison in March, 1778 (Ref: A-244).

JONES, JOSEPH. Two men by this name took the Oath of Allegiance: one before Hon. Thomas Worthington on February 28, 1778, and one before Hon. Nicholas Worthington in March, 1778 (Ref: B-21, 27). One was a Substitute, furnished by Caleb Owings on May 30, 1778, for a 3 year term (Ref: C-208, H-319).

JONES, MORGAN. Private in Captain Richard Chew's Company in Col. John Weems' Battalion, October 5, 1776 (Ref: A-95, I-143). Took the Oath of Allegiance before Hon. Samuel Harrison, Jr. in March, 1778 (Ref: B-28).

JONES, NICHOLAS. Took the Oath of Allegiance before Hon. Nicholas Worthington in March, 1778 (Ref: B-27).

JONES, RICHARD. Enrolled by Captain James Disney, Jr. and passed by Colonel Richard Harwood, Jr. on July 13, 1776 (Ref: H-41). Richard took the Oath of Allegiance before Hon. Nicholas Worthington in March, 1778 (Ref: B-27).

JONES, RICHARD (barber). Enrolled by Captain James Disney, Jr. and passed by Colonel Richard Harwood, Jr. on July 13, 1776 (Ref: H-41).

JONES, SAMUEL. Born in Scotland. He was a Substitute, furnished by Phillip Hammond Hopkins and John Howard Gaither on May 19, 1778, for the duration of the war (Ref: C-213, H-319). He took the Oath of Allegiance before Hon. Thomas Worthington on February 28, 1778 (Ref: B-21).

JONES, THOMAS. Pensioned on May 2, 1818, at age 82, as a Private in the Maryland Line (Ref: Z-27). On March 11, 1834, the Treasurer paid to Thomas Jones, of Anne Arundel County, during life, quarterly, the half pay of a private, for services rendered by him during the revolution (Ref: K-361).

JONES, WILLIAM. Enlisted by Richard Talbot and passed by John Dorsey on July 22, 1776 (Ref: H-39). He took the Oath of Allegiance before Hon. Thomas Worthington on February 28, 1778 (Ref: B-21).

JORDAN, JOHN. He served in the 5th Maryland Line and was accidentally shot and lost his leg on February 15, 1779. He was transferred to the Invalids Regiment and worked as a tailor until discharged on February 15, 1780 (Ref: X-19). Another John Jordan was recruited by Capt. Alexander Truman in late 1780 to serve for the duration of the war (Ref: H-369).

JUDAH, WILLIAM. Second Lieutenant in Capt. Richard Dorsey's Company of Artillery on November 17, 1777 (Ref: H-573).

JUSTICES OF ANNE ARUNDEL COUNTY. On May 29, 1777 commissions were issued to the following Justices of the Peace: Samuel Chew, John Burgess, Nicholas Worthington, George Watts, Richard Harwood, Jr., Henry Ridgely, Elijah Robosson, Samuel Lane, Thomas Brooke Hodgskin, Thomas Watkins, Jr., John Weems, Thomas Watkins, Sr., John Dorsey, Thomas Dorsey, William Brogden, Samuel Harrison, John Brice, William Wilkins, Allen Quynn, Thomas Harwood, Charles Alexander Warfield, Reuben Meriweather, Richard Cromwell, Thomas Henry Hall, Samuel Harrison (of Richard), Thomas Gassaway (of Nicholas), Nicholas Dorsey, Jr., Richard Stringer and Thomas Worthington (Ref: V-263). On June 4, 1777 commissions were issued to the following Justices of the Orphans Court: Samuel Chew, John Burgess, Nicholas Worthington, George Watts, Richard Harwood, Jr., Henry Ridgely and Elijah Robosson (Ref: V-274). On June 10, 1777 commissions were issued to the following Justices of the Orphans Court: John Burgess, Nicholas Worthington, Richard Harwood, Jr., Elijah Robosson, Thomas Watkins, John Bowie, and Allen Quynn (Ref: V-282). The following Justices administered the Oath of Allegiance and Fidelity to the State of Maryland in February and March, 1778: Samuel Harrison, Thomas Worthington (of Nicholas), Thomas Harwood, Richard Harwood, Jr., Samuel Lane, Thomas Dorsey, Reuben Meriweather, John Dorsey, Nicholas Worthington, Elijah Robosson, and Samuel Harrison, Jr. (Ref: A-244, B-21, B-22, B-23, B-24, B-25, B-26, B-27, B-28, B-29). On November 25, 1780 commissions were issued to the following Justices of the Peace: Nicholas Worthington, Richard Harwood, Jr., Elijah Robosson, Samuel Harrison, Allen Quynn, Samuel Harrison (of Richard), Richard Dorsey (of John), Samuel Godman, Richard Harrison (of Richard), Thomas Tongue, Nicholas Maccubbin, Jr., William Hyde, John Burgess, William Brogden, Philemon Dorsey, Brice Howard, Horatio Johnson; and these Judges of the Orphans Court: Nicholas Worthington, Richard Harwood, Jr., Elijah Robosson, Allen Quynn, Nicholas Maccubbin, Jr., William Hyde, and John Burgess (Ref: W-224). On December 4, 1780 the following were commissioned Justices of the Peace: Richard Harwood, Jr., Samuel Godman, Allen Quynn, and Nicholas Maccubbin, Jr. (Ref: W-233).

KAHOE, JOHN. Born in Scotland. He was a Substitute, furnished by Baldwin Lusby on May 15, 1778, to serve to the end of the war (Ref: C-205, H-317).

KEITH, ANDREW. Private in Capt. John Fulford's Company of Artillery which was stationed at Annapolis on December 12, 1776 (Ref: H-572).

KEITH, DANIEL. Disabled soldier in Capt. Popham's Company of the 2nd Canadian (or Col. Moses Hazen's) Regiment, who was discharged on December 14, 1782 because he was "unfit for duty by reason of age" (Ref: X-20). Although this record indicated he was dead, he was paid on August 16, 1783 (Ref: H-598, H-661) and he also received pay on January 13, 1784 and stated that his "discharge was eaten up by rats" (Ref: D-9, D-11), and he was subsequently paid on April 13, 1784, June 9, 1784, September 3, 1784, October 26, 1784 and December 17, 1784 (Ref: D-14, D-18, D-21, D-23, D-25).

KEITH, JOHN. Private in Capt. William Marbury's Company of Artillery in 1777 (Ref: H-575).

KELLIHER, HENRY. Drummer in Capt. Richard Dorsey's Company of Artillery on November 17, 1777 (Ref: H-574).

KELLY (KELLEY), JAMES. Disabled soldier who received pay on April 13, 1784 and June 9, 1784 and September 3, 1784 and October 26, 1784 and December 17, 1784 (Ref: D-13, D-21, D-22, D-25).

KELLY, MATTHEW. Private in Capt. Richard Dorsey's Company of Artillery on November 17, 1777 (Ref: H-574).

KENDALL, JOHN. Took the Oath of Allegiance before Hon. Thomas Worthington on February 28, 1778 (Ref: B-21).

KENDELL, JAMES. Took the Oath of Allegiance before Hon. Samuel Lane on March 1, 1778 (Ref: B-23).

KENNADY, JOHN. Took the Oath of Allegiance before Hon. John Dorsey on March 12, 1778 (Ref: B-26).

KENNEDY, TIMOTHY. Private in Capt. John Fulford's Company of Artillery which was stationed at Annapolis on December 12, 1776 (Ref: H-572).

KENNIDY, PETER. Took the Oath of Allegiance before Hon. Richard Harwood, Jr. on March 1, 1778 (Ref: B-23).

KERBEY, JOHN. Took the Oath of Allegiance before Hon. Thomas Worthington on February 28, 1778 (Ref: B-21).

KERBY, JOSHUA. Took the Oath of Allegiance before Hon. Reuben Meriweather on March 2, 1778 (Ref: B-24).

KERR, DAVID (1749, Galloway, Scotland - November 2, 1814, Easton, Maryland). He immigrated to Virginia in 1769 and to Maryland in 1773, first to Anne Arundel County and then to Talbot County in 1784. He married first in 1773 to Hammutal Bishop, and secondly in 1777 to Rachel Bozman, widow of James Edmondson. His children were: Charles Hammond Kerr, John Leeds Kerr, David Kerr, James Kerr, and Sophia Kerr Muse. During the war he became a First Lieutenant in Capt. George Watts' Company of Militia on February 22, 1776 (Ref: F-223, N-178). After the war he was very active in legislative and political offices in Talbot County (Ref: P-505 contains additional data).

KILTY, JOHN (1756 - May 27, 1811). Son of Capt. John Kilty and Ellen Ahearn. He married Catherine Quynn, daughter of Allen Quynn, in 1792, and had seven children: William Kilty, Richard Kilty, George Kilty, Augustus Kilty, Ellen Kilty Schmuck, Mary Kilty, and Elizabeth Kilty Wilson. John was very active in the Revolutionary War: Ensign in Capt. Norwood's Company in the Maryland Militia in 1776; 2nd Lieutenant, 4th Maryland Line, 1776-1777; prisoner at battle of Germantown, 1777; 1st Lieutenant in Baylor's Corps, 3rd

Regiment, Continental Dragoons, 1777 to 1782; and, Captain, 1782. John was a founding member of the Society of the Cincinnati in 1783, and also held many offices after the war including his appointment as Supervisor of the Revenue of the United States by President George Washington in 1795, and Register of the Land Office, Western Shore, 1803-1811 (Ref: P-510, G-117, H-40). Took the Oath of Allegiance before Hon. Samuel Lane on March 1, 1778 (Ref: B-23).

KILTY, JOHN (died circa 1785). Captain of the ship "Polly" which made regular voyages to Annapolis from at least 1766, and active in the preparations for Maryland's naval forces during the early years of the Revolution. Married Ellen Ahearn and had sons John and William; perhaps others (Ref: P-510).

KILTY, WILLIAM (1757-1821). Son of Capt. John Kilty and Ellen Ahearn. He was appointed a Surgeon's Mate in April, 1776, and then Surgeon in the 5th Maryland Line, 1778-1780, and 4th Maryland Line, 1781-1783. He later became a lawyer and compiled "The Laws of Maryland" in 1799. He married Elizabeth Middleton in 1790 (Ref: P-510). He was also Chancellor of Maryland in 1820 and a member of the Society of the Cincinnati of Maryland (Ref: Y-304).

KING, JOHN. Born in Scotland. He was a Substitute, furnished by Dr. Ephraim Howard on May 18, 1778 to serve to the end of the war (Ref: C-213, H-319).

KING, JOHN JR. Private in Capt. John Fulford's Company of Artillery stationed at Annapolis on December 12, 1776 (Ref: H-572).

KING, MICHAEL. Took the Oath of Allegiance before Hon. John Dorsey on March 12, 1778 (Ref: B-26).

KING, THOMAS. Enrolled by Capt. James Disney, Jr. and passed by Col. Richard Harwood on July 13, 1776 (Ref: H-41). He took the Oath of Allegiance before Hon. Richard Harwood, Jr. on March 1, 1778 (Ref: B-23). In June, 1809, the Treasurer was ordered to pay "to Thomas King, immediately $50.00, and a sum equal to the half pay of a sergeant during his life, quarterly, payments to commence this day. Thomas King, belonging to the artillery company of the city of Annapolis and who has been a soldier in the Revolution, and who was wounded therein, in discharging his duty on this 10th day of June, has been so unfortunate as to lose his right hand, by the firing of a cannon which entitles him to the peculiar care of this State...having a family dependent in him for support." In November session, 1811, "half pay of a sergeant was granted by legislature to Thos. King, in June session 1809, for support of his family, be henceforth paid by the Treasurer, in quarterly payments, to his wife, Mary King." (Ref: K-363).

KIRBEY, JAMES. Took the Oath of Allegiance before Hon. Reuben Meriweather on March 2, 1778 (Ref: B-24). He was deceased by April 5, 1815 when the final distribution of his estate was made by Jacob Jones, administrator, with the following each receiving sevenths of the estate balance: James Kirby, John Kirby, William Kirby,

Nathan Kirby, Robert Kirby, Jacob Jones (husband of Sarah Kirby), and the children of Silvanus Warfield (Ref: U-44).

KIRBY, WILLIAM. Took the Oath of Allegiance before Hon. Samuel Harrison in March, 1778 (Ref: A-244).

KIRK, THOMAS. Took the Oath of Allegiance before Hon. John Dorsey on March 12, 1778 (Ref: B-26).

KIRTON, JAMES. Took the Oath of Allegiance before Hon. Thomas Worthington on February 28, 1778 (Ref: B-21).

KITTIN, EDWARD. He took the Oath of Allegiance before Hon. Thomas Dorsey on March 2, 1778 (Ref: B-24).

KNIGHTON, GASSAWAY. Took the Oath of Allegaince before Hon. Richard Harwood, Jr. on March 1, 1778 (Ref: B-23). One Gassaway Knighton was deceased by January 12, 1838 when the final distribution of his estate was made by John Knighton, executor, to John Knighton, Nicholas Knighton, Thomas Knighton, and Francis Brashears, husband of Eleanor Knighton (Ref: U-96).

KNIGHTON, NICHOLAS. Enrolled by Capt. Thomas Watkins on October 21, 1776 for service to the State (Ref: I-144, MS.1814). He took the Oath of Allegiance before Hon. Richard Harwood, Jr. on March 1, 1778 (Ref: B-23).

KNOCK, JOHN. Enlisted by Joseph Burgess for the Flying Camp on July 20, 1776 (Ref: H-40).

KNOLES, EDWARD. Took the Oath of Allegiance before Hon. Elijah Robosson in March, 1778 (Ref: B-28).

LACKLAND, JOSHUA. Took Oath of Allegiance before Hon. Nicholas Worthington in March, 1778 (Ref: B-27). Still alive in April, 1789 (Ref: U-3).

LAMB, JOHN. Private in Capt. John Fulford's Company of Artillery which was stationed at Annapolis on December 12, 1776 (Ref: H-572).

LAMBETH, HENRY. Born in Maryland. Enrolled by John S. Belt in July, 1776. Height: 5' 7" (Ref: H-40, which spells his name "Henry Lamboth") Took the Oath of Allegiance before Hon. Samuel Lane on March 1, 1778 (Ref: B-23).

LAMBETH, JOHN. Took the Oath of Allegiance before Hon. Samuel Harrison in March, 1778 (Ref: A-244).

LAMBETH, JOHN (OF WILLIAM). Took the Oath of Allegiance before Hon. Samuel Lane on March 1, 1778 (Ref: B-23).

LAMBETH, STEPHEN. Took the Oath of Allegiance before Hon. Samuel Harrison, Jr. in March, 1778 (Ref: B-28).

LANE, BENJAMIN. Took the Oath of Allegiance before Hon. Thomas Harwood on February 28, 1778 (Ref: B-22).

LANE, BENJAMIN (of Calvert County). Took the Oath of Allegiance before Hon. Samuel Lane on March 1, 1778 (Ref: B-23).

LANE, GABRIL. Took Oath of Allegiance before Hon. Thomas Harwood on February 28, 1778 (Ref: B-22).

LANE, HARRISON JR. Took the Oath of Allegiance before Hon. Samuel Harrison in March, 1778 (Ref: A-244). He was deceased by June 10, 1815 when final distribution of his estate was made by Thomas Lane, admin., to Thomas Lane, Joseph Lane, Wilemina Lane, Elizabeth Lane, and Richard Lane (Ref: U-44).

LANE, HARRISON SR. Took the Oath of Allegiance before Hon. Samuel Harrison in March, 1778 (Ref: A-244).

LANE, JOHN JR. Took the Oath of Allegiance before Hon. Samuel Lane on March 1, 1778 (Ref: B-23).

LANE, RICHARD JR. Took the Oath of Allegiance before Hon. Samuel Lane on March 1, 1778 (Ref: B-23).

LANE, SAMUEL. One of the Justices who administered the Oath of Allegiance in March, 1778 (Ref: B-23). Also appointed a Justice of the Peace on November 19, 1778 (Ref: O-241).

LANE, THOMAS. Private in Captain Richard Chew's Company of Col. John Weems' Battalion on October 5, 1776 (Ref: A-95, I-143). Thomas took the Oath of Allegiance before Hon. Thomas Harwood on February 28, 1778 (Ref: B-22).

LANE, THOMAS (OF HARRISON). Took the Oath of Allegiance before Hon. Samuel Harrison in March, 1778 (Ref: A-244). He was possibly the Thomas Lane who was a petitioner to form a company of militia at Herring Creek on March 6, 1776, and a private in Capt. Richard Weems' Company (Ref: I-143, MS.1814).

LANGLEY, WILLIAM. Enlisted by Thomas Mayo on July 20, 1776 (Ref: H-41). Took Oath of Allegiance before Hon. John Dorsey on March 12, 1778 (Ref: B-26).

LANNUM, WILLIAM. Took the Oath of Allegiance before Hon. Thomas Worthington on February 28, 1778 (Ref: B-21).

LANSDALE, ISAAC. Born in Maryland. Enrolled by Capt. Edward Tillard on July 10, 1776. Height: 5' 7" (Ref: H-39).

LANSDALE, THOMAS LANCASTER (August 14, 1777, Anne Arundel County - 1785, Prince George's County). He married Martha ----- and had 4 children: Isaac L. Lansdale, Eleanor Lansdale Berry, Elizabeth Lansdale Hall, and Thomas Lansdale. Commissioned 1st Lieutenant in the Flying Camp in Baltimore County in 1776, Captain in 4th

Maryland Line in 1778, Major in 3rd Maryland Line in 1781, and served until November 15, 1783 (Ref: T-449, H-52, H-53).

LAPPE, JOHN. Enrolled by Capt. Thomas Watkins on October 21, 1776 for service to the State (Ref: I-144, MS.1814).

LARAVIER, JEAN. Recruited by James Brice in 1777 (Ref: H-313).

LAREY (LEARY), DANIEL. Born in Scotland. "Daniel Leary" was a Substitute, furnished by Caleb Dorsey (of Thomas) on May 18, 1778, to serve to the end of the war (Ref: C-213, H-319). "Daniel Larey" took the Oath of Allegiance before Hon. John Dorsey on March 12, 1778 (Ref: B-26).

LARKIN, THOMAS. Resident of Herring Creek who was among those who petitioned to form a militia company on March 6, 1776, and was subsequently a private in Capt. Richard Weems' Company (Ref: I-143, MS.1814). He took the Oath of Allegiance before Hon. Samuel Harrison, Jr. in March, 1778 (Ref: B-28).

LARKINS, WILLIAM. Private in Captain Richard Chew's Company of Colonel John Weems' Battalion on October 5, 1776 (Ref: A-95, I-143). He took the Oath of Allegiance before Hon. Samuel Harrison, Jr. in March, 1778 (Ref: B-28).

LARSEN, THOMAS COPPER. Private in Capt. Gilbert Middleton's Independent Company of Militia of Annapolis on March 20, 1779 (Ref: I-144, O-325).

LATTIN, JOHN. Took Oath of Allegiance before Hon. Thomas Harwood on February 28, 1778 (Ref: B-22).

LATTIN, THOMAS. Enrolled by Capt. James Disney, Jr. and Col. Richard Harwood on July 13, 1776 (Ref: H-41). He was deceased by October 25, 1823 when the final distribution of his estate was made by Richard Estep, executor, to Mary Lattin (widow's third), and remainder to Plummer Lattin (Ref: U-65).

LAUGHLIN, THOMAS. A resident of Herring Creek who was a petitioner to form a militia company on March 6, 1776, and was subsequently a private in Captain Richard Weems' Company (Ref: I-143, MS.1814).

LAURENCE, RICHARD. Took the Oath of Allegiance before Hon. Thomas Worthington on February 28, 1778 (Ref: B-21).

LAVELY, JACOB. Enlisted by Michael Burgess and passed by Col. Hyde on July 20, 1776 (Ref: H-41).

LAVY, JOHN. He was enrolled by John Kilty in July, 1776 (Ref: H-40).

LAWRENCE, LEVIN (1750-1805). Married Sarah Dorsey in 1786 and they had seven children: Caleb Lawrence, Rebecca Lawrence Waters, John Lawrence, Larkin Lawrence, Hammond Dorsey Lawrence, Carolina Lawrence Owings, and Sally Lawrence Keene (Ref: T-451). He was one of the petitioners to the Maryland Convention to form an independent rifle company in July, 1776, and later became First Lieutenant in Capt. Thomas Watkins' Militia Company and the Annapolis Artillery (Ref: B-3, F-223, T-452). He was deceased by November 14, 1811, when final distribution of his estate was made by Sarah Lawrence and Larkin Dorsey, administrators, with sevenths of the remaining balance to Caleb Lawrence, Rebecca Lawrence, John Lawrence, Larkin Lawrence, Sally Ann Lawrence, Hammond Lawrence, and Caroline Lawrence (Ref: U-41).

LAWRENCE, RICHARD. Took the Oath of Allegiance before Hon. Thomas Dorsey on March 2, 1778 (Ref: B-24).

LAWSON, JAMES. Private in Capt. John Fulford's Company of Artillery stationed at Annapolis on December 12, 1776 (Ref: H-572).

LAWTON, JOHN. Took Oath of Allegiance before Hon. Elijah Robosson in March, 1778 (Ref: B-28).

LEADBOURN, GEORGE. Recruited by James Brice in 1777 (Ref: H-313).

LEASON, JOHN. Enlisted by Joseph Burgess for the Flying Camp on July 20, 1776 (Ref: H-40).

LEATCH, JAMES (of Calvert County). Took the Oath of Allegiance before Hon. Samuel Lane on March 1, 1778 (Ref: B-23).

LEATHERBURY, ABEL. Took the Oath of Allegiance before Hon. Reuben Meriweather on March 2, 1778 (Ref: B-24).

LEATHERWOOD, THOMAS. Took the Oath of Allegiance before Hon. John Dorsey on March 12, 1778 (Ref: B-26). He was deceased by November 29, 1811 when the final distribution of his estate was made to Mrs. Mary Leatherwood (widow's third), with remaining fifths to Elizabeth Shipley, Ann Leatherwood, Samuel Leatherwood, Priscilla Leatherwood, and Mary Leatherwood (Ref: U-41).

LEE, JOHN. Enrolled by Capt. Thomas Watkins on October 21, 1776 for service to the State (Ref: I-144, MS.1814). Took the Oath of Allegiance before Hon. Richard Harwood, Jr. on March 1, 1778 (Ref: B-23). On July 11, 1811, John White was administrator de bonis non of John Lee, and distributed halves of the remainder of his estate to Joseph Lee and Mrs. John White (Ref: U-40).

LEE, LEWIS. Took the Oath of Allegiance before Hon. Richard Harwood, Jr. on March 1, 1778 (Ref: B-23).

LEE, THOMAS SIM (1745-1819). On December 16, 1778, Thomas appeared before a Justice of the Anne Arundel County Court and took the oaths qualifying him as an appointee to the Council (Ref: J-127). However, he served in many offices in Prince George's and Frederick Counties, and became Governor of Maryland, 1779-1782 and 1792-1794, but he was not a native Anne Arundel Countian. (Therefore, see Source P-529, 530 for additional information).

LEE, WILLIAM. Born in Scotland. He was a Substitute, furnished by William Brodgen on May 20, 1778, to serve for three years (Ref: C-213, H-319).

LEEKE, HENRY SR. Took the Oath of Allegiance before Hon. Thomas Worthington on February 28, 1778 in Anne Arundel County (Ref: B-21). In December, 1816 the Treasurer was ordered to pay "to Henry Leeke of Montgomery County, an old Revolutionary War soldier, quarterly, during his life, the half pay of a sergeant as a compensation for his services." On February 16, 1820, the Treasurer was ordered to pay to James Brown of Montgomery County, the sum of ten dollars, which appears to be the balance due Henry Leeke, late of Montgomery County, deceased, who was a pensioner (Ref: K-364, K-365).

LEEKE, JOSEPH SR. Took the Oath of Allegiance before Hon. Thomas Worthington on February 28, 1778 (Ref: B-21). On August 9, 1796, Henry Leeke, executor of Joseph Leeke, distributed the whole of the balance agreeably to the will and testament of the deceased to Anne Leeke and Henry Leeke (Ref: U-14).

LEEKE, NICHOLAS. Took the Oath of Allegiance before Hon. Samuel Harrison in March, 1778 (Ref: A-244).

LEETH, PETER. Took the Oath of Allegiance before Hon. Samuel Lane on March 1, 1778 (Ref: B-23).

LEFRANK, CESAR. Commissioned a Second Lieutenant on the Galley "Conqueror" on June 16, 1777 under command of Capt. John David (Ref: V-290).

LEGRAND, JOHN. Took the Oath of Allegiance before Hon. Reuben Meriweather on March 2, 1778 (Ref: B-25).

LEIPER, ANDREW. Took the Oath of Allegiance before Hon. Samuel Harrison in March, 1778 (Ref: A-244).

LETTON, THOMAS. Took the Oath of Allegiance before Hon. Richard Harwood, Jr. on March 1, 1778 (Ref: B-23).

LETZINGER, GEORGE. Private in Capt. Richard Dorsey's Company of Artillery on November 17, 1777 (Ref: H-574).

LEWIN, SAMUEL. Private in Capt. Richard Chew's Company of Col. John Weems' Battalion on October 5, 1776 (Ref: A-95, I-143).

LEWIS, JESSE. Private in Captain William Marbury's Company of Artillery in 1777 (Ref: H-575).

LEWIS, JOB. Took the Oath of Allegiance before Hon. Nicholas Worthington in March, 1778 (Ref: B-27).

LEWIS, JOHN. Two men with this name took the Oath of Allegiance: one before Hon. Thomas Worthington on February 28, 1778 and another before Hon. Samuel Lane on March 1, 1778 (Ref: B-21, B-23).

LEWIS, JONATHAN. He was a Substitute, furnished by Thomas Watkins, and then discharged around June 5, 1778 (Ref: C-208, H-319).

LEWIS, KEELE. Took the Oath of Allegiance before Hon. Richard Harwood, Jr. on March 1, 1778 (Ref: B-23).

LEWIS, THOMAS. He took the Oath of Allegiance before Hon. Thomas Worthington on February 28, 1778 (Ref: B-21). Private in Captain Gilbert Middleton's Independent Co. of Annapolis Militia, March 20, 1779 (Ref: I-144, O-325).

LEVY, SAMUEL. Enrolled by Henry Ridgely, Jr. and passed by Col. Josias Carvil Hall on August 26, 1776 (Ref: H-41).

LICETY (?), JOHN. His name appears on a list of defectives from the Maryland Line in October, 1780 (Ref: H-414).

LIGHT, JOHN. Took Oath of Allegiance before Hon. Elijah Robosson in March, 1778 (Ref: B-28).

LIGHTFOOT, JOHN. Took the Oath of Allegiance before Hon. John Dorsey on March 12, 1778 (Ref: B-26).

LILLIE, ROBERT. Took the Oath of Allegiance before Hon. Reuben Meriweather on March 2, 1778 (Ref: B-23).

LINSEY (LINDSY), JOHN. Enlisted by Edward Spurrier and then passed by Thomas Dorsey on July 20, 1776 (Ref: H-41).

LINSTED, JOHN. Took Oath of Allegiance before Hon. Elijah Robosson in March, 1778 (Ref: B-28). On December 20, 1822 the final distribution of his estate was made to Susannah Linstead (widow), with fourths to George W. Linsted, William Linsted, Susannah Linsted, and Charlotte Rockhold (Ref: U-63).

LINTHICUM, BURTON. Took Oath of Allegiance before Hon. Nicholas Worthington in March, 1778 (Ref: B-27).

LINTHICUM, FRANCIS. Took the Oath of Allegiance before Hon. Thomas Harwood on February 28, 1778 (Ref: B-22).

LINTHICUM, JOHN. Took the Oath of Allegiance before Hon. Nicholas Worthington in March, 1778 (Ref: B-27).

LINTHICUM, JOS. Took the Oath of Allegiance before Hon. Nicholas Worthington in March, 1778 (Ref: Original lists in Maryland State Papers, Red Book 21, MdHR4587. Note: Source B-27 questionably lists his name "Tro Linthicum?").

LINTHICUM, RICHARD (April 12, 1752, Anne Arundel County - August 24, 1817, Dorchester County). Married Mary Lee in 1778. He served in the 38th Militia Battalion of Broad Creek, and was Drummer in 1780 (Ref: T-465).

LINTHICUM, THOMAS. Took Oath of Allegiance before Hon. Nicholas Worthington in March, 1778 (Ref: Original lists in Maryland State Papers, Red Book 21, MdHR4587. Note: Source B-27 questionably lists it "Thomas Tro Linthicum").

LITCHFIELD, WILLIAM. Took the Oath of Allegiance before Hon. Thomas Dorsey on March 2, 1778 (Ref: B-24).

LITTELL, JOSEPH. Took the Oath of Allegiance before Hon. Elijah Robosson in March, 1778 (Ref: B-28).

LITTLE, JAMES. Took the Oath of Allegiance before Hon. Elijah Robosson in March, 1778 (Ref: B-28).

LLOYD, EDWARD (1744-1796). On November 12, 1778, Edward appeared before a Justice of Anne Arundel County Court and took the oath qualifying him as a member of the Council (Ref: J-124). However, he served in many offices in Talbot County, while maintaining a townhouse in Annapolis after 1772. Thus, he was not a native Anne Arundel Countian (Source P-537 has more data).

LLOYD, HENRY. Took the Oath of Allegiance before Hon. Samuel Harrison in March, 1778 (Ref: A-244).

LOGEY, JAMES. Enlisted by John Worthington Dorsey and passed by John Dorsey on July 22, 1776 (Ref: H-39).

LORAH, JOHN. Second Lieutenant in Capt. Daniel Dorsey's Company by June 29, 1776 (Ref: N-534). "2nd Lt. John Lorah must be John O'Hara, who resigned and James Howard was appointed by the Council of Safety on July 24, 1776. It is printed in the Journal of the Convention, but it must be a mistake." (Quoted verbatim from Ref: H-38).

LOVITT, WILLIAM. Drafted in October, 1780, to serve until December 10, 1780 (Ref: H-369).

LOW, JOSEPH. Took the Oath of Allegiance before Hon. Reuben Meriweather on March 2, 1778 (Ref: B-23).

LOWERY, CHARLES. Enrolled by Captain Thomas Watkins on October 21, 1776 for service to the State (Ref: I-144, MS.1814).

LOWTHER, DANIEL. Took the Oath of Allegiance before Hon. Elijah Robosson in March, 1778 (Ref: B-28).

LUCAS, JOHN. On February 12, 1820, the Treasurer was to pay "to John Lucas, of Anne Arundel County, an old revolutionary soldier, quarterly, half pay of a Sergeant, as a further remuneration for services rendered his country during her struggle for independence." On March 6, 1832, the Treasurer was ordered to "pay Rachel Lucas, of Anne Arundel County, widow of John Lucas, a soldier of the Revolutionary War, during life, half yearly, half pay of a private for her husband's services during said war." (Ref: K-367,

K-368). He was pensioned on June 12, 1818, and died September 2, 1823 (Ref: Z-27).

LUND, WILLIAM. Possibly born in England. He was recruited by James Brice, Anne Arundel County Lieutenant, on January 12, 1778 (Ref: C-215, H-313).

LUPTON, GEORGE. Took the Oath of Allegiance before Hon. John Dorsey on March 12, 1778 (Ref: B-26).

LUSBY, BALDWIN. Took the Oath of Allegiance before Hon. Nicholas Worthington in March, 1778 (Ref: B-27, which gives his name as "Baldwin Luzby"). He was deceased by April 9, 1791, when the final distribution of his estate was made by Robert Lusby, executor, to Elizabeth Lusby (widow's third), five shillings each to Eleanor Rawlings and Nancy Maccauley, and fifths of the remaining estate balance to Robert Lusby, John Lusby, Debra Lusby, Susannah Lusby, and Peggy Lusby (Ref: U-6).

LUSBY, ROBERT. Private in Capt. William Marbury's Company of Artillery in 1777 (Ref: H-575). He took the Oath of Allegiance before Hon. Nicholas Worthington in March, 1778 (Ref: Original list in Maryland State Papers, Red Book 21, MdHR4587, which gives his name as "Robert Luzby". However, Source B-27 mistakenly gives his name as "Robert Langley"). He was also commissioned a Second Lieutenant in Capt. Henry Bateman's Company of the Severn Battalion on August 15, 1778, at which time his name was properly spelled "Robert Lusby" (Ref: I-144, J-113, O-208). On June 19, 1789 the final distribution of his estate was made to Deborah Lusby (widow's third) with sevenths of the balance to Susannah Lusby, Edward Lusby, James Lusby, Samuel Lusby, Polly Lusby, Henry Lusby, and William Lusby (Ref: U-3).

LUSBY, VINCENT. Enrolled by Captain James Disney, Jr. and passed by Colonel Richard Harwood on July 13, 1776 (Ref: H-41). On March 5, 1777 he sent a petition to the Council of Safety as follows: "On the 15th day of July 1776 your petitioner entered into the service of his country under the command of Captain James Disney of this county. That on the 16th day of November following he was taken prisoner and so continued until the 3rd day of January 1777. That from the time of his being taken prisoner down to the present time he hath not received one farthing of wages. Wherefore he prays your Honours to take his case under your serious consideration and grant him such relief in the premises as to your Honours shall seem meet. And your petitioner as in duty bound will pray etc." (Ref: V-162). He took the Oath of Allegiance before Hon. Richard Harwood, Jr. on March 1, 1778 (Ref: B-23). On August 24, 1805 final distribution of his estate was made to Ann Lusby, deceased's only child, who received the whole balance (Ref: U-29).

LUX, ROBERT. Took the Oath of Allegiance before Hon. Reuben Meriweather on March 2, 1778 (Ref: B-25).

LYBRANT, CHRISTIAN. Private in Capt. Gilbert Middleton's Independent Company of Militia of Annapolis on March 20, 1779 (Ref: I-144,

O-325).

MACCUBBIN, CHARLES. Private in Capt. Gilbert Middleton's Independent Company of Militia of Annapolis on March 20, 1779 (Ref: I-144, O-325).

MACCUBBIN, JOSEPH. First Lieutenant in Captain George Watts' Company in the Severn Battalion of Militia on February 22, 1776, and commissioned Captain on March 1, 1778 (Ref: A-176, C-202, F-223, N-178). On August 14, 1802 the final distribution of his estate was made to Doris Maccubbin (widows third) with balance to Charlotte Maccubbin and Nicholas Maccubbin (Ref: U-20).

MACCUBBIN, MOSES. Took Oath of Allegiance before Hon. Nicholas Worthington in March, 1778 (Ref: Maryland State Papers, Red Book No. 21, p. 8D. Note: His name is mistakenly omitted from the published list in Reference B-27).

MACCUBBIN, NICHOLAS JR. Commissioned an Ensign on March 6, 1776, in Captain James Brice's Independent Company in the City of Annapolis (Ref: N-203). He was commissioned a Captain on October 6, 1777 (Ref: V-392). On August 22, 1792 the final distribution of his estate was made to Mrs. Sarah Maccubbin, now Mrs. James Cleary (widow's third), with the remainder of the estate balance to Nicholas Zachariah Maccubbin (Ref: U-8).

MACCAULEY, JOHN. Took the Oath of Allegiance before Hon. Thomas Worthington on February 28, 1778 (Ref: B-21).

MACCAULEY (MCCAULEY), THOMAS. Enlisted by Edward Spurrier and then passed by Thomas Dorsey on July 20, 1776 (Ref: H-41). He took the Oath of Allegiance before Hon. Thomas Worthington on February 28, 1778 (Ref: B-21). In 1833 in Harrison County, Kentucky, "Thomas McCawley" applied for a pension, stating he was born in 1757, enlisted in Anne Arundel County, and moved to Harrison County from Anne Arundel in 1818. He received pension S31248. (Ref: L-46).

MACCAULEY (MCCAULEY), ZACHARIAH. Enlisted by Edward Spurrier and then passed by Thomas Dorsey on July 20, 1776 (Ref: H-41).

MACCENEY (MCSENEY), JACOB. Born in Maryland. Was enrolled by Captain Edward Tillard on July 10, 1776. Height: 5' 10" (Ref: H-29). He took the Oath of Allegiance before Hon. Thomas Harwood on February 28, 1778 (Ref: B-22).

MACCENEY, ZACHARIAH. Took the Oath of Allegiance before Hon. Thomas Harwood on February 28, 1778 (Ref: B-22). On October 28, 1829 Benjamin McCeney, administrator de bonis non of Zachariah McCeney, made final distribution of his estate (fifths) to Sarah Owens, Benjamin McCeney, Jacob McCeney, Mary Clayton, and Edward McCeney (Ref: U-79).

MACCOY, JOHN. Took the Oath of Allegiance before Hon. Elijah Robosson in March, 1778 (Ref: B-28).

MACCOY, WILLIAM. Took the Oath of Allegiance before Hon. Elijah Robosson in March, 1778 (Ref: B-28).

MACDANIEL, ALLEN. Took the Oath of Allegiance before Hon. Thomas Worthington on February 28, 1778 (Ref: B-21).

MACDANIEL, COLUMBUS. Took Oath of Allegiance before Hon. Thomas Worthington on February 28, 1778 (Ref: B-21).

MACDONALD, BARTHOLOMEW. Enlisted by Richard Talbot and passed by John Dorsey on July 22, 1776 (Ref: H-39).

MACE, THOMAS. Resident of Herring Creek who petitioned to form a company of militia on March 6, 1776, and subsequently served in Capt. Richard Weems' Company (Ref: I-143, MS.1814). He took the Oath of Allegiance before Hon. Samuel Lane on March 1, 1778 (Ref: B-23).

MACGILL, JAMES. Took the Oath of Allegiance before Hon. Thomas Worthington on February 28, 1778 (Ref: B-21).

MACGILL, PATRICK. Took the Oath of Allegiance before Hon. Thomas Worthington on February 28, 1778 (Ref: B-21).

MACKBEE (MOCKBEE), STEPHEN. Took the Oath of Allegiance before Hon. Reuben Meriweather on March 2, 1778 (Ref: B-24). On December 24, 1804 "Stephen Mockabee" was executor of the estate of Rachel Nichols (Ref: U-18).

MACKENZIE (MACKINZIE, MCKENZIE), AARON. Took the Oath of Allegiance before Hon. Reuben Meriweather on March 2, 1778 (Ref: B-24). He was draughted in 1780 to serve until December 10, 1780 (Ref: H-369).

MACKENZIE (MACKINZIE), DANIEL. Took the Oath of Allegiance before Hon. Reuben Meriweather on March 2, 1778 (Ref: B-24).

MACKENZIE (MACKINZIE), MICHAEL. Took Oath of Allegiance before Hon. Reuben Meriweather on March 2, 1778 (Ref: B-24).

MACKUBIN, JAMES. Took the Oath of Allegiance before Hon. Nicholas Worthington in March, 1778 (Ref: B-27).

MACKUBIN, JOHN CRAY. Took Oath of Allegiance before Hon. Nicholas Worthington in March, 1778 (Ref: B-27, which questionably gives his name as "McCreagh ? Mackubin," but in the original lists in Maryland State Papers, Red Book 21, MdHR4587, the name looks like "Jo. Creagh Mackubin," not McCreagh Mackubin. In fact, Ref: W-537 gives his name as "John Cray McKubin" when he was paid for an unspecified service to the State of Maryland on August 3, 1781).

MACKUBIN, RICHARD. Took Oath of Allegiance before Hon. Nicholas Worthington in March, 1778 (Ref: Maryland State Papers, Red Book No. 21, p. 8D. Note: His name is mistakenly omitted from the published list in Reference B-27).

MACMANI, NATHANIEL. Enrolled by Captain Thomas Watkins on October 21, 1776. (Ref: I-144, MS.1814).

MACNAMARA (MCNAMARA), DARBY. Born in Scotland. In 1778 he was a Substitute, furnished by John Bullen on May 8th to serve a three year term (Ref: C-206, H-317). In November session, 1798, the Treasurer was ordered to "pay Darby McNamara, an old infirm and disabled soldier, annual sum of $57.00, during life, in lieu of $399.00, the principal and interest due on three state certificates issued to him for depreciation of his pay, which certificates were lost---quarterly, beginning December 10, 1798." In November session, 1799, the Treasurer was ordered to "pay to Darby McNamara, a poor disabled soldier of the 1st Maryland Regiment, 25 lbs., 6 sh., 11 d., with interest from August 1, 1780, for a depreciation certificate issued to him for that amount and lost." In November session, 1802, the Treasurer was ordered to "pay annually to Darby McNamara the sum of fifteen pounds current money, in quarterly payments, in consideration of his many services as a soldier in the late Revolutionary War, by which he has been rendered entirely unable to obtain a subsistence." (Ref: K-370, K-371).

MADDEN, CHRISTOPHER. Born in Scotland. He was a Substitute, furnished by Captain Charles Hammond and Elijah Gaither on April 26, 1778, to serve for three years (Ref: C-211, H-318).

MAGEE, THOMAS. Disabled soldier paid in Anne Arundel County on August 16, 1783, with the record indicating "on order Baltimore" (Ref: D-8), and was also paid on January 13, 1784 and April 13, 1784 (Ref: D-12, D-13). He was a Private in Col. Hazen's Regiment and lost his sight (no details). He was discharged from the military on December 14, 1782 (Ref: X-25).

MAGOWAN, WALTER. Took the Oath of Allegiance before Hon. Elijah Robosson in March, 1778 (Ref: B-28).

MALLER, MICHL. Enrolled by Captain Thomas Watkins on October 21, 1776 (Ref: I-144, MS.1814).

MAN, JAMES. He was a Substitute, furnished by William Simmons on June 5, 1778 to serve for nine months (Ref: C-208, H-319).

MANADIER, BENJAMIN. Pensioned on March 4, 1831, at age 77, as a Surgeon's Mate in the Maryland Line during the Revolutionary War (Ref: Z-45).

MANNICA, PHILLIP. Took the Oath of Allegiance before Hon. Thomas Worthington on February 28, 1778 (Ref: B-21).

MANSELL, SAMUEL. Took the Oath of Allegiance before Hon. Reuben Meriweather on March 2, 1778 (Ref: B-24).

MANTLE, MICHAEL. Took the Oath of Allegiance before Hon. Reuben Meriweather on March 2, 1778 (Ref: B-24).

MARBURY, WILLIAM. Captain of company of artillery in 1777 (Ref: H-575).

MARK, ROBERT. Enlisted by Edward Spurrier and passed by Thomas Dorsey on July 20, 1776 (Ref: H-41).

MARONY, DAVID. Private in Capt. Richard Dorsey's Company of Artillery, and noted as being sick on the muster rolls of November 17, 1777 (Ref: H-574).

MARR, JAMES. Took the Oath of Allegiance before Hon. Samuel Lane on March 1, 1778 (Ref: B-23).

MARR, JOHN. Was enrolled by Captain Thomas Watkins on October 21, 1776 (Ref: I-144, MS.1814).

MARR, ORWELL (ORRELL). Born in Maryland. Enrolled by Samuel Chew on July 25, 1776. Height: 5' 8" (Ref: H-40). He took the Oath of Allegiance before Hon. Samuel Lane on March 1, 1778 (Ref: B-23).

MARRIOTT, JOHN. At Elk Ridge on March 29, 1776, Edward Gaither, Jr. stated, in his letter to the Council of Maryland, that "Mr. John Marriott, who was First Lieutenant to Capt. Elisha Riggs, is deceased" (Ref: N-299). He had just been appointed First Lieutenant on February 7, 1776 (Ref: N-139).

MARRIOTT, JOHN. He was an Ensign in Capt. Philip Warfield's Company in the Severn Battalion on August 15, 1778 (Ref: I-144, J-113, O-208). Took Oath of Allegiance before Hon. Nicholas Worthington in March, 1778 (Ref: B-27). On February 16, 1802 the final distribution of his estate (fifths) was made by his executor, Richard Marriott, to John Marriott, Rachel Marriott, Ruth Marriott, Elizabeth Marriott, and Richard Marriott (Ref: U-19).

MARRIOTT, SILVANUS. Took Oath of Allegiance before Hon. Nicholas Worthington in March, 1778 (Ref: B-27).

MARRIOTT, THOMAS. Took the Oath of Allegiance before Hon. Nicholas Worthington in March, 1778 (Ref: B-27).

MARSH, BENJAMIN. He was a Substitute, supplied by Thomas Watkins, Jr. and James Marr, on June 10, 1778 for a three year term (Ref: C-209, H-320).

MARSHALL, EDWARD. Enlisted by Thomas Mayo on July 20, 1776 (Ref: H-41).

MARSHALL, JOHN. Took the Oath of Allegiance before Hon. Elijah Robosson in March, 1778 (Ref: B-28).

MARSHALL, STEPHEN. Took the Oath of Allegiance before Hon. Thomas Worthington on February 28, 1778 (Ref: B-21).

MARTIN, NICHOLAS. Took the Oath of Allegiance before Hon. Elijah Robosson in March, 1778 (Ref: B-28). Master of the Sloop "Morris and Wallace" which had 4 carriage guns and 4 swivels navigated by 15 men, and owned by Charles Wallace and others at the City of Annapolis in March, 1778 (Ref: V-557).

MARTIN, PETER. Took the Oath of Allegiance before Hon. John Dorsey on March 12, 1778 (Ref: B-26).

MASH, RICHARD. Took the Oath of Allegiance before Hon. Thomas Dorsey on March 2, 1778 (Ref: B-24).

MASON, EDWARD. Took the Oath of Allegiance before Hon. Reuben Meriweather on March 2, 1778 (Ref: B-24).

MASSENBACH, FELIX LEWIS. Commissioned a Second Lieutenant in Capt. Fulford's Company of Matrosses on February 20, 1776 (Ref: N-173).

MATHEWSON, ALEXANDER. Sergeant and disabled soldier who was paid in Anne Arundel County on December 11, 1783 (Ref: D-10). He was wounded (no details given) and was subsequently discharged at Newburgh on January 4, 1783. His papers were signed by George Washington (Ref: X-26).

MATHIAS, JAMES. Private in Capt. Richard Dorsey's Company of Artillery, and noted as being "in gaol for housebreaking" on the muster rolls of November 17, 1777 (Ref: H-574).

MATTHEWS, JOHN. Corporal and disabled soldier who was paid in Anne Arundel County on January 13, 1784, April 13, 1784, June 9, 1784, Sept. 3, 1784, October 26, 1784 and December 17, 1784 (Ref: D-11, D-14, D-18, D-21, D-23, D-25). He was discharged at Frederick on November 29, 1783 (Ref: X-22).

MATTOX, CHARLES. Enlisted by Thomas Mayo on July 20, 1776 (Ref: H-41).

MATTOX, CORNELIUS. Enlisted by Richard Talbot and passed by John Dorsey on July 22, 1776 (Ref: H-39).

MATTOX, JACOB. Took the Oath of Allegiance before Hon. Elijah Robosson in March, 1778 (Ref: B-28). On May 13, 1788, the final distribution of the estate of "Jacob Mattocks" was made by his administrator, Leonard Foreman, to his widow (unnamed), with fourths of the remainder to Jonathan Mattocks, Charles Mattocks, Charity Mattocks, and Susannah Mattocks (Ref: U-1).

MAW, EDWARD. Private in Captain Gilbert Middleton's Independent Company of Militia of Annapolis on March 20, 1779 (Ref: I-144, O-325).

MAW, ELIZABETH. On August 25, 1777 she was paid by the Council of Maryland in the amount of 7 lbs., 2 sh., for unspecified services (Ref: V-343).

MAW, WILLIAM. Private in Captain Gilbert Middleton's Independent Company of Militia of Annapolis on March 20, 1779 (Ref: I-144, O-325).

MAXWELL, RICHARD. Born in Scotland. He was a Substitute, furnished by Thomas Worthington on May 7, 1778 to serve to war's duration (Ref: C-212, H-319).

MAY, GEORGE. Enrolled by Captain Thomas Watkins on October 21, 1776 (Ref: I-144, MS.1814). Took the Oath of Allegiance before Hon. Reuben Meriweather on March 2, 1778 (Ref: B-24).

MAY, HANNAH. Served as a Nurse in the Annapolis hospital (Ref: Y-307).

MAY, HENRY. Took the Oath of Allegiance before Hon. Richard Harwood, Jr. on March 1, 1778 (Ref: B-23).

MAYHEW, SAMUEL. Took the Oath of Allegiance before Hon. Reuben Meriweather on March 2, 1778 (Ref: B-25).

MAYNARD, JAMES P. Private in Captain William Marbury's Company of Artillery in 1777 (Ref: H-575).

MAYO, ISAAC. Took the Oath of Allegiance before Hon. Thomas Worthington on February 28, 1778 (Ref: B-21). On April 14, 1798, final distribution of his estate was made by his executrix Sarah Ann Mayo, now Sarah Ann Waters (widow's third), with balance to Sarah Mayo and George Mayo (Ref: U-17).

MAYO, JOHN. Took the Oath of Allegiance before Hon. Richard Harwood, Jr. on March 1, 1778 (Ref: B-23).

MAYO, JOSEPH. He was paid by the Council of Maryland on February 3, 1778 for an unspecified service (Ref: V-482). He took the Oath of Allegiance before Hon. Elijah Robosson in March, 1778 (Ref: B-28). On June 9, 1788, the final distribution of his estate was made to Henrietta Mayo (widow's third), with thirds of the balance to Joshua Mayo, John Mayo and Isaac Mayo (Ref: U-1).

MAYO, JOSEPH JR. Took the Oath of Allegiance before Hon. Elijah Robosson in March, 1778 (Ref: B-28).

MAYO, JOSEPH SR. Took the Oath of Allegiance before Hon. Richard Harwood, Jr. on March 1, 1778 (Ref: B-23).

MAYO, JOSHUA. Took the Oath of Allegiance before Hon. Richard Harwood, Jr. on March 1, 1778 (Ref: B-23).

MAYO, THOMAS. Served on the Committee of Observation in 1775 (Ref: F-222). Second Lieutenant in Capt. John Boone's Militia Company, and then First Lieutenant in Capt. Thomas Hammond's Company in 1776 (Ref: F-223, H-39). He recruited twenty men for military service in July, 1776 (Ref: H-41).

MCADAMS, JOHN. Born in America. He was enlisted and passed by James Brice on January 17, 1778 in Anne Arundel County (Ref: C-215, H-313).

MCCALL, WILLIAM. Born in England. He was a Substitute, furnished by Colonel Edward Lloyd on April 27, 1778, to serve for the duration of the war (Ref: C-204, H-317).

MCCARTIN, WILLIAM. Enlisted by Thomas Mayo on July 20, 1776 (Ref: H-41).

MCCLEN, ALEXANDER. Took Oath of Allegiance before Hon. Nicholas Worthington in March, 1778 (Ref: B-27).

MCCORMACK, THOMAS. Born in Scotland. He was a Substitute, furnished by Robert Shipley on May 6, 1778 to serve to the war's duration (Ref: C-212, H-318).

MCDANIEL, STEPHEN. Took the Oath of Allegiance before Hon. Reuben Meriweather on March 2, 1778 (Ref: B-24).

MCDARNELL, JOSEPH. Born in Scotland. He was a Substitute, furnished by Rezin Hammond on May 11, 1778, to serve to war's duration (Ref: C-212, H-319).

MCDONALD, JOHN. Took the Oath of Allegiance before Hon. Reuben Meriweather on March 2, 1778 (Ref: B-24).

MCDONALD, JOSEPH. Took the Oath of Allegiance before Hon. John Dorsey on March 12, 1778 (Ref: B-26).

MCDOWELL, HUGH. Private in Capt. Richard Dorsey's Company of Artillery, and noted as being sick on the rolls of November 17, 1777 (Ref: H-574).

MCGRILL, EDWARD. Private in Capt. Gilbert Middleton's Independent Company of Militia of Annapolis on March 20, 1779 (Ref: I-144, O-325).

MCGUIRE, MICHAEL. Disabled soldier who was to be paid in Anne Arundel County on December 11, 1783, but the record indicated he was dead (Ref: D-10). His widow "Mary Maguire" petitioned for payment through Benjamin Ward, power of attorney, on July 11, 1784, stating he was in 2nd Md Line (Ref: X-21, 23).

MCINTOCH, GEORGE. Enrolled by Henry Ridgely, Jr. and passed by Col. Josias C. Hall on August 26, 1776 (Ref: H-41).

MCKINLEY, JAMES. Born in Scotland. He was a Substitute, furnished by Amos Dorsey on May 20, 1778, to serve to war's duration (Ref: C-214, H-319).

MCLANE, JOHN. Recruited and passed by James Brice in 1777 (Ref: H-313).

MCLAUGHLIN, CORNELIUS. Born in Scotland. He was a Substitute, furnished by William Haislip on May 5, 1778, to serve to war's end (Ref: C-212, H-318).

MCLEOD, HUGH. Disabled soldier who was paid in Anne Arundel County on April 13, 1784, June 9, 1784, September 3, 1784, October 26, 1784 and December 17, 1784 (Ref: D-13, D-18, D-21, D-23, D-25). He was wounded (no details) and subsequently discharged on January 5, 1780 (Ref: X-24).

MCMULLAIN, ALEXANDER. Private in Capt. Richard Dorsey's Company of Artillery on the rolls of November 17, 1777 (Ref: H-574).

MCNAMARA, NICHOLAS. Disabled soldier who was issued clothing on December 11, 1780 and was paid on May 19, 1783, August 16, 1783, January 13, 1784, April 13, 1784, June 9, 1784, September 3, 1784, October 26, 1784 and December 17, 1784 (Ref: W-240, D-6, D-8, D-12, D-13, D-18, D-21, D-23, D-25).

MCNEAR (MCNEARE), THOMAS. Private in Captain William Marbury's Company of Artillery in 1777 (Ref: H-575). He took the Oath of Allegiance before Hon. Richard Harwood, Jr. on March 1, 1778 (Ref: B-23).

MCNORTON, WILLIAM. Born in Maryland. Enrolled by John S. Belt in July, 1776. Height: 5' 7 1/2" (Ref: H-40).

MEAD, HORATIO. Took the Oath of Allegiance before Hon. Samuel Lane on March 1, 1778 (Ref: B-23).

MEAD, SAMUEL. He was a Deputy Collector of Clothing in 1778 (Ref: V-519).

MEDCALF, JAMES. Resident of Herring Creek who petitioned to form a company of militia on March 6, 1776 and subsequently served in Capt. Richard Weems' Company (Ref: I-143, MS.1814). He took the Oath of Allegiance before Hon. Samuel Harrison in March, 1778 (Ref: A-244).

MEDCALF, JOHN. Took the Oath of Allegiance before Hon. Samuel Harrison in March, 1778 (Ref: A-244).

MEDCALF (MEDCALFE), ROBERT. Born in England. He was enlisted by Thomas Gordon in Anne Arundel County on March 7, 1778 (Ref: C-216, H-313).

MEDCALF, THOMAS. Took the Oath of Allegiance before Hon. Thomas Harwood on February 28, 1778 (Ref: B-22).

MEDCALF (MEDCLEF), WILLIAM. Resident of Herring Creek who petitioned to form a militia company on March 6, 1776 and subsequently served in Capt. Richard Weems' Company (Ref: I-143, MS.1814). He took the Oath of Allegiance before Hon. Elijah Robosson in March, 1778 (Ref: B-28).

MEED, JOSHUA. Took the Oath of Allegiance before Honorable Elijah Robosson in March, 1778 (Ref: B-28).

MEEK, ARON. Took the Oath of Allegiance before Honorable Elijah Robosson in March, 1778 (Ref: B-28).

MEEK, JOHN. Took the Oath of Allegiance before Hon. Nicholas Worthington in March, 1778 (Ref: B-27).

MEEK, JOHNS. Drafted in 1780 to serve to December 10, 1780 (Ref: H-369).

MEEK, JOSEPH. Took the Oath of Allegiance before Hon. Nicholas Worthington in March, 1778 (Ref: B-27).

MEEK, JOSEPH JR. Took the Oath of Allegiance on March 23, 1778 (Ref: V-547).

MEEK, WESTAL. Took the Oath of Allegiance before Hon. Nicholas Worthington in March, 1778 (Ref: Maryland State Papers, Red Book No. 21, p. 8D. Note: His name is mistakenly omitted from the published list in Reference B-27). "Wastal Meek" was a son of James who died before July 3, 1790 (Ref: U-5).

MEHENY, FLORENCE. Took Oath of Allegiance before Hon. Nicholas Worthington in March, 1778 (Ref: B-27).

MELSON, DANIEL. On March 13, 1777 he petitioned the Council of Safety stating he was wrongfully imprisoned, he was not an enemy of this country, and that he would take the Oath of Allegiance (Ref: V-171, V-172). He took the Oath of Allegiance on January 5, 1778 (Ref: V-454).

MELSON, WILLIAM. Captain of the Schooner "Liberty" on April 11, 1777, and granted permission by the Council of Maryland to proceed from the port of Annapolis to the port of Hispaniola (Ref: V-205).

MENCHON, HUMPHRY. Born in Maryland. Enrolled by John S. Belt in July, 1776. Height: 5' 2" (Ref: H-40).

MERCER, FRANCIS. One of the petitioners to the Maryland Convention to form an independent rifle company in July, 1776 (Ref: B-3).

MERCER, JOHN. Took the Oath of Allegiance before Hon. Nicholas Worthington in March, 1778 (Ref: Maryland State Papers, Red Book No. 21, p. 8D. Note: His name is mistakenly omitted from the published list in Reference B-27).

MERCIER, ANDREW. Took Oath of Allegiance before Hon. Reuben Meriweather on March 2, 1778 (Ref: B-25). Executor of Ruth Mercier in 1837 (Ref: U-93).

MERCIER, WELDON. Took the Oath of Allegiance before Hon. Reuben Meriweather on March 2, 1778 (Ref: B-25).

MERIWEATHER, REUBEN (December 15, 1743, Goochland County, Virginia - 1794, Anne Arundel County, Maryland). Son of Nicholas Meriweather and Mary Prior. He married Sarah Anne Dorsey (of Edward) and their son Nicholas Meriweather married Elizabeth Hood. Reuben was a member of the Committee of Observation in 1775 and one of the Justices who administered the Oath of Allegiance in March, 1778. He was appointed a Justice of the Peace on November 19, 1778. (Ref: B-24, E-80A, E-81A, F-222, O-241). He was one of three persons named in Anne Arundel County on August 19, 1779, to receive subscriptions under the Act for enlarging the powers of the Governor and Council (Ref: O-499. Note: Source B-239 indicates that Reuben Meriweather and John Gilliss had a book of affirmations of allegiance for Quakers, Mennonists and Dunkers, and certified that it contained the names of all males over eighteen who had affirmed before Reuben Meriweather on March 1, 1778. However, upon looking in the Maryland State Papers, Red Book 19 (MdHR4584) at the Maryland State Archives, the only document found was the certification itself. The actual list of names referred to by Meriweather and Gilliss was not found there). In 1806 the final distribution of his estate was made to Sarah Meriweather (widow's third) and remaining sevenths to Thomas Beall Dorsey Meriweather, Sally Meriweather, Nicholas Meriweather, Polly Meriweather, Elizabeth Meriweather, Eleanor Meriweather, and Louisa Meriweather (Ref: U-30).

MERRICK, BENJAMIN. Took the Oath of Allegiance before Hon. Thomas Worthington on February 28, 1778 (Ref: B-21).

MERRICK, HENRY. Took the Oath of Allegiance on March 25, 1778 (Ref: V-550).

MERRIKEN (MERRIKIN), HUGH. Took the Oath of Allegiance before Hon. Elijah Robosson in March, 1778 (Ref: B-28).

MERRIKEN (MERRIKIN), JOSEPH. Captain in the Severn Battalion of Militia. On May 23, 1777, he protested the appointment of Capt. James Tootell as Major, stating that he (Merrikin) had four months more time as a Captain then did Tootell. Joseph was, however, subsequently commissioned a Major on March 1, 1778, in the Severn Militia Battalion (Ref: A-162, A-176, C-202). He was paid for recruiting on January 15, 1778 (Ref: V-467), and in March, 1779, was appointed a Purchasing Agent (Ref: O-333). On April 26, 1779, he was appointed County Coroner (Ref: O-366). On June 9, 1788, final distribution of his estate was made (sixths) to Ann Merriken, Sarah Merriken, Joseph Merriken, Robert Merriken, Thomas Merriken, and John Merriken (Ref: U-1).

MERRIKEN (MERRIKIN), JOSHUA. Second Lieutenant in Captain Thomas Hammond's Company in the Severn Battalion of Militia in 1776-1777, and was in Captain Caleb Owings' Company on March 1, 1778 (Ref: A-176, C-202, H-39, I-144). He took the Oath of Allegiance on March 2, 1778 (Ref: V-525). Commissioned a Captain in the Severn Battalion on August 15, 1778 (I-144, J-113, O-208).

MERRIKEN (MERRIKIN), WILLIAM. Took Oath of Allegiance before Hon. Nicholas Worthington in March, 1778 (Ref: B-27). On February 16, 1805, the final distribution of his estate was made with halves of the remaining balance to his daughters Sarah Merriken and Elizabeth Duvall (Ref: U-28).

MIDDLETON, GILBERT. On March 28, 1776 "Mr. Gilbert Middleton" was paid by the Council of Safety for providing for Col. Hall's Battalion of Militia. On April 12, 1776 "Mr. Gilbert Middleton" was paid by the Treasurer for hiring of a boat. On May 2, 1776 "Mr. Edward Parker of Cecil County was ordered to send down to the City of Annapolis by Mr. Gilbert Middelton all the coarse linen manufactured for the use of the province" (Ref: N-294, N-328, N-400). On October 6, 1777 he was commissioned Second Lieutenant in Capt. Benjamin Harwood's Company (Ref: V-392), and he was the Captain of an Independent Company of Militia of Annapolis by March 20, 1779 (Ref: I-144, O-325). In 1781 a Gilbert Middleton was Captain of the State Boat "Plater" and served until August (Ref: W-448, W-449). On January 25, 1823, the Treasurer was directed to "pay to Gilbert Middleton, of Baltimore, half pay of a Captain for his services during the Revolutionary War." On February 9, 1822(?) the Treasurer was directed "to pay Sarah Middleton, of Baltimore, pension, the half pay of a Captain, as a further compensation for the service rendered by her husband during the Revolutionary War" (Ref: K-375).

MIDDLETON, JOSEPH. Private in Capt. Gilbert Middleton's Independent Company of Militia of Annapolis on March 20, 1779 (Ref: I-144, O-325).

MIDDLETON, WILLIAM. First Corporal in Capt. Gilbert Middleton's Independent Company of Militia of Annapolis on March 20, 1779 (Ref: I-144, O-325).

MIER, JOHN. Took the Oath of Allegiance before Hon. Nicholas Worthington in March, 1778 (Ref: The Maryland State Papers, Red Book No. 21, p. 8D. Note: His name is mistakenly omitted from the published list in Reference B-27).

MILDURPH, JOHN. His name appeared on a list of defectives from the Maryland Line on November 3, 1781 (Ref: H-415).

MILES, JOHN. Born in Maryland. Enrolled by Capt. Edward Tillard on July 10, 1776. Height: 5' 9" (Ref: H-39). He took the Oath of Allegiance before Hon. John Dorsey on March 12, 1778 (Ref: B-26).

MILES, JOSHUA. Disabled soldier of the Artillery "who has long been in the hospital and not likely to be fit for service is discharged" on January 15, 1778 (Ref: V-467).

MILES, SAMUEL. Took the Oath of Allegiance before Hon. Thomas Worthington on February 28, 1778 (Ref: B-21).

MILES, THOMAS. Took the Oath of Allegiance before Hon. Samuel Lane on March 1, 1778 (Ref: B-23).

MILES, WILLIAM. Born in Maryland. Enlisted by Captain Edward Tillard and passed by Richard Harwood, Jr. on July 16, 1776 (Ref: H-40). He took the Oath of Allegiance before Hon. Samuel Lane on March 1, 1778 (Ref: B-23).

MILITIA OFFICER COMMISSIONS. Although most Anne Arundel County militia lists are extant, there are records of the commissioning of officers as follows: Commissioned issued on February 15, 1776 to Capt. Abraham Simmons, 1st Lt. Thomas Tongue, 2nd Lt. Thomas Morton, and Ensign Abell Hill in the South River Battalion. Commissions issued on February 22, 1776 to Capt. James Tootell, 1st Lt. Philemon Warfield, 2nd Lt. Lancelot Warfield, and Ensign Thomas Warfield; Capt. George Watts, 1st Lt. David Kerr, 2nd Lt. Joseph Maccubbin, and Ensign Joshua Cromwell; Capt. Henry Hall, 1st Lt. John Worthington (of Brice), 2nd Lt. Nicholas Worthington, and Ensign Gilbert Yieldhall; and Ensign Absalom Anderson of Capt. Thomas Mullikin's Company in the Severn Battalion. Commissions issued on April 13, 1776 to 1st Lt. Joshua Burgess, 2nd Lt. John Norwood, and Ensign Thomas Cornelius Howard of Capt. Brice Howard's Company. Commissions issued on April 17, 1776 to Capt. Richard Weems, 1st Lt. Gideon Dare, 2nd Lt. Joseph Allengham, and Ensign Benjamin Harrison (Ref: N-161, N-178, N-329, N-336). Commissions issued on January 26, 1777 to Col. Nicholas Worthington, Lt. Col. Elijah Robosson and Major James Tootell of the Severn Battalion. Commissions issued on January 28, 1777 to Capt. Philemon Warfield, 1st Lt. Lancelot Warfield, 2nd Lt. Thomas Warfield, and Ensign Joseph Warfield in the Severn Battalion. Commissions issued on June 12, 1777 to 2nd Lt. Joshua Gray, Jr. and Ensign Benjamin Fish of Capt. Boone's Company, and 1st Lt. Richard Cromwell, 2nd Lt. Joshua Merrikin, and Ensign George Hammond of Capt. Owens' Company. Commissions issued on August 25, 1777 to Capt. James Walker, 1st Lt. Horatio Johnson, 2nd Lt. Samuel Norwood, and Ensign Elie Brown in the 22nd Battalion and Ensign Benjamin Hood of Capt. Ellicott's Company. Commissions issued on August 28, 1777 to Capt. Charles Hammond (of John), 1st Lt. Basil Burgess, Ensign John Ray in Capt. John Burgess' Company (sic); 2nd Lt. Nicholas Ridgely and Ensign George Geoghan of Capt. Richard Stringer's Co.; 1st Lt. Henry Griffin and 2nd Lt. Henry Ayton of Capt. Benjamin Warfield's Company; 1st Lt. Nicholas Watkins, 2nd Lt. James Haward (sic), and Ensign Basil Isreal of Capt. John Dorsey's Company; and 2nd Lt. Charles Fox in Capt. Ellicott's Company in the 22nd Battalion. Commissions issued on August 30, 1777 to Quartermaster William Hammond of Col. Thomas Dorsey's Battalion. Commissions issued on September 2, 1777 to Capt. John Gray, 1st Lt. William Heath, 2nd Lt. Henry Selby, and Ensign William Hancock (son of William) in the Severn Battalion. Commissions issued on September 3, 1777 to Dr. Ephraim Howard as Surgeon in Col. Thomas Dorsey's Battalion, and to Walter Warfield as Mate to Dr. Ephraim Howard. Commission issued on September 6, 1777 to Capt. Thomas Watkins in the South River Battalion. Commission issued on October 3, 1777 to Ensign Robert Hudson of Capt. Hammond's Company in the Elk Ridge Battalion. Commissions issued on October 6, 1777 to: Capt. Nicholas Maccubbin, 1st Lt. John Brice, 2nd Lt. Samuel Harvey Howard, 3rd Lt. John Davidson, Capt. Benjamin Harwood, 1st Lt. Charles Wallace Howard,

2nd Lt. Gilbert Middleton, 3rd Lt. John Callahan, all of Independent Companies of Militia in Annapolis. Commissions issued on March 2, 1778 in the Severn Battalion to Col. Elijah Robosson, Lt. Col. James Tootel, Major Joseph Merrikin; Capt. Joseph Maccubbin, 1st Lt. Francis Cromwell, 2nd Lt. Caleb Hazle, Ensign Richard Robosson; Capt. Philemon Warfield, 1st Lt. Lancelot Warfield; 2nd Lt. Thomas Warfield; Ensign Joseph Warfield; Capt. Vachel Gaither, 1st Lt. Abraham Anderson; 2nd Lt. Stephen Bassford; Ensign Thomas Fowler Bassford; Capt. John Boone, Ensign Benjamin Fish; Capt. Caleb Owings, 1st Lt. Richard Cromwell; 2nd Lt. Joshua Merrikin, Ensign George Hammond; Capt. Charles Boone, 1st Lt. Stephen Boone, 2nd Lt. Nicholas Shepherd, Ensign William Bishop; Capt. Nicholas Worthington, 1st Lt. Henry Bateman, Jr., 2nd Lt. John Sears, Ensign Caleb Burgess. Commissions issued in the Elk Ridge Battalion to Col. Thomas Dorsey, Lt. Col. John Dorsey, Major Edward Gaither; Capt. Andrew Ellicott, 1st Lt. Joseph Evans; Capt. John Burgess; Capt. John Worthington Dorsey, 1st Lt. Thomas Ricketts, 2nd Lt. John Norwood, Ensign John Shipley; Capt. Richard Stringer, 1st Lt. William Spurrier; Capt. Benjamin Warfield, 1st Lt. Henry Ayton, 2nd Lt. Robert Warfield, Ensign Charles Warfield; Capt. John Dorsey, 1st Lt. Nathaniel Owings, 2nd Lt. Samuel Brown. Commissions issued in the West River Battalion to Col. John Weems, Lt. Col. Richard Harwood, Major William Brogden; Capt. Thomas Watkins, 1st Lt. Samuel Brogden, 2nd Lt. John Ijams, Jr., Ensign William Davis; 1st Lt. Thomas Noble Stockett, 2nd Lt. Samuel Watkins and Ensign William Harwood in Capt. Thomas Watkins' Company; Capt. Abraham Simmons, 1st Lt. Thomas Tongue, 2nd Lt. Thomas Morton, Jr., Ensign Abel Hill; Capt. Richard Weems, 1st Lt. Gideon Dare, 2nd Lt. Benjamin Harrison, Ensign John Chew; Capt. Richard Chew, 1st Lt. William Chew, 2nd Lt. Samuel Chew, Ensign Richard Harrison; Capt. John Deale, 1st Lt. Benjamin Norman, 2nd Lt. William Crandal, Ensign Roger Phipps; Capt. William Simmons, 1st Lt. Aaron Welsh, 2nd Lt. Robert Welsh, Ensign Charles Drury (Ref: V-77, V-83, V-286, V-343, V-347, V-351, V-359, V-364, V-387, V-525, V-526, C-199, C-200, C-201, C-202, C-203). Commissions issued in the West River Battalion on March 17, 1781 to Capt. Samuel Watkins, 1st Lt. Robert Pain Davis, 2nd Lt. Robert Smith, and Ensign Aaron Rawlings, and on April 21, 1781 to Major Richard Chew. Commissions issued in the Severn Battalion on April 23, 1781 to 1st Lt. Benjamin Talbot, 2nd Lt. Thomas Orrick and Ensign John Linthicum of Capt. Vachel Gaither's Company; Capt. Samuel Jacob; 1st Lt. Benjamin Fish, 2nd Lt. Zachariah Jacob, Ensign Charles Pecker in Capt. Charles Boone's Company; and Ensign Nathan Moss in Capt. John Gray's Company. Commissions issued in the West River Battalion on May 2, 1781 to 1st Lt. Robert Smith, 2nd Lt. Aaron Rawlings, Ensign Robert Steward in Capt. Samuel Warfield's Company; Capt. Benjamin Harrison, 1st Lt. John Chew, 2nd Lt. Nathaniel Chew, Ensign Ferdinando Battee; Capt. Samuel Chew, 1st Lt. Richard Harrison of Richard, 2nd Lt. John Birkhead, Ensign Gilbert Hamilton Smith; Capt. Aaron Welsh, 1st Lt. Charles Drury, 2nd Lt. Robert Welsh, Ensign Jonathan Brashears. Commissions issued on July 30, 1781 in the Severn Battalion to Capt. George (Charles?) Pecker, 1st Lt. Stephen Boone, 2nd Lt. George Sank, and Ensign Robert Moss (Ref: W-354, W-409, W-411, W-422, W-423, W-527).

MILLAR, JAMES. Born in England. He was enlisted by Edward Edgerly in Anne Arundel County on April 8, 1778 (Ref: C-216, H-314).

MILLARD, THOMAS. Enrolled by Henry Ridgely, Jr. and passed by Col. Josias C. Hall on August 26, 1776 (Ref: H-41).

MILLER, ADAM. Took the Oath of Allegiance before Hon. Nicholas Worthington in March, 1778 (Ref: B-27).

MILLER, BENJAMIN. Enlisted by Thomas Mayo on July 20, 1776 (Ref: H-41).

MILLER, JOHN. Took the Oath of Allegiance before Hon. Nicholas Worthington in March, 1778 (Ref: B-27). A marriage proven through Maryland Revolutionary Pension Records is a John Miller to Mary Anne Welch on December 4, 1790, in Anne Arundel County (Ref: G-119).

MILLER, WILLIAM. Disabled soldier of the 3rd Maryland Regiment paid in Anne Arundel County on April 12, 1784, June 9, 1784, Sep. 3, 1784, Oct. 26, 1784 and Dec. 17, 1784 (Ref: D-13, D-18, D-21, D-23, D-25). He was "judged unfit by the doctors" and subsequently discharged on June 21, 1777 (Ref: X-27).

MILLS, CORNELIUS. Third Lieutenant in Capt. Gilbert Middleton's Independent Company of Militia of Annapolis on March 20, 1779 (Ref: I-144, O-325). He was also paid for his recruiting services in 1778 (Ref: V-467, 485, 557).

MILLS, FREDERICK. Took the Oath of Allegiance before Hon. Samuel Harrison in March, 1778 (Ref: A-244). On April 20, 1803, the final distribution of his estate was made by Mrs. Ann Mills, administratrix, with fourths to Achsah Mills, Ann Mills, Elizabeth Mills, and Frederick Mills (Ref: U-18).

MILLS, THOMAS. Took the Oath of Allegiance before Hon. Reuben Meriweather on March 2, 1778 (Ref: B-24).

MILLS, ZACHARIAH. On February 12, 1820, the Treasurer was directed to "pay to Zachariah Mills, of Anne Arundel County, an old revolutionary soldier, quarterly, for life, the half pay of a private, as a further remuneration for those services rendered his country during her arduous struggle for independence." (Ref: K-375). Pensioned on September 21, 1818, at age 64, as a Private in the Maryland Line, he died in September, 1823 (Ref: Z-27).

MINITREE, GIFFORD. Recruited and passed by James Brice in 1777 (Ref: H-313).

MITCHEL, HURIAH. Took the Oath of Allegiance before Hon. Nicholas Worthington in March, 1778 (Ref: B-27).

MITCHELL, PATRICK. Took the Oath of Allegiance before Hon. Reuben Meriweather on March 2, 1778 (Ref: B-25).

MITCHELL, ROBERT. Private in Capt. Richard Dorsey's Company of Artillery, and noted as being "in gaol for house breaking" on the muster rolls of November 17, 1777 (Ref: H-547).

MOBBERLY, REZIN. Took the Oath of Allegiance before Hon. Thomas Worthington on February 28, 1778 (Ref: B-21).

MOBBERLY, THOMAS. Took the Oath of Allegiance before Hon. Thomas Worthington on February 28, 1778 (Ref: B-21).

MOFFITT, THOMAS. He was a Substitute, furnished to Col. Adams in 1780, to serve to December 10, 1780, and subsequently served in the Continental Army in 1781 (Ref: H-370, H-410).

MOLONY, JOHN. Enrolled by Henry Ridgely, Jr. and passed by Col. Josias C. Hall on August 26, 1776 (Ref: H-41).

MONKS, MICHAEL. Born in Scotland. He was a Substitute, furnished by Denton Hammond on May 14, 1778, to serve to war's duration (Ref: C-213, H-319).

MOODY, LEVY. Recruited by Col. Adams in 1780 for 3 year term (Ref: H-369).

MOORE, JOHN. Private in the 7th Maryland Line. He was wounded (no details) and transferred to the Invalids Corps on July 17, 1778, and subsequently discharged at Philadelphia on April 23, 1784 (Ref: X-28).

MOORE, JOHN. Corporal in the Maryland Line. Wounded in the right shoulder at Camden on August 16, 1780, and wounded in the hip at the battle of Guilford on March 15, 1781. Discharged on December 19, 1782 (Ref: X-29).

MOORE, PETER. Born in Scotland. He was a Substitute, furnished by Benjamin Towbairn on May 6, 1778, to serve for three years (Ref: C-205, H-317).

MOORE, SILVANUS. One of the petitioners to the Maryland Convention to form an independent rifle company in July, 1776 (Ref: B-28).

MOREE, JAMES. Private in Captain John Fulford's Company of Artillery at Annapolis on December 12, 1776 (Ref: H-572).

MOREE, ROBERT. Private in Captain John Fulford's Company of Artillery at Annapolis on December 12, 1776 (Ref: H-572).

MORELAND, RICHARD. Took the Oath of Allegiance before Hon. Elijah Robosson in March, 1778 (Ref: B-28, V-532).

MOREWARD (MORIWARD), JOHN. Took the Oath of Allegiance before Hon. Reuben Meriweather on March 2, 1778 (Ref: B-24).

MORFITT, GEORGE. Enrolled by Henry Ridgely, Jr. and passed by Col. Josias C. Hall on August 26, 1776 (Ref: H-41).

MORGAN, JOHN. Born in Maryland. Enrolled by Samuel Chew on July 25, 1776. Height: 5' 4" (Ref: H-40).

MORGAN, PATRICK. Took the Oath of Allegiance before Hon. Elijah Robosson in March, 1778 (Ref: B-28).

MORLEY, JOSEPH. Took the Oath of Allegiance before Hon. Reuben Meriweather on March 2, 1778 (Ref: B-24).

MORRISON, GEORGE. Resident of Herring Creek who was among those to petition for a militia company on March 6, 1776, and subsequently served in Captain Richard Weems' Company (Ref: I-143, MS.1814).

MORTEZ, DAVID. Captain of the Sloop "Jervis Powlonex" on April 14, 1777, and granted permission by the Council of Maryland to proceed from the port of Annapolis to the Island of Coracoa (Ref: V-210).

MORTON, THOMAS JR. 2nd Lieutenant in Captain Abraham Simmons' Company in the South River Battalion on February 15, 1776, and the West River Battalion in 1778 (Ref: C-199, F-223, N-161). Thomas took the Oath of Allegiance before Hon. Samuel Harrison in March, 1778 (Ref: A-244).

MOSS, NATHAN. Drafted in 1780 to serve to December 10, 1780 (Ref: H-369). On June 13, 1788 the final distribution of his estate was made to Delilah Moss (widow's third) with fourths of the remaining balance to Rachel Moss, Sarah Moss, Willoby Moss, and Richard Moss (Ref: U-1, U-2). Commissioned Ensign in Capt. John Gray's Company on April 23, 1781 (Ref: W-411).

MOSS, RICHARD. Drafted in 1780 to serve to December 10, 1780 (Ref: H-369). On June 16, 1808 the final distribution of his estate was made (thirds) to John Crane, Sarah Moss, and Reuben Crane (Ref: U-35).

MOSS, ROBERT. Commissioned Ensign in Capt. Pecker's Company in the Severn Battalion on July 30, 1781 (Ref: W-527).

MOSS, THOMAS. Enlisted by Thomas Mayo on July 20, 1776 (Ref: H-41). He was probably a son of Samuel Skidmore Moss who died in 1792 (Ref: U-8).

MOXLEY, NEHEMIAH (February 17, 1737 - February 18, 1836). Married Elizabeth Norwood in 1760, and three of their sons were William, Jacob, and Ezekiel Moxley (1772-1847, married Catherine Forney in 1792, and their descendants moved to Kentucky and Ohio in the early 1800s. Ref: HCP-106). Nehemiah was one of the zealous patriots in 1775 who helped burn the vessel "Peggy Stewart" in Annapolis over a tea tax protest (Ref: E-1749, E-2878A). Took the Oath of Allegiance before Hon. Thomas Worthington in 1778 (Ref: B-21).

MOYSTON, EDWARD. Enrolled by Henry Ridgely, Jr. and passed by Col. Josias C. Hall on August 26, 1776 (Ref: H-41).

MUIR, ADAM. Appointed Naval Officer of the Sixth District in the room of Mr. Campbell, deceased (Ref: V-317).

MUIR, JOHN. Active in military affairs in 1777, and appointed Purchaser of Clothing in the room of Samuel Harvey Howard who refused on June 16, 1781. (Ref: V-401, W-476). On October 3, 1781, John Muir of Annapolis was given passport to navigate the "Swallow" with its cargo of salt (Ref: W-631).

MULLIKEN (MULLIKIN), BELT. He took the Oath of Allegiance before Hon. Thomas Worthington on February 28, 1778 (Ref: B-21). On April 7, 1804, the final distribution of his estate was made to Mary Mulliken (widow's third), with tenths of estate to Benjamin Hall Mulliken, Martha Waters, Sophia Duckett, Margaret Mulliken, Richard D. Mulliken, Ann D. Mulliken, Basil D. Mulliken, Kitty D. Mulliken, Rignal Mulliken, and Barruch Mulliken (Ref: U-27).

MULLIKEN (MULLIKIN), JEREMIAH. He took Oath of Allegiance before Hon. Thomas Worthington on February 28, 1778 (Ref: B-21).

MULLIKEN (MULLIKIN), THOMAS (1741-1805). Married Elizabeth Williams in 1761 and had a daughter, Mary Mullikin Tydings (Ref: T-537). He was a Captain in the Severn Battalion by February 22, 1776 (Ref: N-178). He took the Oath of Allegiance before Hon. Nicholas Worthington in March, 1778 (Ref: B-27).

MUNDUS, MACHAEL. Recruited by Capt. Alexander Truman in October, 1780, for a three year term (Ref: H-369).

MUNRO, DANIEL. On February 13, 1778 he was issued three pairs of shoes for having enlisted three men for the 1st Maryland Regiment (Ref: V-487).

MURPHEY, MICHAEL. Took the Oath of Allegiance before Hon. Thomas Worthington on February 28, 1778 (Ref: B-21).

MURPHY, ANTHONY. Private in Captain John Fulford's Company of Artillery at Annapolis on December 12, 1776 (Ref: H-572).

MURPHY, JOHN. Born in Scotland. He was a Substitute, furnished by Edward Hall (of Henry) and Thomas Henry Hall on May 10, 1778, to serve for three years or the duration of the war (Ref: C-210, H-318).

MURPHY, TIMOTHY. Private in Captain Richard Dorsey's Company of Artillery on the rolls of November 17, 1777 (Ref: H-574).

MURRAY, JAMES (1739-1819). One of the Association of Freemen of Maryland in 1775 and served on a committee for the establishment of a firearms factory. Since he was a physician he became Colonel in medical service in 1776 and was a chief reliance of the Governor and Council of Maryland throughout the war. In 1780 he was physician to the State Dispensary and all the military recommendations for medical discharge from the service went to him. He was Commissioner of Stores, and inoculated the men for smallpox in

1780-1781. On June 19, 1781 he sustained a fractured ankle and resigned from service, but was soon reinstated and served until war's end. He served in the State Hospitals in various capacities and was appointed Surgeon Examiner for the Medical Board on January 25, 1781. After the war he continued his practice in Annapolis and was a founder of the Medico-Chirurgical Faculty of the State of Maryland (Ref: Y-304 and Archives of Maryland, Vols. 63 and 65).

MURRAY, DANIEL. Private in Captain William Marbury's Company of Artillery in 1777 (Ref: H-575).

MURRAY, WILLIAM (1751, Chestertown, Maryland - 1820). Brother of Dr. James Murray of Annapolis. He was also a physician and served in the Annapolis Hospital. He was a founder of the Medico-Chirurgical Faculty of the State of Maryland (Ref: Y-304; Archives of Maryland, Vols. 63 and 65). Took the Oath of Allegiance before Hon. Elijah Robosson in March, 1778 (Ref: B-28).

MUSLER, ADAM. Recruited by John Sears in 1780 for 3 year term (Ref: H-369).

MYERS, JACOB. Born in Ireland. He was a Substitute, furnished by William Worden on April 16, 1778, to serve for three years (Ref: C-204, H-317).

MYHAN, DENNISS. Private in Captain John Fulford's Company of Artillery at Annapolis on December 12, 1776 (Ref: H-572).

NABB, JOSEPH. Fifer in the 1st Maryland Line, 1780-1783 (Ref: H-433, H-549. Note: He may have been from the Eastern Shore. There is a Nabb's Creek in northern Anne Arundel County, so he could have been there at this time).

NEAL (NEALE), THOMAS. "Thomas Neal" took the Oath of Allegiance before Hon. Samuel Harrison, Jr. in March, 1778 (Ref: B-28). "Thomas Neale" was one of those who formed a militia company on March 6, 1776 at Herring Creek, and subsequently served in Capt. Richard Weems' Company (Ref: I-143, MS.1814).

NEALE, JOHN. Born in Ireland. Recruited by Cornelius Mills and passed by James Brice on April 11, 1778 (Ref: C-216, H-314).

NEARY, JOHN. Recruited and passed by James Brice in 1777 (Ref: H-313).

NEAVE, JOHN. Took the Oath of Allegiance before Hon. Richard Harwood, Jr. on March 1, 1778 (Ref: B-23).

NEIL, THOMAS. Born in Scotland. He was a Substitute, furnished by Stephen Stewart and Benjamin Harrison on May 8, 1778, to serve a three year term. (Ref: C-206, H-317).

NELSON, THOMAS. Private in Capt. Richard Dorsey's Company of Artillery, and on the rolls of November 17, 1777 (Ref: H-574).

NEWMAN, FREEMAN. Private in Capt. Richard Dorsey's Company of Artillery, and on the rolls of November 17, 1777 (Ref: H-574).

NEWTON, JOHN. Recruited by Capt. Alexander Truman in October, 1780, to serve for three years in the Army. (Ref: H-369. Note: Also see John Nuton, q.v.) On February 7, 1818, the Treasurer was directed to pay "to John Newton, an old soldier, during life, quarterly, the half pay of a private, for his service during the Revolutionary War" (Ref: K-378). His pension application (S35536) was filed in Hardin County, Kentucky. He enlisted in Anne Arundel County in October, 1776, serving under Capt. John Smith in the 2nd Maryland Line for 6 years and 9 months. In 1819 he was 63 years old (Ref: L-45).

NICHOLS, EASY. He was a Substitute, furnished by John Deale on June 10, 1778 to serve for three years (Ref: C-208, H-320).

NICHOLS, WILLIAM. Enrolled by Capt. James Disney, Jr. and passed by Colonel Richard Harwood on July 13, 1776 (Ref: H-41). Private in the artillery company of Capt. John Fulford stationed at Annapolis on December 12, 1776 (Ref: H-572).

NICHOLSON, BENJAMIN JR. Took Oath of Allegiance before Hon. Richard Harwood, Jr. on March 1, 1778 (Ref: B-23).

NICHOLSON, FRANCIS. Took the Oath of Allegiance before Hon. Richard Harwood, Jr. on March 1, 1778 (Ref: B-23).

NICHOLSON, HENRY. Born in America. Recruited and passed by James Brice on April 12, 1778 (Ref: C-216, H-314).

NICHOLSON, JOHN JR. Took the Oath of Allegiance before Hon. Richard Harwood, Jr. on March 1, 1778 (Ref: B-23).

NICHOLSON, JOHN SR. Took the Oath of Allegiance before Hon. Richard Harwood, Jr. on March 1, 1778 (Ref: B-23). On January 7, 1818 the final distribution of his estate was made by John Nicholson, Jr., executor, to Mary Nicholson (widow's third), with fourths of the remaining balance to John Nicholson, Nicholas Nicholson, Joseph Nicholson and James Nicholson (Ref: U-51).

NICHOLSON, STEPHEN. Born in Scotland, he was a Substitute, furnished by John Brogden and John Plummer on April 24, 1778, to serve for three years (Ref: C-207, H-318). Took the Oath of Allegiance before Hon, Richard Harwood, Jr. on March 1, 1778 (Ref: B-23). Stephen Nicholson also enrolled October 21, 1776 under Capt. Thomas Watkins to serve the State (Ref: I-144, MS.1814).

NICHOLSON (NICHOLASON), WILLIAM. Enrolled by Capt. James Disney, Jr. and passed by Col. Richard Harwood on July 13, 1776 (Ref: H-41).

NOCK, THOMAS (of Baltimore County). Took the Oath of Allegiance before Hon. Reuben Meriweather on March 2, 1778 (Ref: B-25).

NORMAN, BENJAMIN. First Lieutenant in Capt. John Deale's Company in the West River Battalion in 1778 (Ref: C-200). He took the Oath of Allegiance before Hon. Thomas Harwood on February 28, 1778 (Ref: B-22).

NORMAN, JOHN. Took Oath of Allegiance before Hon. Thomas Harwood on February 28, 1778 (Ref: B-22).

NORMAN, JOSEPH (c1765 - c1815). A resident of West River, he married first to Ruth Randal in 1791 and second to Mary Wayson in 1811. His children were Rispah Randal Norman Welsh, Jane Norman Evans, and Ann Norman Lamb. Joseph was a Private in the 5th Maryland Line in 1782 (Ref: T-546, H-427).

NORMAN, NICHOLAS. Took the Oath of Allegiance before Hon. Thomas Harwood on February 28, 1778 (Ref: B-22).

NORMAN, THOMAS. Took the Oath of Allegiance before Hon. Thomas Harwood on February 28, 1778 (Ref: B-22).

NORRIS (NORRISS), JOHN. Took Oath of Allegiance before Hon. Thomas Harwood on February 28, 1778 (Ref: B-22).

NORRIS, RICHARD. Took the Oath of Allegiance before Hon. Samuel Harrison in March, 1778 (Ref: A-244).

NORRIS, THOMAS. Took the Oath of Allegiance before Hon. Samuel Harrison on March 2, 1778 (Ref: B-24).

NORRIS, ZACHARIAH. Private in Capt. Gilbert Middleton's Independent Company of Militia of Annapolis on March 20, 1779 (Ref: I-144, O-325).

NORTH, THOMAS. Enrolled by Capt. Thomas Watkins on October 21, 1776 to serve the State (Ref: I-144, MS.1814). He took the Oath of Allegiance before Hon. John Dorsey on March 12, 1778 (Ref: B-26).

NORTHEY, BENJAMIN. Took Oath of Allegiance before Hon. John Dorsey on March 12, 1778 (Ref: B-26).

NORTON, DAVID. Took the Oath of Allegiance before Hon. Reuben Meriweather on March 2, 1778 (Ref: B-25).

NORWOOD, EDWARD (1750, England - December 16, 1816, Anne Arundel County). He married Sarah Odell of Prince George's County and a daughter, Mary Norwood, married Thomas H. Wright of Baltimore. Edward was commissioned a Captain on February 7, 1776 in the Anne Arundel County Militia, and by 1777 was in the Fourth Maryland Line under Gen. William Smallwood. He served on the Committee of Observation in 1775 (Ref: E-94, F-222, H-38, N-139, O-534).

NORWOOD, JEREMIAH. Took Oath of Allegiance before Hon. John Dorsey on March 12, 1778 (Ref: B-26).

NORWOOD, JOHN. Second Lieutenant in Capt. Brice Howard's Company in 1776 and Captain John Worthington Dorsey's Company in Elk Ridge Battalion of Militia in 1778 (Ref: C-201, F-223). Took the Oath of Allegiance before Hon. Reuben Meriweather on March 2, 1778 (Ref: B-25).

NOWELL, RICHARD. Took the Oath of Allegiance before Hon. Samuel Harrison, Jr. in March, 1778 (Ref: B-28).

NOWELL, WILLIAM. Born in Maryland. Enrolled by Samuel Chew on July 25, 1776. Height: 5' 10 1/2" (Ref: H-40).

NOWRY, ANTHONY. Recruited by Col. J. H. Stone and passed by James Brice on November 18, 1778 (Ref: C-217, H-314).

NUTLEY, HENRY. Took the Oath of Allegiance before Hon. John Dorsey on March 12, 1778 (Ref: B-26).

NUTON, JOHN. Enlisted by Joseph Burgess for the Flying Camp on July 20, 1776 (Ref: H-40). He took the Oath of Allegiance before Hon. Elijah Robosson in March, 1778 (Ref: B-28. Note: Also refer to John Newton, q.v.).

O'BRIAN, PHILLIP. Private in Capt. John Fulford's Company of Artillery at Annapolis on December 12, 1776 (Ref: H-572).

O'CONNER, MICHAEL. Enlisted by John Worthington Dorsey and passed by John Dorsey on July 22, 1776 (Ref: H-39).

O'CONNER, PATRICK. Took the Oath of Allegiance before Hon. Elijah Robosson in March, 1778 (Ref: B-28).

ODLE, RICHARD. Took the Oath of Allegiance before Hon. Samuel Lane on March 1, 1778 (Ref: Original list in Maryland State Papers, Red Book 21. Note: His name is mistakenly omitted from the published list in Reference B-23).

O'DONALY, CORNIALUS. Enrolled by Capt. Thomas Watkins on October 21, 1776 to serve the State (Ref: I-144, MS.1814).

O'D----L, R-----. Private in Capt. Richard Dorsey's Company of Artillery on November 17, 1777 (Ref: H-574, which notes that some parts are torn off).

OGDEN, JAMES. Took the Oath of Allegiance before Hon. John Dorsey on March 12, 1778 (Ref: B-26).

OGLE, BENJAMIN (January 27, 1748/9 - July 7, 1809). Son of Samuel Ogle and Anne Tasker. Married Henrietta Margaret Hill in 1770 and had 4 children: Samuel Ogle, Benjamin Ogle, Ann Ogle Tayloe, and Mary Ogle Bevans Conner. Benjamin Ogle was a prominent Marylander and held many offices, including: Upper House, 1773 to 1776; Council, 1773 to 1776; Executive Council, 1783; Governor, 1798-1801; Maryland State Elector, 1806. During the Revolution he was Third Lieutenant in Capt. Samuel Harvey Howard's Independent

Company of Militia of Annapolis, commissioned on June 18, 1781 (Ref: P-618).

OGLE, JOHN. Took the Oath of Allegiance before Hon. Samuel Lane on March 1, 1778 (Ref: B-23).

O'HARA, JAMES. On August 5, 1777 the Council of Maryland ordered that "James O'Harra who enlisted in Capt. Ramsay's Company of Smallwood's Battalion, having since from sickness, become blind and incapable of service, is therefore discharged. That James O'Harra draw rations while he continues in Annapolis and until further directions." (Ref: V-325). He was paid in Anne Arundel County on May 19, 1783, August 16, 1783, December 11, 1783, January 13, 1784, April 13, 1784, and June 9, 1784 (Ref: D-6, 8, 10, 11, 13, 18).

O'HARA (O'HARIO), DENNIS. Enlisted by John Worthington Dorsey and passed by John Dorsey on July 22, 1776 (Ref: H-39).

OLDNEY, JOHN. Took the Oath of Allegiance before Hon. John Dorsey on March 12, 1778 (Ref: B-26).

O'NEAL, DANIEL. Born in New England. Last resided in Annapolis, Maryland. Enlisted July 26, 1782 to serve on the Barge "Fearnought" under Capt. Levin Spedden. Height: 5' 10". Dark complexion. (Ref: H-612).

ONION, CHARLES. Took the Oath of Allegiance before Hon. Thomas Worthington on February 28, 1778 (Ref: B-21). Charles Onion was drafted in October, 1780, to serve until December 10, 1780 (Ref: H-369).

ONION, JOHN. Enrolled by Capt. Thomas Watkins on October 21, 1776, to serve the State (Ref: I-144, MS.1814). He took the Oath of Allegiance before Hon. John Dorsey on March 12, 1778 (Ref: B-26). John Onion married in 1787 to Julia Pendergast (widow) in Anne Arundel County (Ref: G-120).

O'QUIN, RICHARD. Disabled soldier in the German Regiment who was wounded in the leg at the battle of White Plains in 1776. He was not discharged until August 10, 1782. His papers were signed by George Washington (Ref: X-30). Richard was paid in Anne Arundel County on December 11, 1783 (Ref: D-10).

ORBER, JOHN. Private in Capt. John Fulford's Company of Artillery stationed at Annapolis on December 12, 1776 (Ref: H-572).

ORME, MOSES. On March 8, 1833, the Treasurer was directed to "pay to Moses Orme, of Anne Arundel County, a soldier of the Revolutionary War, during life, quarterly, half pay of a private, in consideration of the services rendered by him during said war" (Ref: K-379).

ORRICK, THOMAS. Took the Oath of Allegiance before Hon. Nicholas Worthington in March, 1778 (Ref: B-27). Commissioned a 2nd

Lieutenant in Capt. Vachel Gaither's Company in the Severn Battalion on April 23, 1781 (Ref: V-411).

OSBAND, SAMUEL. Took the Oath of Allegiance before Hon. Samuel Harrison, Jr. in March, 1778 (Ref: B-28).

OWENS, HENRY. Son of James Owens and Eliza -----. Henry took the Oath of Allegiance before Hon. Samuel Lane on March 1, 1778 (Ref: B-23).

OWENS, ISAAC (May 9, 1729 - September 21, 1805). Married Priscilla ----- in 1756 and had 13 children: Elizabeth Owens Owens, Ann Owens Childs, Charles Owens, Priscilla Owens Welch, Benjamin Owens, Margaret Owens Lowry, Isaac Owens, Thomas Owens, John Owens, Artridge Owens, William Owens, Nicholas Owens, and Joseph Owens (Ref: T-554). He was a Private in the Militia and took the Oath of Allegiance before Hon. Samuel Lane on March 1, 1778 (Ref: B-23, T-554). On June 10, 1807 the final distribution of his estate was made by Thomas Owens, his executor, with legacies to the children of Ann Childs, and Priscilla Welch, and the children of Margaret Lowrey, and the fourths of the remaining balance to Betsy Childs, Thomas Owens, William Owens, and Nicholas Owens (Ref: U-32).

OWENS, JAMES (c1722 - 1786). Married twice: first to Eliza ----- in 1743 and had eight children: Sarah Owens Gardiner, Edward Owens, Jane Owens Owens, James Owens, Henry Owens, Elizabeth Owens, Ann Owens McDaniel, and Mary Owens Shepherd. Married second to Ann Pritchard in 1771 and had five more children: Benjamin Owens, Archibald Owens, Elizabeth Owens Beall, Martha Owens, and William Owens (Ref: T-554). James took the Oath of Allegiance before Hon. Samuel Lane on March 1, 1778 (Ref: B-23).

OWENS, JAMES JR. Son of James Owens and Eliza -----. He took the Oath of Allegiance before Hon. Samuel Lane on March 1, 1778 (Ref: B-23).

OWENS, JAMES SR. (1748-1797). Married Elizabeth Owens circa 1771 and had 4 children: Nicholas Owens, James Owens, Priscilla Owens Woodward, and Mary Owens Shepherd. Private in Maryland Line, 1780-1783 (Ref: T-555, E-21).

OWENS, JOHN. Took Oath of Allegiance before Hon. Thomas Harwood on February 28, 1778 (Ref: B-22).

OWENS, JOSEPH. Two men by this name took the Oath of Allegiance on March 1, 1778: one before Hon. Samuel Lane, and one before Hon. Nicholas Worthington (Ref: B-23, B-27).

OWINGS FAMILY. The Owings family held land and resided in both Anne Arundel County and Baltimore County. For information on those not included in this book, see Henry C. Peden, Jr.'s "Revolutionary Patriots of Baltimore Town and Baltimore County, 1775-1783" (Westminster: Family Line Publications).

OWINGS, CALEB. Captain in the Severn Battalion of Militia under Col. Nicholas Worthington on June 19, 1777, and under Colonel Elijah Robosson on March 1, 1778 and August 15, 1778 (Ref: A-176, C-202, I-144, J-113, O-208). Took the Oath of Allegiance before Hon. John Dorsey on March 12, 1778 (Ref: B-26).

OWINGS, HENRY. Took the Oath of Allegiance before Hon. Reuben Meriweather on March 2, 1778 (Ref: B-24).

OWINGS, NATHANIEL. Ensign in Capt. Elisha Riggs' Company in March, 1776, and First Lieutenant in Capt. John Dorsey's Company in the Elk Ridge Battalion of Militia in 1778 (Ref: C-201, O-299). He took the Oath of Allegiance on March 12, 1778 before Hon. John Dorsey (Ref: B-26).

PACA, WILLIAM (October 31, 1740, Baltimore, now Harford, County - October 13, 1799, Queen Anne's County). Son of John Paca and Elizabeth Smith. Married first to Ann Mary Chew and had three children: Henrietta Maria Paca, John Philemon Paca, and William Paca. He also had a natural daughter, Hester, in Philadelphia in 1775. In 1777 he married to Ann Harrison, who died in 1780. William Paca represented Annapolis and Anne Arundel County at the Maryland Convention in 1774, 1775 and 1776. He held many offices, including: Lower House of Anne Arundel County, 1768-1774; Senate, Western Shore, 1776-1777; Senate, Eastern Shore, 1778-1780; Lower House of Queen Anne's County, 1786 to 1791; Council of Safety, 1775; Judge of the General Court, 1778; Special Council for the State, 1780; Commissioner of Confiscated British Property, 1781; and, Governor of Maryland, 1782-1785 (Ref: A-77, J-4, P-633, P-634).

PAGE, JOHN. Born in Scotland. He was a Substitute, furnished by Ely Dorsey, Jr. on April 21, 1778, to serve to the war's duration (Ref: C-211, H-318).

PAGE, RICHARD. Enlisted by Edward Spurrier and passed by Thomas Dorsey on July 20, 1776 (Ref: H-41).

PAINTER, CHARLES. Took Oath of Allegiance before Hon. Nicholas Worthington in March, 1778 (Ref: Original list in Maryland State Papers, Red Book 21. Note: His name is mistakenly spelled "Charles Printor" in Source B-28).

PAINTER, DANIEL. Took the Oath of Allegiance before Hon. John Dorsey on March 12, 1778 (Ref: B-26).

PALMORNE, BENJAMIN. Enrolled by Capt. Thomas Watkins on October 21, 1776 for service to the State (Ref: I-144, MS.1814).

PALMOUR, WILLIAM. He was a Substitute delivered to Colonel Adams in October, 1780, to serve until December 10, 1780 (Ref: H-369).

PANACLIFT, JOHN. Born in Scotland. He was a Substitute, furnished by Thomas Snowden on May 9, 1778, to serve to war's duration (Ref: C-207, H-318).

PARKER, GEORGE. Enrolled by Captain Edward Tillard on July 10, 1776. Height: 5' 7 1/2" (Ref: H-39).

PARKER, GERRARD. Born in Scotland. He was a Substitute, furnished by Benjamin Warfield on May 19, 1778, to serve to war's duration (Ref: C-207, H-318).

PARKER, JONATHAN. Private in Capt. Gilbert Middleton's Independent Company of Militia of Annapolis on March 20, 1779 (Ref: I-144, O-325).

PARKER, JOSIAH. Took the Oath of Allegiance before Hon. Samuel Lane on March 1, 1778 (Ref: B-23).

PARKER, ROBERT. Private in Capt. William Marbury's Company of Artillery in 1777 (Ref: H-575).

PARROTT (PARRIT), THOMAS. He took the Oath of Allegiance before Hon. Samuel Harrison in March, 1778 (Ref: A-244). On February 13, 1827, the final distribution of the estate of Thomas Parrott was made by his administrator, John Wood, to Mary Parrott (widow's third), with sixths to Thomas Parrott, Knighton Parrott, John Parrott, the heirs of Walter Carr, John Stallings (by right of his unnamed wife), and children of John A. Riely (Ref: U-72).

PARROTT (PARRETT, PARRATT), WILLIAM. Enrolled by Edward Tillard on July 10, 1776. Height: 5' 6" (Ref: H-39).

PARSLEY (PAISLEY?), THOMAS. Took the Oath of Allegiance before Hon. Nicholas Worthington in March, 1778 (Ref: Original list in Maryland State Papers Red Book 21, p. 8D. Note: This name is mistakenly omitted from Source B-28).

PARSON, JOHN. Took Oath of Allegiance before Hon. Samuel Harrison in March, 1778 (Ref: A-244).

PARSONS, JOHN. On March 13, 1777 he petitioned the Council of Maryland, stating he was wrongfully imprisoned, he was not an enemy of this country, and that he would take the Oath of Allegiance (Ref: V-171, 172). Took Oath of Allegiance before Hon. Thomas Harwood on February 28, 1778 (Ref: B-22).

PARSONS, WILLIAM. Recruited by James Brice on January 12, 1778 (Ref: H-313).

PARTRIDGE, SAMUEL. Enlisted by John Worthington Dorsey and passed by John Dorsey on July 22, 1776 (Ref: H-39).

PATTAN, THOMAS. Enrolled by Henry Ridgely, Jr. and passed by Col. Josias C. Hall on August 26, 1776 (Ref: H-41).

PATTERSON, ROBERT. Born in Scotland. He was a Substitute, furnished by John Snowden on May 12, 1778, to serve to war's duration (Ref: C-207, H-318).

PEABODDY, JOHN. Private in Capt. Gilbert Middleton's Independent Company of Militia of Annapolis on March 20, 1779 (Ref: I-144, O-325).

PEAK, NATHAN. Recruited and passed by James Brice in 1777 (Ref: H-313).

PEALE, JAMES. Son of Charles Peale (1709-1750) and Margaret Triggs. James was commissioned an Ensign in Col. Smallwood's Maryland Regiment in July, 1776, and was in the battle of Long Island, and also at Trenton, Princeton, Valley Forge and Monmouth. He was commissioned Captain in the 1st Maryland Regiment on March 27, 1777 and resigned on June 2, 1779. He was a member of the Society of the Cincinnati (Ref: The Albert Charles Peale Genealogical Collection G5043 at the Maryland Historical Society in Baltimore).

PEALE, ST. GEORGE (died 1778). Son of Charles Peale (1709-1750) and Margaret Triggs. His siblings were: Charles Willson Peale; Margaret Jane Peale, who married Col. Nathaniel Ramsey; James Peale; and, Elizabeth Digby Peale, who married Capt. Robert Polk, a privateer who died in battle in late 1777. St. George was a clerk in the Land Office of Maryland prior to the Revolution, becoming Chief Clerk and then the Register of the Land Office on April 21, 1777 (Ref: V-250). On March 6, 1776, he was commissioned 1st Lieutenant in Captain James Brice's Independent Company of Militia of Annapolis. He also served as Commissary of Military Supplies in 1776-1778. He died testate in 1778 (due to exposure) and his will is recorded in Baltimore County (Ref: N-203, and A. C. Peale Genealogical Collection G5043 at Md. Hist. Soc.).

PEARCE, DANIEL. Two men by this name took the Oath of Allegiance: one before Hon. Richard Harwood, Jr. on March 1, 1778, and another before Hon. Reuben Meriweather on March 2, 1778 (Ref: B-23, B-25). One Daniel Pearce was born in Scotland and was a Substitute furnished by Basil Rolf and William Pearce on April 24, 1778 to serve 3 years or war's duration (Ref: C-210, H-318).

PEARCE, JOSEPH. Took the Oath of Allegiance before Hon. Richard Harwood, Jr. on March 1, 1778 (Ref: B-23).

PEARCE, WALTER. Took the Oath of Allegiance before Hon. Reuben Meriweather on March 2, 1778 (Ref: B-24, which questions the legibility of his surname. Note: Part of the original list in Maryland State Papers, Red Book No. 21, at the Maryland State Archives is now missing, including Walter's name).

PEARCE, WILLIAM. Took the Oath of Allegiance before Hon. Richard Harwood, Jr. on March 1, 1778 (Ref: B-23).

PEARSON, JOHN. Private in Capt. Richard Dorsey's Company of Artillery on November 17, 1777 (Ref: H-574).

PEARSON, THOMAS. Corporal in Capt. Richard Dorsey's Company of Artillery on November 17, 1777 (Ref: H-574).

PECKER, CHARLES. Commissioned an Ensign in Capt. Charles Boone's Company in the Severn Battalion on April 23, 1781 (Ref: W-411).

PECKER, GEORGE. Commissioned a Captain in the Severn Battalion of Militia in the room of Charles Boone on July 30, 1781 (Ref: W-527).

PEGEGRAM, WILLIAM. In November, 1811, the Treasurer was directed to "pay to William Pegegram, of Anne Arundel County, an old Revolutionary soldier, the half pay of a common soldier, during his life, as further remuneration for the services rendered his country" (Ref: K-381).

PENN, BENJAMIN (1753, Maryland - May 10, 1827, Jefferson County, Kentucky). He married Rebecca Ryan (1760-1840) in 1774 in Montgomery County, Maryland and had eleven children: Axey Penn Marshall, Ann Penn McCann, Zacheus Penn, Ephraim Penn, Polly Penn Warfield, Charles Penn, Benjamin Penn, Betsy Penn Onann, Noah Penn, Joseph Penn, and Rebecca Penn Shadwick. In May, 1776, he enlisted at Elk Ridge and served in the 1st and 2nd Maryland Regiments (his name might appear as Benjamin Payne in some records), under Captain Joseph Burgess. Source H-41 indicates he was enrolled by Henry Ridgely, Jr. and passed by Col. Josias C. Hall on August 26, 1776. After the war, Benjamin moved to Franklin County, Kentucky and applied for his pension in 1820. He was in Harrison County, Indiana prior to 1825, and transferred to Jefferson County, Kentucky in 1826, where he died in 1827. His widow received pension W8510 in Franklin County, Kentucky in 1836; died in 1840 (Ref: HCP-115).

PENN, EDWARD. Two men with this name took the Oath of Allegiance before Hon. Thomas Worthington on February 28, 1778 (Ref: B-21).

PENN, JACOB. Took the Oath of Allegiance before Hon. Thomas Worthington on February 28, 1778 (Ref: B-21).

PENN, JOSEPH. Took the Oath of Allegiance before Hon. Thomas Dorsey on March 2, 1778 (Ref: B-24). On May 29, 1792, the final distribution of his estate was made to Mary Penn (widow's third), with sixths to Rachel Penn, Mary Penn, Joshua Penn, Sarah Penn, Joseph Penn, and Peggy Penn (Ref: U-8).

PENN, JOSHUA. Took the Oath of Allegiance before Hon. Thomas Worthington on February 28, 1778 (Ref: B-21).

PENN, RICHARD. Took the Oath of Allegiance before Hon. Nicholas Worthington in March, 1778 (Ref: B-27).

PENN, SHADRICK. Took the Oath of Allegiance before Hon. Thomas Worthington on February 28, 1778 (Ref: B-21).

PENNINGTON, CHARLES. Drafted in October, 1780, to serve to December 10, 1780 (Ref: H-369).

PERKINSON, JOHN. Enrolled by Capt. Thomas Watkins on October 21, 1776, for service to the State (Ref: I-144, MS.1814).

PERRY, ROBERT. Took Oath of Allegiance before Hon. Thomas Harwood on February 28, 1778 (Ref: B-22).

PERRY, WILLIAM. Took the Oath of Allegiance before Hon. Thomas Worthington on February 28, 1778 (Ref: B-21).

PHELPS, BASIL (BAZILL). Took the Oath of Allegiance before Hon. Richard Harwood, Jr. on March 1, 1778 (Ref: B-23). Married Barbara Davis in 1791 and had 3 children: Edward Gaither Phelps, Sarah Phelps, and Anne Phelps. Basil died after 1796. (Ref: U-9. Note: Another source states he married Leah Gaither, daughter of Edward (but this may be an earlier Basil Phelps, according to the research notes by genealogist Robert W. Barnes, 1991).

PHELPS, BENJAMIN. Enrolled by Capt. James Disney, Jr. and passed by Colonel Hyde on July 13, 1776 (Ref: H-41). Took the Oath of Allegiance before Hon. Richard Harwood, Jr. on March 1, 1778 (Ref: B-23). One Benjamin Phelps was born in Scotland and became a Substitute, furnished by William Harwood and Nicholas Harwood on April 24, 1778, to serve three years or the duration of the war (Ref: C-210, H-318).

PHELPS, EZEKIEL. Took the Oath of Allegiance before Hon. Richard Harwood, Jr. on March 1, 1778 (Ref: B-23). On December 10, 1825, the final distribution of his estate was made to Margaret Phelps (widow's third), with fourths to Wilson Phelps, Walter Phelps, Mary Scott and Middleton Phelps (Ref: U-69). According to Geneva M. Phelps' "An Annal Begins," Ezekiel married Margaret Watkins and had 4 children: Nelson Phelps, Mary Ann Phelps Scott, Middleton Phelps and Walter Watkins Phelps (per genealogist Robert W. Barnes, 1991).

PHELPS, ISAIAH (ISIAH). He took the Oath of Allegiance before Hon. Nicholas Worthington in March, 1778 (Ref: B-27). Listed in the 1776 Census of All Hallows Parish with one white male, three white females, and three white children (Information contributed by genealogist Robert W. Barnes, 1991).

PHELPS, JOHN. Two men with this name took the Oath of Allegiance before Hon. Nicholas Worthington in March, 1778 (Ref: B-27, B-28). Note: Original list in Maryland State Papers, Red Book 21, p. 8D, shows a third John Phelps who took the Oath, but the published list in Source B-28 mistakenly omits it). One John Phelps was listed in the 1783 tax list in Town Neck Hundred, while another John Phelps was a bachelor in South River Hundred. One John Phelps was administrator of Archibald Phelps in 1784 and one purchased property of Richard Phelps circa 1795 (Data from genealogist Robert W. Barnes, 1991).

PHELPS, JOSEPH. Took the Oath of Allegiance before Hon. Nicholas Worthington in March, 1778 (Ref: Original lists in Maryland State Papers, Red Book 21, p. 8D. Note: This name is mistakenly omitted from published Source B-28). He was a bachelor in 1783 tax list, and married Sophia Taylor in 1791 and Catherine Thompson in 1801. Joseph Phelps, of Annapolis, died testate in 1833 and his wife

Catherine Phelps died testate in 1838, naming daughters Ann Catherine Phelps, Mary Phelps, and Julia Phelps, one of whom married Richard R. Goodwin (Information from genealogist Robert W. Barnes, 1991).

PHELPS, JOSHUA. Took the Oath of Allegiance before Hon. Nicholas Worthington in March, 1778 (Ref: Original list in Maryland State Papers, Red Book 21, p. 8D. Note: This name is mistakenly omitted from published Source B-28).

PHELPS, JOSIAH. Took the Oath of Allegiance before Hon. Reuben Meriweather on March 2, 1778 (Ref: B-25).

PHELPS, RICHARD. Took the Oath of Allegiance before Hon. Richard Harwood, Jr. on March 1, 1778 (Ref: B-23). Richard is in the 1776 Census of All Hallows Parish with one white male and one white female, and in the 1783 tax list he is in South River Hundred. He died by November, 1795, when the inventory of his estate was signed by next of kin John Phelps and Joshua Phelps. At the sale of his property, the following Phelps purchased property: George Phelps, Jacob Phelps, Jno, Phelps, Margaret Phelps, William Phelps, and Zachariah Phelps (Information from genealogist Robert W. Barnes, 1991).

PHELPS, ROBERT. Took the Oath of Allegiance before Hon. Richard Harwood, Jr. on March 1, 1778 (Ref: B-23). He died testate in 1799, leaving his entire estate to his brother George Phelps, of Frederick County (Information from genealogist Robert W. Barnes, 1991).

PHELPS, WALTER. Took the Oath of Allegiance before Hon. Nicholas Worthington in March, 1778 (Ref: Original lists in Maryland State Papers, Red Book 21, MdHR 4587. Note: Source B-27 mistakenly gives the name "Trotter Phelps"). He married Ruth -----, and had three children: Ruth Phelps, William Phelps, and George Phelps (Information from genealogist Robert W. Barnes, 1991).

PHELPS, WILLIAM. Two men by this name took the Oath of Allegiance on March 1, 1778: one before Hon. Richard Harwood, Jr. and another before Hon. Nicholas Worthington (Ref: B-23, B-28). One William Phelps was enlisted by Richard Talbot and passed by John Dorsey on July 22, 1776 (Ref: H-39). There were several William Phelps, so reference could be to one or different ones with respect to these marriages: Sarah Fowler in 1778; Elizabeth Morgan in 1785; and, Ann Dannison in 1815. William Phelps, of Annapolis, died testate in 1804, and naming his wife Elizabeth Phelps as his sole heir and executrix (Information from genealogist Robert W. Barnes, 1991).

PHILIPS, PAUL. He was drafted in October, 1780, to serve until December 10, 1780 (Ref: H-369).

PHILIPS, SAMUEL. Took Oath of Allegiance on September 10, 1777 (Ref: V-368).

PHILPOTT, THOMAS. Enrolled by Capt. Thomas Watkins on October 21, 1776, for service to the State (Ref: I-144, MS.1814). He took the Oath of Allegiance before Hon. Richard Harwood, Jr. on March 1, 1778 (Ref: B-23).

PHIPS, BENJAMIN. Took Oath of Allegiance before Hon. Samuel Lane on March 1, 1778 (Ref: B-23).

PHIPS, JOHN. Two men with this name took the Oath of Allegiance on March 1, 1778: one before Hon. Richard Harwood, Jr., and another before Hon. Samuel Harrison, Jr. (Ref: B-23, B-28). One John Phips was administrator of Paul Busy in August, 1803, when final estate distribution was made (Ref: U-18).

PHIPS (PHIPPS), NATHANIEL. Took the Oath of Allegiance before Hon. Samuel Harrison in March, 1778 (Ref: A-244). On August 7, 1822 final distribution of his estate was made by administrators Ann Phipps and Jacob Wainwright to Ann Phipps (widow's third), with fifths to Thomas Phipps, Randolph Phipps, Mary Ann Phipps, John Wilson Phipps, and Nicholas Phipps (Ref: U-63).

PHIPS (PHIPPS), ROGER. Commissioned an Ensign in Capt. John Deale's Company in the West River Battalion of Militia on March 1, 1778 (Ref: C-200).

PHIPS, THOMAS. Took the Oath of Allegiance before Hon. Richard Harwood, Jr. on March 1, 1778 (Ref: B-23).

PIERCE, AQUILA. Born in America. Recruited by John Ijams and passed by James Brice on April 12, 1778 (Ref: C-216, H-314).

PIERPOINT, CHARLES JR. Took the Oath of Allegiance before Hon. John Dorsey on March 12, 1778 (Ref: B-26, which spells the name as "Peirpoint." Note: Original list in Maryland State Papers Red Book 22 spells it "Pierpoint").

PILLARD, WILLIAM. Took Oath of Allegiance before Hon. Samuel Lane on March 1, 1778 (Ref: B-23).

PINCKNEY, WILLIAM (March 17, 1764, Annapolis - February 25, 1822, Washington, D.C.). Married Ann Marie Rogers and they had 8 children: Isabelle Pinckney White, Charles Pinckney, Edward Pinckney, Frederick Pinckney, William Pinckney, Henry Pinckney, Emily Pinckney Jones and Betsy Pinckney Williams. William served in the mounted guard at the fort in Annapolis (Ref: T-578).

PINDELL, JOHN. Took Oath of Allegiance before Hon. Thomas Harwood on February 28, 1778 (Ref: B-22).

PINDELL, NICHOLAS. Enrolled by Capt. Thomas Watkins on October 21, 1776, for service to the State (Ref: I-144, MS.1814). On February 18, 1830, "Governor and Council were directed to ascertain amount due Nicholas Pindell, a rev. soldier, at time of his death; and Treas. Western Shore is required to pay to Gassaway Pindell, admr. of Nicholas Pindell, such sum as shall be found due to said Pindell at death" (Ref: K-381). On August 10, 1831, the final distribution of his estate was made by Gassaway Pindell, administrator, to Margaret Pindell, Elizabeth Pindell, Gassaway Pindell, Philip Pindell, Thomas Pindell, and John Pindell (Ref: U-83).

PINDELL (PINDEL), SAMUEL. Maimed soldier who was paid in Anne Arundel County on Dec. 11, 1783, January 13, 1784, April 13, 1784, June 9, 1784, Sept. 3, 1784, Oct. 26, 1784 and Dec. 17, 1784 (Ref: D-10, 11, 14, 18, 21, 22, 25).

PINE, FREDERICK. Private in Capt. Richard Dorsey's Company of Artillery, and reported sick on the rolls of November 17, 1777 (Ref: H-574).

PINKSTON, THOMAS. His name appears on a list of defectives from the Maryland Line in September, 1781 (Ref: H-415).

PIPER, JAMES. Disabled soldier who was paid in Anne Arundel County on August 16, 1783, with the record noting he was "on order Baltimore" (Ref: D-8).

PITCHFORD, EDWARD. Took Oath of Allegiance before Hon. Nicholas Worthington in March, 1778 (Ref: Original list in Maryland State Papers, Red Book 21, p. 8D. Note: This name is mistakenly omitted from published Source B-28).

PITCOCK (PETCOCK), MOSES. Enlisted by John Worthington Dorsey and passed by John Dorsey on July 22, 1776 (Ref: H-39). He took the Oath of Allegiance before Hon. John Dorsey on March 12, 1778 (Ref: B-26).

PITSLAND, RICHARD. Private in Capt. Richard Dorsey's Company of Artillery, reported on the rolls of November 17, 1777 as being "sick in the country with bilious fever" (Ref: H-547).

PITTS, THOMAS. Took the Oath of Allegiance before Hon. Nicholas Worthington in March, 1778 (Ref: B-28).

PLANE, JACOB. On February 24, 1830, the Treasurer was directed to "pay to Catherine Plane, of Anne Arundel County (widow of Jacob Plane who was a soldier in the Revolutionary War), during widowhood, quarterly, the half pay of a private, for the services of her late husband (Ref: K-381, 382). "Jacob Plain" married Catherine Folks on April 24, 1788 (Ref: G-121).

PLUMMER, CUPIT. Born in Scotland. He was a Substitute, furnished by Thomas Hopkins, Jr. on May 2, 1778, to serve three years or war's duration (Ref: C-210, H-318).

PLUMMER, JOHN. He took the Oath of Allegiance before Hon. Thomas Harwood on February 7, 1778 (Ref: B-22).

PLUMMER, JOHN. The Council of Maryland recorded that John Plummer took the Oath of Fidelity and Support to the State on April 9, 1778 (Ref: O-22).

PLUMMER, OBED. Born in Scotland. He was a Substitute, furnished by Benjamin Harwood on May 2, 1778, for 3 years or war's duration (Ref: C-210, H-318).

POLAND, WILLIAM. Private in Capt. John Fulford's Company of Artillery at Annapolis on December 12, 1776 (Ref: H-572).

POLTON, JOHN. Took the Oath of Allegiance before Hon. Nicholas Worthington in March, 1778 (Ref: B-27).

POMAIROL, ANTOINE. Recruited and passed by James Brice in 1777 (Ref: H-313).

POOLE, CHARLES. Took the Oath of Allegiance before Hon. Reuben Meriweather on March 2, 1778 (Ref: B-25).

POOLE, JAMES. One of the petitioners to the Convention of Maryland to form an independent rifle company in July, 1776 (Ref: B-3). He took the Oath of Allegiance before Hon. Reuben Meriweather on March 2, 1778 (Ref: B-25).

POOLE, MATHEW (of Baltimore County). Took the Oath of Allegiance before Hon. Reuben Meriweather on March 2, 1778 (Ref: B-25).

POOLE, PETER (of Baltimore County). Took the Oath of Allegiance before Hon. Reuben Meriweather on March 2, 1778 (Ref: B-25).

POOLE, RICHARD (of Baltimore County). Took the Oath of Allegiance before Hon. Reuben Meriweather on March 2, 1778 (Ref: B-25).

POOLE, RICHARD. Took the Oath of Allegiance before Hon. Thomas Worthington on February 28, 1778 (Ref: B-21).

POOLE, SAMUEL. Two men by this name took the Oath of Allegiance: one before Hon. Richard Harwood, Jr. on March 1, 1778, and another before Hon. Reuben Meriweather on March 2, 1778 (Ref: B-23, B-25).

POOLE, THOMAS. Took the Oath of Allegiance before Hon. Thomas Worthington on February 28, 1778 (Ref: B-21).

POPE, JAMES. On December 11, 1780 the Council of Maryland ordered that James Pope, a blind soldier of the 3rd Regiment, be issued a pair of breeches and a pair of shoes (Ref: W-240). He was paid in Anne Arundel County on May 19, 1783, December 11, 1783, April 13, 1784, June 9, 1784, September 3, 1784, October 26, 1784 and December 17, 1784 (Ref: D-6, 10, 13, 18, 21, 23, 25).

POPHAM, BENJAMIN. On March 12, 1827, the Treasurer was directed to "pay to Benjamin Popham, of Anne Arundel County, during life, half yearly, half pay of a Private, for his services during the Rev. War" (Ref: K-382). Pensioned on March 4, 1831, at age 81, as Private in the Maryland Line (Ref: Z-45).

PORTER, ADAM. Took the Oath of Allegiance before Hon. Reuben Meriweather on March 2, 1778 (Ref: B-24).

PORTER, JAMES. Took the Oath of Allegiance before Hon. Reuben Meriweather on March 2, 1778 (Ref: B-24).

PORTER, JOHN. Took the Oath of Allegiance before Hon. Nicholas Worthington in March, 1778 (Ref: B-27).

PORTER, PETER. Took the Oath of Allegiance before Hon. Thomas Worthington on February 28, 1778 (Ref: B-21).

PORTER, PETER SR. Took the Oath of Allegiance before Hon. Reuben Meriweather on March 2, 1778 (Ref: B-25).

PORTER, PETER (of Baltimore County). Took the Oath of Allegiance before Hon. Reuben Meriweather in Anne Arundel County on March 2, 1778 (Ref: B-24).

PORTER, RICHARD. Took the Oath of Allegiance before Hon. Thomas Dorsey on March 2, 1778 (Ref: B-24).

PORTER, THOMAS. One of the petitioners to the Convention of Maryland to form an independent rifle company in July, 1776 (Ref: B-3). He took the Oath of Allegiance before Hon. John Dorsey on March 12, 1778 (Ref: B-26).

PORTIUS, ROBERT. Took the Oath of Allegiance before Hon. John Dorsey on March 12, 1778 (Ref: B-26).

PORTLAND, JAMES. Drafted in October, 1780, to serve until December 10, 1780. (Ref: H-369).

POTEE, SILVANUS. Enrolled by Capt. Thomas Watkins on October 21, 1776, for service to the State (Ref: I-144, MS.1814).

POTTER, WILLIAM. Took the Oath of Allegiance before Hon. Thomas Worthington on February 28, 1778 (Ref: B-21). William was recruited by Capt. Alexander Truman in October, 1780 to serve for three years in the Army (Ref: H-368).

POULAIN, GERMAIN. Recruited and passed by James Brice in 1777 (Ref: H-313).

POWELL, EDWARD. Enrolled by Captain Thomas Watkins on October 21, 1776, for service to the State (Ref: I-144, MS.1814).

POWELL, HENRY. Enrolled by Capt. Edward Tillard on July 10, 1776. Height: 5' 8 1/2" (Ref: H-39). Took the Oath of Allegiance before Hon. Samuel Lane on March 1, 1778 (Ref: B-23).

POWELL, JAMES. Took the Oath of Allegiance before Hon. Samuel Lane on March 1, 1778 (Ref: B-23).

POWELL, JOHN. Took the Oath of Allegiance before Hon. Richard Harwood, Jr. on March 1, 1778 (Ref: B-23).

POWELL, JOSEPH. Born in Scotland. He was a Substitute, furnished by John Davidson and Samuel Green on May 8, 1778, to serve a three year term (Ref: C-206, H-317).

POWELL, PETER. Born in Scotland. He was a Substitute, furnished by Thomas Duvall on May 11, 1778, to serve to war's duration (Ref: C-212, H-319).

POWELL, WILLIAM. Two men by this name took the Oath of Allegiance on March 1, 1778: one before Hon. Samuel Lane, and another before Hon. Elijah Robosson (Ref: B-23, B-28). One was a Private in Captain John Fulford's Company of Artillery stationed at Annapolis on December 12, 1776 (Ref: H-572).

POWER, JOHN. Private in Capt. Richard Dorsey's Company of Artillery reported sick on the rolls of November 17, 1777 (Ref: H-574).

POWERS, STEPHEN JR. Took Oath of Allegiance before Hon. Reuben Meriweather on March 2, 1778 (Ref: B-24).

POWERS, STEPHEN SR. Took Oath of Allegiance before Hon. Reuben Meriweather on March 2, 1778 (Ref: B-25).

PRESTON, FRANCIS. Took the Oath of Allegiance before Hon. Thomas Dorsey on March 2, 1778 (Ref: B-24).

PRICE, THOMAS. Enlisted by Michael Burgess and passed by Colonel Hyde on July 20, 1776 (Ref: H-41). On April 10, 1800, final distribution of his estate was made to Mary Price, now wife of Paul Hartman of Baltimore County (her widow's third), with sixths of the remaining balance to Elizabeth (name illegible), Edward Price, Letty (name illegible), Harriet Price, Thomas Price, and Sophia Price (Ref: U-22, U-23).

PRICE, WALTER LANE. He was pensioned on October 12, 1819, at age 79, as a Lieutenant in the United States Navy, and died April 13, 1832 (Ref: Z-27).

PRICE, WILLIAM. Took the Oath of Allegiance before Hon. Thomas Worthington on February 28, 1778 (Ref: B-21).

PRICHARD, JOHN. Took the Oath of Allegiance before Hon. Elijah Robosson in March, 1778 (Ref: B-28).

PRIESTLY, MARY. Nurse on the State Ship "Defence" in 1774 (Ref: Y-307).

PRITCHETT, WILLIAM. Private in Capt. John Fulford's Company of Artillery at Annapolis on December 12, 1776 (Ref: H-572).

PRIVATEERS. The defense of Maryland was enhanced by an act of Congress on March 23, 1776 which authorized the fitting out of private armed vessels, and thus serving the dual purpose of pursuing personal enterprises while defending their commerce and protecting the people from depredations by the enemy. Under this 1776 act, "privateering" became a business coupled with patriotism. Under this condition many citizens of Baltimore and Annapolis served on the sea in their privately armed vessels and displayed the same valor as those who served in the army. The Archives of Maryland between April 1, 1777 and March 14, 1783 mentions the following who were authorized privateers from Annapolis (although most vessels were from Baltimore) as listed in J. Thomas Scharf's "The History of Baltimore City and County," pages 99 to 103: Capt. Nicholas Martin of the sloop "Morris and Wallace" commissioned on October 19, 1777, with fifteen men, four guns and four swivels; Capt. John Frazier of the sloop "Despatch" commissioned on March 30, 1779; Capt. Nicholas Martin of the sloop "Porpus" commissioned on April 23, 1779 with six guns and four swivels; Capt. Thomas Walker of the sloop "Despatch" commissioned on June 19, 1779 and on February 28, 1780 with six men and four swivels; Capt. Robert Dashiell of the schooner "Lady Lee" commissioned on October 19, 1780 with fourteen men and four guns; and, Capt. Robert Walsh of the schooner "Mantopony" commissioned on May 10, 1781 with eight men and two guns. (Note: This source also lists about 240 other captains who were commissioned in Baltimore, Dorchester County, Talbot County, Worcester County, Philadelphia, and Alexandria between 1777 and 1783, as gleaned from the Archives of Maryland, adding also that "these privateers were the nurse of the infant navy of the country"). In April, 1780, Commodore Thomas Grason was authorized to press vessels into service for the transportation of troops from Annapolis to Virginia. His officers were Captain Joseph Middleton, Lieutenant James Ewing, and Lieutenant James Skinner (J. T. Scharf's "History of Baltimore City and County," p. 99).

PROCTOR, JOSEPH. Took the Oath of Allegiance before Hon. Thomas Harwood on February 28, 1778 (Ref: B-22).

PROVERD, WILLIAM. Took the Oath of Allegiance before Hon. Thomas Worthington on February 28, 1778 (Ref: B-21).

PRUDDEN, SAMUEL. Captain of the Schooner "Polly" on April 14, 1777, when he was granted permission by the Council of Maryland to proceed from the port of Annapolis to the Island of Coracoa (Ref: V-210).

PRYSE, EDWARD. Private in Capt. William Marbury's Company of Artillery in 1777 (Ref: H-575).

PUE, MICHAEL. Served on the Committee of Observation in 1775 (Ref: F-222). He took the Oath of Allegiance before Hon. John Dorsey on March 12, 1778. (Ref: B-26).

PURDELL, ROBERT. Born in America. Recruited by James Brice on January 19, 1778 (Ref: C-215, H-313).

PURDY, EDMOND. Took the Oath of Allegiance before Hon. Richard Harwood, Jr. on March 1, 1778 (Ref: B-23).

PURDY, EDWARD. Enlisted by Joseph Burgess for the Flying Camp on July 20, 1776 (Ref: H-40).

PURDY, HENRY. Took the Oath of Allegiance before Hon. Richard Harwood, Jr. on March 1, 1778 (Ref: B-23). On March 30, 1837 the final distribution of his estate was made by James Iglehart, administrator, to Sarah Purdy (her widow's third), with fifths of the balance to the children of William Purdy (deceased), John Purdy, Alfred Purdy, Samuel Purdy, and Richard Mitchell in right of his wife Mary Ann Purdy (Ref: U-94).

PURDY, WILLIAM. Took the Oath of Allegiance before Hon. Richard Harwood, Jr. on March 1, 1778 (Ref: B-23).

PURNELL, WILLIAM. Took the Oath of Allegiance before Hon. Elijah Robosson in March, 1778 (Ref: B-28).

PYBUS (PIBUS), JOHN. "John Pybus" took Oath of Allegiance before Hon. Samuel Harrison in March, 1778 (Ref: A-244). "John Pibus" was a petitioner to form a militia company at Herring Creek on March 6, 1776 and subsequently served in Capt. Richard Weems' Company (Ref: I-143, MS.1814).

QUANTRILE, PRETTYMAN. Took Oath of Allegiance before Hon. Thomas Worthington on February 28, 1778 (Ref: B-21).

QUAY, JAMES. Born in America. Enlisted by Daniel Munro and passed by James Brice on February 27, 1778 (Ref: C-215, H-313).

QUINN, JOSEPH. Disabled soldier of the Invalids Corps who was discharged at Frederick Town on November 29, 1783 (Ref: X-31). He received pay in Anne Arundel County on January 13, 1784, April 13, 1784, June 9, 1784, September 3, 1784, October 26, 1784 and December 17, 1784 (Ref: D-12, D-13, D-18, D-21, D-22, D-25). "Joseph Quynn" was a Substitute, furnished by James Maccubbin on May 30, 1778, to serve for three years (Ref: C-208, H-319).

QUYNN (QUINN), ALLEN (c1726 - November 8, 1803). Married Elizabeth -----, and had seven children: William Quynn, Allen Quynn, John Quynn, Catherine Quynn Kilty, Mary Quynn Gassaway, Sophia Quynn, and Elizabeth Quynn Claude. Allen was a prominent citizen of the City of Annapolis. He was appointed Justice of Anne Arundel County on June 10, 1777, and served as Anne Arundel County Coroner, resigning June 3, 1778 (Ref: O-121, Q-177, T-594, and Anne Arundel County Orphans Court Proceedings, 1777-1779, p. 1, MdHR9524). On November 19, 1778 he was appointed a Justice of the Peace, which position he held until 1803, and also Justice of the Orphans Court in Anne Arundel County, which position he held until 1794. In 1775, he served on the Committee of Observation, and on the committee to erect fortifications for the City of Annapolis (Ref: O-241, P-670, P-671). Allen was also appointed Messenger to the Council on April 20, 1776 (Ref: N-357).

RANDALL, AQUILLA JR. Commissioned a Second Lieutenant in Capt. Elisha Riggs' Company of Militia on March 30, 1776 (Ref: N-299).

"Acquilla Randle, Jr." took the Oath of Allegiance before Hon. John Dorsey on March 12, 1778 (Ref: B-26).

RANDALL, AQUILLA (ACQUILA) SR. Took the Oath of Allegiance before Hon. Reuben Meriweather on March 2, 1778 (Ref: B-24). In 1804 the final distribution of his estate (fifths) was made to Nathan Randall, Christopher Randall, John Randall, Aquilla Randall, and Brice Randall (Ref: U-27).

RANDALL, JOHN (of Annapolis). He was appointed Commissary to the Maryland Troops on February 13, 1778, holding the rank of Colonel (Ref: V-493). He married Deborah Knapp in 1783, and three of their children were Alexander Randall, Barton Randall, and Henrietta Randall Magruder (Ref: E-18, E-23, E-37, G-43). He also took the Oath of Allegiance as did two other men with this same name: one before Hon. Thomas Worthington on February 28, 1778, another before Hon. Thomas Dorsey on March 2, 1778, and another before Hon. Reuben Meriweather on March 2, 1778 (Ref: B-21, B-24).

RANDALL, JOHNSEY. Took the Oath of Allegiance before Hon. Thomas Worthington on February 28, 1778 (Ref: B-21).

RANDALL, RICHARD. Private in Capt. Richard Chew's Company in Col. John Weems Battalion on October 5, 1776 (Ref: A-95, I-143). He also took the Oath of Allegiance before Hon. Samuel Harrison, Jr. in March, 1778 (Ref: B-28).

RANER, JAMES. Took Oath of Allegiance before Hon. Elijah Robosson in March, 1778 (Ref: B-28).

RANER, JOHN. Took Oath of Allegiance before Hon. Elijah Robosson in March, 1778 (Ref: B-28).

RASH, GEORGE. Took the Oath of Allegiance before Hon. Thomas Dorsey on March 1, 1778 (Ref: B-24).

RATCLIFF, JOSEPH. Took the Oath of Allegiance before Hon. John Dorsey on March 12, 1778 (Ref: B-26).

RATCLIFT, CHARLES. Private in Capt. Gilbert Middleton's Independent Company of Militia of Annapolis on March 20, 1779 (Ref: I-144, O-325).

RAWLINGS, AARON. Took the Oath of Allegiance before Hon. Richard Harwood, Jr. on March 1, 1778 (Ref: B-23). On October 17, 1800 the final distribution of his estate was made to Mary Rawlings (widow) who received the whole of the estate during her natural life or after her marriage, and then to be divided among his children: John Rawlings, Aaron Rawlings, Moses Rawlings, Richard Rawlings, Nathan Rawlings, Susanna Rawlings, Elizabeth Rawlings, Anne Rawlings, Mary Lusby, and Rebecca Rawlings (Ref: U-23).

RAWLINGS, AARON (OF WILLIAM). Took the Oath of Allegiance before Hon. Richard Harwood, Jr. on March 1, 1778 (Ref: B-23).

RAWLINGS, FRANCIS. Took Oath of Allegiance before Hon. Nicholas Worthington in March, 1778 (Ref: B-27).

RAWLINGS, GASSAWAY. Took the Oath of Allegiance before Hon. Thomas Harwood on February 28, 1778 (Ref: B-22).

RAWLINGS, ISAAC. On June 18, 1779, the Treasurer of the Western Shore was directed to "pay to Lieut. Isaac Rawlings 100 pounds to bear his expenses in going after deserters from the Annapolis Matrosses." (Ref: O-458).

RAWLINGS, JONATHAN. Private in Capt. William Marbury's Company of Artillery in 1777 (Ref: H-575). He took the Oath of Allegiance before Hon. Thomas Harwood on February 28, 1778 (Ref: B-22).

RAWLINGS, MOSES (born in Anne Arundel County, Maryland and died in Hampshire County, Virginia in May, 1809, with burial in Cumberland, Maryland). Moses married Elizabeth McMahon and they had at least one son, Moses Rawlings. During the Revolutionary War, he served as a Lieutenant in Frederick County under Capt. Cresap, and subsequently rose to the rank of Colonel in command of his own regiment. He served with distinction in the Maryland Continental Line throughout the war, fighting in many battles, with many Anne Arundel Countians in his command. (Ref: E-281, and Archives of Maryland, Vol. 18).

RAWLINGS, RICHARD. Three men with this name took the Oath of Allegiance: one before Hon. Thomas Harwood on February 28, 1778, one before Hon. Richard Harwood, Jr. on March 1, 1778, and one before Hon. Nicholas Worthington in March, 1778 (Ref: B-22, B-23, B-28). One Richard Rawlings was deceased by November 2, 1803 when the final distribution of his estate was made to his widow, Elizabeth W. Rawlings, with the remainder to Mary Rawlings, John Rawlings, Aaron Rawlings, Moses Rawlings, Susanna Rawlings, Eliza Rawlings Atwell, Mary Rawlings Lusby, and Rebecca Rawlings Duvall (Ref: U-18).

RAWLINGS, SAMUEL. Took the Oath of Allegiance before Hon. Samuel Harrison, Jr. in March, 1778 (Ref: B-29).

RAWLINGS, STEPHEN. Took the Oath of Allegiance before Hon. Richard Harwood, Jr. on March 1, 1778 (Ref: B-23). On May 12, 1792 the final distribution of his estate was made to Eleanor Rawlings, now Mrs. Zachariah Tucker (widow's third) with remaining thirds to Thomas Rawlings, Lurana Rawlings and Eleanor Rawlings (Ref: U-8).

RAWLINGS, WILLIAM. Took the Oath of Allegiance before Hon. Richard Harwood, Jr. on March 1, 1778 (Ref: B-23).

RAY, JESSE. Private in Capt. William Marbury's Company of Artillery in 1777. (Ref: H-575).

RAY, JOHN. Born in 1756 and enlisted in Anne Arundel County in 1776. Moved to Kentucky in 1779 and settled in Bullitt County in 1780. Applied for his pension in 1832 while residing in Union

County, Kentucky. John's wife was Margaret -----. (Ref: L-54, G-43. His application (R8612) may have been rejected, according to some sources. Also consult reference HCP-120.)

RAY, JOHN, JR. (1750-1817). Married Frances ----- in 1784 and had one son, William Ray. John Ray was commissioned a Second Lieutenant in Capt. Basil Burgess' Company in the Elk Ridge Battalion in March of 1779 (Ref: O-333, T-599). He also took the Oath of Allegiance before Hon. Thomas Worthington on February 28, 1778 (Ref: B-21).

RAY, JOHN SR. (1707 - c1799). Married Sarah Wilson in 1731 and had children John Ray, Elizabeth Ray Hanson, Sarah Ray, Mary Ray, and "five other sons and three daughters" (Ref: T-599). He took the Oath of Allegiance before Hon. Thomas Worthington on February 28, 1778 (Ref: B-21).

RAY, JOSEPH. Took the Oath of Allegiance before Hon. Thomas Worthington on February 28, 1778 (Ref: B-21).

RAY, RICHARD. Took the Oath of Allegiance before Hon. Thomas Worthington on February 28, 1778 (Ref: B-21).

RAY, WILLIAM. Born in Maryland. Enrolled by John S. Belt in July, 1776. Height: 5' 6" (Ref: H-40).

RAY, WILLIAM JR. Took the Oath of Allegiance before Hon. Thomas Worthington on February 28, 1778 (Ref: B-21). He died prior to 1785 and final estate distribution was made on September 26, 1787 to his widow (unnamed), with sevenths to Elizabeth Ray, Priscilla Ray, Nicholas Ray, Sarah Ray, Anne Ray, Rebecca Ray, and Matthew Ray (Ref: U-25; also see William Ray, Sr., q.v.).

RAY, WILLIAM SR. Took the Oath of Allegiance before Hon. Thomas Worthington on February 28, 1778 (Ref: B-21). On May 12, 1785 the final distribution of his estate was made to John Ray, Joseph Ray, Nicholas Ray, Ann Ray, and the heirs of William Ray (Ref: U-25, U-26).

READ, FRANCIS. Recruited by Capt. Alexander Truman in October, 1780 to serve for three years (Ref: H-369).

REAR, WILLIAM. Enrolled by Capt. James Disney, Jr. and passed by Colonel Richard Harwood on July 13, 1776 (Ref: H-41).

REDMAN, ALICE. Served as a Nurse in the Annapolis hospital (Ref: Y-307).

REED, JAMES. Enrolled by Capt. Thomas Watkins on October 21, 1776 for service to the State (Ref: I-144, MS.1814).

REED, JOHN. He was paid by the Council of Maryland on November 4, 1777 for furnishing horses for riding express to Virginia (Ref: V-408). Took Oath of Allegiance before Hon. Samuel Harrison, Jr. in March, 1778 (Ref: B-29).

REED, WILLIAM. Private in Capt. Richard Dorsey's Company of Artillery on the rolls of November 17, 1777 (Ref: H-574, G-43). Took the Oath of Allegiance before Hon. Richard Harwood, Jr. on March 1, 1778 (Ref: B-23).

REID, JAMES (of Annapolis). In his deposition on January 23, 1777 he stated that on August 27, 1776 he heard from William Gordon that one William Nevin had written a letter to Lord Dunmore offering his services in acquainting him with the lay of the city and where to land his forces (Ref: V-72).

RENCHER, JOHN GRANT. Took Oath of Allegiance before Hon. Thomas Worthington on February 28, 1778 (Ref: B-21).

RESTON (RISTON), HENRY. "Henry Reston" took Oath of Allegiance before Hon. Thomas Dorsey on March 1, 1778 (Ref: B-24). "Henry Riston" was enrolled by Captain Thomas Watkins on October 21, 1776, for service to the State (Ref: I-144, MS.1814).

REWARK, JAMES (born 1744). Private, Maryland Line. Married Susannah Tucker in 1784 in Anne Arundel County (Ref: G-43, G-121).

REYNOLDS (RENOLS, RANOLS), CHRISTOPHER. He was wounded twice while serving on board the sloop "Porpoise" (no details given), and he was discharged on January 10, 1783. His papers were signed by George Washington (Ref: X-32, X-33). He was paid in Anne Arundel County on January 13, 1784, April 13, 1784, June 9, 1784, September 3, 1784, October 26, 1784, and December 17, 1784 (Ref: D-12, D-13, D-18, D-21, D-22, D-25).

REYNOLDS, JAMES. Took the Oath of Allegiance before Hon. John Dorsey on March 12, 1778 (Ref: B-26).

REYNOLDS, JOHN. Private in Captain John Fulford's Company of Artillery at Annapolis on December 12, 1776 (Ref: H-572).

REYNOLDS, ROBERT. On February 16, 1776 he was paid by the Council of Safety for providing wood for their use (Ref: N-163, N-336). He took the Oath of Allegiance before Hon. Thomas Worthington on February 28, 1778 (Ref: B-21). Served as a Private in Captain Gilbert Middleton's Independent Company of Militia of Annapolis on March 20, 1779 (Ref: I-144, O-325).

REYNOLDS, THOMAS. Enlisted by Edward Spurrier and passed by Thomas Dorsey on July 20, 1776 (Ref: H-41). Took the Oath of Allegiance before Hon. Thomas Worthington on February 28, 1778 (Ref: B-21).

REYNOLDS, TOBIAS (1761 - c1833). Private in the Maryland Line (Ref: G-44). On February 7, 1818, the Treasurer was directed to "pay to Tobias Reynolds, of Anne Arundel County, an old soldier, quarterly, a sum of money equal to the half pay of a private in the Revolutionary War" (Ref: K-385). On July 23, 1833 the final distribution of his estate (eighths) was made to Lewis Reynolds, Allen Reynolds, Sarah Reynolds, Rebecca Stewart, Goven Reynolds, James Deaver (for the use of Rezin Hopkins), Leonard Osborne (for the use of Andrew Elliott), and Margaret Kelly (Ref: U-87).

REYNOLDS, WILLIAM (c1710 - April, 1777). A prominent Annapolis merchant and member of the South River Club. Married first in 1739 to Deborah Syng, a widow, and had 5 children: John Reynolds, Thomas Reynolds, Robert Reynolds, Joseph Reynolds, and William Reynolds. Married second to his housekeeper, Mary Howell, circa 1757 and had a daughter, Margaret Reynolds, who married Capt. Alexander Truman, a Revolutionary War officer, in 1781. Capt. Truman served throughout the war and was a member of the Society of the Cincinnati in 1783. While on a peace mission to Ohio in 1792, Major Truman was killed by Indians. William Reynolds owned Reynolds Tavern in Annapolis, a meeting place for Revolutionary War soldiers. Tradition states that he had a run in with George Washington who had, shall we say, shown certain affections for William's wife, adding credence to "George Washington slept here" stories (prior to the Revolution and his fathering of our country). William loaned a horse to the military in 1776, and died testate in 1777 (Ref: E-2332FF and research by Henry C. Peden Jr., a descendant and this compiler; Robert H. McIntire's "Annapolis Maryland Families," p. 580; Reference N-316; and, Information presented by Cmdr. Elmer M. Jackson, Jr., of Annapolis, 1991).

REYNOLDS, WILLIAM. Enlisted by Edward Spurrier and passed by Thomas Dorsey on July 20, 1776 (Ref: H-41). Took Oath of Allegiance before Hon. Nicholas Worthington in March, 1778 (Ref: B-27).

REYNOLDS, WILLIAM (of Baltimore County). Took the Oath of Allegiance before Hon. Reuben Meriweather on March 2, 1778 (Ref: B-25).

RHODES, JOHN. Enrolled by Captain Thomas Watkins on October 21, 1776, for service to the State (Ref: I-144, MS.1814).

RICH, SAMUEL. Born in Scotland. He was a Substitute, furnished by Joseph Warfield on May 18, 1778, to serve to war's duration (Ref: C-213, H-319).

RICHARDS, PETER. Private in Capt. Richard Dorsey's Company of Artillery on the rolls of November 17, 1777 (Ref: H-574).

RICHARDS, ROBERT. Took the Oath of Allegiance before Hon. Thomas Harwood on February 28, 1778 (Ref: B-22).

RICHARDSON, ADAM. Private in Capt. Gilbert Middleton's Independent Company of Militia of Annapolis on March 20, 1779 (Ref: I-144, O-325).

RICHARDSON, GEORGE. Born in Scotland. He was a Substitute, furnished by Philip Thomas, Jr. on May 9, 1778, to serve 3 years (Ref: C-206, H-317).

RICHARDSON, JOSEPH. Enrolled by Capt. Thomas Watkins on October 21, 1776 for service to the State (Ref: I-144, MS.1814). Two men with this name took the Oath of Allegiance on March 1, 1778: one before Hon. Richard Harwood, Jr., and one before Hon. Samuel Lane (Ref: B-23, B-29).

RICHARDSON, PHILIP. Took the Oath of Allegiance before Hon. Richard Harwood, Jr. on March 1, 1778 (Ref: B-23).

RICKETTS, NICHOLAS. Sergeant in Capt. Richard Dorsey's Company of Artillery on the rolls of November 17, 1777 (Ref: H-573).

RICKETTS, RICHARD. Enrolled by Capt. James Disney, Jr. and passed by Colonel Richard Harwood on July 13, 1776 (Ref: H-41).

RICKETTS, THOMAS. Took the Oath of Allegiance before Hon. Reuben Meriweather on March 2, 1778 (Ref: Original list in Maryland State Papers, Red Book 22. Note: This name is mistakenly spelled "Thomas Ruketts" in Reference B-24). First Lieutenant in Capt. John Burgess' Company in the Elk Ridge Battalion of Militia on March 1, 1778 (Ref: C-201).

RICKORDS, JOHN. Enlisted by Joseph Burgess for the Flying Camp and passed on July 20, 1776 (Ref: H-40).

RICKORDS, WILLIAM. Took the Oath of Allegiance before Hon. Elijah Robosson in March, 1778 (Ref: B-28).

RID, JAMES. Private in Captain Richard Dorsey's Company of Artillery on November 17, 1777 (Ref: H-574).

RIDGELY FAMILY. The Ridgely family was prominent in colonial Anne Arundel County and Baltimore County. Any information not found in this book about the Ridgely men who served in Anne Arundel County may be found in Henry C. Peden, Jr.'s book "Revolutionary Patriots of Baltimore Town and Baltimore County, 1775-1783," pp. 226-227 (Westminster: Family Line Publications).

RIDGELY, ABSALOM (May 17, 1743 - 1818). Son of Henry Ridgely and Catherine Lusby. Married Ann Robertson in 1755 and they had 14 children: Elizabeth Ridgely Weems, John Ridgely, Ann Ridgely, Henry Ridgely, Absalom Ridgely, Mary Ridgely Hooper, Charles Ridgely, Frances Ridgely, Ann Ridgely, Henry Ridgely, David Ridgely, Richard Ridgely, Nicholas Ridgely, and Catherine Ridgely Gaither. Absalom took the Oath of Allegiance in 1778 (Ref: S-137). On March 20, 1779 he was a Private in Capt. Gilbert Middleton's Independent Company of Militia of Annapolis (Ref: I-144, O-325; not listed in S-137).

RIDGELY, BASIL. Son of William and Margaret Ridgely. On February 3, 1776, he enlisted in the Flying Camp, and served under Captain Patrick Sims. He was commissioned an Ensign in the 1st Maryland Line, and served until resigning on December 7, 1777. He took the Oath of Allegiance before Hon. John Dorsey on March 12, 1778 (Ref: B-26, H-155, S-112).

RIDGELY, CHARLES. Two men with this name took the Oath of Allegiance: one before Hon. Thomas Worthington on February 28, 1778

(Ref: B-21), and one before Hon. Nicholas Worthington in March, 1778 (Ref: Original lists in Maryland State Papers, Red Book 21, p. 8D. Note: This name is mistakenly omitted from the published list found in Reference B-28, which source has only one Charles Ridgely listed when there were actually two such names). One Charles Ridgely (of William) was born in 1746 in Anne Arundel County and died in 1810 in Baltimore County. He was a Justice of the Peace from 1779 to 1784 in Baltimore County, and Speaker of the House (Ref: S-111).

RIDGELY, CHARLES (c1748/9, Anne Arundel County - December 17, 1786, Baltimore County). Son of John Ridgely and Mary Dorsey. Married Rebecca Lawson and had six children: Charles Ridgely, Rachel Ridgely, Elizabeth Ridgely Young, Rebecca Ridgely Barney, Dorothy Ridgely, and Mary Ridgely Horne. Charles took the Oath of Allegiance before Hon. Thomas Worthington on February 28, 1778, as "Charles Ridgely of John" (Ref: B-21, S-113). He also served on the Committee of Observation in Baltimore County in 1774 (Ref: P-685).

RIDGELY, CHARLES GREENBURY (October 3, 1735 - September, 1781). Son of Henry Ridgely and Elizabeth Warfield. Married Sarah MacGill and had six children: Mary Davidge Ridgely, Charles Ridgely, Anne Ridgely Griffith, Sarah Ridgely Cole, Elizabeth Ridgely Griffith, and Archibald Ridgely. He took the Oath of Allegiance before Hon. John Worthington of Nicholas on February 28, 1778 (Ref: S-135, S-136).

RIDGELY, FREDERICK. A physician from upper Anne Arundel County, he began the practice of medicine in Baltimore in 1775, became a Surgeon to the Fourth Maryland Line, and served in the Yorktown campaign in 1781 (Ref: Y-305).

RIDGELY, GREENBURY. Took the Oath of Allegiance before Hon. Thomas Dorsey on March 2, 1778 (Ref: B-24).

RIDGELY, GREENBURY (December 15, 1726 - February, 1783). Son of Henry Ridgely and Elizabeth Warfield. He married Lucy Stringer and had 10 children: Henry Ridgely, Richard Ridgely, Frederick Ridgely, Anne Ridgely Sappington, Lydia Ridgely, Henry Ridgely, Elizabeth Ridgely Griffith, Greenbury Ridgely, Nicholas Ridgely, and Sarah Ridgely (S-131, S-132). In 1775, he served on the Committee of Observation (Ref: F-222). He took the Oath of Allegiance before Hon. Thomas Worthington on February 28, 1778 (Ref: B-21, although Reference S-132 states it was before Hon. John Worthington of Nicholas).

RIDGELY, HENRY. 1st Lieutenant in Capt. James Disney's Company in July, 1776 and styled "Henry Ridgely, Jr." (Ref: H-39, H-41, N-534). Took the Oath of Allegiance before Hon. Elijah Robosson in March, 1778 (Ref: B-28. See the information on Henry Ridgely, Jr., q.v., in case it might apply to him).

RIDGELY, HENRY (May 17, 1728 - June 29, 1791). Son of Henry Ridgely and Elizabeth Warfield. Married Anne Dorsey in 1750 and had 9 children: Henry Ridgely (#1), Elizabeth Ridgely Warfield, Ann

Ridgely, Polly Ridgely, Henry Ridgely (#2), Henrietta Ridgely (#1), Henrietta Ridgely (#2), Joshua Ridgely and Sarah Ridgely. Henry served in the colonial militia from 1753 to 1773, rising to the rank of Major, and possibly Colonel (Ref: S-134). He served on the Committee of Observation in 1776 (Ref: F-222), and took the Oath of Allegiance before Hon. Thomas Worthington on February 28, 1778 (Ref: B-21, although Source S-134 states it was before John Worthington of Nicholas). He was appointed a Justice of the Peace on November 19, 1778 (Ref: O-241). He also served in the Lower House, Anne Arundel County, 1779-1780. He was active in organizing militia companies in northern Anne Arundel County in 1774 and 1775, but was exempted from militia duty in 1776 (Ref: P-688).

RIDGELY, HENRY JR. (July 9, 1758 - circa 1805). Son of Henry Ridgely and Anne Dorsey. He took the Oath of Allegiance before Hon. Thomas Worthington on February 28, 1778 (Ref: B-21, S-134). On February 14, 1805 final estate distribution was made to Rachel Ridgely (widow's third), with remainder to Achsah Claridge, Charles Ridgely, Ann Maccubbin, Eleanor Maccubbin, Rachel Ridgely, Henrietta Ridgely, William Ridgely, Nicholas Ridgely, David G. Ridgely, and Rachel Ridgely (Ref: U-28. See entry on Henry Ridgely, q.v.).

RIDGELY, JOHN (c1740 - c1817). Son of William Ridgely and Mary Orrick. He married Anne Griffith and had six children: Bazil Ridgely, Charles Ridgely, Anne Ridgely Marriott, William Ridgely, Lloyd Ridgely, and Caroline Ridgely Todd. He took the Oath of Allegiance on March 1, 1778, before Hon. Thomas Dorsey (Ref: B-24, S-159, S-160).

RIDGELY, JOHN. Took the Oath of Allegiance before Hon. Nicholas Worthington in March, 1778 (Ref: B-28).

RIDGELY, RICHARD (August 3, 1753/55 - February 26, 1824). Son of Greenbury Ridgely and Lucy Stringer. Born in Anne Arundel County, moved to Baltimore County circa 1780, and returned to Anne Arundel County circa 1790. Married in 1778 to Elizabeth Dorsey, and they had 7 children: Edward D. Ridgely, Richard Ridgely, Daniel Ridgely, Deborah Ridgely Neilson, Sophia Ridgely Battee, Ann Ridgely Dashiell, Elizabeth Ridgely Dare, and Matilda Ridgely Baer. Richard was very active in political affairs, including: Senate, Western Shore, 1776-1781, 1786-1791, 1801-1806; Lower House, Annapolis, 1801-1802; Council of Safety, Assistant Clerk in 1776, and Clerk in 1777; Executive Council Clerk, 1777; Maryland Senate Clerk, 1777-1779; Maryland State Elector, Baltimore Town, 1786; Commissioner, Baltimore Town, 1781 to 1788; Warden, Port of Baltimore, 1783; Common Councilman, Annapolis, 1796; Associate Judge, 3rd District, 1811-1824; Captain, Baltimore Militia, 1781; Delegate to the Constitutional Convention, 1784-1785 (Ref: P-690, T-610).

RIDGELY, NICHOLAS. Commissioned an Ensign on February 28, 1776, and Second Lieutenant in Captain Richard Stringer's Company of the 22nd (Elk Ridge) Battalion of Militia on August 28, 1777. Resigned on April 13, 1781 (Ref: K-385, N-191). Two men with this name took the Oath of Allegiance: one before Hon. Thomas Worthington on

February 28, 1778, and one before Hon. Thomas Dorsey on March 2, 1778 (Ref: B-21, B-24).

RIDGELY, RICHARD. Appointed Clerk to the Council of Maryland on March 25, 1777 and took the Oath of Allegiance to the State (Ref: V-188).

RIDGELY, WILLIAM. Took Oath of Allegiance before Hon. Nicholas Worthington in March, 1778 (Ref: B-28).

RIDGELY, WILLIAM, of Elk Ridge (died in August, 1779). Son of Robert Ridgely and Sarah Howard. He married Margaret -----, and had eight children: Basil Ridgely, William Ridgely, Zephaniah Ridgely, Charles Ridgely, Nancy Ridgely Oram, Sarah Ridgely Gaither, Rachel Ridgely, and Amelia Ridgely. William took the Oath of Allegiance before Hon. Thomas Worthington on February 28, 1778. He died in August, 1779 (Ref: S-105, B-21).

RIDGELY, WILLIAM (1703/5 - October, 1780). Son of William Ridgely and Jane Westall. Married Mary Orrick in 1726 and had 10 children: Nicholas Ridgely, Priscilla Ridgely Griffith, Jane Ridgely Hand, Mary Ridgely Pumphrey, Sophia Ridgely Pumphrey, John Ridgely, Henry Ridgely, Greenbury Ridgely, Anne Ridgely Rigby, and William Ridgely. He took the Oath of Allegiance before Hon. John Dorsey on March 12, 1778 (Ref: S-155, B-26, T-610, and Original lists in Maryland State Papers, Red Book No. 22, MdHR 4587).

RIDGELY, WILLIAM (c1742 - May, 1821). Son of William Ridgely. He married Elizabeth Dorsey and they had 8 children: Sarah Ridgely Welling, Charles Greenbury Ridgely, Rachel Ridgely Dorsey, Samuel Ridgely, William Pitt Ridgely, Elizabeth Ridgely Griffith, Amelia Ridgely Warfield Griffith, and Philemon Dorsey Ridgely. William took the Oath of Allegiance before Hon. Thomas Worthington on February 28, 1778 (Ref: B-21, S-109). On April 23, 1828 final distribution of his estate was made by Henry Welling, executor, with sixths of the balance to Charles G. Ridgely, Philemon D. Ridgely, Rachel Dorsey and Sarah Welling, and a third of a sixth of the remaining balance to Catharine D. Warfield, George W. Warfield, William R. Warfield, Remus Griffith, Ruth H. Cummins, and Lydia Cran (Ref: U-75).

RIDGEWAY, WILLIAM. Enlisted by John Worthington Dorsey and passed by John Dorsey on July 22, 1776 (Ref: H-39). On August 3, 1781 he petitioned the Council of Maryland and questioned the validity of "a fine imposed by a court martial in 1779 in the sum of ten pounds for which the Sheriff had executed him, that he belongs to a company in Anne Arundel, and that he never was warned in nor before a court martial to take his trial." He also enclosed a certificate from Charles Fox in this regard (Ref: W-539).

RIFFLE, JACOB. Took the Oath of Allegiance before Hon. Reuben Meriweather on March 2, 1778 (Ref: B-24).

RIGBY, JAMES TOWNLY. Took Oath of Allegiance on March 2, 1778 (Ref: V-525).

RIGGS, ELISHA. Commissioned a Captain in the Militia on February 7, 1776. (Ref: N-139, N-299).

RIGGS, JAMES. Took the Oath of Allegiance before Hon. Thomas Worthington on February 28, 1778 (Ref: B-21).

RIGGS, LYNON. Took the Oath of Allegiance before Hon. Thomas Dorsey on March 2, 1778 (Ref: B-24).

RILEY, JAMES. Born in Ireland. Recruited by Cornelius Mills and passed by James Brice on March 5, 1778 (Ref: C-216, H-313).

RILEY, LAWRENCE. Born in Ireland. Recruited by Cornelius Mills and passed by James Brice on February 27, 1778 (Ref: C-215, H-313).

RILEY (RYLY), MARK. "Mark Riley" took Oath of Allegiance before Hon. Thomas Worthington on February 28, 1778 (Ref: B-21). "Mark Ryly" was enrolled by Captain Thomas Watkins on October 21, 1776, for service to the State (Ref: I-144, MS.1814).

RILEY, THOMAS. Took the Oath of Allegiance before Hon. Thomas Worthington on February 28, 1778 (Ref: B-21).

RITCHIE, BENJAMIN. Born in Scotland. He was a Substitute, furnished by John Sellman on May 18, 1778, to serve to war's duration (Ref: C-205, H-317).

ROBERTS, EDWARD. Private in Capt. William Marbury's Company of Artillery in 1777 (Ref: H-575).

ROBERTS, HENRY. Born in Maryland. Enrolled by Samuel Chew on July 25, 1776 (Ref: H-40).

ROBERTS, JOSEPH. Took Oath of Allegiance before Hon. John Dorsey on March 12, 1778 (Ref: B-26). He was born in Scotland and furnished as a Substitute by Matthias Hammond on May 11, 1778, until the war's end (Ref: C-212, H-318).

ROBERTS, RICHARD. Born in England. He was a Substitute, furnished by John Gray on April 24, 1778, for a three year term (Ref: C-204, H-317).

ROBERTS, WILLIAM. Two men by this name took the Oath of Allegiance on March 1, 1778: one before Hon. Richard Harwood, Jr., and one before Hon. Samuel Lane (Ref: B-23). Two men by this name were born in Scotland and both were Substitutes to serve three years in the American Army. One was furnished by Zachariah Childs on May 4, 1778, and the other by Samuel Childs on May 20, 1778 (Ref: C-206, C-210, H-317, H-318). Another William Roberts (born in Maryland) was enrolled by Samuel Chew on July 25, 1776. Height: 5' 6" (Ref: H-40).

ROBERTSON, WILLIAM. Private in Capt. William Marbury's Company of Artillery in 1777 (Ref: H-575).

ROBERTSON, ZACHARIAH, Born 1763 and enlisted in Anne Arundel County in 1781 in the Maryland Line. He applied for his pension while living in Pendleton County, Kentucky in 1820, age 57, and received pension S35632 (Ref: L-46). His wife's name was Elizabeth ------, and their six children were: Rachel Robertson, Margaret Robertson, Matilda Robertson, James Robertson, Delilah Robertson, and Pruda Robertson. There appears to be a discrepancy in his age as he may have been age 74 in 1819 (also consult reference HCP-126).

ROBINSON, CHARLES. Disabled soldier who was paid in Anne Arundel County on Sept. 3, 1784, October 26, 1784 and December 17, 1784 (Ref: D-21, 23, 25). One Charles Robinson was deceased by October 30, 1833 when final estate distribution was made, with half to the heirs of Hannah Stewart, namely Sarah Stewart, Susan Waller, Charles R. Stewart, Rachel Linthicum and Mary Ann Holland, and half to the heirs of Thomas Robinson, namely Benjamin Robinson, Thomas Robinson, and Ann Robinson (Ref: U-88).

ROBINSON, DAVID (1756 - after 1814). Son of Hamilton Robinson and Rebecca Jones. He married Katherine Johnson and had one daughter, Sophia Robinson Hilger. He served as Waterman on the barge "Intrepid" during the Revolution in 1781 and he also served in the War of 1812 (Ref: E-337, H-610, T-615).

ROBINSON, GEORGE. Enrolled by Henry Ridgely, Jr. and passed by Col. Josias C. Hall on August 26, 1776 (Ref: H-41).

ROBINSON, HAMPTON. Took Oath of Allegiance on March 9, 1778 (Ref: V-531).

ROBINSON, LAWRENCE. Took Oath of Allegiance before Hon. Nicholas Worthington in March, 1778 (Ref: Originals list in Maryland State Papers, Red Book 21, p. 8D. Note: Name is mistakenly omitted from published list in Ref: B-28).

ROBINSON, PATRICK. Enlisted by John Worthington Dorsey and passed by John Dorsey on July 22, 1776 (Ref: H-39).

ROBINSON, RICHARD. Enrolled by Capt. James Disney, Jr. and passed by Colonel Richard Harwood on July 13, 1776 (Ref: H-41). Took the Oath of Allegiance before Hon. Nicholas Worthington in March, 1778 (Ref: B-28).

ROBINSON, THOMAS. Private in Capt. Richard Dorsey's Company of Artillery on the rolls of November 17, 1777 (Ref: H-574). On April 22, 1816 the final distribution of his estate was made to Elizabeth Robinson (widow's third), with fifths of the balance to Benjamin Robinson, Ann Robinson Linthicum, James Robinson, Charles Robinson and Thomas Robinson (Ref: U-47).

ROBINSON, THOMAS. Born in Scotland. He was a Substitute, furnished by Joseph Wilkins on May 3, 1778, to serve a three year term (Ref: C-206, H-317).

ROBSON (ROBISON), JOHN. Took Oath of Allegiance before Hon. Samuel Harrison, Jr. in March, 1778 (Ref: B-29).

ROBOSSON, CHARLES (born 1758). Married Rebecca Hanson (widow) in 1786 (Ref: G-45, G-122). On February 27, 1839, the Treasurer was directed to "pay to Rebecca Robosson, of Baltimore City, widow of Charles Robosson, a First Lieutenant in the Revolutionary Army, half pay of a First Lieutenant of the revolution, during life, quarterly, commencing Jan. 1, 1839" (Ref: K-386).

ROBOSSON, ELIJAH. Second Major in 1776 and Lieutenant Colonel in the Severn Battalion of Militia on June 19, 1777. He was subsequently commissioned a Colonel on March 1, 1778 (Ref: A-176, C-202, F-224). Elijah was one of the Justices who administered the Oath of Allegiance in Anne Arundel County in March, 1778 (Ref: B-28). On June 10, 1777, he was appointed Justice of the Orphans Court (Ref: A.A. Orphans Court Proc., 1777-1779, p. 1, MdHR9524). He was appointed a Justice of the Peace on November 19, 1778 (Ref: O-241). On June 20, 1799 final distribution of his estate was made to Mary Robosson (widow) with the remaining balance to Elizabeth Robosson, Ann Robosson (now wife of Dr. Reverdy Ghiselin), and Elijah Robosson (Ref: U-25).

ROBOSSON, GEORGE JR. Took the Oath of Allegiance before Hon. Elijah Robosson in March, 1778 (Ref: B-28, which shows his name as "George Robosson II").

ROBOSSON, GEORGE SR. Took the Oath of Allegiance before Hon. Elijah Robosson in March, 1778 (Ref: B-28, which shows his name as "George Robosson I").

ROBOSSON, OBED. Took the Oath of Allegiance before Hon. Elijah Robosson in March, 1778 (Ref: B-28).

ROBOSSON, ONEIL. Took the Oath of Allegiance before Hon. Elijah Robosson in March, 1778 (Ref: B-28).

ROBOSSON, RICHARD. Took the Oath of Allegiance before Hon. Elijah Robosson in March, 1778 (Ref: B-28). Ensign in Capt. Joseph Maccubbin's Company in the Severn Battalion of Militia on March 1, 1778 (Ref: C-202, which mistakenly gives his name as "Richard Bobosson," an obvious typographical error).

ROBOSSON, THOMAS. Took the Oath of Allegiance before Hon. Elijah Robosson in March, 1778 (Ref: B-28).

ROBOSSON, VACHEL. Took the Oath of Allegiance before Hon. Elijah Robosson in March, 1778 (Ref: B-28). On June 6, 1793, final distribution of his estate was made to Elizabeth Robosson (widow), with fourths of the balance to John Robosson, Sarah Robosson, Vachel Robosson and Dorsey Robosson (Ref: U-10).

ROBUCK, WILLIAM. Enrolled by Capt. Thomas Watkins on October 21, 1776, for service to the State (Ref: I-144, MS.1814).

ROCKHOLD, CHARLES. Took the Oath of Allegiance before Hon. Elijah Robosson in March, 1778 (Ref: B-28). On November 16, 1793, final distribution of his estate was made to Jane Rockhold, now wife of John Robinson (widow's third) and thirds of the remaining balance to Thomas Rockhold, Charles Rockhold, and Elizabeth Rockhold (Ref: U-11).

ROCKHOLD, CLARK JR. Took the Oath of Allegiance before Hon. Elijah Robosson in March, 1778 (Ref: B-28). On September 11, 1793, final distribution of the estate of Clark Rockhold was made by Mrs. Sarah Todd, administratrix de bonis non, with negroes to Thomas Clarke Rockhold and Rachel Rockhold, plus 15 pounds to Thomas Fields Rockhold, and fifths to Charles Rockhold, John Rockhold, Sarah Rockhold, Solorah Rockhold and Mary Rockhold (Ref: U-10).

ROCKHOLD, CLARK SR. Took the Oath of Allegiance before Hon. Elijah Robosson in March, 1778 (Ref: B-28).

ROCKHOLD, JOHN. Took the Oath of Allegiance before Hon. Elijah Robosson in March, 1778 (Ref: B-28).

ROGERS, JOHN. Took the Oath of Allegiance before Hon. Thomas Worthington on February 28, 1778 (Ref: B-21). On June 15, 1796 the final distribution of his estate was made, with sevenths of the balance to Nicholas G. Rogers, Samuel Rogers, Ann Rogers Warfield, Charles Rogers, Mary Rogers, Catherine Rogers, and John Rogers (Ref: U-14).

ROGERS, WILLIAM. Private in Capt. Ramsay's Company in 1776 and was "wounded at Camden on August 16, 1780 and returned home the following winter." He was discharged on November 15, 1783 (Ref: X-34), and he was paid in Anne Arundel County on September 3, 1784, October 26, 1784 and December 17, 1784 (Ref: D-21, D-23, D-25).

ROSS, GEORGE. Took the Oath of Allegiance before Hon. Samuel Harrison, Jr. in March, 1778 (Ref: B-29).

ROUSBATCH, SAMUEL. Took the Oath of Allegiance before Hon. Samuel Harrison in March, 1778 (Ref: A-244).

ROWDON, JOHN. Took the Oath of Allegiance before Hon. Reuben Meriweather on March 2, 1778 (Ref: B-25).

ROWLAND, JAMES. Took the Oath of Allegiance before Hon. Thomas Worthington on February 28, 1778 (Ref: B-21).

ROWLES, WILLIAM. Took Oath of Allegiance in 1780 (Ref: Richard B. Miller's "Some Little Known Data Regarding Maryland Signers of Oath of Fidelity," Maryland Genealogical Society Bulletin, Vol. 27, No. 1, 1986, p. 119).

RUSSELL, BENJAMIN. Took the Oath of Allegiance before Hon. Samuel Lane on March 1, 1778 (Ref: B-23). On November 5, 1796 the final distribution of his estate was made to Keziah Russell (widow's third), with sevenths of the balance to James Russell, Jane Russell (wife of Samuel Carr), Sarah Russell (wife of Joseph Whittington), Mary Russell (wife of Vansant Screvener), Providence Russell, Richard Russell, and Jemima Russell (Ref: U-15).

RUSSELL, WILLIAM. Took the Oath of Allegiance before Hon. Reuben Meriweather on March 2, 1778 (Ref: B-25).

RYAN, JACOB. Enrolled by Henry Ridgely, Jr. and passed by Col. Josias C. Hall on August 26, 1776 (Ref: H-41). He took the Oath of Allegiance before Hon. Thomas Worthington on February 28, 1778 (Ref: B-21).

RYAN, NATHAN. Enlisted by Edward Spurrier and passed by Thomas Dorsey on July 20, 1776 (Ref: H-41). Took the Oath of Allegiance before Hon. Thomas Worthington on February 28, 1778 (Ref: B-21).

RYAN, ROBERT. Took the Oath of Allegiance before Hon. Thomas Worthington on February 28, 1778 (Ref: B-21).

RYOM, WILLIAM. Took the Oath of Allegiance before Hon. Richard Harwood, Jr. on March 1, 1778 (Ref: B-23).

ST. LAWRENCE, FRANCIS. Took the Oath of Allegiance before Honorable Nicholas Worthington in March, 1778 (Ref: Original list in the Maryland State Papers Red Book 21, MdHR4587. Source B-27 mistakenly left the name off its list).

ST. LAWRENCE, WILLIAM. Took the Oath of Allegiance before Honorable Nicholas Worthington in March, 1778 (Ref: Original list in the Maryland State Papers Red Book 21, MdHR4587. Source B-27 mistakenly spelled name "St. Laurans").

SALLY, WILLIAM. Was enlisted by Thomas Mayo on July 20, 1776 (Ref: H-41).

SAND, GABRIEL. Captain of the Schooner "The Industry" on April 14, 1777, and was permitted to proceed from Annapolis to Island of Coracoa (Ref: V-210).

SANDERS, EDWARD. Took the Oath of Allegiance before Hon. Samuel Harrison in March, 1778 (Ref: A-244).

SANDERS, JAMES JR. Took the Oath of Allegiance before Hon. Richard Harwood, Jr. on March 1, 1778 (Ref: B-23).

SANDERS, JAMES SR. Took the Oath of Allegiance before Hon. Richard Harwood, Jr. on March 1, 1778 (Ref: B-23).

SANDERS, WILLIAM. Took the Oath of Allegiance before Hon. Richard Harwood, Jr. on March 1, 1778 (Ref: B-23).

SANDS, JOHN. Private in Capt. William Marbury's Company of Artillery in 1777 (Ref: H-575). On July 1, 1811 the final distribution of his estate was made to Delilah Sands, now wife of Isaac Holland (widow's third), with fifths of the balance to Ann Holland,

Eliza Sands, Washington Sands, Jane Sands, and Thomas Sands (Ref: U-40).

SANDS, ROBERT. Took the Oath of Allegiance before Hon. Samuel Harrison in March, 1778 (Ref: A-244).

SANDS, THOMAS. Private in Captain Gilbert Middleton's Independent Company of Militia of Annapolis on March 20, 1779 (Ref: I-144, O-325).

SANDS, WILLIAM. Private in Capt. Gilbert Middleton's Independent Company of Militia of Annapolis on March 20, 1779 (Ref: I-144, O-325).

SANK, GEORGE. Took Oath of Allegiance on March 9, 1778 (Ref: V-531). He was a 2nd Lieutenant in Capt. Pecker's Company on July 30, 1781 (Ref: W-527).

SANSBERRY, RICHARD. Born in Maryland. Enrolled by Capt. Edward Tillard and passed on July 10, 1776. Height: 5' 6" (Ref: H-39).

SAPPINGTON, JOHN. Three men with this name took the Oath of Allegiance: one before Hon. Richard Harwood, Jr. on March 1, 1778, another before Hon. John Dorsey on March 12, 1778, and another before Hon. Nicholas Worthington in March, 1778 (Ref: B-23, B-26, B-28). One John Sappington was deceased by August 5, 1823 when final distribution of his estate (sevenths) was made to John Sappington, Martha Sappington, Caleb Sappington, Rebecca Sappington, Ann Sappington, Elizabeth Sappington, and Caroline Sappington (Ref: U-65). This is probably the John Sappington (1758-1816) who married Elizabeth ---- and had seven children: John Sappington, Robert Sappington, Ann Sappington, Rebecca Sappington, Martha Sappington Haslup, Elizabeth Sappington Sewell, and Caroline Sappington Young (Ref: T-628).

SAPPINGTON, FRANCIS BROWN, M.D. (1754-1839). Married Anne Ridgely in 1783 in Anne Arundel County and a son, Col. Thomas Sappington was born in Frederick County in 1792. Francis was a Major in the militia during the Revolution, and is buried in Mt. Olivet Cemetery in Frederick, Maryland (Ref: E-2790).

SAPPINGTON, NATHANIEL. Took the Oath of Allegiance before Hon. Nicholas Worthington in March, 1778 (Ref: B-28). Still alive in 1801 (Ref: U-21).

SAPPINGTON, RICHARD, M. D. He was appointed an Assistant Surgeon in 1777 and Surgeon in August, 1780 in the 3rd Maryland Line. Served in the Army until 1782, and was wounded. His first wife was Margaret Hamilton and his second wife was Cassandra Frances Durbin in 1784. Children were: John Sappington, William Sappington, Gerrard Sappington, Robert Sappington, Mary Sappington, John K. Sappington, Edward Sappington, Thomas Sappington, and Frederick Sappington. Richard died in Harford County, Maryland in 1828 (Ref: T-628, Y-305, and Henry C. Peden, Jr.'s "Revolutionary Patriots of Harford County, Maryland, 1775-1783, page 198 (Bel Air, Maryland:

Published by the Author, 1985). He also took the Oath of Allegiance before Hon. Nicholas Worthington in Anne Arundel County in March, 1778 (Ref: B-27).

SAPPINGTON, RICHARD. He was paid by the Council of Maryland on November 3, 1777, for riding express from Annapolis to Philadelphia (Ref: V-408).

SAPPINGTON, THOMAS. Took Oath of Allegiance before Hon. Thomas Worthington on February 28, 1778 (Ref: B-21).

SAUNDERS, JAMES II (1729-1794). Married Susanna Ricketts in 1769 and had 2 children: James Saunders and Elizabeth Saunders. James took the Oath of Allegiance in 1778 (according to Ref: T-629).

SAUNDERS, JOHN. Private in Captain John Fulford's Company of Artillery at Annapolis on December 12, 1776 (Ref: H-572).

SAVAGE, WILLIAM. Took the Oath of Allegiance before Hon. Thomas Dorsey on March 2, 1778 (Ref: B-24).

SAVORY, PHILIP. Born in Ireland. He was recruited by Cornelius Mills and passed by Lt. Col. James Tootell on May 9, 1778 (Ref: C-217, H-314).

SAWYER, RICHARD. Took the Oath of Allegiance before Hon. Samuel Harrison in March, 1778 (Ref: A-244).

SCOOT, RICHARD. Took the Oath of Allegiance before Hon. Thomas Dorsey on March 1, 1778 (Ref: B-24).

SCOTT, ADAM. Took the Oath of Allegiance before Hon. Thomas Worthington on February 28, 1778 (Ref: B-21).

SCOTT, ALEXANDER. Enlisted by Richard Talbot and passed by John Dorsey on July 22, 1776 (Ref: H-39).

SCOTT, DAVID. One of the petitioners to the Convention of Maryland to form an independent rifle company in July, 1776 (Ref: B-3). He took the Oath of Allegiance before Hon. John Dorsey on March 12, 1778 (Ref: B-26).

SCOTT, GEORGE. One of the petitioners to the Convention of Maryland to form an independent rifle company in July, 1776 (Ref: B-3). He took the Oath of Allegiance before Hon. Thomas Dorsey on March 2, 1778 (Ref: B-24).

SCOTT, HENRY. Private in Capt. John Fulford's Artillery Company at Annapolis on December 12, 1776 (Ref: H-572).

SCOTT, JOHN. Born in Scotland. He was a Substitute, furnished by Richard Harwood on May 2, 1778, to serve 3 years (Ref: C-205, H-317). Took the Oath of Allegiance before Hon. Thomas Harwood on February 28, 1778 (Ref: B-22).

SCRIVENOR (SCRIVENER), FRANCIS. He took the Oath of Allegiance before Hon. Samuel Harrison in March, 1778 (Ref: B-29). On June 15, 1808, the final distribution of his estate (sevenths) was made to his children: Elizabeth Whittington, Mary Scrivener, Sarah Ward, Ann Dowell, Thomas Scrivener, John Scrivener, and George Scrivener (Ref: U-35).

SCRIVENOR (SCRIVENER), JOHN. Three men with this name took the Oath of Allegiance: one before Hon. Samuel Lane on March 1, 1778, one before Hon. John Dorsey on March 12, 1778, and one before Hon. Samuel Harrison in March, 1778 (Ref: B-23, B-26, B-29). One was born in Scotland and was a Substitute, furnished by William Fisher on May 20, 1778, to serve three years (Ref: C-206, H-317). Another was born in Maryland and was enrolled by Samuel Chew and passed on July 25, 1776. Height: 6' 1" (Ref: H-40).

SCRIVENOR, LEWIS. Took the Oath of Allegiance before Hon. Samuel Harrison in March, 1778 (Ref: B-29).

SCRIVENOR, RICHARD. Took the Oath of Allegiance before Hon. Samuel Harrison in March, 1778 (Ref: B-29).

SCRIVENOR, ROBERT. Born in America. He was recruited and passed by James Brice on April 12, 1778 (Ref: C-216, H-314).

SCRIVENOR, WILLIAM. Two men by this name took the Oath of Allegiance before Hon. Samuel Harrison in March, 1778 (Ref: A-244, B-29).

SEARLES, DANIEL. Private in Capt. Richard Chew's Company in Col. John Weems' Battalion on October 5, 1776 (Ref: A-95, I-143).

SEARS, JOHN. Second Lieutenant in Captain Nicholas Worthington's Company of Militia in the Severn Battalion in 1777 and First Lieutenant in Capt. Henry Bateman's Company in 1778 (Ref: C-203, I-144, J-113, O-208). On January 26, 1828, the Treasurer was directed to "pay to Mary Sears, of Harford County, during life, half yearly, half pay of a Lieutenant, a further remuneration for her husband John Sears' services during the rev. war" (Ref: K-389).

SEFTON, EDWARD. Took Oath of Allegiance before Hon. Richard Harwood, Jr. on March 1, 1778 (Ref: B-23). Private in Capt. Gilbert Middleton's Independent Company of Militia of Annapolis on March 20, 1779 (Ref: I-144, O-325).

SEFTON, JOHN (c1734-1799). Married Elizabeth Woolton in 1756 and had seven children: Edmond Sefton, Edmond Sefton, William Sefton, John Sefton, Thomas Sefton, Richard Sefton, Charles Sefton, and James Sefton (Ref: T-640, which mistakenly spelled his name "Septon"). Took the Oath of Allegiance before Hon. Richard Harwood, Jr. on March 1, 1778 (Ref: B-23). In February, 1801, final distribution of his estate was made with legacies to Richard Sefton, James Sefton, Thomas Sefton, Charles Sefton, Sarah Sefton (daughter-in-law) and granddaughters Elizabeth Sefton and Maria Sefton (Ref: U-21).

SEFTON, WILLIAM. Two men with this name took the Oath of Allegiance before Hon. Richard Harwood, Jr. on March 1, 1778 (Ref: B-23).

SELBY, BENJAMIN. Took the Oath of Allegiance before Hon. Nicholas Worthington in March, 1778 (Ref: B-28). On July 27, 1788, a distribution of his estate (sevenths) to Joseph Selby, Benjamin Selby, Polly Selby, Rebecca Selby, Ann Selby, Jemima Selby and Elizabeth Selby. On May 27, 1789 final distribution was made (sixths) to Mary Selby (wife of Lancelot Green), Joseph Selby, Ann Selby (wife of Edward Stewart), Rebecca Selby, Jemima Selby, and Elizabeth Selby. Benjamin Selby was mentioned in 1788 but not in 1789 (Ref: U-2, 3).

SELBY, HENRY. Ensign in Capt. John Hammond's Company in the Severn Battalion of Militia on June 19, 1777 (Ref: A-176). Commissioned a Second Lieutenant on September 2, 1777 in Capt. John Gray's Company (Ref: V-359). He took the Oath of Allegiance before Hon. Elijah Robosson in March, 1778 (Ref: B-28).

SELBY, JONATHAN. Took the Oath of Allegiance before Hon. Nicholas Worthington in March, 1778 (Ref: B-28). On May 12, 1827, the final distribution of his estate was made to Mary Selby (widow's third), with the remaining balance to Susan Selby and Sarah Selby (Ref: U-73).

SELBY, MORDECAI. Took the Oath of Allegiance before Hon. Reuben Meriweather on March 2, 1778 (Ref: B-25).

SELBY, MORDECAI JR. Took Oath of Allegiance before Hon. Reuben Meriweather on March 2, 1778 (Ref: B-25).

SELBY, NICHOLAS. Took the Oath of Allegiance before Hon. Reuben Meriweather on March 2, 1778 (Ref: B-25). Drafted in October, 1780, to serve until December 10, 1780 (Ref: H-369).

SELLMAN, GASSAWAY. Took the Oath of Allegiance before Hon. Samuel Harrison in March, 1778 (Ref: A-244).

SELLMAN, JOHN. Took the Oath of Allegiance before Hon. Richard Harwood, Jr. on March 1, 1778 (Ref: B-23).

SELLMAN, JONATHAN (1757, Anne Arundel County - 1817, Baltimore County). He married Elizabeth Dawson in 1783 and they had 2 children: Charlotte Sellman Crook and Patty Sellman Welch. Jonathan took the Oath of Allegiance in 1778 (according to Ref: T-639).

SELLMAN, JONATHAN JR. (March 2, 1753 - May 21, 1810). He married first to Rachel Lucas in 1783 and second to Elizabeth Harwood in 1794. His children were Alfred Sellman, Richard Sellman, John Henry Sellman, Ann (Elizabeth) Sellman Welch and Margaret Sellman Brogden (Ref: T-639). His deposition taken on August 27, 1776, stated he was "exercising some men of the flying camp when approached by Matthias Hammond and Thomas Harwood who advised all the men to lay down their arms and vote for Rezin Hammond as one who would defend their rights" (Ref: A-82). Jonathan also took the Oath of Allegiance before Hon. Richard Harwood, Jr., on March 1, 1778 (Ref: B-23). He was a 2nd Lieutenant in Capt. James Disney's Company in the 3rd Maryland Line in June, 1776, and was at Valley Forge (Ref: E-2664, H-39, N-534). On October 18, 1827, the final distribution of his estate was made by Alfred Sellman, administrator de bonis non, to Ann Sellman (widow's third), with sixths of the remainder to Alfred Sellman, Joseph N. Stockett, Richard Sellman, Thomas Welch, David M. Brogden, and John H. Sellman (Ref: U-74).

SELLMAN, LEONARD. Took Oath of Allegiance before Hon. Nicholas Worthington in March, 1778 (Ref: B-28). Still alive in March, 1817 (Ref: U-50).

SELLMAN, WILLIAM. Resident of Herring Creek who petitioned to form a militia company on March 6, 1776, and subsequently served in Captain Richard Weems' Company (Ref: I-143, MS.1814). There were two men with this name who took the Oath of Allegiance: one before Hon. Thomas Harwood on February 28, 1778 and one before Hon. John Dorsey on March 12, 1778 (Ref: B-22, B-26). One William Sellman (1720-1796) married Charity Knighton in 1745 and they had two children: William Sellman and Jonathan Sellman (Ref: T-639).

SEWARD, DANIEL. Took the Oath of Allegiance on March 9, 1778 (Ref: V-531).

SEWELL, AUGUSTUS (AUGUSTIN?). Took Oath of Allegiance before Hon. Nicholas Worthington in March, 1778 (Ref: B-28). On January 26, 1820, the final distribution of the estate of "Augustin Sewell" was made with a legacy to John M. Sewell and the fifths of the remainder to Augustin Sewell, George Sewell, Julia Worthington, Eleanor Sewell, and Mary Baldwin (Ref: U-57).

SEWELL, BENJAMIN. Took Oath of Allegiance before Hon. Nicholas Worthington in March, 1778 (Ref: B-28).

SEWELL, CHARLES. He was enlisted by Richard Talbot and passed by John Dorsey on July 22, 1776 (Ref: H-39).

SEWELL, GREENBURY. Took Oath of Allegiance before Hon. Nicholas Worthington in March, 1778 (Ref: B-28).

SEWELL, JAMES (died 1790). Married Rachel Gassaway, widow of Nicholas, and had a son, James Sewell, Jr. James served as a Private in Col. William's Regiment in the 2nd Maryland Line from 1780 to 1783 (Ref: T-641).

SEWELL, JAMES. Pensioned as a Private in the Maryland Line on May 16, 1817, at $60 per month from March 4, 1803. In December, 1817, the Treasurer was directed to "pay to James Sewell, an old rev. soldier, quarterly, half pay of a private, as a further remuneration for his services" (Ref: K-390). A "James Sewall" was pensioned as a Private on March 4, 1831 (Ref: Z-45) and an Invalid soldier named James Sewall was pensioned in Anne Arundel County on March 4, 1803, and again on April 24, 1816, as a Private (Ref: Z-2).

SEWELL, JOHN (1740-1805). He married Mary Warfield Marriott in 1760 and they had 4 children: John Sewell, Achsah Sewell Mallonee, Sarah Sewell, and Mary Sewell (Ref: T-641). John took the Oath of Allegiance before Hon. Nicholas Worthington in March, 1778 (Ref: B-28).

SEWELL, JOSEPH. Born in 1753 in Elk Ridge, Anne Arundel (now Howard) County, Maryland, and enlisted in Wilkes County, North Carolina on April 1, 1776 or 1777. Two years after the war he moved to Carter County, Tennessee, where he lived for thirty years before moving to Cumberland County, Kentucky. He applied for pension S31354 in November, 1832, age 79 (Ref: L-33, HCP-130).

SEWELL, JOSEPH. Took the Oath of Allegiance before Hon. Nicholas Worthington in March, 1778 (Ref: B-28).

SEWELL, JOSEPH SR. Took Oath of Allegiance before Hon. Nicholas Worthington in March, 1778 (Ref: B-28).

SEWELL, PHILIP. Took the Oath of Allegiance before Hon. Nicholas Worthington in March, 1778 (Ref: B-27).

SEWELL, VACHEL. Took the Oath of Allegiance before Hon. Nicholas Worthington in March, 1778 (Ref: B-28).

SEWELL, WILLIAM. In November, 1811, the Treasurer of the Western Shore was directed to "pay to William Sewell, of Annapolis, late a soldier in the rev. war, or order during life, quarterly payments, half pay of a private." On February 22, 1822, the Treasurer of the Western Shore was directed to "pay to William Sewell, of Talbot County, half pay of a private, for his rev. war services." On February 6, 1832, the Treasurer of the Western Shore was directed to "pay to Rebecca Sewell, widow of William Sewell, a soldier of the rev. war, during life, half yearly, the half pay of a private, for the services rendered by her said husband" (Ref: K-390). William married Rebecca Disney on December 9, 1790 in Anne Arundel County (Ref: G-122).

SHAAFF, ARTHUR. Private in Captain William Marbury's Company of Artillery in 1777 (Ref: H-575). Still alive in May, 1814 (Ref: U-44).

SHAAFF, JOHN T. Private in Captain William Marbury's Company of Artillery in 1777 (Ref: H-575). He could be the Dr. John Thomas Shaaff who was executor of Bennett Lake in 1814, with Arthur Shaaff serving as surety (Ref: U-44).

SHADDOWS, DAVID. Took the Oath of Allegiance before Honorable John Dorsey on March 12, 1778 (Ref: B-26).

SHANKS, JOHN (1754 - March 23, 1829, Nelson County, Kentucky). He served in the Revolutionary War in 1780 and, as a disabled soldier, was paid in Anne Arundel County on April 13, 1784 and September 3, 1784 and October 26, 1784 and December 17, 1784 (Ref: D-14, D-21,

D-23, D-25) and was first pensioned on April 14, 1789. He subsequently moved to Kentucky where he applied for and received pension S37393 in Meade County in 1826 or 1827. He had moved to Kentucky to be with his children and their families. Bounty land warrant 262-100 was later issued to his widow, Ann Shanks (Ref: L-58, HCP-130). He was medically discharged at Frederick on November 29, 1783 (Ref: X-35).

SHANLEY, JACOB. Soldier in the 7th Maryland Line who was wounded at battle of Germantown. His discharge was signed by George Washington on November 1, 1783 (Ref: X-36). He was paid in Anne Arundel County on September 3, 1784 and October 26, 1784 and December 17, 1784 (Ref: D-21, D-22, D-25).

SHAW, JOHN. Sergeant Major who was wounded and transferred to the Invalids Corps (no date given) and discharged at Philadelphia on June 18, 1781 (Ref: X-37). He was paid in Anne Arundel County on January 13, 1784, April 13, 1784, June 9, 1784, September 3, 1784, October 26, 1784, and December 17, 1784 (Ref: D-12, D-14, D-18, D-21, D-23, D-25).

SHAW, JOHN. Second Lieutenant in Capt. John Walker's Company in the Severn Battalion of Militia on September 19, 1778 (Ref: I-114, J-113, O-208). Took Oath of Allegiance before Hon. Elijah Robosson in March, 1778 (Ref: B-28). One John Shaw died before December 5, 1831, when final distribution of his estate was made to Thomas Shaw, Mary Shaw, James Shaw (dec'd.), George Shaw (dec'd.), and Thomas Franklin in right of his wife Elizabeth (Ref: U-83).

SHEAN, TIMOTHY. His name appeared on a list of defectives from the Maryland Line on August 16, 1780 (Ref: H-415).

SHEARBUT, BENJAMIN BATTEE. Resident of Herring Creek who petitioned to form a company of militia on March 6, 1776, and subsequently served in Captain Richard Weems' Company (Ref: I-143, MS.1814). Took the Oath of Allegiance before Hon. Samuel Lane on March 1, 1778 (Ref: B-23).

SHEARBUT, RICHARD. Resident of Herring Creek who petitioned to form a militia company on March 6, 1776, and subsequently served in Captain Richard Weems' Company (Ref: I-143, MS.1814).

SHEARBUT, THOMAS. Resident of Herring Creek who petitioned to form a militia company on March 6, 1776, and subsequently served in Captain Richard Weems' Company (Ref: I-143, MS.1814).

SHECKELLS, JOHN. Took the Oath of Allegiance before Hon. Thomas Harwood on February 28, 1778 (Ref: B-22).

SHECKELLS, SAMUEL. Took the Oath of Allegiance before Hon. Samuel Lane on March 1, 1778 (Ref: B-23).

SHEDBOLT, WILLIAM. Enlisted by Joseph Burgess for the Flying Camp and passed on July 20, 1776 (Ref: H-40).

SHEETS, MARTIN. Took the Oath of Allegiance before Hon. Thomas Worthington on February 28, 1778 (Ref: B-21).

SHEKELL, FRANCIS. Took the Oath of Allegiance before Hon. Thomas Harwood on February 28, 1778 (Ref: B-22).

SHEKELL, JOHN. Took the Oath of Allegiance before Hon. Thomas Harwood on February 28, 1778 (Ref: B-22). On December 9, 1792, final distribution of his estate (eighths) was made to Francis Shekell, Elizabeth Shekell (wife of Benjamin Basford), Abraham Shekell, Rebecca Magruder, Mary Shekell, Susannah Ray, Deborah Dowley, and Richard Shekell (Ref: U-9).

SHEKELL, RICHARD. Took the Oath of Allegiance before Hon. Thomas Harwood on February 28, 1778 (Ref: B-22).

SHEKELL, SAMUEL. Took the Oath of Allegiance before Hon. Thomas Harwood on February 28, 1778 (Ref: B-22).

SHELDA, CHRISTOPHER. Took the Oath of Allegiance before Hon. Samuel Harrison in March, 1778 (Ref: A-244).

SHEPARD, HENRY. Took the Oath of Allegiance before Hon. Samuel Lane on March 1, 1778 (Ref: B-23).

SHEPHERD, NATHANIEL. Enlisted by Thomas Mayo on July 20, 1776 (Ref: H-41).

SHEPPARD, NICHOLAS. Second Lieutenant in Capt. Charles Boone's Company of Militia in the Severn Battalion on March 1, 1778 (Ref: C-203).

SHEPPERD, THOMAS. Took the Oath of Allegiance before Hon. Thomas Worthington on February 28, 1778 (Ref: B-21).

SHIPLEY, ADAM. Took the Oath of Allegiance before Hon. John Dorsey on March 12, 1778 (Ref: B-26).

SHIPLEY, ADAM (of Baltimore County). Took the Oath of Allegiance before Hon. Reuben Meriweather on March 2, 1778 (Ref: B-25).

SHIPLEY, BENJAMIN. Took the Oath of Allegiance before Hon. Reuben Meriweather on March 2, 1778 (Ref: B-24).

SHIPLEY, BENJAMIN (of Baltimore County). Took the Oath of Allegiance before Hon. Reuben Meriweather on March 2, 1778 (Ref: B-24).

SHIPLEY, GEORGE JR. One of the petitioners to the Convention of Maryland to form an independent rifle company in July, 1776 (Ref: B-3). He took Oath of Allegiance before Hon. Reuben Meriweather on March 2, 1778 (Ref: B-24).

SHIPLEY, GREENBURY (of Baltimore County). Took the Oath of Allegiance before Hon. Reuben Meriweather on March 2, 1778 (Ref: B-24).

SHIPLEY, HENRY. Enrolled by Capt. Thomas Watkins for service to the State on October 21, 1776 (Ref: I-144, MS.1814). Took the Oath of Allegiance before Hon. Reuben Meriweather on March 2, 1778 (Ref: B-24).

SHIPLEY, JOHN (circa 1743 - before 1815). Married Keziah Porter in 1766 and had a son, John Shipley. He was one of the petitioners to the Convention of Maryland to form an independent rifle company in July, 1776 (Ref: B-3). He took the Oath of Allegiance before Hon. John Dorsey on March 12, 1778 (Ref: B-26). Commissioned an Ensign in Captain Brice Howard's Company on May 15, 1776 and served in Capt. John Worthington Dorsey's Company in the Elk Ridge Battalion in 1778. In March, 1779, he was commissioned a First Lieutenant in Capt. Vachel Stevens' Company (Ref: C-201, E-2679, N-426, O-333). John's second wife was Eleanor Purnell and his children were Ann Shipley Harrison, Adam Shipley, John Shipley, Rezin Shipley, Larkin Shipley, Peter Shipley, Richardson Shipley, Peggy Shipley, Enos Shipley, Sarah Shipley, Elizabeth Shipley, and Polly Shipley (Ref: T-647).

SHIPLEY, JOHN. Took the Oath of Allegiance before Hon. Reuben Meriweather on March 2, 1778 (Ref: B-24).

SHIPLEY, JOSHUA. Took the Oath of Allegiance before Hon. Thomas Dorsey on March 2, 1778 (Ref: B-24).

SHIPLEY, PETER. One of the petitioners to the Convention of Maryland to form an independent rifle company in July, 1776 (Ref: B-3).

SHIPLEY, PETER (of Baltimore County). Took the Oath of Allegiance before Hon. Reuben Meriweather on March 2, 1778 (Ref: B-24).

SHIPLEY, RICHARD SR. Took the Oath of Allegiance before Hon. Thomas Dorsey on March 2, 1778 (Ref: B-24).

SHIPLEY, ROBERT. Took the Oath of Allegiance before Hon. Reuben Merieweather on March 2, 1778 (Ref: B-24).

SHIPLEY, SAMUEL. Took the Oath of Allegiance before Hon. John Dorsey on March 12, 1778 (Ref: B-26).

SHIPLEY, SAMUEL (of Baltimore County). He took the Oath of Allegiance before Hon. Reuben Meriweather on March 2, 1778 (Ref: B-24).

SHIPLEY, SAMUEL JR. (of Baltimore County). Took the Oath of Allegiance before Hon. Reuben Meriweather on March 2, 1778 (Ref: B-24).

SHIPLEY, TALBOT. Took the Oath of Allegiance before Hon. Reuben Meriweather on March 2, 1778 (Ref: B-25).

SHIPLEY, VACHEL. Took the Oath of Allegiance before Hon. Reuben Meriweather on March 2, 1778 (Ref: B-25).

SHIPLEY, WILLIAM. One of the petitioners to the Convention of Maryland to form an independent rifle company in July, 1776 (Ref: B-3). Took the Oath of Allegiance before Hon. Reuben Meriweather on March 2, 1778 (Ref: B-24). On March 25, 1823, the final distribution of his estate was made to Susan Goldsborough, Denton Geohagan (in right of wife), Elias Shipley, William Sellman (in right of wife), Thomas Shipley, Joshua Shipley, Denton Shipley, Thomas J. Warfield (in right of wife), Henry Goldsborough (in right of wife), Upton D. Welch (in right of wife), and Robert Shipley (Ref: U-64).

SHIPLEY, WILLIAM JR. Took Oath of Allegiance before Hon. Reuben Meriweather on March 2, 1778 (Ref: B-24).

SHOEBROOK (SHOBROOK), PHILIP. He was recruited by Cornelius Mills and passed by James Brice on January 27, 1778 (Ref: C-215, H-313). He was wounded and sent to the Invalids Corps. He was discharged at Philadelphia on November 6, 1783, stating he had served over five years in the Army (Ref: X-38).

SHOEMAKER, GIDEON. Private in Captain Richard Chew's Company of Col. John Weems' Battalion on October 5, 1776 (Ref: A-95, I-143).

SHORT, ABRAHAM. Took the Oath of Allegiance before Hon. Richard Harwood, Jr. on March 1, 1778 (Ref: B-23).

SHOUGHNESEY(?), ------. Private in Capt. Richard Dorsey's Artillery Company on November 17, 1777 (Ref: H-574).

SHRINK, ANDREW. Sergeant in Capt. Richard Dorsey's Company of Artillery on November 17, 1777 (Ref: H-573).

SHULES, THOMAS. Took the Oath of Allegiance before Hon. Samuel Harrison in March, 1778 (Ref: A-244).

SIEBERT, JUSTICE. Private in Capt. Gilbert Middleton's Independent Company of Militia of Annapolis on March 20, 1779 (Ref: I-144, O-325).

SIMMONS, ABRAHAM. Captain in the South River Battalion in 1776 and Colonel John Weems' Battalion in 1778 (Ref: C-199, N-161, N-232). He took the Oath of Allegiance before Hon. Samuel Harrison in March, 1778 (Ref: A-244).

SIMMONS, DAVID. Born in America. He was a Substitute, furnished by Caleb Burgess on April 15, 1778, to serve for three years (Ref: C-204, H-317).

SIMMONS, GEORGE. Born in Maryland. Enrolled by Captain Edward Tillard and passed on July 10, 1776. Height: 5' 5" (Ref: H-39). George took the Oath of Allegiance before Hon. Samuel Lane on March 1, 1778 (Ref: B-23).

SIMMONS, ISAAC. Two men by this name took the Oath of Allegiance: one before Hon. Thomas Harwood on February 28, 1778 and another one before Hon. Samuel Harrison in March, 1778 (Ref: B-22, B-29).

SIMMONS, JAMES. Private in Captain John Fulford's Company of Artillery at Annapolis on December 12, 1776 (Ref: H-572).

SIMMONS, JEREMIAH CHAPMAN. He took the Oath of Allegiance before Hon. Samuel Harrison in March, 1778 (Ref: Original lists in Maryland State Papers, Red Book 19, MdHR4584. Source A-244 mistakenly gave his name as "Jerome Chapman Simmons"). On March 3, 1796 the final distribution of his estate was made to Elizabeth Simmons (widow's third), with fifths of the remaining balance to Jeremiah Chapman Simmons, Elizabeth Simmons, Richard Simmons, Margaret Simmons, and William Simmons (Ref: U-13).

SIMMONS, JOHN. Took the Oath of Allegiance in 1780 (Ref: Richard B. Miller's "Some Little Known Data Regarding Maryland Signers of the Oath of Fidelity" in Maryland Genealogical Society Bulletin, Vol. 27, No. 1, 1986, p. 120).

SIMMONS, WILLIAM. Two men by this name took the Oath of Allegiance in March, 1778: one before Hon. Samuel Lane and one before Hon. Samuel Harrison (Ref: A-244, B-23). One was a Captain in the West River Battalion in 1778 (Ref: C-200), and the other was enrolled by Captain Edward Tillard and passed on July 10, 1776. Born in Maryland. Height: 5' 7" (Ref: H-39). One William Simmons was pensioned on March 4, 1831, age 72, as a Private (Ref: Z-45).

SIMMONS, WILLIAM JR. Took the Oath of Allegiance before Hon. Samuel Harrison in March, 1778 (Ref: A-244).

SIMON, JOSEPH. Took the Oath of Allegiance before Hon. Nicholas Worthington in March, 1778 (Ref: B-27).

SIMPSON, AMOS. Took the Oath of Allegiance before Hon. John Dorsey on March 12, 1778 (Ref: B-26).

SIMPSON, BENJAMIN. Enrolled by Capt. Thomas Watkins for service to the State on October 21, 1776 (Ref: I-144, MS.1814). He took the Oath of Allegiance before Hon. John Dorsey on March 12, 1778 (Ref: B-26).

SIMPSON, CHARLES. Took the Oath of Allegiance before Hon. Thomas Worthington on February 28, 1778 (Ref: B-21).

SIMPSON, FRANCIS. Took the Oath of Allegiance before Hon. Thomas Worthington on February 28, 1778 (Ref: B-21).

SIMPSON, GREENBURY. Took the Oath of Allegiance before Hon. John Dorsey on March 12, 1778 (Ref: B-26). He was drafted from the 51st Class of Militia in Anne Arundel County under the Act of May, 1781, made oath that he was drafted in the 47th Class under Act of October, 1780, and "procured John Jordan to enlist for the war to whom he gave forty pounds, part gold and part paper equal to gold, and that he had a mother sixty odd years of age and three sisters the eldest about fourteen, two have not been able to do anything for two years past, the next to her about twelve and the youngest about ten years of age, who depend on his labour only for support." The Council discharged him on August 29, 1781 from this draft (Ref: W-586).

SIMPSON, WILLIAM. Took the Oath of Allegiance before Hon. Thomas Worthington on February 28, 1778 (Ref: B-21).

SKELLY, DANIEL. He was enlisted by Capt. Edward Tillard and passed by Richard Harwood, Jr. on July 16, 1776 (Ref: H-40).

SKELLY (SKELLE), WILLIAM. He took the Oath of Allegiance before Hon. Thomas Worthington on February 28, 1778 (Ref: B-21).

SKIFFINGTON, ROGER. Born in Ireland. He was recruited and passed by James Brice on January 12, 1778 (Ref: C-215, H-313).

SKINNER, JAMES JOHN. Sergeant in Capt. John Fulford's Company of Artillery at Annapolis on December 12, 1776 (Ref: H-572).

SKINNER, JOHN. Private in Capt. Richard Chew's Company of Col. John Weems' Battalion on October 5, 1776 (Ref: A-95, I-143).

SLACK, JOHN. Born in Maryland. Enrolled by John S. Belt and passed in July, 1776. Height: 5' 3 1/2" (Ref: H-40).

SLIGHT, JOHN. His name appeared on a list of defectives from the Maryland Line on March 15, 1781 (Ref: H-416).

SLY (SLYE), JOHN. Private in Capt. Richard Dorsey's Company of Artillery on November 17, 1777 when reported sick with "peupneumony" (Ref: H-574, 618).

SLYE (SLIGH), WILLIAM. Disabled soldier who was paid in Anne Arundel County on May 20, 1783 and "on order Baltimore" on August 16, 1783. Also paid on Dec. 11, 1783, Jan. 13, 1784, April 13, 1784, June 9, 1784, Sept. 3, 1784, Oct. 26, 1784 and Dec. 17, 1784 (Ref: D-6, 8, 10, 12, 14, 18, 21, 23, 25).

SMART, JONAS. Enlisted by John Worthington Dorsey and passed by John Dorsey on July 22, 1776 (Ref: H-39).

SMITH, ANTHONY. Enrolled by Capt. Thomas Watkins for service to the State on October 21, 1776 (Ref: I-144, MS.1814). Took the Oath of Allegiance before Hon. Richard Harwood, Jr. on March 1, 1778 (Ref: B-23).

SMITH, COSMAN. Took the Oath of Allegiance before Hon. Reuben Meriweather on March 2, 1778 (Ref: B-24).

SMITH, GEORGE. Took the Oath of Allegiance before Hon. Reuben Meriweather on March 2, 1778 (Ref: B-24).

SMITH, GILBERT HAMILTON. Private in Capt. Richard Chew's Company of Colonel John Weems' Battalion on October 5, 1776 (Ref: A-95, I-143). He took the Oath of Allegiance before Hon. Samuel Harrison in March, 1778 (Ref: B-29).

SMITH, HENRY. Private in Captain William Marbury's Company of Artillery in 1777 (Ref: H-575).

SMITH, JAMES. Commissioned a First Lieutenant in Captain William Brown's Company of Matrosses on January 15, 1777 (Ref: V-50).

SMITH, JAMES. Soldier in the 3rd Maryland Line who was wounded in the foot (no date given) and discharged at Annapolis on July 15, 1782 (Ref: X-39). Paid on January 13, 1784, April 13, 1784, September 3, 1784, October 26, 1784 and December 17, 1784 in A. A. County (Ref: D-11, 13, 21, 23, 25).

SMITH, JOHN. Two men with this name took the Oath of Allegiance: one before Hon. Richard Harwood, Jr. on March 1, 1778, and another before Hon. Samuel Harrison in March, 1778 (Ref: B-23, B-29). One was born in Maryland and was enrolled by John S. Belt in July, 1776. Height: 5' 5 1/2" (Ref: H-40). Another was enrolled by Captain Thomas Watkins for service to the State on October 21, 1776 (Ref: I-144, MS.1814). On February 19, 1819 the Treasurer was directed to "pay to John Smith, of Anne Arundel County, late a soldier of the revolution, during life, the half pay of a private." On February 26, 1825 the Treasurer was directed to "pay to John Smith, of Anne Arundel Co., half pay of a private, further remuneration for his war services." On March 14, 1832 the Treasurer was directed to "pay to Sarah Smith, of Anne Arundel County, widow of John Smith, a soldier of the rev. war, during widowhood, half pay of a private for the services of her husband" (Ref: K-393, K-394). John Smith married Sarah Tydings in 1785 in Anne Arundel Co. (Ref: G-122).

SMITH, JOSEPH. Born in America. He was a Substitute, furnished by Adam Reb on May 11, 1778, to serve until war's end (Ref: C-204, H-317).

SMITH, JOSEPH. Born in Scotland. He was a Substitute, furnished by Joseph Howard, Jr. on May 6, 1778, to serve for three years (Ref: C-205, H-317).

SMITH, JOSEPH. Private in Captain John Fulford's Company of Artillery at Annapolis on December 12, 1776 (Ref: H-572).

SMITH, JOSEPH. Soldier in the 1st Maryland Line who was wounded at Camden on August 16, 1780. By permission of Gen. William Smallwood, he returned home and was discharged from the service at Annapolis on August 13, 1781 (Ref: X-40). He was paid in Anne Arundel County on April 13, 1784, September 3, 1784, October 26, 1784, December 17, 1784 (Ref: D-14, D-21, D-22, D-25).

SMITH, MICHAEL. Recruited by Captain Alexander Truman in October, 1780, to serve for three years (Ref: H-369). One Michael Smith was a Drummer in the Maryland Line, and appeared on the pension rolls of 1820 (Ref: K-394).

SMITH, NATHAN. Born in Ireland. He was recruited by Cornelius Mills and passed by Lt. Col. James Tootell on May 9, 1778 (Ref: C-217, H-314).

SMITH, PHILEMON. Took the Oath of Allegiance before Hon. Samuel Harrison in March, 1778 (Ref: A-244).

SMITH, REZIN. Took Oath of Allegiance before Hon. Elijah Robosson in March, 1778 (Ref: B-28).

SMITH, RICHARD. In Annapolis, on March 3, 1777, he petitioned the Council that he had been in Capt. Fulford's Company for 12 months and desired to serve on the ship "Conqueror" as he was offered the rank of Sergeant in the Marines, and his father also served on said vessel (Ref: V-156). Took the Oath of Allegiance before Hon. Elijah Robosson in March, 1778 (Ref: B-28).

SMITH, ROBERT JOHN. Took the Oath of Allegiance before Hon. Richard Harwood, Jr. on March 1, 1778 (Ref: B-23). He was administrator of John Carvill in 1793 (Ref: U-10).

SMITH, SAMUEL. Born in Ireland. Recruited by Cornelius Mills and passed by James Brice on April 11, 1778 (Ref: C-216, H-314). Two men with this name took the Oath of Allegiance: one before Hon. Thomas Harwood on February 28, 1778 and one before Hon. Elijah Robosson in March, 1778 (Ref: B-22, B-28).

SMITH, THOMAS. Private in Captain Richard Dorsey's Company of Artillery on November 17, 1777 (Ref: H-574). Two men with this name took the Oath of Allegiance in March, 1778: one before Hon. Elijah Robosson and one before Hon. Samuel Harrison (Ref: A-244, B-28).

SMITH, VALENTINE. Disabled soldier paid in Anne Arundel County on August 16, 1783 and noted as being "out of state" (Ref: D-8).

SMITH, WILLIAM. Born in America. He was recruited by Thomas Gordon and passed by James Brice on March 9, 1778 (Ref: C-216, H-313).

SMITH, WILLIAM. Born in Ireland. He was recruited by Cornelius Mills and passed by James Brice on May 9, 1778 (Ref: C-217, H-314).

SMITHE, ROBERT. Enrolled by Capt. Thomas Watkins for service to the State on October 21, 1776 (Ref: I-144, MS.1814).

SNAIRN, LEWIS, He was a Substitute passed on June 2, 1778 for a nine month term in Capt. William Simmons' Company (Ref: C-208, H-319).

SNOW, CHARLES. Born in Scotland. He was a Substitute, furnished by Henry May on May 12, 1778, for a three year term (Ref: C-205, H-317).

SNOWDEN, JOHN. Took the Oath of Allegiance before Hon. Thomas Worthington in March, 1778 (Ref: B-28). On September 24, 1817 the final distribution of his estate was made to Rachel Snowden (widow's third), with sevenths of the balance to Richard P. Snowden, Gerard A. (or H.) Snowden, Ann Maria Snowden (wife of Joseph R. Hopkins), John T. Snowden, Margaret H. Snowden, Rezin A. Snowden, and Rachel Snowden (Ref: U-51).

SNOWDEN, THOMAS. Took the Oath of Allegiance before Hon. Thomas Worthington in March, 1778 (Ref: B-28).

SOLLERS, ABRAHAM. Took the Oath of Allegiance before Hon. Samuel Lane on March 1, 1778 (Ref: B-23).

SOLLERS (SOLLARS), JACOB. Born in Maryland. He was enrolled by Capt. Edward Tillard and passed on July 10, 1776. Height: 5' 3" (Ref: H-39).

SOLLERS (SOLLARS), ROBERT. Born in Maryland. He was enrolled by Samuel Chew and passed on July 25, 1776. Height: 5' 2 1/2" (Ref: H-40). He took the Oath of Allegiance before Hon. Samuel Lane on March 1, 1778 (Ref: B-23).

SORRELL, JOHN. Took the Oath of Allegiance before Hon. Richard Harwood, Jr. on March 1, 1778 (Ref: B-23).

SOUTH, ALEXANDER. Born in England. He was a Substitute, furnished by Capt. Nicholas Maccubbin on May 13, 1778, to serve to the war's end (Ref: C-204, H-317).

SOUTHER, VALENTINE. He was discharged from the Independent Regulars on May 14, 1777 because he was not fifteen years old (Ref: V-252. Note: Perhaps he was the "Pheltr(?) Souther" recruited by James Brice in 1776 (Ref: H-313).

SPARKS, RICHARD. Enlisted by John Worthington Dorsey and passed by John Dorsey on July 22, 1776 (Ref: H-39).

SPARROW, THOMAS. Third Sergeant in Captain Gilbert Middleton's Independent Company of Militia of Annapolis on March 20, 1779 (Ref: I-144, O-325).

SPEAKE, FRANCIS. Captain of the ship "John" by February, 1776 (Ref: H-163).

SPENCER, CHARLES. Took the Oath of Allegiance before Hon. Samuel Harrison in March, 1778 (Ref: B-29).

SPICER, WILLIAM. Drafted in October, 1780, to serve until December 10, 1780. (Ref: H-369).

SPICKNELL, WILLIAM. Took the Oath of Allegiance before Hon. Samuel Harrison in March, 1778 (Ref: B-29).

SPRIGG, JOHN. A physician in Anne Arundel County who was paid by the Council of Maryland for an unspecified military service in 1780/1790 (Ref: Y-305).

SPRIGG, THOMAS (November, 1715, Prince George's County - December 29, 1781). Son of Thomas Sprigg and Margery Wight. Married Elizabeth Galloway in 1737 and had one son, Richard Sprigg. Thomas was appointed a Delegate to the 1st Maryland Convention in 1774 but did not attend, and served on the Committee of Observation in 1774-1775. He affirmed (Quaker) to the Oath of Allegiance before Hon. Thomas Harwood on February 28, 1778 (Ref: B-22, P-765, P-766).

SPURRIER, AARON. Took Oath of Allegiance before Hon. Reuben Meriweather on March 2, 1778 (Ref: B-24). Commissioned Second Lieutenant in Capt. Robert Warfield's Company in the Elk Ridge Battalion in March, 1779 (Ref: O-333).

SPURRIER, EDWARD. Ensign in Capt. James Disney's Company in the 3rd Maryland Line in June, 1776 (Ref: H-39, H-41, N-534).

SPURRIER, GREEN (December 20, 1737 - 1787, Baltimore, Maryland). He married Avis Leeks and a son, Joshua John Spurrier, was born in Anne Arundel County in 1768. Green Spurrier took the Oath of Allegiance in 1778 (Ref: E-2944).

SPURRIER, JOSEPH. Took the Oath of Allegiance before Hon. Thomas Worthington on February 28, 1778 (Ref: B-21).

SPURRIER, THOMAS JR. Took the Oath of Allegiance before Hon. John Dorsey on March 12, 1778 (Ref: B-26).

SPURRIER, THOMAS SR. Took Oath of Allegiance before Hon. Thomas Worthington on February 28, 1778 (Ref: B-21).

SPURRIER, WILLIAM. Commissioned First Lieutenant in Capt. Richard Stringer's Company of Militia in the Elk Ridge Battalion on February 28, 1776, and served through at least 1778 (Ref: C-201, N-191). He also took the Oath of Allegiance before Hon. Thomas Dorsey on March 2, 1778 (Ref: B-24).

STACK, SAMUEL. Took the Oath of Allegiance before Hon. Thomas Worthington on February 28, 1778 (Ref:B-21).

STALKER, GEORGE. Took the Oath of Allegiance before Hon. Richard Harwood, Jr. on March 1, 1778 (Ref: B-23).

STALLINGS, LANCELOT. Private in Capt. Richard Chew's Company of Col. John Weems' Battalion on October 5, 1776 (Ref: A-95, I-143).

STALLIONS, JOHN. Took the Oath of Allegiance before Hon. Reuben Meriweather on March 2, 1778 (Ref: B-25).

STANSBURY, ELISHA. Took Oath of Allegiance before Hon. Nicholas Worthington in March, 1778 (Ref: B-27).

STANTON, JOHN. He was recruited by Col. J. H. Stone and passed on November 18, 1778 (Ref: C-217, H-314). On February 23, 1829, the Treasurer of the Western Shore was directed to "pay to John Stanton, a soldier of the rev. war, during life, half yearly, half pay of a private, further remuneration for his services during the Revolutionary War." (Ref: K-395).

STEEL, JOHN. Took the Oath of Allegiance before Hon. Richard Harwood, Jr. on March 1, 1778 (Ref: B-23).

STELL (STEEL?), JOHN. Born in England. He was recruited by John Ijams and passed by James Brice on March 24, 1778 (Ref: C-216, H-314).

STEPHENS, BENJAMIN. Took Oath of Allegiance before Hon. Reuben Meriweather on March 2, 1778 (Ref: B-24).

STERRETT, JOHN (1751-1787). On April 9, 1778 the Council of Maryland reported "Benjamin Griffith is appointed Purchasing Agent in Baltimore County in the room of John Sterrett who declined by reason of having lately removed into Anne Arundel County" (Ref: O-22, P-771, and Henry C. Peden's "Revolutionary Patriots of Baltimore Town and Baltimore County, 1775-1783," p. 259).

STEUART, DAVID. Took the Oath of Allegiance before Hon. Richard Harwood, Jr. on March 1, 1778 (Ref: B-23).

STEUART, JAMES. Took the Oath of Allegiance before Hon. Richard Harwood, Jr. on March 1, 1778 (Ref: B-23).

STEUART, ROBERT. Took the Oath of Allegiance before Hon. Richard Harwood, Jr. on March 1, 1778 (Ref: B-23).

STEVENS, CHARLES. Took the Oath of Allegiance before Hon. Elijah Robosson in March, 1778 (Ref: B-28).

STEVENS, DAWSON. Took the Oath of Allegiance before Hon. Reuben Meriweather on March 2, 1778 (Ref: B-25).

STEVENS, JOHN. Took the Oath of Allegiance before Hon. Elijah Robosson in March, 1778 (Ref: B-28).

STEVENS, LEWIS. Private in Capt. Richard Chew's Company of Col. John Weems' Battalion on October 5, 1776 (Ref: A-95, I-143).

STEVENS, REZIN (of Baltimore County). Took the Oath of Allegiance before Hon. Reuben Meriweather on march 2, 1778 (Ref; B-25).

STEVENS, VACHEL. Took the Oath of Allegiance before Hon. John Dorsey on March 12, 1778 (Ref: B-26). On December 9, 1778, "Vachel Stevens of Elk Ridge" was appointed Surveyor of Anne Arundel County (Ref: O-262). He was Captain in the Elk Ridge Battalion of Militia in March, 1779 (Ref: O-333), and by September 4, 1781, he was serving as Commissary of Purchases (Ref: W-599).

STEVENS, VACHEL (OF BENJAMIN). Enlisted by Michael Burgess and passed by Col. Hyde on July 20, 1776 (Ref: H-41).

STEVENS, WILLIAM. Born in Scotland. He was a Substitute, furnished by Amos Davis on May 5, 1778, to serve to the war's end (Ref: C-207, H-318). Took Oath of Allegiance before Hon. John Dorsey on March 12, 1778 (Ref: B-26).

STEVENSON, AARON. Recruited by Colonel Adams in October, 1780, to serve for three years (Ref: H-370).

STEWARD, STEPHEN. Took the Oath of Allegiance before Hon. Samuel Harrison in March, 1778 (Ref: B-29). In 1776 he was "requested to purchase necessary militia stores of Annapolis Hospital according to memorandum of Dr. Tootell (Ref: F-223).

STEWARD, STEPHEN JR. Took the Oath of Allegiance before Hon. Samuel Harrison in March, 1778 (Ref: B-29).

STEWART, CALEB. Enrolled by Capt. Thomas Watkins for service to the State on October 21, 1776 (Ref: I-144, MS.1814). Took the Oath of Allegiance before Hon. Richard Harwood, Jr. on March 1, 1778 (Ref: B-23). He was pensioned on March 4, 1831, at age 78, as a Private in the Maryland Line (Ref: Z-45).

STEWART, CHARLES. Took the Oath of Allegiance before Hon. Richard Harwood, Jr. on March 1, 1778 (Ref: B-23).

STEWART, CHARLES JR. Took the Oath of Allegiance before Hon. Richard Harwood, Jr. on March 1, 1778 (Ref: B-23).

STEWART, DAVID. Took the Oath of Allegiance before Hon. Nicholas Worthington in March, 1778 (Ref: B-28). He was drafted in October, 1780 to serve until December 10, 1780 (Ref: H-370).

STEWART, JOHN N. Private in the Maryland Militia. Pensioned on November 19, 1814, as an Invalid in Anne Arundel County, and died in 1821 (Ref: Z-2).

STEWART, ROBERT. Enrolled by Capt. Thomas Watkins for service to the State on October 21, 1776 (Ref: I-144, MS.1814).

STEWART, STEPHEN. Took the Oath of Allegiance before Hon. Thomas Dorsey on March 2, 1778 (Ref: B-24).

STOAKS, PATRICK. ENlisted by Michael Burgess and passed by Col. Hyde on July 20, 1776 (Ref: H-41).

STOCKETT, HENRY (January 30, 1759, Anne Arundel County - May, 1808, Baltimore County). Son of Lewis and Katharine Stockett. He married Barbara McKinzie in Baltimore in 1794 and had two children: Henry Stockett and Mary Stockett Flint. He enlisted as a Fifer in the 4th Maryland Line on December 6, 1776 becoming Fife Major on July 1, 1778. He was discharged on December 6, 1779 and subsequently served in recruiting for the Continental Army. After the war he became a seaman and was styled "Captain" (Ref: R-388, R-389).

STOCKETT, LEWIS (August 6, 1724 - October, 1785). Son of Thomas Stockett and Damaris Welsh. He married first to Katharine -----, and had three children: Henry Stockett, Thomas Stockett and Mary Stockett. He married secondly to Ann Ijams and they had 5 children: John Stockett, Rebecca Stockett Beard, Ann Stockett, Richard Stockett and William Ijams Stockett. Lewis took the Oath of Allegiance before Hon. Richard Harwood, Jr. on March 1, 1778 (Ref: B-23, R-383, R-384, P-779). On November 7, 1788 the final distribution of his estate was made to Ann Stockett (widow's third), with sixths of the balance to Mary Stockett, Rebecca Stockett, John Stockett, Ann Stockett, Richard Stockett, and William Ijams Stockett (Ref: U-2).

STOCKETT, THOMAS NOBLE (July 12, 1747 - May 16, 1802). Son of Thomas Stockett and Elizabeth Noble. He married Mary Harwood in 1770 and had ten children: Mary Harwood Stockett Alexander, Richard Galen Stockett, Thomas Mifflin Stockett, Joseph Noble Stockett, Helen Stockett McGill, Margaret Stockett, William Shippen Stockett, John Shaaf Stockett, Ann Stockett Warfield, and Eleanor Stockett Watkins. He was commissioned a First Lieutenant in Captain Thomas Watkin's Company in the South River Battalion in 1776. Since he was trained in medicine, Thomas was appointed to Second Surgeon's Assistant in Colonel William Richardson's Battalion of the Flying Camp on September 26, 1776. He was also a Captain in Colonel John Weems' Battalion of Militia in 1778. He had to retire from the army on account of ill health (Ref: R-386, R-387, F-223, C-199, N-158, T-683, Y-305 and Dr. J. M. Toner's "Medical Men of the Revolution," p. 127). Thomas also took the Oath of Allegiance before Hon. Richard Harwood, Jr. on March 1, 1778 (Ref: B-23).

STOCKSTER, JOHN. Took the Oath of Allegiance before Hon. Thomas Worthington on February 28, 1778 (Ref: B-21).

STONE, JOHN. Born in Maryland. He was enrolled by Capt. Edward Tillard in July, 1776 (Ref: H-39). He took the Oath of Allegiance before Hon. Samuel Harrison in March, 1778 (Ref: A-244).

STONE, JOHN HOSKINS (1750, Charles County - October 5, 1804, Annapolis). Son of David Stone and Elizabeth Jenifer. Although born in Charles County, John resided in Annapolis from 1781 to 1798, in Baltimore until 1803 and then in Annapolis until his death in 1804. He married Mary Couden in 1781 and they had four children: Robert Couden Stone, Anne Stone Turner, Couden Stone and Elizabeth Stone Causin. He served in many offices during the Revolutionary period in both Charles County and Anne Arundel County. As for the latter, he was on the Executive Council from 1779 to 1785 and Governor from

1794 to 1797. He was Colonel in Gen. Smallwood's Maryland Regiment in 1777 and was wounded at the battle of Germantown. When he died in 1804 "the men of the Society of the Cincinnati were ordered to wear crepe on this occasion" (Ref: P-784 and National Genealogical Society Quarterly, Vol. 25, No. 2, p. 56).

STONE, THOMAS. Born in Maryland. Enrolled by John Kilty in July, 1776 (Ref: H-40).

STONER, SAMUEL. Enlisted by Joseph Burgess for the Flying Camp and passed on July 20, 1776 (Ref: H-40).

STOREY, SOLOMON. Took the Oath of Allegiance before Hon. Thomas Harwood on February 28, 1778 (Ref: B-22).

STOVER, SAMUEL. Took the Oath of Allegiance before Hon. Thomas Worthington on February 28, 1778 (Ref: B-21).

STRINGER, RICHARD. Commissioned Captain in the Elk Ridge Battalion of Militia on February 28, 1776, and served through at least 1778 (Ref: C-201, K-397, N-191). Took Oath of Allegiance before Hon. John Dorsey on March 12, 1778 (Ref: B-26). Served on the Committee of Observation in 1775 (Ref: F-222).

STRUM, ISRAEL. He was a Substitute passed on May 30, 1778 for a three year term in Capt. Charles Boone's Company (Ref: C-208, H-319).

STUART (STEWART), JAMES (1755-1845). A physician who assisted in smallpox inoculation in Annapolis in 1782 with Dr. Murray and Dr. Tootel. He moved to Baltimore after 1782 (Ref: Y-305).

STURT, GEORGE. Enlisted by Joseph Burgess for the Flying Camp and passed on July 20, 1776 (Ref: H-40).

SULLIVAN, JOHN. Born in Scotland. He was a Substitute, furnished by Richard Dorsey (of John) on May 4, 1778, to serve three years (Ref: C-211, H-318).

SULLIVAN, JOHN JR. Private in Capt. William Marbury's Artillery Company in 1777 (Ref: H-575).

SUMMERLAND, WILLIAM. Drafted in October, 1780, to serve until December 10, 1780 (Ref: H-370).

SUTHERLAND, WILLIAM. Born in America. He was recruited and passed by James Brice on January 8, 1778 (Ref: C-215, H-313). One marriage proven through Maryland pension applications was William Sutherland to Katherine Ensminger on August 6, 1789 in Rockbridge County, Virginia (Ref: G-124).

SUTTON, THOMAS. Took the Oath of Allegiance before Hon. Thomas Dorsey on March 2, 1778 (Ref: B-24).

SUTTON, WILLIAM. Disabled soldier paid in Anne Arundel County on January 13, 1784 (Ref: D-11).

SWAIN, ISAAC. Took the Oath of Allegiance before Hon. Richard Harwood, Jr. on March 1, 1778 (Ref: B-23).

SWANARD, JOHN. Took the Oath of Allegiance before Hon. John Dorsey on March 12, 1778 (Ref: B-26).

SWAN, JOHN. Enrolled by Captain Thomas Watkins for service to the State on October 21, 1776 (Ref: I-144, MS.1814).

SWANN, JOHN THOMAS. Took the Oath of Allegiance before Hon. Richard Harwood, Jr. on March 1, 1778 (Ref: B-23).

SWIVNOR (SCRIVNOR?), ROBERT. Took the Oath of Allegiance before Hon. Richard Harwood, Jr. on March 1, 1778 (Ref: B-23).

SYBLE, HENRY. Private in Capt. William Marbury's Artillery Company in 1777. (Ref: H-575).

SYKES, WILLIAM (of Baltimore County). Took the Oath of Allegiance before Hon. Reuben Meriweather on March 2, 1778 (Ref: B-24).

SYKES, WILLIAM. Born in England. He was recruited by Thomas Ricketts and passed by James Brice on March 20, 1778 (Ref: C-216, H-313).

TALBOTT, BENJAMIN. Took the Oath of Allegiance before Hon. Elijah Robosson in March, 1778 (Ref: B-28). On October 16, 1789 the final distribution of his estate was made to Sarah Talbott, now Mrs. William Merriken (widow's third), with half of the residue to Thomas Talbott and half of the residue to Ann Talbott, wife of Elijah Robinson (Ref: U-4).

TALBOTT, EDWARD, of Baltimore County (born July 15, 1723, Anne Arundel County and died August 29, 1799, Baltimore County). Married Temperance Merryman in 1745 and a daughter Temperance Merryman married Richard Britton in 1782. He took the Oath of Allegiance before Hon. Reuben Meriweather on March 2, 1778 (Ref: B-24). He also served on the Council of Safety in Baltimore County in 1776, and was a member of the Convention of Maryland in 1775 (Ref: E-237).

TALBOTT, ELISHA. Private in Captain John Fulford's Company of Artillery at Annapolis on December 12, 1776 (Ref: H-572).

TALBOTT, JAMES (of Baltimore County). He took the Oath of Allegiance before Hon. Reuben Meriweather on March 2, 1778 (Ref: B-24).

TALBOTT, RICHARD JR. Took the Oath of Allegiance before Hon. John Dorsey on March 12, 1778 (Ref: B-26).

TALBOTT, RICHARD SR. Ensign in Captain Edward Norwood's Company in the Third Maryland Line by June, 1776 (Ref: H-38, H-39, N-534). He took the Oath of Allegiance before Hon. John Dorsey on March 12, 1778 (Ref: B-26).

TAME, EDWARD. Born in England. He was a Substitute, furnished by Dr. James Murray on May 12, 1778, to serve a three year term (Ref: C-204, H-317).

TANGUARY (JANQUARY?), ABRAHAM. Took the Oath of Allegiance before Honorable Samuel Harrison in March, 1778 (Ref: B-29).

TARVEY, THOMAS. Took the Oath of Allegiance before Hon. Nicholas Worthington in March, 1778 (Ref: Original lists in Maryland State Papers, Red Book 21, MdHR4587. Source B-27 questionably spelled the name "Thomas Frivey?").

TAYLOR, EDWARD. Took the Oath of Allegiance before Hon. Nicholas Worthington in March, 1778 (Ref: B-28).

TAYLOR, JAMES. Private in Capt. Gilbert Middleton's Independent Company of Militia of Annapolis on March 20, 1779 (Ref: I-144, O-325).

TAYLOR, JOHN. On March 8, 1834, the Treasurer was directed to "pay to John Taylor, of Anne Arundel County, quarterly, half pay of a private, for the service rendered by him during the Revolutionary War." On March 8, 1836, the Treasurer was directed to "pay to Sega Taylor, of Anne Arundel County, the amount due her late husband, John Taylor, upon the pension list of this State, at the time of his death." On April 1, 1836, the Treasurer was also directed to "pay to Sydney Taylor, widow of John Taylor, a rev. soldier, the half pay of a private for the services of her husband." (Ref: K-398). A marriage proven through Maryland Revolutionary War pension applications is that of a John Taylor to Leggy Crutchley on October 11, 1824 (Ref: G-124).

TAYLOR, SAMUEL. Took the Oath of Allegiance before Hon. Nicholas Worthington in March, 1778 (Ref: Original list in Maryland State Papers, Red Book 21, MdHR4587, which indicated his name was "Samuel Talor." However, Source B-28 stated his name was "Samuel Caleb Taylor" but no such name found on list).

TAYLOR, SNOWDEN. Enrolled by Captain James Disney, Jr. and passed by Colonel Richard Harwood, Jr. on July 13, 1776 (Ref: H-41).

TAYLOR, SOLOMON. Born in Maryland. Enrolled by Samuel Chew on July 25, 1776. Height: 5' 7" (Ref: H-40). Took the Oath of Allegiance before Hon. Thomas Harwood on February 28, 1778 (Ref: B-22).

TAYLOR, THOMAS. Born in Maryland. Enrolled by Capt. Edward Tillard on July 10, 1776. Height: 5' 9" (Ref: H-39).

TAYLOR, WILLIAM. Born in Scotland. He was a Substitute, furnished by Gerrard Hopkins and William Hall on May 2, 1778, to serve 3 years or to the end of the war (Ref: C-210, H-318). Took the Oath of Allegiance before Hon. John Dorsey on March 12, 1778 (Ref: B-26).

TAYLOR, WILLIAM. Private in Capt. William Marbury's Company of Artillery in 1777 (Ref: H-575).

THACKARD, REZIN. Born in America. He was a Substitute, furnished by James West on April 27, 1778, to serve until war's end (Ref: C-204, H-317).

THACKREL, NICHOLAS. Took Oath of Allegiance before Hon. Nicholas Worthington in March, 1778 (Ref: B-27).

TEARN, JOSEPH. Enlisted by John Worthington Dorsey and passed by John Dorsey on July 22, 1776 (Ref: H-39).

TERRENCE, WILLIAM. Soldier who was in the Light Infantry Company of William Smallwood's Battalion, and "being unable for further duty," was discharged from the service by the Council of Maryland on July 8, 1777 (Ref: V-312).

THIRD AND FOURTH MARYLAND REGIMENTS. These regiments of the Continental Army was organized in 1777 and consisted of soldiers from the counties of Anne Arundel, Prince George's, Baltimore, Harford, Somerset and Talbot. Judging by their surnames and the names of their captains, it appears as though the following were from Anne Arundel County, although further research may be required to substantiate that connection, and also consult the Archives of Maryland, Vol. 18, as this list is not all inclusive: John Allen, William Allen, Joseph Burgess, Joshua Burgess, Peter Bushell, Philip Brisington, John Brown, Jehu Bowen, John Barnett, Richard Bidwell, Esau Bicknell, Christopher Busby, Isaac Brown, John Craig, Richard Chew, John Coland, John Colegate, Lawrence Cregan, Simmons Cappock, James Crampton, John Chevick, Roger Cord, John Dunster, William Denbugh, William Downes, Barnaba Doran, Peter Deliazon, Thomas Durnor, William Denmass, Francis Deane, William Douglass, William Eaton, Samuel Elliott, Thomas Ennis, Thomas Edwards, Thomas Eades, Peter Emanuel, Coleman Finley, Richard Feraby, Richard Frewen, William Flanagan, Richard Fenwick, Nicholas Gassaway, Anthony Geoghegan, Robert Gregory, Hugh Gainer, Henry Gassaway, George Griffith, Hugh Gill, John Gollier, Robert Gray, Alexander Gardiner, Francis Garrish, William Gamble, John Gwinn, Samuel Godman, Richard Goff, James Gray, Daniel Harding, John Hood, Edward Hatfield, William Hedge, Richard Harris, William Hull, Thomas Hickey, Thomas Huddleston, Joseph Hennis, George Hamilton, Thomas Hellam, Isaac Hynes, John Hodges, Thomas Harris, Abraham Johnson, Joseph Johnson, Miles Johnson, Joseph Jenkins, Robinson Jacobs, Samuel Jones, Richard Jacks, Francis James, Isaac King, Duncan Keith, Richard Kelly, Thomas Kenney, John Knox, Thomas Keats, John King, James Logie, David Lawler, John Lennox, John Lucas, Jacob Leavley, John Lawler, Daniel Leary, Michael Leary, John Lester, Joel McAllester, John McNeall, Thomas Murphey, Mathew Moore, George McIntosh, John Marks, Robert Mallows, John Murphey, Christopher Madden, Thomas McCormick, John Murry, Patrick McGinity, John Miles,

Edward Merican, Patrick Murphy, Lawrence McKenny, Patrick Nugent, Philip Norris, Thomas Newton, Anthony Nicholson, Thomas Noland, Richard Nelson, James Nowland, Edward Norwood, Robert Newcomb, Cooper Oram, John Oram, Samuel Oram, Edward Oldham, Hugh O'Neil, Dennis O'Connor, Daniel O'Quinn, William Purcell, Edward Parrish, Samuel Popham, William Petterfer, Thomas Potts, Daniel Price, Stephen Purnell, William Peach, John Page, Robert Patterson, Jerrold Parker, Joseph Quynn, John Queen, James Quinland, Samuel Ridgely, Charles Reynolds, Richard Reynolds, John Riely, Henry Ramsey, William Riely, John Rowley, John Reading, James Rowe, Robert Richardson, Joseph Roberts, Joseph Rogers, James Ringrose, Michael Rourke, Benedict Reynolds, John Russell, John Simmons, John Smith, Thomas Sappington, Joseph Smith, William Scoot, William Smith, James Smith, Alexander Scott, Jonathan Sellman, Edward Spurrier, Patrick Stokes, Richard Stewart, John Smith, Samuel Street, Lab. C. Smith, William Stevens, Peter Shulmear, Nathan Smith, William Stead, Snowden Taylor, John Truman, Thomas Thomas, Nathaniel Twining, William Townshend, Caleb Tydings, John Taylor, Griffith Taylor, Thomas Turner, John Troy, James Tiser, John Thomas, Peter Topping, Patrick Welch, William Watkins, Thomas Wood, William Wilson, John Welsh, James Watkins, John Wood, Dorsey Wood, Francis Winstanly, Frederick West, John Wells, John Webster, Jacob Wilderman, James Wallingsford, Joseph Webb, William Wood, James Warwick, William Warwick, Joseph Waldron, Joseph Whitehouse, Jarvis Williams, John Williams, Benjamin Yarnall, John Young, and Benjamin Young (Ref: Archives of Maryland, Vol.18, pp. 78-180).

THOMAS, ELLIS. Pensioned on March 4, 1831, at age 79, as a Sergeant in the Maryland Line (Ref: Z-45).

THOMAS, EVAN. Took the Oath of Allegiance before Hon. John Dorsey on March 12, 1778 (Ref: B-26).

THOMAS, JAMES. Born in Scotland. He was a Substitute, furnished by Thomas Pryss on May 20, 1778, to serve to the war's end (Ref: C-214, H-319).

THOMAS, JEREMIAH. Took the Oath of Allegiance before Hon. Richard Harwood, Jr. on March 1, 1778 (Ref: B-23). "Jerre Thomas" was enrolled by Captain Thomas Watkins for service to the State on October 21, 1776 (Ref: I-144).

THOMAS, JOHN. Born in Scotland. He was a Substitute, furnished by Captain Caleb Owings on May 5, 1778, to serve to war's end (Ref: C-206, H-317).

THOMAS JOHN. First Major in Col. John Weems' Battalion in 1776 (Ref: F-224). Took the Oath of Allegiance before Hon. Thomas Harwood on February 7, 1778. (Ref: B-22).

THOMAS, JOHN. Enrolled by Capt. James Disney, Jr. and passed by Col. Richard Harwood on July 13, 1776 (Ref: H-41).

THOMAS, PHILIP JR. Took the Oath of Allegiance before Hon. Samuel Harrison in March, 1778 (Ref: B-29).

THOMPSON, ALEXANDER. Private in Capt. Gilbert Middleton's Independent Company of Militia of Annapolis on March 20, 1779 (Ref: I-144, O-325).

THOMPSON, FRANCIS. Recruited and passed by James Brice in 1777 (Ref: H-313).

THOMPSON, JOHN. Private in Captain William Marbury's Company of Artillery in 1777 (Ref: H-575). A marriage proven through the Maryland Revolutionary War pension applications is that of John Thompson to Elizabeth Connaway in Anne Arundel County on January 3, 1786 (Ref: G-124).

THOMPSON, RICHARD. Private in Capt. Gilbert Middleton's Independent Company of Militia of Annapolis on March 20, 1779 (Ref: I-144, O-325).

THOMPSON, ROBERT. Private in Capt. Richard Dorsey's Company of Artillery on November 17, 1777 (Ref: H-574).

THOMPSON, WILLIAM. Took the Oath of Allegiance before Hon. Reuben Meriweather on March 2, 1778 (Ref: B-25).

THOMSON, SAMUEL. Corporal in Capt. Richard Dorsey's Company of Artillery on November 17, 1777 (Ref: H-574).

THORNTON, JOSEPH (of Baltimore County). Took the Oath of Allegiance before Hon. Reuben Meriweather on March 2, 1778 (Ref: B-25).

THORNTON, SAMUEL. Took the Oath of Allegiance before Hon. Thomas Worthington on February 28, 1778 (Ref: B-21).

THORNTON, WILLIAM. Took the Oath of Allegiance on April 9, 1778 (Ref: O-22).

THORPE, JOHN. Captain of the Schooner "Rebecca and Sally" and belonging to Charles Ridgely and others, was given clearance to proceed from the port of Annapolis to the Island of St. Eustatius on April 14, 1777 (Ref: V-210).

TILLARD, EDWARD (1756-1820). Married Sarah Estep and had a daughter Elizabeth Tillard (Ref: T-708). Edward was Quartermaster in Col. John Weems' Militia Battalion in 1776 (Ref: F-224). By March, 1776, he was a Captain in Col. John Weems' Militia Battalion, and by June, 1776, he was a Captain in the 3rd Maryland Regiment and actively involved in recruiting (Ref: H-38, H-39, H-40, N-232, N-534). He was Major in the 6th Maryland Line and Lieutenant Colonel in the 4th Maryland Line in 1779 (Ref: T-708). On January 22, 1820, the Treasurer was directed to "pay to Sarah Tillard, widow of Lieutenant Colonel Tillard, of the Maryland Line during the Revolutionary War, during life, quarterly, a sum of money equal to the half pay of a Captain." On February 11, 1835, the Treasurer was directed to "pay to Capt. Otho Thomas, of Frederick County, for benefit of the heirs of Sarah Tillard, late a pensioner, the $57.33 due her at the time of her death." (Ref: K-399).

TILLARD, THOMAS (December 22, 1742 - December, 1806). Son of William Tillard (Taylard) and Martha Simmons. He married Janet Hamilton in 1776 and they had six children: Thomas Hamilton Tillard, William Smallwood Tillard, John Hamilton Tillard, Matilda Tillard Simmons Drury, Sarah Tillard Pindell, and Ann Tillard. Thomas served as a Delegate to the Maryland Convention, 1775 and in Lower House of Anne Arundel County, 1777-1778. He was commissioned a Second Major and a First Major (both in January, 1776) in the South River Battalion of Militia under Col. John Weems. He resigned in December, 1776 to run for elective office. He was appointed a Major in the Anne Arundel County Militia in 1794 (Ref: K-399, F-222, F-224, P-834, P-835).

TIMS, JOHN. Took the Oath of Allegiance before Honorable Samuel Harrison in March, 1778 (Ref: B-29).

TINDALL (TINDALE), SAMUEL. Soldier of the Maryland Line who was wounded (no details given) and was paid full pay through August 15, 1783 (Ref: X-41).

TISER, JAMES. Born in Scotland. He was a Substitute, furnished by George Mansell on April 26, 1778, to serve to the war's end (Ref: C-211, H-318).

TODD, ALEXANDER. Took the Oath of Allegiance before Hon. Reuben Meriweather on March 2, 1778 (Ref: B-24).

TODD, LANCELOT SR. He took the Oath of Allegiance before Hon. John Dorsey on March 12, 1778 (Ref: B-26). On May 1, 1798, the final distribution of his estate was made with third to Thomas Drane, third to James Drane, and third to Rezin Todd and Mary Todd, the representatives of John Todd (Ref: U-17).

TODD, RHESA. He took the Oath of Allegiance before Hon. Reuben Meriweather on March 2, 1778 (Ref: B-24).

TODD, RICHARD. He took the Oath of Allegiance before Hon. Elijah Robosson in March, 1778 (Ref: B-28).

TODD, THOMAS. On September 16, 1776, he was recommended for 2nd Lieutenant in Captain Thomas Watkins' Company in the Elk Ridge Battalion of Militia (Ref: A-88, F-223). He took the Oath of Allegiance before Hon. John Dorsey on March 12, 1778 (Ref: B-26). On September 2, 1792 the final distribution of his estate was made by Samuel Jacob, administrator de bonis non, to his widow (unnamed), with thirds of the estate balance to John Toft, Mary Toft, and Eleanor Toft, now the wife of Caleb Fennell (Ref: U-9).

TOFT, THOMAS. Took the Oath of Allegiance before Hon. Nicholas Worthington in March, 1778 (Ref: B-28. See previous entry in event it may be relevant).

TONGUE, THOMAS (June 9, 1746 - February 6, 1826). Married Elizabeth Roberts in 1769 and had a daughter, Elizabeth Tongue Allein (Ref: T-711). Thomas was commissioned First Lieutenant in the South River Battalion on February 15, 1776 and served in Col. John Weems' Battalion of Militia in 1778 (Ref: C-199, N-161). A Thomas Tongue was drafted in October, 1780 to serve until December 10, 1780. It could have been him or another Thomas (Ref: H-370).

TOOTELL, JAMES. He was commissioned a Captain on February 22, 1776, became a Major in June, 1777, and then a Lieutenant Colonel on March 1, 1778 in the Severn Battalion (Ref: A-176, C-202, N-178. Note: Source C-202 erroneously spelled his name "James Footel," and Source N-427 also misspelled the name: "Ordered that the Treasurer pay to "James Tootle" 49 pounds, 17 shillings, for building magazine"). He was also appointed a Collector of Clothing on November 27, 1777 (Ref: V-426). He took the Oath of Allegiance before Hon. Nicholas Worthington in March, 1778 (Ref: B-28). On November 10, 1809 the final distribution of his estate (fifths) was made to Elizabeth Plater, Hellen Tootell, Ann Tootell, Mary Childs, and Rosanna Tootell (Ref: U-37).

TOOTELL, RICHARD (of Annapolis). He served with Dr. James Murray as examiner and application surgeon to the Council in 1776. He was appointed Surgeon to a militia battalion in 1777. When ordered with the troops to Long Island he resigned because "he was too old a man for the hardships of the field." He was restored to the Examining Board in 1778 (Ref: Y-305, V-130, V-291).

TOPHOUSE, THOMAS. Born in England. Enrolled by John S. Belt in July, 1776. Height: 5' 2" (Ref: H-40).

TOPPING, JOHN. Took the Oath of Allegiance before Hon. John Dorsey on March 12, 1778 (Ref: B-26).

TOPPING, PETER. Born in Scotland. He was a Substitute, furnished by Philip Hammond on May 15, 1778, to serve to the war's end (Ref: C-207, H-318).

TOWNSEND, WILLIAM. Took the Oath of Allegiance before Hon. John Dorsey on March 12, 1778 (Ref: B-26).

TRACEY, ROBERT. Born in Scotland. He was a Substitute, furnished by Seth Warfield, Jr. on April 26, 1778, to serve to the war's end (Ref: C-211, H-318).

TRIGG, CHARLES. Took the Oath of Allegiance before Hon. Elijah Robosson in March, 1778 (Ref: B-28).

TROTT, JOHN. Took the Oath of Allegiance before Honorable Samuel Harrison in March, 1778 (Ref: B-29).

TROTT, SABRET. Took the Oath of Allegiance before Hon. Samuel Harrison in March, 1778 (Ref: B-29).

TROTT, THOMAS. Took the Oath of Allegiance before Hon. Samuel Harrison in March, 1778 (Ref: B-29). On June 11, 1793 the final distribution of his estate was made to Allison Trott (widow's third) with eighths of remainder to Elizabeth Trott, James Trott, Sarah Trott, Nancy Trott, Ester Trott, Thomas Trott, Allison Trott and Rebecca Trott (Ref: U-10).

TRUMAN, ALEXANDER (circa 1750 - April, 1792). Son of Henry Truman and Ann Magruder, and grandson of Thomas Truman and Sarah Briscoe. Alexander was an Ensign and then a Captain in the 2nd and 6th Maryland Lines from June, 1776 to January 1, 1783. Although born in Prince George's County, Alexander served in and recruited soldiers from Anne Arundel County where met and married Margaret Reynolds, daughter of William Reynolds of Annapolis, in 1781. They had 3 children: Alexander M. Truman, Mary Ann Truman Rogers, and Thomas Truman. An Original Member of the Society of the Cincinnati in 1783, he re-joined the U. S. Army after the Revolutionary War and became a Major in 1792. While on a peace mission from President George Washington to Ohio in April, 1792, he was killed by Indians. His descendants settled in Kentucky and Missouri (Ref: H-363, H-369, H-379, HCP-147, and Henry C. Peden, Jr.'s "Truman and Related Families of Early Maryland" (1986).

TRUMAN (TRUEMAN), JOHN. 1st Lieutenant in the Maryland Line, and a disabled soldier who was paid in Anne Arundel County on April 13, 1784 and June 9, 1784 and September 3, 1784 and October 26, 1784 and December 17, 1784 (Ref: D-13, 18, 21, 23, 25). In November, 1785, the General Assembly "granted half pay of a Lieutenant, for disability acquired in the service, to John Truman, a Lieutenant in the Md. Line in the Continental Army (Ref: K-401).

TUCK, WILLIAM. Private in Capt. Gilbert Middleton's Independent Company of Militia of Annapolis on March 20, 1779 (Ref: I-144, O-325).

TUCK, WILLIAM. Doorkeeper to the Council of Safety in 1777 (Ref: V-184).

TUCKER, ISAAC. Private in Capt. Richard Chew's Company of Col. John Weems' Battalion of Militia on October 5, 1776 (Ref: A-95, I-143). He took the Oath of Allegiance before Hon. Samuel Harrison in March, 1778 (Ref: B-29).

TUCKER, JOHN. He took the Oath of Allegiance before Hon. Samuel Harrison in March, 1778 (Ref: A-244). On August 14, 1799 the final distribution of his estate was made to Ann Tucker (widow's third), with fifths of the remaining balance to Thomas Tucker, John Tucker, James Tucker, William Tucker, and Sarah Tucker (Ref: U-24).

TUCKER, JOSEPH. Private in Captain John Fulford's Company of Artillery at Annapolis on December 12, 1776 (Ref: H-572).

TUCKER, SEABORN. Private in Capt. Richard Chew's Company of Col. John Weems' Battalion of Militia on October 5, 1776 (Ref: A-95, I-143).

TUCKER, WILLIAM. Resident of Herring Creek who petitioned the Convention of Maryland to form a militia company on March 6, 1776 and subsequently served in Captain Richard Weems' Company (Ref: I-143, MS.1814). He took the Oath of Allegiance before Hon. Samuel Harrison in March, 1778 (Ref: A-244). On December 17, 1819 the final distribution of his estate (sixths) was made by his administrator, Abel Tucker, to Mary Ann Tucker, Rachel Tucker, Thomas Tucker, Nancy Tucker, Jane Tucker, and Sarah Tucker (Ref: U-56, U-57).

TUCKER, ZACHARIAH. Took Oath of Allegiance on March 2, 1778 (Ref: V-525).

TUNER (SUNER?), MATTHIAS. Disabled soldier paid in Anne Arundel County on April 13, 1784 and June 9, 1784 and September 3, 1784 and October 26, 1784 and December 17, 1784 (Ref: D-13, 18, 21, 23, 25).

TURNER, ABRAHAM. Private in Capt. Richard Chew's Company of Col. John Weems' Battalion of Militia on October 5, 1776 (Ref: A-95, I-143). He took the Oath of Allegiance before Hon. Samuel Harrison in March, 1778 (Ref: B-29). "Abram Turner" was a Substitute, passed on June 10, 1778, for a nine month term in Capt. Richard Chew's Company (Ref: C-209, H-320).

TURNER, JOHN. Private in Captain Richard Dorsey's Company of Artillery on November 17, 1777 (Ref: H-574).

TURNER, JOSEPH. Took the Oath of Allegiance before Hon. Reuben Meriweather on March 2, 1778 (Ref: B-25).

TURNER, THOMAS. Private in Capt. Richard Chew's Company of Col. John Weems' Battalion of Militia on October 5, 1776 (Ref: A-95, I-143). He took the Oath of Allegiance before Hon. Samuel Harrison in March, 1778 (Ref: B-29).

TURNER, WILLIAM. Private in Capt. Richard Chew's Company of Col. John Weems' Battalion of Militia on October 5, 1776 (Ref: A-95, I-143). Took the Oath of Allegiance before Hon. Richard Harwood, Jr., March 1, 1778 (Ref: B-23).

TURNER, ZACHARIAH. Enlisted by Capt. Edward Tillard and passed by Richard Harwood, Jr. on July 16, 1776. Height: 5' 6 1/2" (Ref: H-40). On October 15, 1802 final distribution of his estate was made to Johanna Turner (her widow's third), with fourths of the remaining balance to Abraham Turner, William Turner, John Turner, and Richard Turner (Ref: U-20).

TURNER, ZEPHANIAH (1737-1794). Although a native Charles Countian, Zephaniah resided in Annapolis from 1778 to 1783 when he was Auditor General. He also served in many offices in Charles County (See data in Ref: P-844, P-845).

TWINER, JOHN. Took the Oath of Allegiance before Hon. Thomas Dorsey on March 2, 1778 (Ref: B-24).

TYDIE, WILLIAM (of Baltimore County). Took the Oath of Allegiance before Hon. Reuben Meriweather on March 2, 1778 (Ref: B-25).

TYDINGS, CALEB. He was a Substitute, furnished by Colonel Adams, in October, 1780 to serve until December 10, 1780 (Ref: H-370). "Caleb Tidings" appears on a list of discharged soldiers raised for the Continental Army in 1781, and was paid accordingly (Ref: H-412).

TYDINGS, CELE. Enrolled by Capt. Thomas Watkins for service to the State on October 21, 1776 (Ref: I-144, MS.1814). In November, 1811, the Treasurer was directed to "pay to Kealey Tydings, late a Sergeant in the Md. Line during the rev. war, half pay of a Sergeant, as a further remuneration for those services rendered his country during the American war" (Ref: K-401).

TYDINGS, JOHN. Took the Oath of Allegiance before Hon. Richard Harwood, Jr. on March 1, 1778 (Ref: B-23). On November 20, 1816 the final distribution of his estate (tenths) was made to Ferdinando Tydings, Samuel Tydings, Ann Tydings, Horatio Tydings, Richard Tydings, Catherine Tydings, Mary Ann Bright, Sophia Skidmore, Elizabeth Purdy and Margaret Watkins (Ref: U-49).

TYDINGS, RICHARD. Took the Oath of Allegiance before Hon. Richard Harwood, Jr. on March 1, 1778 (Ref: B-23).

TYDINGS, RICHARD JR. Took the Oath of Allegiance before Hon. Richard Harwood, Jr. on March 1, 1778 (Ref: B-23).

TYLER, JERVIS. Took the Oath of Allegiance before Hon. Thomas Worthington on February 28, 1778 (Ref: B-21).

UNCLES, BENJAMIN. On February 22, 1822, the Treasurer was directed to "pay to Benjamin Uncles, a revolutionary soldier, half pay of a private, for his Revolutionary War services." On January 28, 1838, the State Treasurer was directed to "pay to Rebecca Uncles, widow of Benjamin Uncles, the half pay of a private during her life, as a further remuneration for his services." On March 10, 1847, the State Treasurer was directed to "pay to Mrs. Sarah Earlougher $6.67, it being the balance of pension money due from this State to Rebecca Uncles, deceased, at the time of her death." (Ref: K-401). Also, marriages proven through Revolutionary War pensions indicates that Benjamin Uncles married Margaret Plaister in Frederick Co. circa 1781 (Ref: G-124).

VALLETTE, ELIE. He was the Register of Wills of Anne Arundel County for many years during the colonial and the revolutionary periods (Ref: Anne Arundel County Orphans Court Proceedings, 1777-79, MdHR9524, p. 2, June 10, 1777). He was paid by the Council of Safety on February 23, 1776 for removing and caring for the records of the Commissary's Office (Ref: N-141, N-180). On July 29, 1777 he was paid by the Council of Maryland "for damages done to his house and for rent whilst occupied by the soldiers" (Ref: V-320).

VALLEY FORGE. Some men from Anne Arundel County who served in Capt. Richard Dorsey's Company of Artillery were at Valley Forge, and the following is a list of that company as it stood at Valley Forge on June 3, 1778 (but not all of them were from Anne Arundel County): Capt. Richard Dorsey, Capt.-Lt. Ebenezer Finley, First Lt. Robert Wilmott, Second Lt. Nicholas Ricketts, Second Lt. Young Wilkinson. Sergeants: Samuel Thompson, John Howard, David Walsh, John Wheeler, James Rice and Robert Thompson; Corporals: Thomas Neilson, Philip Jones, David White, William Delaney, Thomas Smith and John Wilkins; Drummer Henry Kelliker; Bombardiers: John Pierson, David Maroney, Alexander McMullan and John Clarke; Gunners: Timothy Donovan, Daniel Donogue, John Turner, Thomas Grainger, John Brady, John Ackerly. Matrosses: Dennis Flannegan, Edward Coughland, James Berry, Patrick Shoughness, John Bryant, John Jallome, John Sandall, Howel Lewis, William Grimes, William Reed, William Day, William Wade, Frederick Pine, Andrew Shrink, Robert O'Donald, Robert Britt, John Fitzpatrick, Hugh McDowell, Richard Wilkinson, Daniel Redden, Freeman Newman, Matthew Kelly, Daniel Neil, James Jack, Thomas Randall, Michael Connor, Thomas Pierce, Mathew McMahan, John Taylor, Stephen Fennel, John Handlin, William Forbes, and Bryan Ferrel (Ref: W. T. R. Saffell's "Records of the Revolutionary War," New York: Pudney & Russell Publishers, 1858, pp. 230-231. Note: For others from Anne Arundel County who served in the 1st and 2nd Maryland Regiments and who may have been at Valley Forge with Gen. William Smallwood, or perhaps who served in one of the four German Regiments from Maryland, consult Archives of Maryland, Vol. 18, and then research the records of the individual of interest at the National Archives. It was not practical for the purpose of this book for this compiler to search the individual records of each and every soldier).

VALLIANT, NICHOLAS. Private in Capt. Gilbert Middleton's Independent Company of Militia of Annapolis on March 20, 1779 (Ref: I-144, O-325).

VANSANT, JOHN. Disabled soldier who was paid in Anne Arundel County on Jan. 13, 1784 and April 13, 1784 and June 9, 1784 and September 3, 1784 and October 26, 1784 and December 17, 1784 (Ref: D-12, 13, 18, 21, 23, 25).

VAUBRAN (DE VAUBRAN), JOHN. His marriage is proven through Revolutionary War pension records which indicate he married Anne Howard in September, 1781 in Anne Arundel County, but no record of his service was given. (Ref: G-125).

VENNOM (VINEM), RAY. He was enrolled by Capt. Thomas Watkins on October 21, 1776 for service to the State (Ref: I-144, MS.1814). He took the Oath of Allegiance before Hon. Richard Harwood, Jr. on March 1, 1778 (Ref: B-23).

VINALL, RICHARD. He was enrolled by Capt. Thomas Watkins on October 21, 1776 for service to the State (Ref: I-144, MS.1814).

WAIGHT, THOMAS. Took the Oath of Allegiance before Hon. Thomas Dorsey on March 2, 1778 (Ref: B-24).

WALDRUM, JOSEPH. Born in Scotland. He was a Substitute, furnished by Dorsey Barnes on April 20, 1778, to serve for three years (Ref: C-210, H-318).

WALKER, GIDEON. He was recruited by Col. Adams in October, 1780, to serve for three years (Ref: H-369).

WALKER, JAMES. Commissioned a Second Lieutenant in Captain Edward Norwood's Company of Militia on February 7, 1776 (Ref: N-139). Two men by this name took the Oath of Allegiance: one before Hon. Samuel Lane on March 1, 1778, and one before Hon. John Dorsey on March 12, 1778 (Ref: B-23, B-26).

WALKER, JOHN. Took the Oath of Allegiance before Honorable Elijah Robosson in March, 1778 (Ref: B-28). He was commissioned a Captain in the Severn Battalion of Militia on August 15, 1778 (Ref: I-144, J-113, O-208). John was appointed a Justice of the Peace on November 19, 1778 (Ref: O-241).

WALKER, JOSEPH JR. Commissioned a First Lieutenant in Captain Elisha Riggs' Company on March 29, 1776 at Elk Ridge, "in the room of John Marriott, who was deceased." (Ref: N-299. Note: One record leaves "Jr." off his name).

WALLACE, CHARLES (April 27, 1727 - February 13, 1812). Son of John Wallace of Annapolis and Anne -----. He married first to Catherine ---- and second to Mary Bull, widow of George Rankin, in 1798. His children are not known, but possibly include Charles Wallace and Catherine Wallace Sprigg. Charles may have had children, but they were apparently dead and died without heirs by the time he wrote his will in 1810. He was a prominent merchant, tavern keeper and land developer in Annapolis. He was a Common Councilman in 1757 through 1765, an Alderman in 1767, Chairman of the Committee of Observation in 1775, member of the Committee to fortify Annapolis in 1776, Commissioner of the Tax, 1778-1783, Judge of the Court of Appeals in 1786, member of the Executive Council, 1783-1785, and Paymaster for Maryland troops, 1776-1780. To cover his debts and legacies, his estate was not settled until 1831 with his wife and grandnieces being the principal heirs (Ref: P-856, P-857).

WALLACE, GEORGE. Took the Oath of Allegiance before Hon. Samuel Harrison in March, 1778 (Ref: A-244).

WALLACE, JOHN. Physician and member of Annapolis convention (Ref: Y-305).

WALLACE, MICHAEL (of Annapolis). Physician and Surgeon's Mate in March, 1776. Surgeon to the Maryland Line and furnished medicines to William Smallwood's Battalion in 1776-1777. Annapolis hospital surgeon in 1777 (Ref: Y-306).

WALLINGSFORT, JAMES. He was a Substitute furnished by Capt. Alexander Truman in October, 1780, to serve until December 10, 1780 (Ref: H-369).

WALSH, DAVID. Private in Captain Richard Dorsey's Company of Artillery on November 17, 1777 (Ref: H-574).

WALSH, EDMOND. Sergeant in Capt. Richard Dorsey's Company of Artillery on November 17, 1777 (Ref: H-573).

WALSTON, BOAZ. On March 13, 1777 he petitioned the Council of Safety to inform them that he was wrongfully imprisoned, that he was not an enemy of this country, and that he would take the Oath of Allegiance (Ref: V-171).

WARD, BENJAMIN. A resident of Herring Creek who was among those who formed a militia company on March 6, 1776, and subsequently served as a private in Capt. Richard Weems' Company (Ref: I-143, MS.1814). Two men with this name took the Oath of Allegiance before Honorable Samuel Harrison in March, 1778 (Ref: A-244, B-29).

WARD, JOHN. Two men with this name took the Oath of Allegiance: one before Honorable Thomas Harwood on February 28, 1778 and one before Hon. Samuel Harrison in March, 1778 (Ref: B-22, B-29).

WARD, SAMUEL. Took the Oath of Allegiance before Honorable Thomas Harwood on February 7, 1778 (Ref: B-22).

WARD, SAMUEL JR. Took the Oath of Allegiance before Hon. Thomas Harwood on February 28, 1778 (Ref: B-22).

WARD, THOMAS. Took the Oath of Allegiance before Hon. John Dorsey on March 12, 1778 (Ref: B-26).

WARD, WEST (?). Private in Capt. Richard Chew's Company of Col. John Weems' Battalion of Militia on October 5, 1776 (Ref: A-95).

WARD, WILLIAM. Two men by this name took the Oath of Allegiance: one before Hon. Thomas Worthington on February 28, 1778, and one before Hon. Richard Harwood, Jr. on March 1, 1778 (Ref: B-22, B-23). One William Ward died by October 16, 1821 when the final distribution of his estate was to Sarah Ward (Wood?), her widow's third, with fourths of the balance to Yate Ward, Elizabeth Ward, William Ward, and Sarah E. Ward (Ref: U-61).

WARDEN, JACOB. Took the Oath of Allegiance before Hon. Elijah Robosson in March, 1778 (Ref: B-28).

WARFIELD AZEL (died in 1813). Son of Seth Warfield and Mary Gaither. Married Elizabeth Welling in 1786 and they had twelve children: Richard Warfield, Azel Warfield, Elizabeth Warfield, William Warfield, Mary Warfield Fisher, Matilda Warfield, Henry Warfield, Eliza Warfield Mercer, Sarah Warfield Shipley, Ann Warfield Dorsey, George W. Warfield, and Charles A. Warfield. Azel took the Oath of Allegiance before Hon. Thomas Worthington on

February 28, 1778 (Ref: Q-386, B-22. Also refer to the other Azel Warfield, q.v.).

WARFIELD, AZEL or ASEL (June 24, 1728 - November, 1785). Son of Alexander Warfield and Dinah Davidge. He married twice: first to Sarah Griffith and had six children: Dr. Charles Alexander Warfield, Dinah Warfield Gassaway, Catherine Warfield Griffith, Walter Warfield, Anne Warfield Waters, and Zachariah Warfield. His second wife was Susanna Magruder (in 1768) and they had 2 children: George Fraser Warfield and Sarah (Susanna) Warfield Waters. Azel was active in the revolution for he received from an armourer 12 gun barrels and 12 locks to be stocked on September 8, 1777, and he was paid by the Treasurer on December 12, 1777 (Ref: Q-419, E-248. Note: Source Q-419 also assigned him the patriotic duty of taking the Oath of Allegiance in 1778 as well as another Azel Warfield also assigned that same event by this same source. Original records, however, indicate there was only one Azel who took the Oath of Allegiance before Hon. Thomas Worthington in 1778). On April 9, 1805 the final distribution of his estate was made to Susanna Warfield (widow's third), with eighths of the balance to Charles Alexander Warfield, Dinah Gassaway, Catharine Griffith, Walter Warfield, Zachariah Warfield, Nancy Waters, George F. Warfield, and Sally Waters (Ref: U-29). Azel Warfield was born in 1726 and died in 1787 (according to Ref: T-734).

WARFIELD, BENI (died in October, 1829). Son of Seth Warfield. He married Arey Dorsey in 1779 and had 7 children: Sarah Warfield, Margaret Warfield, Marion Warfield, Daniel Warfield, Nicholas Dorsey Warfield, Charles Dorsey Warfield, and Alfred Warfield. He took the Oath of Allegiance before Hon. Reuben Meriweather on March 2, 1778 (Ref: Q-382, B-24). Final distribution of the estate of "Bani Warfield" was made on February 21, 1834 (sixths) to Charles D. Warfield, Daniel Warfield, Aldred Warfield, Margaret Warfield, Nicholas D. Warfield, and Nicholas Owens in right of his wife (Ref: U-89).

WARFIELD, BENJAMIN (born c1740 - died in September, 1806). Son of Benjamin Warfield and Rebecca Ridgely. Married Catherine Dorsey and had four sons: Beale Warfield, Benjamin Warfield, Philemon Dorsey Warfield, and Joshua Warfield. Benjamin was a Captain in the Elk Ridge Battalion of Militia in 1777 and 1778 (Ref: Q-370, Q-371, C-201). He took the Oath of Allegiance before Hon. Reuben Meriweather on March 2, 1778 (Ref: B-24). Benjamin was born in 1740 and died in 1814 (according to Ref: T-735).

WARFIELD, BRICE (February 3, 1742, Anne Arundel County - April 30, 1817, Frederick County). He first married Susannah Dickerson and after her death he married Sarah Collins in 1797. His children were Zadock Warfield, Surrat Dickerson Warfield and Rachel Warfield Burgess. Took the Oath of Allegiance before Hon. Thomas Worthington on February 28, 1778 (Ref: Q-376, B-22).

WARFIELD, CALEB (born c1743 - before 1820). Son of Joshua Warfield and Ruth Davis. He married (wife unknown) and had four children: Thomas Warfield, Caleb Warfield, Elizabeth Warfield, and Eleanor

Warfield. He is believed to be the "Calife Warfield" who took the Oath of Allegiance before Hon. Thomas Worthington on February 28, 1778 (Ref: Q-465, Q-466, B-22).

WARFIELD, CHARLES (1738-1790). Son of Alexander Warfield and Dinah Davidge. He was born in Anne Arundel County, married Elizabeth Warfield and settled in Frederick County where he was a Lieutenant in the Linganore Battalion, 1776-1778. (For additional information, see Ref: Q-422).

WARFIELD, CHARLES (February 1, 1752 - June, 1804). Son of John Warfield and Rachel Dorsey. Married Catherine Dorsey, daughter of Col. John Dorsey, and they had 12 children: Fielder Warfield, Eleanor Warfield, Kitty Warfield, Prestley Warfield, Rachel Warfield, Amelia Warfield, John Warfield, Singleton Warfield, Charles Warfield, Tilghman Warfield, Matilda Warfield, and Sarah Warfield (Ref: Q-365, Q-366) Charles was one of the petitioners to the Maryland Convention to form an independent rifle company in July, 1776 (Ref: B-3). On March 1, 1778, he was an Ensign in Captain Benjamin Warfield's Company in the Elk Ridge Battalion (Ref: C-201). He took Oath of Allegiance before Hon. Reuben Meriweather on March 2, 1778 (Ref: B-25).

WARFIELD, CHARLES ALEXANDER, M.D. (December 3, 1751 - January 29, 1813). Son of Azel Warfield and Sarah Griffith. Married Elizabeth Ridgely and they had 7 children: Peregrine Warfield, Gustavus Warfield, Anne Warfield Thomas, Charles Warfield, Elizabeth Warfield Snowden, Henry Ridgely Warfield, and Laura Victoria Warfield Snowden (Ref: Q-431). He was a zealous patriot who led the "Whigs" to Annapolis and burned the brig "Peggy Stewart" in 1774. He served on the Committee of Observation in 1775 (Ref: F-222) and he also took the Oath of Allegiance before Hon. Reuben Meriweather on March 2, 1778 (Ref: B-24). Charles held the rank of Major (Ref: E-283, T-735), and was the Surgeon for Gen. William Smallwood's Maryland Regiment (Ref: Y-306).

WARFIELD, DAVIDGE (February 15, 1729 - June, 1810). Son of Alexander Warfield and Dinah Davidge. He married Ann Worthington and had nine children: Henry Warfield, Sarah Warfield Burgess, Polly Warfield Warfield, Thomas Warfield, Ann Warfield Leek, Rebecca Warfield Simpson, Basil Warfield, Dinah Warfield James, and Absolom Warfield (Ref: Q-420, Q-421). Davidge took the Oath of Allegiance before Hon. Thomas Worthington, February 28, 1778 (Ref: B-22).

WARFIELD, EDMOND (died after 1810). Son of Philip Warfield and Anne Purdy. Married Mary Ann Warfield, daughter of Seth Warfield, in 1792, and had two children: Mary Warfield Hobbs and Anne Warfield Warfield. Took the Oath of Allegiance before Hon. John Dorsey on March 12, 1778 (Ref: Q-381, B-26).

WARFIELD, EDWARD (August 11, 1710 - February, 1787). Son of John Warfield and Ruth Gaither. He married Rachel Riggs in 1741 and they had twelve children: Ephraim Warfield, Edward Warfield, Achsah Warfield Hall, Robert Warfield, James Warfield, Leven Warfield,

Ruth Warfield, Catherine Warfield, Rachel Warfield Hobbs, Sarah Warfield Gaither, Elizabeth Warfield Ray, and Edward Warfield (Ref: Q-359, 360). Edward took the Oath of Allegiance before Hon. Thomas Worthington on February 28, 1778 (Ref: B-22).

WARFIELD, ELISHA (1740/1741, Anne Arundel County, Maryland - July 16, 1818, Fayette County, Kentucky). Son of Benjamin Warfield and Rebecca Ridgely. He married twice: first to Elizabeth Dorsey and they had three children: Polly Warfield Ford, Sally Warfield, and Nicholas Warfield. His second marriage, after the death of his first wife, occurred in August, 1778 and they had four sons: Elisha Warfield, Nicholas Warfield, Benjamin Warfield, and Henry Warfield (Ref: Q-373, Q-374, T-735). He served on the Committee of Observation in 1775 (Ref: F-222), and also took the Oath of Allegiance before Hon. Thomas Worthington on February 28, 1778 (Ref: B-22). He and his family moved to Kentucky in the Summer of 1790 (Refer to Source HCP-150).

WARFIELD, EPHRAIM. First Lieutenant in Capt. Robert Warfield's Company in the Elk Ridge Battalion of Militia in March, 1779 (Ref: O-333).

WARFIELD, JAMES (September 21, 1751 - December 1812). Son of Edward Warfield and Rachel Riggs. He married Ann Gassaway in 1797 and had 6 children: Laban Warfield, James Henry Warfield, George Hanson Warfield, Luther Warfield, Charles M. Warfield, and Elizabeth Warfield Waters. He was enrolled by Captain Thomas Watkins on October 21, 1776 for service to the State (Ref: I-144, MS.1814). He also took Oath of Allegiance before Honorable Thomas Worthington on February 28, 1778 (Ref: Q-377, B-22).

WARFIELD, JOHN (born by 1734 - 1820). Son of Samuel Warfield and Sarah Welch (Welsh). He married Mary Chaney in 1761 and they had nine children: Rachel Warfield Clark, Polly Warfield Forsythe, Samuel Warfield, Richard Warfield, John Warfield, Nancy Warfield Smith, Elizabeth (or Betsy) Warfield Carroll, Eleanor (or Nelly) Warfield Westley, and Benjamin Warfield. John was a 2nd Lieutenant in the Fifth Maryland Regiment (Ref: Q-448. Note: Source E-1822F states he was born in 1740 and died in 1787. Source Q-448 states that John "X" Warfield took the Oath of Allegiance before Hon. Reuben Meriweather in 1778, but the record indicates the name was "John W. Warfield," q.v). John was born in 1730 or 1740 and died circa 1787 (according to Source T-735).

WARFIELD, JOHN (OF RICHARD). Took the Oath of Allegiance before Hon. Nicholas Worthington in March, 1778 (Ref: Original lists in Maryland State Papers, Red Book 21, MdHR4587. Note: Source B-28 erroneously spelled the name as "John Waashole of Zion").

WARFIELD, JOHN WORTHINGTON (February 3, 1742, Anne Arundel County - March, 1811, Montgomery County). A twin of Brice Warfield, and son of Alexander Warfield and Thomasine Worthington, John allegedly married first to Susanna Ridgely and then Mary Holland. His children were Arnold Warfield, Alexander Warfield, Araminta Warfield Cooper Fitzgerald, Nancy Warfield Stevens, and Sarah

Warfield Day (Ref: Q-375). He took the Oath of Allegiance before Hon. Reuben Meriweather on March 2, 1778 (Ref: B-24. Note: Source Q-375 does not assign this oath-taking to him, but to another John Warfield. A review of the original record indicates "John W. Warfield" actually took the Oath).

WARFIELD, JOSEPH. He was one of the petitioners to the Maryland Convention to form an independent rifle company in July, 1776 (Ref: B-3) and he was an Ensign in Capt. Philemon Warfield's Company in the Severn Battalion on June 19, 1777 (Ref: A-176, C-202). There were two Joseph Warfield's who took the Oath of Allegiance: one before Hon. Thomas Worthington on February 28, 1778 and one before Hon. Nicholas Worthington in March, 1778 (Ref: B-22, B-28), and there were two Joseph Warfield's who appear as officers in the Severn Battalion on August 15, 1778 (Ref: I-144, J-113, O-208. See next entry).

WARFIELD, JOSEPH (February 19, 1758, Anne Arundel County - October 19, 1837, Montgomery County). Son of Joshua Warfield and Rachel Howard. He married Elizabeth Dorsey in 1778 and they had 7 children: Elizabeth Warfield Offut, Juliet Warfield Williams, Harriet Warfield, Nicholas Dorsey Warfield, Charlotte Warfield Lawrence, Elizabeth Dorsey Warfield, and Sarah Warfield. At the outbreak of the revolution he was appointed a cadet and joined the forces at Long Island a few days after the American defeat, in Capt. James Disney's Company of Colonel Josias C. Hall's Regiment. He left in December, 1776, at Philadelphia, and returned to Maryland, where he was commissioned a Second Lieutenant in the 5th Maryland Regiment commanded by Col. William Richardson, of the Eastern Shore. He was assigned to Captain John Dean's Company under whom he served until the winter at Valley Forge. He resigned his commission after the battle of Germantown in the spring of 1778. Joseph moved to Montgomery County, Maryland in 1801 (Ref: Q-439, Q-440, G-125. A lot of genealogical information about Joseph Warfield's family can be found in National Genealogical Society Quarterly, Vol, 34, No. 2, p. 69 (1946).

WARFIELD, JOSHUA (1710-1779). Son of Benjamin Warfield and Elizabeth Duvall. Joshua married Ruth Davis and had eight children: Benjamin Warfield, Thomas Warfield, Joshua Warfield, Caleb Warfield, Henry Warfield, Mary Warfield, Elizabeth Warfield Wells and Eleanor Warfield Welsh (Ref: Q-461). Took Oath of Allegiance before Hon. Nicholas Worthington in March, 1778 (Ref: B-28. Note: Source Q-461 does not give him credit for this patriotic gesture).

WARFIELD, LANCELOT (1740 - May, 1804). Son of Richard Warfield and Sarah Gaither. He married first to Polly Robertson (Robosson) and they had four children: Charles Warfield, Lancelot Warfield, Lemuel Warfield, and Sarah Warfield. He married second to Rachel Marriott in 1783 and they had four children: Evan Warfield, John Warfield, Allen Warfield and Rachel Warfield. Lancelot was commissioned a 2nd Lieutenant in 1776 in Capt. James Tootell's Company (Ref: N-178) and then a 1st Lieutenant in Capt. Philemon Warfield's Company in the Severn Battalion in 1777. He was still in service in May, 1781 when he was paid money "due him for guarding prisoners to Frederick

Town" (Ref: A-176, C-202, F-223, Q-450, Q-451, T-736). He took the Oath of Allegiance before Hon. Elijah Robosson in March, 1778 (Ref: B-28). Final distribution of his estate was made in 1810 to Rachel Warfield (widow) with bequests to Charles Warfield, Lemuel Warfield, Sarah Warfield, Lancelot Warfield, John Warfield, Allen Warfield, and Rachel Warfield (Ref: U-38).

WARFIELD, LUKE (died 1780, d.s.p). Son of Richard Warfield and Mary Caldwell (Ref: Q-350). Took the Oath of Allegiance before Hon. Nicholas Worthington in March, 1778 (Ref: B-28).

WARFIELD, NICHOLAS RIDGELY (died 1814, d.s.p.). Son of Benjamin Warfield and Rebecca Ridgely (Ref: Q-354). Took the Oath of Allegiance before Hon. John Dorsey on March 12, 1778 (Ref: B-26). He was commissioned a Captain in the Elk Ridge Battalion of Militia in March, 1779 (Ref: O-333).

WARFIELD, PHILEMON (April 15, 1744 - March, 1794). Son of Alexander Warfield and Dinah Davidge. Married Asenah (Asseneth) Waters and had two daughters: Mary Warfield and Elizabeth Warfield. In 1776 Philemon was a 1st Lieutenant in Capt. James Tootell's Co. (Ref: N-178). On April 14, 1777, he resigned his appointment as a commissioner of blankets because he was needed on his plantation (Ref: A-151, Q-427). On June 19, 1777, he was Captain in Severn Battalion of Militia under Colonel Nicholas Worthington (Ref: A-176, C-202, F-223, I-144, J-113, O-208). Note: Reference Q-427 indicates two Philemon Warfield's who were commissioned officers during the Revolutionary War. If such was the case, then part of the foregoing data may pertain to the other Philemon Warfield whose identity is not given, but who apparently served as Lieutenant in Capt. Henry Hall's Company in 1776. (Also see Source T-736). One took the Oath of Allegiance before Hon. Nicholas Worthington in March, 1778 (Ref: B-28) and one was on the Committee of Observation (Ref: F-222).

WARFIELD, PHILIP (JR). Son of Philip Warfield and Anne Purdy. He married Susannah Hobbs; children not known (Ref: Q-380). Philip took the Oath of Allegiance before Hon. Reuben Meriweather on March 2, 1778 (Ref: B-24).

WARFIELD, PHILIP SR. (1717 - after 1778). Son of John Warfield and Ruth Gaither. He married Anne Purdy and they had 14 children: Philip Warfield, Ephraim Warfield, Edmond Warfield, Lydia Warfield Hobbs, John Warfield, Elizabeth Warfield Duvall, Ruth Warfield, Sarah Warfield Dorsey, William Warfield, Richard Warfield, Mary Warfield, Amelia Warfield Higgins, Rachel Warfield, and Polly Warfield (Ref: Q-361, Q-362). Philip took the Oath of Allegiance before Hon. John Dorsey on March 12, 1778 (Ref: B-26).

WARFIELD, RICHARD. Two men with this name took the Oath of Allegiance: one before Hon. Thomas Worthington on February 28, 1778 and another before Hon. Thomas Dorsey on March 2, 1778 (Ref: B-22, B-24).

WARFIELD, RIDGELY. In March, 1778, he listed military supplies stored at Elk Ridge of tin boxes, gun flints, canteens, grape shot, bullet molds, levels, handspikes, cartridges and paper, wadding, barrels, speaking trumpets, bar lead, blankets, powder, and pikes (Ref: B-29).

WARFIELD, ROBERT (May 1, 1749 - 1817/1818). Son of Edward Warfield and Rachel Riggs. Unmarried. He was one of the petitioners to the Maryland Convention to form an independent rifle company in July, 1776 (Ref: B-3). On March 1, 1778, he was a Second Lieutenant in Captain Benjamin Warfield's Company in the Elk Ridge Battalion of Militia, and subsequently became a Captain in March, 1779 (Ref: Q-359, Q-379, C-201, O-333). Robert also took the Oath of Allegiance before Hon. Reuben Meriweather on March 2, 1778 (Ref: B-24).

WARFIELD, SAMUEL (c1705 - died by 1790). Son of Alexander Warfield and Sarah Pierpont. Married Sarah Welch (Welsh) in 1727 and had seven children: John Warfield, Samuel Warfield, Vachel Warfield, Gerard Warfield, Mary Warfield Pumphrey, Welsh Warfield and Richard Warfield (Ref: Q-446, E-1822G, T-736). Took the Oath of Allegiance before Hon. Thomas Dorsey in 1778 (Ref: B-24).

WARFIELD, SAMUEL JR. Son of Samuel Warfield and Sarah Welsh (Welch). He took the Oath of Allegiance before Hon. Thomas Dorsey on March 2, 1778 in Anne Arundel County. After the revolution he and his brother Gerard Warfield moved to the Redstone District of Pennsylvania (Ref: Q-446, Q-447, B-24).

WARFIELD, SETH SR. (January 15, 1723 - May 14, 1805). Son of Richard Warfield and Marion Caldwell. Married Mary Gaither. Their children: Seth Warfield, Elizabeth Warfield, Beni Warfield, Bela Warfield, Elizabeth Warfield Chapman, Azel Warfield, Mary Warfield Owings, Amos Warfield, Eli Warfield, and Mary Ann Warfield Warfield (Ref: Q-363, E-2714, E-2826). Took Oath of Allegiance before Hon. Thomas Worthington, February 28, 1778 (Ref: B-22). He is also referred to as Seth Warfield, Jr. (according to Source T-736).

WARFIELD, THOMAS (c1753-1818). Was commissioned an Ensign in Capt. James Tootell's Company on February 22, 1776, and then a 2nd Lieutenant in Capt. Philemon Warfield's Company in the Severn Battalion of Militia in 1777-1778 (Ref: A-176, C-202, F-223, I-144, J-113, N-178, T-736). He took the Oath of Allegiance before Hon. Nicholas Worthington in March, 1778 (Ref: B-28).

WARFIELD, VACHEL (September 9, 1747 - 1815). Son of Benjamin Warfield and Rebecca Ridgely. Married Sarah Dorsey and had 9 children: Allen Warfield, Philemon Dorsey Warfield, Lloyd Warfield, Joshua Warfield, Greenbury Ridgely Warfield, Rebecca Warfield, Catherine Warfield Linthicum, Nicholas Warfield, and Larkin Warfield (Ref: Q-371, U-66). Vachel took the Oath of Allegiance before Hon. Thomas Worthington, February 28, 1778 (Ref: B-22).

WARFIELD, VACHEL (died in May, 1817). Son of Samuel Warfield and Sarah Welsh. Married Mary Ryan (widow) prior to 1769 and they had seven children: Sarah Warfield Elliott, Mary Warfield, Allen Warfield, Charles Warfield, William Warfield, Henrietta Warfield Marriott, and Vachel Warfield. Very little is known about his activities during the Revolutionary War but on December 9, 1777 he was paid for the hire of his wagon for State service (Ref: Q-449).

WARFIELD, WALTER, M.D. (June 17, 1760, Anne Arundel County, Maryland - March 10, 1826, Lexington, Kentucky). Son of Azel Warfield and Sarah Griffith. He married a niece of Patrick Henry (name not given) and they left issue. During the revolution Walter served as Surgeon Mate to the Sixth Maryland Regiment in 1777 and Surgeon to the Second Maryland Regiment in 1779. He was an original member of the Society of the Cincinnati. Sometime after 1800 he settled in Fayette County, Kentucky (Ref: Q-433, Y-307, V-359).

WARNER, JOSEPH. Took the Oath of Allegiance before Hon. Samuel Harrison in March, 1778 (Ref: B-29).

WARWICK, JAMES. Enrolled by Henry Ridgely, Jr. and passed by Col. J. Carvil Hall on August 26, 1776 (Ref: H-41).

WASON, JOHN. Took the Oath of Allegiance before Hon. Samuel Harrison in March, 1778 (Ref: A-244).

WATERMAN, PHYLLIS. Served as a Nurse in Annapolis hospitals during the war and is sometimes referred to as a physician (Ref: Y-307).

WATERS, EZEKIEL. Son of Joseph and Mary Waters. Took the Oath of Allegiance before Hon. Thomas Worthington on February 28, 1778 (Ref: R-490, B-22).

WATERS, HENRY. Took the Oath of Allegiance before Hon. Thomas Worthington on February 28, 1778 (Ref: B-22).

WATERS, JOHN. Enrolled by Henry Ridgely, Jr. and passed by Col. J. Carvil Hall on August 26, 1776 (Ref: H-41). Took the Oath of Allegiance on March 21, 1778 (Ref: V-545).

WATERS, JONATHAN (1758 - May 3, 1823). Son of Nathan Waters and Catherine Wilson. Married Sarah Ann Thornton in 1798 and had five children: William Thornton Waters, Thomas Gassaway Waters, Juliana Waters Flusser, Nicholas B. Waters, and James L. Waters. During the Revolutionary War he served as a Marine on the sloop "Lincoln" and was captured by the British and held in New York City. During the war he was wounded and was subsequently paid the half pay of private on February 19, 1819 (Ref: R-483, R-484, K-404, U-68).

WATERS, JOSEPH (d.s.p. 1798). Probably a son of John Waters and Mary Ijams. He took the Oath of Allegiance before Hon. Elijah Robosson in March, 1778. (Ref: R-449, B-28).

WATERS, JOSEPHUS (1742-1800). Son of John Waters and Mary Ijams. Married Mary Edwards in 1776 and they had two sons: Edward Waters and Aquilla Waters (Ref: T-741). Josephus Waters took the Oath of

Allegiance before Hon. Thomas Dorsey on March 2, 1778 (Ref: R-457, B-24).

WATERS, NATHAN (OF JOSEPH). Son of Joseph and Mary Waters. He married Susanna Gaither; children unknown. Took the Oath of Allegiance before Hon. Thomas Worthington on February 28, 1778. May have been the Nathan Waters who died April 19, 1828, and who was the father of David Waters (Ref: R-488, B-22).

WATERS, NATHAN (circa 1735 - 1812). Son of William Waters and Rachel Duvall. He married Catherine Wilson and had seven children: Wilson Waters, Martha Waters, Elizabeth Waters Chisholm, Jonathan Waters, William Waters, Robert Waters, and Mary Waters. He settled in Annapolis and established a leather manufacturing business, furnishing equipment for the Maryland Line during the Revolution. His home was damaged during the war and the Treasurer was directed on December 23, 1777 to pay Archibald Chisholm for damages done to Nathan's house. He was also paid on April 17, 1778 and March 16, 1781 by the Auditor General (Ref: R-480. Note: This source also states he took the Oath of Allegiance in 1778. However, the list published in Reference B-22 indicates the Oath was, in fact, taken by Nathan Waters of Joseph, q.v.).

WATERS, WILSON, M.D. (1757-1836). Son of Nathan Waters and Catherine Wilson. He married first to Joan or Jane Montgomery in 1785 (died 1799) and second to Margaret Davis in 1800. Their children were William Montgomery Waters, Elizabeth Waters, and Ramsay Waters (Ref: R-481) but on March 9, 1836 final distribution of his estate was made to Margaret Waters (widow's third) with thirds of the remainder to Ramsay Waters, Maria Louisa Waters, and John Wilson Waters (Ref: U-92). Dr. Waters' first involvement in the war was in 1776 when he assisted Dr. Benjamin Rush in the care of Maryland soldiers on their return from the New York City campaign. In March, 1777, he was commissioned a Surgeon's Mate and served under the Physician General of the Hospitals of the Middle Department of the Continental Army. He was with Dr. Rush at Philadelphia, Burlington, Stony Run, Lancaster Trenton and Yellow Springs. He resigned in August, 1779 and returned to Maryland. Upon returning, he was commissioned a Surgeon in the Maryland Navy, was captured on the vessel "Matilda" under Capt. James Belt, and was carried as prisoner to New York by the British. Upon his release, he was assigned by Gov. Paca as Surgeon of a Maryland Flotilla on Tangier Island in the Chesapeake Bay. In 1783, he returned to his plantation on Rhodes River (Ref: R-481, R-482). Wilson was pensioned on March 4, 1831, at age 77 (according to Ref: Z-45). On March 16, 1836, the Treasurer was directed to "pay to Margaret Waters, widow of Dr. Wilson Waters, quarterly during her life, the half pay of a surgeon's mate in consideration of her husband's services." (Ref: K-404).

WATKINS, AARON. He was enrolled by Capt. Thomas Watkins on October 21, 1776 for service to the State (Ref: I-144, MS.1814). Took the Oath of Allegiance before Hon. Richard Harwood, Jr. on March 1, 1778 (Ref: B-23).

WATKINS, BENJAMIN. Took the Oath of Allegiance before Hon. Thomas Harwood on February 28, 1778 (Ref: B-22).

WATKINS, CHARLES. Born in Maryland. H e was enrolled by Capt. Edward Tillard in July, 1776. Height: 5' 7" (Ref: H-39). He took the Oath of Allegiance before Hon. Samuel Lane on March 1, 1778 (Ref: B-23).

WATKINS, GASSAWAY (1752 - July 14, 1840, Howard County, Maryland). Married Eleanor Bowie Clagett in 1803 in Baltimore County and they had at least one daughter Priscilla Watkins Kenly. Gassaway was enrolled by Captain James Disney, Jr. and passed by Col. Richard Harwood on July 13, 1776 (Ref:H-41), and commissioned an Ensign in the 3rd Maryland Line in 1777 and Lieutenant in 1778. At the time of his death in 1840 he was President of the Society of the Cincinnati in Maryland (Ref: E-15, E-284). In December, 1815, the State Treasurer was directed to "pay to Gassaway Watkins, late a Captain in the Revolution, a sum equal to the half pay of Captain, in lieu of the sum already allowed him by resolution passed in November, 1811, as a further remuneration for serving for his country's independence." (Ref: K-404). He was pensioned on June 14, 1828, as a Captain in 3rd Md. Line (Ref: Z-53).

WATKINS, GASSAWAY (OF JOHN). He was enrolled by Captain Thomas Watkins on October 21, 1776 for service to the State (Ref: I-144, MS.1814).

WATKINS, GASSAWAY CHAMBERS. He was enrolled by Captain Thomas Watkins on October 21, 1776 for service to the State (Ref: I-144, MS.1814). He took the Oath of Allegiance before Hon. Richard Harwood, Jr. on March 1, 1778. (Ref: B-23).

WATKINS, JEREMIAH (March 8, 1743, Anne Arundel Co., Maryland - May 3, 1833, Montgomery Co., Maryland). Married Elizabeth Waugh in 1762 and had a son Nicholas Watkins, and probably other children (Ref: E-2878). Took the Oath of Allegiance before Hon. Thomas Harwood on February 28, 1778 (Ref: B-22).

WATKINS, JOHN. Enrolled by Captain James Disney, Jr. and passed by Colonel Richard Harwood on July 13, 1776 (Ref: H-41). John Watkins, son of Stephen Watkins, was deceased by January 6, 1819 when final distribution of his estate (fourths) was made by Nicholas Watkins (of Thomas), administrator, to William Watkins, Eleanor Watkins, Rachel Sprigg Watkins, and Elizabeth Watkins (Ref: U-55). Another John Watkins was deceased by June 4, 1807 when final distribution of his estate was made to Ann Watkins (widow) and half of the balance to Rachel Watkins and Julianna Watkins (Ref: U-32).

WATKINS, JOHN JR. Took the Oath of Allegiance before Hon. Thomas Harwood on February 28, 1778 (Ref: B-22).

WATKINS, JOHN SR. Took the Oath of Allegiance before Hon. Thomas Harwood on February 28, 1778 (Ref: B-22).

WATKINS, JOHN (OF JOHN). Took the Oath of Allegiance before Honorable Richard Harwood, Jr. on March 1, 1778 (Ref: B-23).

WATKINS, JOSEPH (1734-1788). Married Ann Brown. He was Major and Commissary of Ordinance Stores in 1777 (Ref: E-345). He took the Oath of Allegiance before Hon. Richard Harwood, Jr. on March 1, 1778 (Ref: B-23, T-741).

WATKINS, NICHOLAS. One of the petitioners to the Maryland Convention to form an independent rifle company in July, 1776 (Ref: B-3). He was commissioned a 1st Lieutenant in Capt. John Dorsey's Company of the 22nd (or Elk Ridge) Battalion of Militia on August 28, 1777 (Ref: K-405). He took the Oath of Allegiance before Hon. John Dorsey on March 12, 1778 (Ref: B-26). Nicholas Watkins was deceased by December 30, 1829, when final distribution of his estate was made by Thomas W. Watkins, administrator de bonis non (sureties Nicholas Watkins, Jr. and Gassway Watkins), half to Lafayette Watkins, and half to the heirs of William Pitt Watkins, namely Harriet Watkins (widow of William P. Watkins) and William T. Watkins, Harriet Ann Watkins, Manelia Watkins, and Olive P. Watkins (Ref: U-80).

WATKINS, RICHARD. Took the Oath of Allegiance before Hon. Richard Harwood, Jr. on March 1, 1778 (Ref: B-23).

WATKINS, SAMUEL. Second Lieutenant in Capt. Thomas Watkins' Company in the South River Battalion of Militia in 1776 (Ref: F-223). He took the Oath of Allegiance before Hon. Richard Harwood, Jr. on March 1, 1778 (Ref: B-23).

WATKINS, STEPHEN (1753 - February 12, 1839). Enrolled by Capt. James Disney, Jr. and passed by Col. Richard Harwood on July 13, 1776 (Ref: H-41). Took the Oath of Allegiance before Honorable Thomas Harwood on February 28, 1778 (Ref: B-22). He applied for pension in Monongalia County, Virginia in 1820 (at age 67), stating he enlisted under Capt. Jonathan Sellman and joined the 4th Maryland Regiment under Col. Smith and Col. Hall and served in the 2nd Maryland Brigade under Gen. Gist. He was discharged in May, 1780, at West Point. He also took the oath of loyalty and declared that his family consisted of Sarah Watkins (43), James Watkins (16), Frances Watkins (15), Arthur Watkins (13), Thomas Watkins (10), Stephen Watkins (8), Gassaway Watkins (6), and Hannah Watkins (3). He further stated that in 1804 he married Sarah Miller (born in 1778) in Monongalia County, Virginia (Ref: National Genealogical Society Quarterly, Vol. 34, No. 2, p. 70 (1946)).

WATKINS, THOMAS. One of the representatives of Anne Arundel County to the Maryland Convention on July 3, 1776 and November 8, 1776 (Ref: J-35). He was appointed Justice on June 10, 1777 (Ref: Anne Arundel Co. Orphans Court Proceedings, 1777-1779, MdHR9524, p. 1), and he took the Oath of Allegiance before Hon. Richard Harwood, Jr. on March 1, 1778 (Ref: B-23. Note: It is possible that some of the foregoing data pertains to Thomas Watkins, Jr. as the "Jr." is not always shown on the name of Thomas Watkins, Jr., q.v.).

WATKINS, THOMAS JR. Took the Oath of Allegiance before Hon. Richard Harwood, Jr. on March 1, 1778 (Ref: B-23). He was a Captain in Col. John Weems' West River Battalion of Militia from 1776 to at least 1779 (Ref: A-88, C-199, F-223, K-405, N-158, N-232, O-496). On September 20, 1776 he reported to the Council of Safety that desertions from his company were due to lack of clothing and blankets. Col. William Richardson reported that Capt. Watkins was "addicted to drink." (Ref: J-49. Note: It is possible that some of this data may pertain to Thomas Watkins, as the "Jr." is not always included).

WATSON, DAVID. Took the Oath of Allegiance before Hon. Samuel Harrison in March, 1778 (Ref: B-29).

WATSON, SAMUEL. Took the Oath of Allegiance before Hon. Nicholas Worthington in March, 1778 (Ref: B-27).

WATSON, WILLIAM. Took the Oath of Allegiance before Hon. Nicholas Worthington in March, 1778 (Ref: B-27). On November 13, 1793 the final distribution of his estate was made to Mary Watson (widow's third), with thirds of the remainder to Charles Watson, William Watson and Mary Watson (Ref: U-11).

WATTS, GEORGE. Commissioned a Captain in the Severn Battalion of Militia on February 22, 1776 and served under Colonel Nicholas Worthington on June 19, 1777 (Ref: A-176, F-223, N-178).

WATTS, JOHN. Enrolled by Capt. James Disney, Jr. and passed by Col. Richard Harwood on July 13, 1776 (Ref: H-41). He took the Oath of Allegiance before Hon. Thomas Dorsey on March 2, 1778 (Ref: B-24).

WATTS, RICHARD. Took the Oath of Allegiance before Hon. Richard Harwood, Jr. on March 1, 1778 (Ref: B-23).

WATTS, SAMUEL. Enrolled by Captain James Disney, Jr. and passed by Colonel Richard Harwood on July 13, 1776 (Ref: H-41).

WATTSON, JOSEPH. Took the Oath of Allegiance before Hon. Thomas Worthington on February 28, 1778 (Ref: B-22).

WAYMAN, EDMOND. Took the Oath of Allegiance before Hon. Richard Harwood, Jr. on March 1, 1778 (Ref: B-23). Still alive in 1793 (Ref: U-10).

WAYMAN, HEZEKIAH. Private in Capt. William Marbury's Company of Artillery in 1777 (Ref: H-575).

WEAKLE, THOMAS. Took the Oath of Allegiance before Hon. Elijah Robosson in March, 1778 (Ref: B-28).

WEBB, JOSEPH. Enlisted by Michael Burgess and passed by Colonel Hyde on July 20, 1776 (Ref: H-41).

WEEDON (WEDON), JOSEPH. Born in Scotland. He was a Substitute, furnished by Charles Worthington (of Nicholas) on May 6, 1778, to serve for the duration of the war (Ref: C-206, H-317).

WEEDON (WHIDDON), OLIVER. He was paid by the Council of Safety for stocking fourteen muskets on April 6, 1776 and January 24, 1777 (Ref: N-316, V-75).

WEEDON, RICHARD. First Lieutenant in Capt. Joseph Merriken's Company in the Severn Battalion of Militia on June 19, 1777 (Ref: A-176). He was paid by the Council of Safety on June 29, 1776 for "supplying the Severn Battalion on the Otter Alarm with provisions" (Ref: N-533).

WEEMS, DAVID (1706-1779). He took the Oath of Allegiance before Hon. Samuel Harrison in March, 1778 (Ref: A-244, P-874).

WEEMS, DAVID JR. Took the Oath of Allegiance before Hon. Samuel Harrison in March, 1778 (Ref: B-29).

WEEMS, JAMES. Physician of lower Anne Arundel County who was appointed by the Council of Maryland and served as Surgeon's Mate in 1782 (Ref: Y-306).

WEEMS, JOHN (March 26, 1727 - November 28, 1794). Son of David Weems and Elizabeth Lane. Married twice: first wife unknown; second wife was Mary Dorsey in 1781 and their children were William Weems, Richard Dorsey Weems, John Beale Weems, Mary Weems McPherson, Sarah Weems Johns, Eleanor Weems and Ann Weems Ridout. John was Colonel of the West River (or South River) Battalion, 1776 to 1779 (Ref: A-95, A-140, C-199, E-2624, F-223, N-206, N-207, N-232, T-746). He took the Oath of Allegiance before Hon. Richard Harwood, Jr. on March 1, 1778 (Ref: B-23). In 1776 he was appointed one of three "collectors of all gold and silver in Anne Arundel County in exchange for continental money for use of Congress" (Ref: F-222, N-132). On July 3, 1776 he was appointed a Judge of Elections (Ref: J-35). On August 19, 1779 he was commissioned by Congress to be one of the three persons to receive subscriptions in Anne Arundel County (Ref: O-499). He was also commissioner of the tax at various times between 1777 and 1790 in Anne Arundel County, and attended the Maryland Convention in 1774 (Ref: P-874, P-875, U-28).

WEEMS, RICHARD. Resident of Herring Creek who petitioned the Convention of Maryland on March 6, 1776 to form an independent militia company and was subsequently Captain in the West River Battalion under Colonel John Weems, from 1776 to at least 1778 (Ref: C-199, F-223, N-336, I-143, MS.1814).

WEEMS, THOMAS. He was a Substitute, passed by James Brice on June 10, 1778, for nine months in Capt. Abraham Simmons' Company (Ref: C-209, H-320).

WEEMS, THOMAS LANE (1737-1779). Son of David Weems and Elizabeth Lane (Ref: P-875). He took the Oath of Allegiance before Hon. Samuel Lane on March 1, 1778 (Ref: B-23).

WEEMS, WILLIAM JR. (1743, Anne Arundel County - 1815, Calvert County). He married first to Mrs. Chapman of Virginia and secondly to Anne Ewell in 1797. His children were William Morris Weems, Elijah Weems, Anne Weems, James Ewell Weems, Marianna Weems Simmons, and Sophie Weems Horrell. He was Commander of the sloop "Little Sam" in 1779 in Anne Arundel County (Ref: T-746). He also took the Oath of Allegiance before Hon. Samuel Harrison in March, 1778 (Ref: A-244).

WEIR, ANDREW. Took the Oath of Allegiance before Hon. Samuel Harrison in March, 1778 (Ref: B-29).

WELCH (WELSH), AARON. Took the Oath of Allegiance before Hon. Thomas Harwood on February 28, 1778 (Ref: B-22). First Lieutenant in Capt. William Simmons Company in the West River Battalion on March 1, 1778 (Ref: C-200). He was deceased by December 3, 1801 when final distribution of his estate was made to Elizabeth Welch (widow's third), with remaining fifths to Aaron Welch, Catharine Welch, John Welch, Rachel Welch and Benjamin Welch (Ref: U-22).

WELCH, BENJAMIN. Took the Oath of Allegiance before Hon. Richard Harwood, Jr. on March 1, 1778 (Ref: B-23).

WELCH, HENRY O'NEAL. Took the Oath of Allegiance before Honorable Nicholas Worthington in March, 1778 (Ref: B-28).

WELCH (WELSH), JACOB. Took the Oath of Allegiance before Honorable Samuel Harrison in March, 1778 (Ref: A-244).

WELCH, JOHN. Three men by this name took the Oath of Allegiance: one before Hon. Thomas Harwood on February 28, 1778, one before Hon. Richard Harwood, Jr. on March 1, 1778, and one before Hon. Samuel Harrison in March, 1778. (Ref: B-22, B-23, B-29; also see "John Welsh," q.v.).

WELCH, JOHN (OF ROBERT). Took the Oath of Allegiance before Honorable Thomas Harwood on February 28, 1778 (Ref: B-22).

WELCH, RICHARD. Took the Oath of Allegiance before Hon. Samuel Harrison in March, 1778 (Ref: B-29).

WELCH, ROBERT. Physician and Surgeon's Mate in 1778 (Ref: Y-306).

WELCH (WELSH), ROBERT. Second Lieutenant in Captain William Simmons' Company in the West River Battalion on March 1, 1778 (Ref: C-200). Took the Oath of Allegiance before Hon. Richard Harwood, Jr. on March 1, 1778 (Ref: B-23).

WELCH, ROBERT (OF JOHN). Took the Oath of Allegiance before Hon. Richard Harwood, Jr. on March 1, 1778 (Ref: B-23).

WELCH, ZACHARIAH. Took the Oath of Allegiance before Hon. Samuel Harrison in March, 1778 (Ref: B-29).

WELLING, WILLIAM. Took the Oath of Allegiance before Hon. Thomas Worthington on February 28, 1778 (Ref: B-22).

WELLS, BENJAMIN. Resident of Herring Creek who petitioned the Convention of Maryland on March 6, 1776 to form an independent militia company and later served in Capt. Richard Weems' Company (Ref: I-143, MS.1814). Took the Oath of Allegiance before Hon. Thomas Harwood on February 28, 1778 (Ref: B-22).

WELLS, DANIEL JR. (1739-1817). Married Susanna ----- and had 9 children: William Wells, Frederick Wells, Ann Wells Monroe, Daniel Wells, John Wells, Mary Wells Carter, Sarah Wells Hyde, Richard Wells, and Elizabeth Wells Waters (Ref: T-748). Took the Oath of Allegiance before Honorable Thomas Dorsey on March 2, 1778 (Ref: B-24). Private in Capt. Gilbert Middleton's Independent Company of Militia of Annapolis on March 20, 1779 (Ref: I-144, O-325). On February 14, 1827 the final distribution of his estate (ninths) was made to William Wells, Frederick Wells, Ann Munroe, the children of Daniel Wells, John Wells, Mary Carter, the children of Sarah Hyde, Richard Wells, and Elizabeth Waters (Ref: U-72. Note: These same people are listed on the same date regarding the distribution of the estate of Susan Wells).

WELLS, JOHN. Enlisted by Edward Spurrier and passed by Thomas Dorsey on July 20, 1776 (Ref: H-41), and stationed at Annapolis in Captain John Fulford's Company of Artillery on December 12, 1776 (Ref: H-572). He was a disabled soldier who was paid in Anne Arundel County on August 16, 1783; the record indicated he was "out of state." (Ref: D-8).

WELLS, JOHN. Private in Capt. Gilbert Middleton's Independent Company of Militia of Annapolis on March 20, 1779 (Ref: I-144, O-325).

WELLS, NATHAN. Enrolled by Samuel Chew on July 25, 1776 (Ref: H-40). On July 14, 1826 the final distribution of his estate was made with a third to his widow (unnamed) and remaining fifths to Sarah Tellott, George Wells, James Wells, Floyd Wells, and Matilda Wells (Ref: U-71).

WELLS, NATHANIEL. Took the Oath of Allegiance before Hon. Samuel Harrison in March, 1778 (Ref: A-244).

WELLS, RICHARD. Resident of Herring Creek who petitioned the Convention of Maryland on March 6, 1776 to form an independent militia company and later served in Captain Richard Weems' Company (Ref: I-143, MS.1814). A second Richard Wells was commissioned Second Lieutenant in the militia on January 3, 1776. He resigned his commission on July 12, 1777 by writing a letter to the Council of Safety advising "that his bad state of health had rendered him impossible to attending to his duty since September last and should God restore his health to a capacity of assisting his country in proportion of its right and privileges, he will always be ready." (Ref: K-404, K-405). Three men by this name took the Oath of Allegiance: one before Hon. Thomas Harwood and one before Hon.

Thomas Worthington on February 28, 1778, and another before Hon. Samuel Harrison in March, 1778 (Ref: A-244, B-22).

WELLS, WILLIAM. Born in Maryland. Enrolled by Capt. Edward Tillard on July 10, 1776. Height: 5' 6 1/4" (Ref: H-39). He took the Oath of Allegiance before Hon. Thomas Harwood on February 28, 1778 (Ref: B-22).

WELSH, JACOB. Resident of Herring Creek who petitioned to the Convention of Maryland on March 6, 1776 to form an independent militia company and later served in Capt. Richard Weems' Company (Ref: I-143, MS.1814).

WELSH, JOHN. Private in Capt. William Marbury's Company of Artillery in 1777 (Ref: H-575).

WELSH, JOHN SR. or III (February 3, 1719 - December 19, 1784). Married Hannah Hammond circa 1742 and they had 11 children: John Welsh, Anne Welsh Duvall, Charles Welsh, Razia Welsh, Samuel Welsh, Henry Welsh, Ruth Welsh Warfield, Hamutal Welsh, Rachel Welsh, Philip Welsh, and Sarah Welsh. John took the Oath of Allegiance before Hon. Thomas Worthington in March, 1778. He was also a Justice of the Peace in 1774-75 (Ref: T-749, E-2826 Supplemental).

WELSH, ROBERT (1731-1786). Married Frances Peacock in 1757 and they had five children: Benjamin Welsh, Robert Welsh, Mary Welsh, Ann Welsh and Catherine Welsh (Ref: T-750, which states he was a Surgeon in Col. Ewing's Battalion in 1776). One Robert Welsh was enlisted by Capt. Edward Tillard and passed by Richard Harwood, Jr. on July 16, 1776 (Ref: H-40).

WENTWORTH, ISAAC. Captain of the Brig "Marian" on April 12, 1777 when given permission to proceed from port of Annapolis to James River (Ref: V-208).

WEST, JAMES. Recruited by Capt. Alexander Truman in October, 1780, to serve for three years (Ref: H-370).

WESTENEYS (WESTEMEY), JOHN. Took the Oath of Allegiance before Hon. Samuel Harrison in March, 1778 (Ref: B-29).

WESTLEY, WILLIAM. Took the Oath of Allegiance before Hon. Samuel Harrison in March, 1778 (Ref: A-244).

WESTON, THOMAS. Enlisted by Richard Talbot and passed by John Dorsey on July 22, 1776 (Ref: H-39). Born in Scotland. He was a Substitute, furnished by Thomas Warfield on May 4, 1778, to serve three years (Ref: C-205, H-317).

WHEDON (WEEDON), OLIVER. On May 25, 1776 "Oliver Weedon" was paid ten pounds and fifteen shillings for stocking 20 muskets and finding 2 gun locks (Ref: N-444). On March 20, 1779, "Oliver Whedon" was a Private in Capt. Gilbert Middleton's Independent Militia Company of Annapolis (Ref: I-144, O-325).

WHEELER, CHARLES. His name appears on a list of defectives from the Maryland Line on November 29, 1781 (Ref: H-416).

WHEELER, HENRY. Took the Oath of Allegiance before Hon. Thomas Worthington on February 28, 1778 (Ref: B-22).

WHEELER, LUKE. Took the Oath of Allegiance before Hon. John Dorsey on March 12, 1778 (Ref: B-26).

WHIPS, BENJAMIN. Enlisted by Joseph Burgess for the Flying Camp on July 20, 1776 (Ref: H-40).

WHIPS, JOHN SR. Took the Oath of Allegiance before Hon. Reuben Meriweather on March 2, 1778 (Ref: B-25).

WHIPS, SAMUEL (of Baltimore County). Took the Oath of Allegiance before Hon. Reuben Meriweather on March 2, 1778 (Ref: B-25).

WHITE, ABSOLOM. Took the Oath of Allegiance before Hon. Samuel Lane on March 1, 1778 (Ref: B-23).

WHITE, ANDREW. He was recruited by James Brice in 1777 (Ref: H-313).

WHITE, CHARLES. He was one of the petitioners to the Maryland Convention to form an independent rifle company in July, 1776 (Ref: B-3). In March, 1779 he was a Captain in the Elk Ridge Battalion of Militia (Ref: O-333). Two men with this name took Oath of Allegiance in March, 1778: one before Hon. Thomas Dorsey and one before Hon. Nicholas Worthington (Ref: B-24, B-27). On February 20, 1799 the final distribution of the estate of Susanna Miller by Mrs. Elizabeth White, administratrix, gave eighths of the estate balance to Elizabeth White, Thomas Babbs, Nancy Babbs, Sarah White, Regancy White, Polly White, Charles White, and Nackey White (Ref: U-24).

WHITE, DAVID. Private in Capt. Richard Dorsey's Company of Artillery on November 17, 1777 (Ref: H-574).

WHITE, EDWARD. Took the Oath of Allegiance before Hon. Richard Harwood, Jr. on March 1, 1778 (Ref: B-23). Born in England. He was enlisted by John Ijams and passed by James Brice on March 24, 1778 (Ref: C-216, H-314).

WHITE, FRANCIS. Took the Oath of Allegiance before Hon. Samuel Harrison in March, 1778 (Ref: A-244). On February 13, 1801 the final distribution of his estate was made to Sarah White (widow's third) with eighths of the remainder to Gideon White, Elizabeth White, Elisha White, Reuben White, Sarah White, Caleb White, Isaac White, and Susanna Hopper (Ref: U-21).

WHITE, GIDEON. Took the Oath of Allegiance before Hon. Thomas Worthington on February 28, 1778 (Ref: B-22). Son of Francis White and Sarah -----, and he and his mother were administrators of Francis White in 1801 (Ref: U-21).

WHITE, HORATIO. Took the Oath of Allegiance before Hon. Thomas Dorsey on March 2, 1778 (Ref: B-24).

WHITE, JAMES. Enlisted by Edward Spurrier and passed by Thomas Dorsey on July 20, 1776 (Ref: H-41). He took the Oath of Allegiance before Honorable John Dorsey on March 12, 1778 (Ref: B-26).

WHITE, JOHN. Born in Maryland. Enrolled by John Belt in July, 1776. Height: 5' 4 1/2" (Ref: H-40). Two men with this name took the Oath of Allegiance before Hon. Thomas Dorsey on March 2, 1778 (Ref: B-24). One John White was deceased by June 10, 1812 when the final distribution of his estate was made to Elizabeth White (widow's third) with sevenths of the remainder to Jonathan White, John White, Joseph White, Mary Ann White, Margaret White, George White, and Robert White (Ref: U-42).

WHITE, JOSEPH JR. Took the Oath of Allegiance before Hon. Thomas Worthington on February 28, 1778 (Ref: B-22).

WHITE, JOSEPH SR. Took the Oath of Allegiance before Hon. Thomas Worthington on February 28, 1778 (Ref: B-22). On December 11, 1788, final distribution of his estate was made to Frances White (widow's third) with fifths of the remaining balance to Joseph White, Robert White, Frances Freeland White, Alfred White, and Roena White (Rf: U-2).

WHITE, SAMUEL. Born in Maryland. Enlisted by Capt. Edward Tillard on July 10, 1776. Height: 5' 6 1/2" (Ref: H-39).

WHITE, THOMAS. Three men by this name took the Oath of Allegiance: one before Hon. Reuben Meriweather on March 2, 1778, another before Hon. John Dorsey on March 12, 1778, and one before Hon. Nicholas Worthington in March, 1778. (Ref: B-25, B-26, B-27).

WHITE, VACHEL. Took the Oath of Allegiance before Hon. Nicholas Worthington in March, 1778 (Ref: B-28).

WHITECROFT (WHETERCROFT), WILLIAM. Took the Oath of Allegiance before Hon. John Dorsey on March 12, 1778 (Ref: B-26).

WHITEHOUSE, JOSEPH. Born in Scotland. He was a Substitute, furnished by John Stearn on May 7, 1778, to serve until war's end (Ref: H-319. Note: Source C-212 mistakenly spelled his name as "Joseph Whitchoase").

WHITHIM, WILLIAM. Enrolled by Capt. Thomas Watkins on October 21, 1776 for service to the State (Ref: I-144, MS.1814).

WHITICOMB, ROBERT. Took the Oath of Allegiance before Hon. Richard Harwood, Jr. on March 1, 1778 (Ref: B-23).

WHITTINGTON, FRANCIS JR. Private in Capt. Richard Chew's Company of Colonel John Weems' Battalion of Militia on October 5, 1776 (Ref: A-95).

WHITTINGTON, FRANCIS SR. Private in Capt. Richard Chew's Company of Colonel John Weems' Battalion of Militia on October 5, 1776 (Ref: A-95).

WHITTINGTON, JAMES. Took the Oath of Allegiance before Hon. Samuel Harrison in March, 1778 (Ref: A-244). On August 27, 1816, final distribution of his estate was made to Mary Whittington (widow); Elizabeth Whittington, wife of John Ward; and, Eleanor Whittington, wife of William Hardesty (Ref: U-48).

WHITTINGTON, JOHN. Two men with this name took the Oath of Allegiance before Hon. Samuel Harrison in March, 1778 (Ref: B-29).

WHITTINGTON, THOMAS. Took the Oath of Allegiance before Hon. Samuel Harrison in March, 1778 (Ref: B-29).

WHITTINGTON, WILLIAM. Private in Capt. Richard Chew's Company of Col. John Weems' Battalion of Militia on October 5, 1776 (Ref: A-95).

WHITTLE, JOHN. Took the Oath of Allegiance before Hon. Thomas Dorsey on March 2, 1778 (Ref: B-24).

WHITTOM, WILLIAM. Private in Capt. Richard Dorsey's Company of Artillery on November 17, 1777 (Ref: H-574).

WILBEY, JOHN. Born in Ireland. He was enlisted by Thomas Gordon and passed by James Brice on April 11, 1778 (Ref: C-216, H-314).

WILKERSON, RICHARD. Pensioned as an Invalid soldier on March 4, 1789 and on April 24, 1816, as a Private in the Revolutionary War and residing in Anne Arundel County (Ref: Z-2. Also refer to "Richard Wilkinson," q.v.).

WILKINS, JOHN. Private in Capt. Richard Dorsey's Company of Artillery on November 17, 1777 (Ref: H-574).

WILKINS, JOSEPH. Took the Oath of Allegiance before Hon. Thomas Worthington on February 28, 1778 (Ref: B-22).

WILKINS, WILLIAM. Paid by the Council of Maryland for money appropriated for fortifications of the City of Annapolis on March 14, 1777, May 5, 1777, August 25, 1777, November 5, 1777 and February 20, 1778 (Ref: V-173, V-240, V-343, V-409, V-514), and as Auditor of Accounts in 1777 (Ref: V-514).

WILKINSON, RICHARD. Private in Capt. Richard Dorsey's Company of Artillery on November 17, 1777 (Ref: H-574). Disabled soldier who was paid in Anne Arundel County on December 11, 1783, April 13, 1784, June 9, 1784, Sept. 3, 1784, October 26, 1784, December 17, 1784 (Ref: D-10, 13, 18, 21, 23, 25). "Richard Wilkerson" was pensioned May 16, 1817 at $40 per month from March 4, 1789, under the Act of June 7, 1785 and received $1085.56 (Ref: K-407).

WILKINSON, YOUNG (1742-1827). Sergeant in Capt. Richard Dorsey's Company of Artillery in 1777 (Ref: H-573). In November, 1810, the State Treasurer was directed to "pay half yearly to Young Wilkerson, of Anne Arundel County, a sum of money equal to half pay of Lieutenant during his life" (Ref: K-407. See Henry C. Peden, Jr.'s "Revolutionary Patriots of Baltimore Town and Baltimore County, 1775-1783," p. 291, for more information on this man).

WILKS, JOSEPH. Sergeant in Capt. Richard Dorsey's Company of Artillery in 1777 (Ref: H-573).

WILLIAMS, ANDREW. Private in Capt. William Marbury's Company of Artillery in 1777 (Ref: H-575).

WILLIAMS, BENJAMIN. Took the Oath of Allegiance before Honorable Nicholas Worthington in March, 1778 (Ref: B-27).

WILLIAMS, CHANEY. Enlisted by Captain James Disney, Jr. and passed by Col. Richard Harwood, Jr. on July 13, 1776 (Ref: H-41).

WILLIAMS, CHARLES. Recruited by Captain Alexander Truman in October, 1780, to serve for 3 years (Ref: H-369).

WILLIAMS, ISAIAH. Recruited by Captain Alexander Truman in October, 1780, to serve for 3 years (Ref: H-370).

WILLIAMS, JARVIS. Born in Scotland. He was a Substitute, furnished by Moses Bekos on May 18, 1778, to serve to the end of the war (Ref: C-213, H-319).

WILLIAMS, JEREMIAH (born 1759). Private in the Maryland Line. His marriage to Mary Gaither in December, 1784 in Anne Arundel County was proven through his Maryland Revolutionary War pension record (Ref: G-55, G-125).

WILLIAMS, JOHN. Enrolled by Captain Thomas Watkins on October 21, 1776 for service to the State (Ref: I-144, MS.1814).

WILLIAMS, JOHN. Private in Capt. William Marbury's Company of Artillery in 1777 (Ref: H-575). One John Williams, an Invalid soldier of Capt. Brown's Company of Artillery, was discharged on July 5, 1777 (Ref: V-308).

WILLIAMS, JOHN. Born in England. He was enlisted by Thomas Ricketts and passed by James Brice on March 20, 1778 (Ref: C-216, H-313).

WILLIAMS, JOHN. He was a Substitute, furnished by Philip Thomas, on May 8, 1778, to serve for three years (Ref: C-206, H-317).

WILLIAMS, JOHN. He was a Substitute, furnished by William Shipley, Jr., on May 5, 1778, to serve until war's end (Ref: C-206, H-317).

WILLIAMS, JOHN. He was a Substitute, furnished by William Wilkins on May 16, 1778, to serve until war's end (Ref: C-207, H-318).

WILLIAMS, JOHN. He was a Substitute, furnished by Charles Warfield, on May 13, 1778, to serve until war's end (Ref: C-212, H-318).

WILLIAMS, JOSEPH. Took the Oath of Allegiance before Hon. Richard Harwood, Jr. on March 1, 1778 (Ref: B-23). On November 11, 1815, final distribution of his estate (sixths) was made to John Ball (grandson), Thomas Williams, Joseph Williams, Sarah Knighton, Ann Bird, and Mary Lednum (Ref: U-46).

WILLIAMS, JOSEPH (OF JOSEPH). Took the Oath of Allegiance before Hon. Richard Harwood, Jr. on March 1, 1778 (Ref: B-23). "Joseph Williams, Jr." enlisted under Capt. James Disney on July 13, 1776 (Ref: H-41). On February 25, 1824 the State Treasurer was directed to "pay to Joseph Williams of Annapolis, a soldier of the Revolutionary War, half pay of Private, further remuneration for his services." On March 21, 1833 the Register of the Land Office issued "to Joseph William of Annapolis, a soldier of the Revolution, a warrant and later patent for 50 acres of vacant land in Allegany County" (Ref: K-409).

WILLIAMS, JOSEPH (OF RICHARD). Took the Oath of Allegiance before Honorable Richard Harwood, Jr. on March 1, 1778 (Ref: B-23).

WILLIAMS, MOSES. Resident of Herring Creek who petitioned the Convention of Maryland on March 6, 1776 to form an independent militia company and later served in Capt. Richard Weems' Company (Ref: I-143, MS.1814).

WILLIAMS, SAMUEL. On March 13, 1777 he petitioned the Council of Safety to inform them that he was wrongfully imprisoned, that he was not an enemy of this country, and that he would take the Oath of Allegiance (Ref: V-171).

WILLIAMS, THOMAS. Enlisted by Henry Ridgely, Jr. and passed by Col. Josias Carvil Hall on August 26, 1776 (Ref: H-41). His name appears on a list of defectives from the Maryland Line in July, 1780 (Ref: H-414).

WILLIAMS, WILLIAM. Born in Maryland. Enrolled by John S. Belt in July, 1776. Height: 5' 3 1/2" (Ref: H-40). He took the Oath of Allegiance before Hon. Nicholas Worthington in March, 1778 (Ref: B-28).

WILLIAMS, WILLIAM. Enlisted by Capt. James Disney, Jr. and passed by Richard Harwood, Jr. on July 13, 1776 (Ref: H-41). He took the Oath of Allegiance in March 1, 1778, before Hon. Richard Harwood, Jr. (Ref: B-23).

WILLIAMS, WILLIAM. Enrolled by Capt. Thomas Watkins on October 21, 1776 for service to the State (Ref: I-144, MS.1814).

WILLIS, DANIEL. Drummer in the 5th Maryland Line. He enlisted on February 9, 1777 and "was wounded in several places" on August 18, 1780 at Sumpter's Defeat. He was taken prisoner, along with Lt. Henry Gassaway of the 4th Maryland Line, who stated that Willis "behaved himself as a good soldier" while he was held prisoner. He was discharged June 20, 1783 (Ref: X-42).

WILLIS, JOHN. Took the Oath of Allegiance before Hon. Thomas Dorsey on March 2, 1778 (Ref: B-24).

WILSON (WILLSON), EDWARD. He took the Oath of Allegiance before Hon. Reuben Meriweather on March 2, 1778 (Ref: B-25).

WILSON, HENRY. A resident of Herring Creek who petitioned the Convention of Maryland to form an independent militia company on March 6, 1776 and later served in Capt. Richard Weems' Company (Ref: I-143, MS.1814). He took the Oath of Allegiance before Hon. Samuel Harrison in March, 1778 (Ref: B-29). Possibly a son of William Wilson who died prior to June, 1800 (Ref: U-23).

WILSON (WILLSON), JAMES. He took the Oath of Allegiance before Hon. Thomas Worthington on February 28, 1778 (Ref: B-22).

WILSON, JOHN. Born in Scotland. He was a Substitute, furnished by Joseph Spurrier on May 9, 1778, to serve until war's end (Ref: C-212, H-318).

WILSON, MATH. Enlisted by Michael Burgess and passed by Colonel Hyde on July 20, 1776 (Ref: H-41).

WILSON, RICHARD. He took the Oath of Allegiance before Hon. Thomas Dorsey on March 2, 1778 (Ref: B-24).

WILSON (WILLSON), SAMUEL. Sergeant and disabled soldier who was paid in Anne Arundel County on August 16, 1783 and January 13, 1784 and April 13, 1784 and June 9, 1784 and September 3, 1784 and October 26, 1784 and December 17, 1784 (Ref: D-8, D-13, D-18, D-21, D-23, D-25).

WILTSHIRE, JONATHAN. Born in England. He was recruited and passed by James Brice on February 10, 1778 (Ref: C-215, H-313). He was a Private in Capt. Gilbert Middleton's Independent Company of Militia of Annapolis on March 20, 1779 (Ref: I-144, O-325).

WINSER, SAMUEL Q. Private in Captain John Fulford's Company of Artillery at Annapolis on December 12, 1776 (Ref: H-572).

WINTERBURN, JOHN. Recruited in October, 1780 to serve 3 years (Ref: H-369).

WOAKLIN, CHARLES. Took Oath of Allegiance before Hon. Nicholas Worthington in March, 1778 (Ref: B-27).

WOAKLIN, WILLIAM. Took Oath of Allegiance before Hon. Nicholas Worthington in March, 1778 (Ref: B-27).

WOOD, DORSEY. He was a Substitute, passed by James Price on May 30, 1778 to serve for nine months in Capt. John Gray's Company (Ref: C-208, H-319).

WOOD, HOPEWELL. Private in Capt. Richard Chew's Company of Col. John Weems' Battalion of Militia on October 5, 1776 (Ref: A-95). He took the Oath of Allegiance before Hon. Samuel Harrison in March, 1778 (Ref: B-29). Married Ann Muse in 1779 (Ref: K-486). Note: Probably a brother of Zebedee Wood).

WOOD, JOHN. Private in Capt. Richard Chew's Company of Colonel John Weems' Battalion of Militia on October 5, 1776 (Ref: A-95).

WOOD, JOHN (1763-1843). Possibly a son of Robert Wood. He married Elizabeth Sunderland, daughter of Benjamin Sunderland and ELizabeth Taylor of Calvert County, on April 22, 1783. They resided in Anne Arundel County near the Calvert County line. John initially served with the Maryland troops under Capt. John Mackall and Col. Fitzhugh for nine months. Later, he was drafted into the militia under Colonel John Weems for the duration of the war. As specified in his pension application (and his widow's W6573), John said he was age 69 in 1832 and although he was a Private, he was also "captain of a newsboat" that sailed between Herring Bay and Baltimore. He and his wife became Methodists circa 1787 and held "clap meetings" at their home, which was located about 2 miles from Reverend John Gibson of Calvert County. In 1790 or 1791 John and family moved to Virginia and settled near Earlysville in Albemarle County. He also served in 1794 during the Whiskey Rebellion. When his widow applied in 1855 for his bounty land, she said she had lived in Virginia for 65 years and John Wood died on July 28, 1843 (she died in 1857). Their children were: Obadiah Wood, Eleaenor Wood Marshall, Robert Wood, Levi Wood, John Wood, Elizabeth Wood Estes, Benjamin Wood, William M. Wood, Sarah Wood Cox, Willis Wood, Isaac Wood, and Jesse Wood. (Data from Stewart E. Wood of Glen Allen, Virginia, and "DAR Patriot Index," Vol. I).

WOOD, MORGAN. Private in Capt. Richard Chew's Company of Colonel John Weems' Battalion of Militia on October 5, 1776 (Ref: A-95). He took the Oath of Allegiance before Hon. Samuel Harrison in March, 1778 (Ref: B-29). He was a son of William Wood, Jr. and Elizabeth ----- (Ref: U-16).

WOOD, WILLIAM. Private in Capt. Richard Chew's Company of Col. John Weems' Battalion of Militia on October 5, 1776 (Ref: A-95). He took the Oath of Allegiance before Hon. Samuel Harrison in March, 1778 (Ref: B-29). He was a son of William Wood, Jr. and Elizabeth ----- (Ref: U-16).

WOOD, WILLIAM. Enlisted by Joseph Burgess for the Flying Camp and passed on July 20, 1776 (Ref: H-40). Took the Oath of Allegiance before Hon. Thomas Dorsey on March 2, 1778 (Ref: B-24). On October 15, 1807 final distribution of his estate (elevenths of the remaining balance) was made to: John Wood; Henry Wood; Samuel Wood; Robert Wood; Sarah Sullivan; Mary Whittington; Dorothy Sunderland; heirs of William Wood; heirs of Susanna Whittington; the heirs of Ann Parrott; and, the heirs of James Wood (Ref: U-34).

WOOD, ZEBEDEE (1750-1788). Son of Hopewell Wood. Married Ann Drury in 1776 (Ref: "Maryland Marriages, 1634-1778," by Robert W. Barnes, 1976, p. 413, and Zebedee's deposition, Chancery Book No. 14, Anne Arundel County, 1785). His children were: Mary Ann Wood, died before 1801; Cassandra Wood Stone, Ann Wood Scott, and Hopewell Wood (Ref: Anne Arundel County Distributions Liber JG #2, f. 156; Chancery Papers 17898-5855 in 1812; U-40). Took the Oath of Allegiance before Hon. Samuel Lane on March 1, 1778 (Ref: B-23).

WOODIN, JOHN. Took the Oath of Allegiance before Hon. Thomas Worthington on February 28, 1778 (Ref: B-22).

WOODWARD, THOMAS. Took the Oath of Allegiance before Hon. Thomas Dorsey on March 2, 1778 (Ref: B-24).

WOODWARD, WILLIAM JR. (1747-1807). Married Jane Ridgely in 1765 and had a son, Henry Woodward (Ref: T-776). He took the Oath of Allegiance before Hon. Nicholas Worthington in March, 1778 (Ref: B-28). In October, 1780, he was drafted to serve in the Army until December 10, 1780 (Ref: H-368). He apparently stayed because he was commissioned an Ensign in Capt. Philemon Warfield's Company in Severn Battalion on February 22, 1781 (Ref: W-322).

WOOLF, JOHN (1744, Annapolis - June 10, 1818, Sabillasville, MD). Courier of documents and a militia officer in Frederick County (Ref: E-2719, K-410).

WOOTTON, THOMAS. Took the Oath of Allegiance before Hon. Nicholas Worthington in March, 1778 (Ref: B-28).

WORTHINGTON, BENJAMIN. He took the Oath of Allegiance before Hon. Nicholas Worthington in March, 1778 (Ref: The original list in Maryland State Papers Red Book 21, p. 8D. Mistakenly left off the published list in Ref: B-27).

WORTHINGTON, BRICE B. JR. Took the Oath of Allegiance before Hon. Nicholas Worthington in March, 1778 (Ref: Original lists in Maryland State Papers, Red Book 21, p. 8D. Mistakenly left off the published list in Ref: B-27. Note: Brice B. Jr. is most probably Brice Thomas Beale Worthington, Jr.).

WORTHINGTON, BRICE THOMAS BEALE (November 2, 1727 - July 17, 1794). Son of Thomas Worthington and Elizabeth Ridgely. He married Anne Ridgely and they had seven children: Henry Worthington, John Worthington, Brice Thomas Beale Worthington, Elizabeth Worthington, Sarah Worthington Simpson, Henrietta Worthington Simpson, and Polly Worthington Worthington. He was quite active in politics and held several offices, including: Member of the Lower House (1756 to 1774), Delegate to the Maryland Convention (1774 to 1776), Senator (1776 to 1781), Member of the Lower House (1781 to 1790), Senator (1791 to 1794), Member of the Council of Safety (1776 to 1777), and Member of the Committee of Observation in 1775 (Ref: A-77, E-106A, J-1, 4, P-912, P-913). Brice also served with the Association of Freemen in 1775 (Ref: T-778).

WORTHINGTON, CHARLES (born 1759). Son of Nicholas Worthington and Catherine Griffith (Ref: P-914, P-915). He took Oath of Allegiance before Hon. Thomas Worthington on February 28, 1778 (Ref: B-22).

WORTHINGTON, HENRY (died in 1808). Son of Brice Thomas Beale Worthington and Anne Ridgely (Ref: P-912). Took the Oath of Allegiance before Hon. Nicholas Worthington in March, 1778 (Ref: The original list in Maryland State Papers Red Book 21, p. 8D. Mistakenly left off the published list in Ref: B-27).

WORTHINGTON, JOHN JR. He took the Oath of Allegiance before Hon. Nicholas Worthington in March, 1778 (Ref: The original list in Maryland State Papers Red Book 21, p. 8D. Mistakenly left off the published list in Ref: B-27).

WORTHINGTON, JOHN (died circa 1817). Son of Brice Thomas Beale Worthington and Anne Ridgely. Married Christina Magruder (Ref: P-912). He was a First Lieutenant in Capt. Henry Hanslap's Company in the Severn Battalion in 1776 (Ref: F-222, but this appears to be a mistake by this source because Source N-178 states he was in Capt. Henry Hall's Company, not Hanslap's Company).

WORTHINGTON, NATH. Enrolled by Capt. Thomas Watkins on October 21, 1776 for service to the State (Ref: I-144, MS.1814).

WORTHINGTON, NICHOLAS (March 29, 1734 - November 1, 1793). Son of Thomas Worthington and Elizabeth Ridgely. Married Catherine Griffith and had 11 children: Thomas Worthington, Nicholas Worthington,, Charles Worthington, Charles Worthington (2), Brice John Worthington, John Griffith Worthington, Elizabeth Worthington, Catherine Worthington Johnson, Elizabeth Worthington (2), Achsah Worthington Goldsborough, and Sarah Worthington (Ref: P-914). Nicholas was one of the Justices who administered the Oath of Allegiance in March, 1778 (Ref: B-27, and Maryland State Papers in MdHR4587). He served in the Lower House, 1774-1793, and was commissioned First Major on January 6, 1776, and then Colonel of the Severn Battalion on June 19, 1777. (Ref: A-176, E-35, E-47A, F-224, T-778). He was appointed a Justice on June 10, 1777 and served until 1792 (Ref: P-915 and A. A. Orphans Court Proceedings, 1777-1779, MdHR9524, p. 1). He served on Committee of Observation in 1775 (Ref: F-222), and was appointed Justice of the Peace in 1778 (Ref: O-241).

WORTHINGTON, NICHOLAS. Second Lieutenant in 1776 and Captain in the Severn Battalion of Militia on March 1, 1778 (Ref: C-203, F-222). Took the Oath of Allegiance before Hon. Nicholas Worthington in March, 1778 (Ref: B-28). He is among the officers of the Severn Battalion on August 15, 1778 (Ref: I-144. He is not listed in Source O-208 as indicated in Source I-144).

WORTHINGTON, NICHOLAS JR. Took the Oath of Allegiance before Hon. Nicholas Worthington in March, 1778 (Ref: B-28).

WORTHINGTON, SAMUEL (1734-1815). Although born and raised in Anne Arundel County, Samuel moved to Baltimore County by 1757 and contributed greatly to the revolutionary war effort. For more information on this man, see Source P-916, and Henry C. Peden, Jr.'s "Revolutionary Patriots of Baltimore Town and Baltimore County, 1775-1783," p. 298 (Family Line Publications, 1988).

WORTHINGTON, THOMAS (1754-1823). Son of Nicholas Worthington and Catherine Griffith. Married Margaret Mullikin (Ref: P-915). Thomas was one of the Justices who administered the Oath of Allegiance in March, 1778 (Ref: B-21, B-28). He was a Justice of the Peace on November 19, 1778 (Ref: O-241). On March 18, 1826 his final estate distribution (sixths) was made to Nicholas Worthington, Brice J. G. Worthington, Charles G. Worthington, the heirs of Thomas Worthington, Ann Worthington, and John G. Worthington (Ref: U-71).

WORTHINGTON, VACHEL. Took the Oath of Allegiance before Honorable Nicholas Worthington in March, 1778 (Ref: B-28).

WRIGHT, BENJAMIN. Ensign in Captain George Watts' Company in the Severn Battalion of Militia in 1776 and 1777 (Ref: A-176, F-223).

WRIGHT, THOMAS. Took the Oath of Allegiance before Hon. Elijah Robosson in March, 1778 (Ref: B-28).

WYLLBE, WILLIAM. Took the Oath of Allegiance before Hon. Thomas Worthington on February 28, 1778 (Ref: B-22).

WYNDHAM, THOMAS. On February 22, 1822, the Treasurer was directed to "pay to Sarah Wyndham, of Annapolis, quarterly, half pay of a Sergeant, for service rendered by her husband in the Revolutionary War" (in the Maryland Line). On March 2, 1842, the Treasurer was directed to "pay to Andrew Slicer, of Annapolis, $20.83, the amount due Sarah Wyndham for pension per Resolution No. 42, 1822 to August 5, 1841, the day of her death" (Ref: K-411, H-173). "Thomas Windham" married Sarah Lamb, widow, in 1785 (Ref: G-55, G-126).

WYVILL, WILLIAM. Took the Oath of Allegiance before Hon. Richard Harwood, Jr. on March 1, 1778 (Ref: B-23).

YATES, JOSHUA. Took the Oath of Allegiance before Hon. Richard Harwood, Jr. on March 1, 1778 (Ref: B-23).

YEALDHALL, BENJAMIN. Took Oath of Allegiance before Hon. Nicholas Worthington in March, 1778 (Ref: B-27). On April 22, 1811, the final distribution of his estate was made with thirds of the remaining balance going to Susanna Yealdhall, Aaron Yealdhall and Harriet Yealdhall (Ref: U-39).

YEALDHALL (YIELDHALL), GILBERT. Gilbert "Yieldhall" was Ensign in Capt. Henry Hall's Company in 1776 (Ref: N-178. Note: Source F-222 erroneously spelled his name as "Gilbert Guldhall" instead of "Yieldhall," and stated he served under Capt. Henry Hanslap, not Capt. Henry Hall). "G. Yealdhall" took Oath of Allegiance before Hon. Nicholas Worthington in March, 1778 (Ref: B-28).

YEALDHALL, ROBERT. Took the Oath of Allegiance before Hon. Thomas Worthington on February 28, 1778 (Ref: B-22).

YEALDHALL, SAMUEL. Took Oath of Allegiance before Hon. Nicholas Worthington in March, 1778 (Ref: Original lists in Maryland State Papers, Red Book 21, MdHR4587. Source B-27 erroneously spelled the name as "Samuel Byer Whale"). On April 23, 1811 the final distribution of his estate was made to Frances Yealdhall (her widow's third) and sevenths of the remaining balance going to Elizabeth Yealdhall, the heirs of Joshua Yealdhall, the heirs of Henry Yealdhall, the heirs of William Yealdhall, Elijah Yealdhall, Frederick Yealdhall, and Aquila Yealdhall (Ref: U-39, U-40).

YEALDHALL, THOMAS. Took Oath of Allegiance before Hon. Nicholas Worthington in March, 1778 (Ref: B-28).

YEALDHALL (YIELDHALL), WILLIAM. On June 25, 1776 the Committee of Observation ordered "William Yieldell, a non-associator, having refused to give bond be committed to the custody of Capt. James Tootell, to be brought before the Convention." (Ref: J-29). On June 26, 1776 the Convention of Maryland then "ordered that William Yieldell be discharged upon giving bond with sureties approved by the Committee of Observation of Anne Arundel County and upon paying the charges of his imprisonment." (Ref: J-31). He took the Oath of Allegiance before Hon. Nicholas Worthington in March, 1778 (Ref: B-27).

YEALDHALL, WILLIAM JR. Took the Oath of Allegiance before Honorable Nicholas Worthington in March, 1778 (Ref: B-28).

YOUNG, JOHN. Took Oath of Allegiance before Hon. Thomas Harwood on February 28, 1778 (Ref: B-22). Born in Scotland. He was a Substitute, furnished by Ely Elder on May 15, 1778, to serve until war's end (Ref: C-213, H-319).

YOUNG, JOSHUA. Took the Oath of Allegiance before Hon. John Dorsey on March 12, 1778 (Ref: B-26). On December 12, 1837 the final distribution of his estate was made to Orpha Young (widow's third) with tenths of the remaining balance to Jason Young, Catharine Hitchcock, Orpha Miller, Joshua Young, Elizabeth Hitchcock, William Young, Samuel Robinson, James C. Hitchcock, John Roberts, and William McMeeken (Ref: U-96).

YOUNG, JOSHUA JR. Took the Oath of Allegiance before Honorable John Dorsey on March 12, 1778 (Ref: B-26).

YOUNG, RICHARD. Took the Oath of Allegiance before Hon. Thomas Worthington on February 28, 1778 (Ref: B-22).

YOUNG, ROBERT. Private in Capt. Richard Chew's Company of Col. John Weems' Battalion of Militia on October 5, 1776 (Ref: A-95). He took the Oath of Allegiance before Hon. Samuel Harrison in March, 1778 (Ref: B-29).

YOUNG, WILLIAM. Took the Oath of Allegiance before Hon. Reuben Meriweather on March 2, 1778 (Ref: B-24). On January 10, 1799 the final distribution of his estate was made to Rachel Young (widow's third) with ninths of the remaining balance to Lurana Young, William Young, Richard Young, Rachel Young, Mary Young, Nathan Young, Comfort Young, Benjamin Young, and Joshua Young (Ref: U-24).

INDEX

-A-
ACKERLY,
  John, 204
ADAMS,
  Ann Cavy, 67
  Colonel (Col.),
   45, 78, 92,
   138, 147, 191,
   203, 205
  Daniel Jenifer,
   1
  John, 64
  Joshua, 1
  Major, 1
  Peter, 36, 64,
   104
  Rebecca Dorsey,
   56
AHEARN,
  Ellen, 114, 115
AKERLY,
  John, 1
ALCOCK,
  Robert, 1
ALDRICH,
  Nathaniel, 1
ALDRIDGE,
  Nathan, 1
  Nicholas, 1
  Zachariah, 1
ALEXANDER,
  Charles, 1
  Mary Harwood
   Stockett, 192
ALLCOCK,
  Martin, 68
ALLEIN,
  Adam, 1
  Elizabeth
   Tongue, 200
ALLEN,
  --, 42
  Adam, 1
  Azel, 1
  John, 1, 196
  Ruth, 1
  Susanna, 1
  William, 64, 196
ALLENDER,
  Joshua, 68
ALLENGEM,
  Joseph, 2
ALLENGHAM,
  Joseph, 135

ALLENJEM,
  Stephen, 2
ALLINGHAM,
  Joseph, 2
  Stephen, 2
ALLMAN,
  William, 68
ALTON,
  Jonathan, 2
ANCKERS,
  Snowden, 3
ANDERSON,
  Abraham, 2, 136
  Absalom, 2, 135
  Andrew, 2
  Ann, 2
  Anne, 98
  Edward Edwards, 2
  Elizabeth, 2, 60
  Elizabeth
   Edwards, 59
  James, 2
  Joshua, 2
  Richard, 2
  Robert, 2
  Samuel, 2
  Sarah Edwards, 59
  Susanna, 2
  Thomas, 2
  William, 2, 60
  William Clarke, 2
ANDRIS,
  William, 2
ANGUS,
  John, 2
ANKERS,
  Edward, 3
  Snowden, 3
ANLEY,
  Joseph, 3
ANNAN,
  William, 3
ANNIM,
  William, 3
ANTHONY,
  Negro, 3
APPINGSTALL,
  William, 3
APPLEBY,
  Bignel, 3
  Bigner, 3
ARCHIBLAD,
  Robert, 3
ARMIGER,
  Benjamin, 3

  Jesse, 3
  John, 3
  John F., 3
  Leonard, 3
  Mary, 3
  Rachel, 3
  Richard, 3
  Samuel, 3
  Sarah Ann, 3
  Susannah, 3
  Thomas, 3
  William, 3
ARNOLD,
  William, 3
ASHBAW,
  Henry, 110
ASHBURNHAM,
  Hannah, 107
ASHEN,
  Michael, 3
ASHMEAD,
  Joseph, 4
  Sarah, 78
ASHMORE,
  Charles, 4
ASKEW,
  Peregrine, 27
ATKINSON,
  Catherine, 4
  Elizabeth, 4
  Francis, 4
  John, 4
  Nathan, 4
  Rachel, 4
  Thomas, 4
ATTWELL,
  Benjamin, 4
  Catherine, 4
  Daniel, 4
  Joseph, 4
  Mary, 4
  Robert, 4
  Samuel, 4
  William, 4
ATWELL,
  Benjamin, 4
  Daniel, 4
  Eliza Rawlings,
   161
  Elizabeth, 4
  John, 4
  Joseph, 4
  Margaret, 4
  Rachel, 4
  Robert, 4

INDEX

Samuel, 4, 5
Sarah, 4
William, 4, 5
AUBER,
  John, 5
AVERY,
  John, 5
AYRES,
  Rebecca Dorcas
    Howard, 99
AYTON,
  Anna Howard, 101
  Henry, 5, 78,
    135, 136

-B-

BABBER,
  James, 5
BABBS,
  John, 64
  Nancy, 222
  Thomas, 222
BACON,
  William, 5
BACQUES,
  James, 27
BAER,
  Elizabeth W.
    Dorsey, 48
  Matilda Ridgely,
    167
BAGNALL,
  Thomas, 5
BAGNESS,
  Jacques, 5
BAILEY,
  James, 64
BAKER,
  Abednego, 5
  Edward Blair, 68
  Elizabeth, 52
  Henry, 64
  Nancy, 96
  Thomas, 5
  William, 68
  Zebediah, 5
BALDERSON,
  Bartholomew, 5
BALDWIN,
  Ann, 31
  Elizabeth, 5
  Henry, 5
  James, 6
  Maria, 5
  Mary, 178

Samuel, 6
Sarah, 5
Thomas, 6, 31
William, 5
William H., 5
BALEY,
  John, 64
  Thomas, 65
BALL,
  Allen, 6
  Elizabeth Dorsey,
    52
  John, 6, 226
  Sarah Dorsey, 53
BALLMAN,
  Henry, 10
BALLOD,
  Richard, 6
BANKS,
  Elenor Dorsey, 54
BANNON,
  John, 6
BAQUES,
  Jacques, 5
BARBER,
  Charles, 6
  Samuel, 6
BARBOR,
  Charles, 6
  George, 6
  John, 6
BARDEN,
  William, 68
BAREY,
  Cornelius, 8
BARITT,
  Ralh, 6
BARLOW,
  John, 6
  Zacharias, 6
BARNES,
  Adam, 6, 7
  Anthony, 7
  Aquila, 7
  Dorsey, 7, 205
  Elijah, 7
  Ellis, 7, 8
  Ely, 7
  Hammutal, 7
  James, 6, 7
  John, 7
  Leah Hood, 97
  Michael, 7
  Nathan, 7, 8
  Peter, 7, 8

Philimon, 8
Philip, 8
Rachel, 7, 8
Richard, 8
Robert, 6, 8
Robert W., 7, 151,
  152, 229
Robert William, 7
Thomas, 8
Vachel, 8
William, 7
BARNETT,
  John, 68, 196
  Robert, 8
BARNEY,
  Mary Chase, 31
  Rebecca Ridgely,
    166
BARNSBY,
  William, 8
BARRETT,
  Thomas, 8
BARRY,
  Basil, 8
  Bazil, 8
  Cornelius, 8
  Edward, 9
  Jacob, 9
  James, 9
  Mordecai, 9
  William, 9
BARTLEY,
  James, 9
BARTON,
  Isaac, 9
  John, 9
  Mark, 9
BASFORD,
  Benjamin, 9, 10,
    181
  Elizabeth, 105
  Elizabeth Shekell,
    181
  Frederick, 10
  Jemima, 10
  John, 9, 10
  Rachel, 10
  Richard, 10
  Stephen, 9
  Stephen Bell, 9
  Thomas, 9, 10
  Thomas Fowler, 10
  William, 64
  Zachariah, 10

INDEX

BASS,
  David, 25
BASSFORD,
  Stephen, 136
  Thomas Fowler, 136
BATCHELRY,
  Joseph, 68
BATEMAN,
  Amzi, 10
  Ann, 10
  Benjamin, 10
  Elizabeth, 10
  George, 64
  Henry, 10, 42, 123, 136, 176
  Lemuel, 10
  Martha, 83
  Rachel, 10
  William, 10
BATES,
  John, 68
  Raler, 10
BATTEE,
  Dinah, 75, 76
  Elizabeth, 10, 55
  Fardenando, 10
  Fardinan, 10
  Ferdinando, 10, 136
  John, 91
  Lucinda, 91
  Sophia Ridgely, 167
BATTERSON,
  Thomas, 11
BAXTER,
  John, 11
  Lidey Burgess, 23
BAYLEY,
  Elizabeth Dorsey Hawkins, 54
BEACHAM,
  William, 11
BEACHUM,
  William, 11
BEAL,
  John, 65
BEALL,
  Christopher, 11, 64
  Elizabeth Owens, 146

  Rezin, 1
  Russell, 11
BEALMEAR,
  Elizabeth Anderson, 2
  Francis, 11
BEALMERE,
  Francis, 11
BEARD,
  Elizabeth, 11
  John, 11
  John Stockett, 11
  Jonathan, 11
  Luranah, 11
  Mary, 11
  Matthew, 11
  Rebecca, 11
  Rebecca Stockett, 192
  Richard, 11
  Robert, 11
  Stephen, 11
  Susanna, 11
  Thomas, 11, 12
  William, 12
BEAVER,
  John, 12
BECRAFT,
  Abraham, 12
BEECHGOOD,
  James, 12
BEHOO,
  Moses, 12
BEKOS,
  Moses, 225
BELFORD,
  Jeremiah, 68
BELLISON,
  William, 12
BELT,
  James, 78, 214
  John, 17, 223
  John S., 36, 39, 62, 75, 109, 116, 131, 132, 162, 185, 186, 200, 226
  John Sprigg, 12, 68
BENNETT,
  Joel, 12
  Joseph, 12
  Sayers James, 12
BENNETTE,
  Edward, 12

  George, 12
BENNINGTON,
  Thomas, 12
BENSON,
  Elizabeth, 13
  John, 12, 13
  Rachel, 13
  Richard, 13
  Sarah, 13
  Thomas, 13
  William, 13
BERRY,
  Edward, 27
  Eleanor Lansdale, 117
  Elizabeth Dorsey, 55
  Harriet Dorsey, 55
  James, 204
  Robert, 13
  William, 13
BERTHAUD,
  Adam, 13
BETHARD,
  Jerman, 13
BEVANS,
  Mary Ogle, 144
BICKNELL,
  Eleanor Gaither, 71
  Esau, 196
  Juliette Gaither Clarke, 74
  Thomas, 69
BIDDLE,
  Richard, 13, 68
BIDWELL,
  Richard, 196
BIRCKHEAD,
  Abraham, 13
  Francis, 13
  John, 13, 14
  Joseph, 14
  Matthew, 14
  Nehemiah, 14
  Seaborn, 14
  Thomas, 14
BIRD,
  Ann, 226
BIRKHEAD,
  Elizabeth, 14
  John, 13, 136
  Mary, 14
  Nehemiah, 14
  Sarah, 14

INDEX

Seaborn, 14
Thomas, 14
BIRMINGHAM,
  Patrick, 68
BISETT,
  Thomas, 14
BISHOP,
  Elizabeth, 102
  Greenbury, 14
  Hammutal, 114
  John, 14
  Solomon, 14, 37
  William, 14, 136
BLACK,
  Elizabeth
    Burgess, 23
  Rudolph, 14
BLAINE,
  Matilda Dorsey, 51
BLAIR,
  John, 15
BLAKE,
  Alex, 15
  Dorothy, 28
  Jacob, 65
BLAND,
  Gilbert, 15
  Thomas, 15
BLEWER,
  James, 15
  John, 68
BLOOM,
  John, 15
BLOUNT,
  Edward, 15
BOARMAN,
  Thomas, 64
BOAZER,
  Samuel, 68
BOBOSSON,
  Richard, 171
BOCARD,
  Peter, 64
BOLTON,
  Nancy Ijams, 104
BOND,
  John, 15
BONE,
  Susannah Jacob, 107
BONEY,
  Philip, 15
BOON,
  Charles, 15

Ignatius, 64
John, 15, 64
BOONE,
  Ann, 87
  Capt., 135
  Charles, 14, 15, 136, 150, 181, 193
  John, 15, 65, 80, 84, 107, 129, 136
  Margaret, 50
  Mary Cromwell, 39
  Rebecca, 99
  Robert, 87
  Stephen, 15, 87, 136
BORDLEY,
  William, 15
BOSFORD,
  Stephen, 9
  Thomas Fowler, 10
BOSTICK,
  Barton, 15
  William, 16
BOTTS,
  Joseph, 16
BOUIS,
  Charles E., 67
BOURNE,
  Catherine, 59
  Henry, 59
BOWDEN,
  Arthur, 68
BOWEN,
  Jehu, 196
  Robert, 68
  Sutliff, 16
BOWIE,
  James, 16
  John, 16, 113
BOWLER,
  Thomas, 27
BOWLING,
  John, 16
BOYCE,
  Abraham, 68
BOYD,
  Benjamin, 65
BOYLE,
  John, 16
BOYS,
  Matthew, 16
BOZMAN,
  Rachel, 114

BRADFORD,
  George, 21
BRADLEY,
  James, 16
BRADY,
  John, 16, 204
  William, 16
BRAITHWAITE,
  John, 16
BRANNON,
  Owen, 16
BRANNUM,
  Richard, 16
BRANON,
  Richard, 16
BRASHEARS,
  Benjamin, 16
  Charles, 17
  Dowell, 17
  Eleanor, 116
  Francis, 116
  Jesse, 17
  Jonathan, 17, 136
  Judson, 17
  Levi, 17
  Lilburn, 17
  Margery, 17
  Nancy, 17
  Nathan, 17
  Waymack, 17
  Wilkerson, 17
  William, 17
BRASHEEARS,
  Zadock, 17
BRAY,
  John, 17
BREWER,
  Allen Thomas, 18
  Ann, 18
  Brice Beal, 18
  Eliza, 18
  Elizabeth, 18
  Ennas, 18
  Hannah Jacob, 107
  John, 17, 18
  John Mercer, 18
  Joseph, 17, 18
  Lot, 18
  Mary Ann, 18
  Mary Birkhead, 14
  Nicholas, 17, 18
  Roady, 18
  Sarah Stockett, 18
  Susanna, 18
  Thomas Stockett,

INDEX

18
  William, 18
BRIAN,
  William, 18
BRICE,
  Ann Carroll, 18
  Edmund, 18
  Henry, 18
  James, 18, 34,
    37, 41, 47, 61,
    63, 66, 69, 70,
    74, 92, 93,
    101, 118, 119,
    123, 124, 130,
    137, 141, 142,
    144, 148, 149,
    153, 155, 156,
    158, 159, 169,
    176, 183, 185,
    187, 188, 190,
    193, 194, 198,
    218, 222, 224,
    225, 227
  Jamess Frisby,
    18
  John, 18, 73,
    113, 135
  Juliana
    Jennings, 108
  Julianna, 18
  Margaretta
    Clare, 18
  Nicholas, 18
  Rachel, 84, 85,
    86
  Sarah Ann, 18
  Thomas Jennings,
    18
BRIGHT,
  James, 19
  Mary Ann, 203
  William, 68
BRISCOE,
  Philip, 64
  Sarah, 201
BRISINGTON,
  Philip, 196
BRISSINGTON,
  Abram, 19
BRITT,
  Robert, 19, 204
BRITTAIN,
  James, 19
BRITTON,
  John, 19

  Richard, 194
  Temperance
    Merryman, 194
BROGDEN,
  Capt., 104
  David M., 19, 178
  James, 19
  John, 19, 42, 142
  Jonathan Sellman,
    19
  Margaret Sellman,
    177
  Mary, 19
  Samuel, 19, 136
  William, 19, 90,
    113, 120, 136
BROOKE,
  Elizabeth, 28, 29
  Susannah Dorsey,
    48
BROOKS,
  Margaret
    Davidson, 42
  Walter, 19
BROWN,
  Alley, 20
  Ann, 20, 216
  Basil, 64
  Benjamin, 20
  Capt., 30, 225
  Christopher, 68
  Daniel, 19
  Elie, 135
  Ely, 19
  Harriet, 20
  Isaac, 196
  James, 20, 120
  Jennett, 20
  John, 20, 64, 196
  John Riggs, 20
  Joshua, 20, 28
  Joshua D., 21
  Lloyd, 21
  Margarey Gaither,
    72
  Matilda Hammond,
    86
  Rachel, 18, 20
  Richard, 20, 68
  Robert, 20
  Samuel, 20, 136
  Sarah A., 21
  Sarah Gassaway,
    75
  Susannah, 20

  Thomas, 20
  Valentine, 20
  William, 20, 21,
    64, 186
  Zachariag, 21
  Zachariah, 21
  Zecharia, 21
BRYAN,
  Daniel, 21
  Joseph, 21
  Thomas, 21
BRYANT,
  George, 21
  John, 204
  Richard, 21
BRYCE,
  Mary, 58
BUCK,
  James, 21
BULL,
  Mary, 205
BULLEN,
  John, 21, 90, 126
  Luke, 47
BURGEE,
  Jane Ijams, 103
BURGESS,
  Absalom, 24
  Absolom, 23
  Achsah, 22, 23
  Alexander, 22
  Ann D., 24
  Anne, 22, 24
  Anne Dorsey, 24
  Basil, 1, 21, 22,
    23, 24, 74, 135,
    162
  Benjamin, 21
  Caleb, 22, 136,
    183
  Catherine, 22
  Charles, 24
  Cynthia, 21
  Edward, 22, 24
  Eleanor, 21, 23
  Eleanor Burgess,
    23
  Eleanor Dorsey, 50
  Elizabeth, 22, 23,
    24
  Elizer Ann, 22
  George, 24
  Harriet, 24
  Hetty W., 24
  Honor, 23

240 INDEX

James, 23
Jane, 22, 23
John, 21, 22, 23, 113, 135, 136, 165
John Dorsey, 21
Joseph, 7, 8, 22, 23, 24, 59, 94, 95, 107, 116, 119, 144, 150, 159, 165, 180, 193, 196, 222, 228
Joseph V., 23
Joshua, 23, 24, 135, 196
Juliet, 24
Lidey, 23
Margaret, 22
Mary, 22, 23, 24
Mary Ridgely Dorsey, 55
Mary V., 24
Matilda, 22
Michael, 7, 19, 23, 24, 30, 71, 73, 105, 107, 109, 118, 157, 191, 217, 227
Michael D., 23
Mordecai, 23, 24
Nancy, 23
Osgood, 21
Peregrine, 24
Philemon, 23
Rachel Warfield, 207
Rebecca, 23, 24
Rebecca Dorsey, 55
Rebecca O., 24
Richard, 23, 24
Roderick, 23
Ruth, 23
Sally, 23
Samuel, 22, 24
Sarah, 22, 23, 24, 72, 73, 74
Sarah Warfield, 208
Sheridan, 23
Susan, 22
Susanna, 22
Thomas, 22, 23
Thomas D., 24

Upton, 23
Vachel, 23, 24, 64
William, 23, 24
BURGOE,
  Jacob, 24
  John, 24
  Robert, 24
BURGOON,
  Jacob, 24
  John, 24
  Robert, 24
BURGOONE,
  Robert, 24
BURHILL,
  John, 24
BURKE,
  Jane, 61
  Patrick, 24
  Richard, 25
BURKHEAD,
  Abraham, 13
BURN,
  Michael, 25
BURNES,
  Luke, 25
BURNS,
  Luke, 25
BURR,
  Luke, 25
BURTON,
  Charles, 25
  Edward, 25
  Elizabeth, 25
  Francis, 25
  James, 25
  John, 25
  Mary, 25
  Nancy, 25
  Sarah, 25
  Thomas, 25
  William, 25
BUSBY,
  Christopher, 196
BUSHELL,
  Peter, 196
BUSY,
  Paul, 153
BUTCHER,
  John, 25
BUTLER,
  James, 25
  Joseph, 25, 68
  Noble, 25
  Vacey, 26

William, 26, 65
BYFIELD,
  Thomas, 26

-C-
CADLE,
  Ann, 84
  Benjamin, 26
  Eleanor, 26
  Elizabeth, 26, 61
  Horace, 26
  James, 26, 61
  Priscilla, 26
  Samuel, 26
  Thomas, 26
  William, 26
CAIN,
  Hugh, 26
CALDWELL,
  Marion, 212
  Mary, 211
  William, 26
CALE,
  John, 26
CALHOON,
  Alexander, 26
CALLAHAN,
  John, 26, 136
CAMBDEN,
  Richard, 26
CAMDEN,
  Richard, 26
CAMP,
  John, 27
CAMPBELL,
  Daniel, 27
  Mr., 140
  William, 5, 27, 35, 71
CAN,
  James, 27
CANADA,
  Thomas, 64
CANE,
  Hugh, 26
CANN,
  George, 27
  James, 27
CANNOR,
  Francis, 27
  William, 27
CANTRELL,
  Alexander, 30
CANTWELL,
  Richard, 68

INDEX

CAPPOCK,
  Samuel, 27
  Simmons, 196
  Simon, 28
CARBURY,
  Peter, 28
CARDIFF,
  Thomas, 65
CAREY,
  William, 28
CARR,
  Abigail, 63
  Benjamin, 28
  Daniel, 28
  Jacob, 28
  James, 28
  Jane Russell, 173
  John, 28, 64
  Mary, 28
  Mary Armiger, 3
  Mary Burgess, 23
  Samuel, 173
  Walter, 28, 148
  William, 28
CARRALL,
  John, 30
CARROL,
  Henry, 30
CARROLL,
  Anne B., 29
  Anne Jennings, 108
  Brian, 28
  Catherine, 29
  Charles, 28, 29, 30
  Daniel, 29
  Dennis, 29, 68
  Elizabeth, 29
  Elizabeth Warfield, 209
  Henry, 30
  James, 29
  John, 29, 30, 64
  Joseph, 68
  Louisa R., 29
  Mary, 29
  Mary Clare, 30
  Nicholas, 30
CARTER,
  Samuel, 27
CARTY,
  Timothy, 30
  William, 68

CARVAR,
  James, 68
CARVEL,
  Alexander, 30
CARVELL,
  John, 30
  William, 30
CARVILL,
  John, 187
CARWIN,
  James, 30
CARY,
  James, 30
CASTLE,
  James, 26
CATHEL,
  Josiah, 30
CATHERSIDE,
  Abram, 30
CATON,
  Mary Carroll, 29
CATRELL,
  Alexander, 30
CAUSIN,
  Elizabeth Stone, 192
CAYHILL,
  David, 30
CHAFFEY,
  John, 30
CHALMBNERS,
  John, 31
CHALMERS,
  John, 31
  Thomas, 31
CHAMBERS,
  Edward, 31
  Mary, 38
CHANEY,
  John, 64
  Mary, 209
  Richard, 64
  Zachariah, 32
CHAPLAIN,
  John, 31
CHAPLIN,
  Hugh, 31
CHAPMAN,
  Abraham, 31
  Charles, 31
  Elizabeth, 19
  Elizabeth Warfield, 212
  Frances Dorsey, 53

Mrs., 219
Rebecca, 76
Thomas, 31
CHASE,
  Ann, 31
  Elizabeth, 31
  Fanny, 31
  Mary, 31
  Matilda, 31
  Nancy, 31
  Samuel, 31
  Thomas, 31
  Thomass, 31
  Walker, 94
CHATLING,
  William, 31
CHATTERTON,
  John, 68
CHEEVER,
  John, 27
CHENEY,
  Andrew Francis, 32
  Anne Cromwell, 39
  Benjamin, 32
  Elizabeth, 2
  Isaiah, 32
  John, 13, 64
  Joseph, 32
  Richard, 68
  Samuel, 32
  Susan, 2
  Zachariah, 32
  Zepheniah, 32
CHESTER,
  Samuel, 32
CHESTON,
  Ann, 74
CHEVICK,
  John, 196
CHEW,
  Ann, 33
  Ann Mary, 147
  Anne, 74
  Benjamin, 32
  Elizabeth, 33
  Henrietta Maria, 33, 74
  John, 32, 136
  John Croley, 33
  Lock, 32
  Nathaniel, 32, 136
  Richard, 13, 14, 32, 33, 65, 68, 71, 82, 89, 102, 107, 110, 112,

117, 118, 120, 136, 160, 176, 183, 185, 186, 189, 190, 196, 201, 202, 206, 223, 224, 228, 232
  Samuel, 16, 26, 31, 33, 39, 63, 75, 77, 79, 95, 113, 127, 136, 139, 144, 169, 176, 188, 195, 220
  Samuel Lloyd, 33
  Sarah, 22
  William, 33, 136
CHILD,
  Benjamin, 33
  Cephas, 33
  John, 33
  Samuel, 33
  William, 33
  Zachariah, 33
CHILDS,
  Ann, 33
  Ann Owens, 146
  Barbary, 33
  Benjamin, 33
  Betsy, 146
  Cephas, 33
  Elizabeth, 33
  George, 64
  Henry, 33, 81, 103
  John, 33
  Martha P., 33
  Mary, 33, 200
  Nelly, 33
  Ruth, 103, 104
  Samuel, 33, 169
  Sarah, 33
  Sephas, 33
  William, 33
  Zachariah, 33, 169
CHISHOLM,
  Archibald, 33, 214
  Catharine, 34
  Charlotte, 34
  Elizabeth, 33
  Elizabeth Waters, 214
  Emily, 34

CHIVAS,
  Andrew, 68
CHURCH,
  John, 68
CLAGETT,
  Eleanor Bowie, 215
  Ephraim, 22
  Margaret Burgess, 22
CLANCEY,
  Daniel, 64
  Dennis, 34
CLANSEY,
  Michael, 34
CLARIDGE,
  Achsah, 167
CLARK,
  Edward, 34
  James, 34, 68
  John, 27, 34
  Rachel Warfield, 209
  Richard, 68
  Thomas, 34
  William, 34
CLARKE,
  James, 34
  John, 204
  Juliette Gaither, 74
  Margaret Howard Duckett, 100
  Robert, 34
CLARVO,
  John, 34
CLAUDE,
  Abraham, 11
  Elizabeth Quynn, 159
CLAYTON,
  Mary, 124
CLEARY,
  James, 124
  Sarah, 124
CLEMENTS,
  Henry, 64
  James, 64
  John, 64
  William, 64
CLEMMENTS,
  Francis T., 34
CLIVEY,
  Isaac, 34

CLOONEY,
  John, 68
COAL,
  Sarah, 35
COALE,
  Alfred, 35
  Anna Maria, 35
  Charles Ridgely, 35
  Francis, 34
  Harriet, 35
  John, 34
  Joseph, 35
  Thomas, 35
  William, 35
COALTER,
  Daniel, 35
COCKBURN,
  Alexander, 35
COCKERTON,
  John, 35
COCKEY,
  Edward, 55
COE,
  Mary, 35
  William, 35
COFFIN,
  Arthur, 35
COLAND,
  John, 196
COLBERT,
  Daniel, 35
COLE,
  Elizabeth Chase Dugan, 31
  James, 35
  Joseph, 35, 68
  Levi, 35
  Sarah Ridgely, 166
  Thomas, 35
COLEGATE,
  John, 196
COLIN,
  John, 68
COLLAHAN,
  James, 19
COLLENSON,
  Edward, 36
COLLINS,
  George, 36
  James, 4
  John, 36
  Sarah, 207
  William, 36

COLLIOR,
  Thomas, 36
COLSON,
  Robert, 38
COMBLY,
  Benjamin, 36
COMEGYS,
  Evaline Mary
  Dorsey, 56
COMPTON,
  John, 27
CONAWAY,
  John, 36
CONDON,
  Martin, 36
CONDRAM,
  Thomas, 36
CONNALSON,
  Joseph, 36
CONNAR,
  William, 36
CONNAWAY,
  Elizabeth, 198
CONNELLY,
  John, 64
CONNER,
  Caleb, 36
  James, 36
  Mary Ogle
   Bevans, 144
  Patrick, 36
CONNOLLY,
  Benjamin, 36
  Francis, 36
  James, 36
  Jennie, 36
  John, 36
  John J., 36
  Michael, 37
  Milly, 36
  Sandford, 36
  Sarah, 36
CONNOR,
  James, 37
  John, 37
  Michael, 27, 204
  Thomas, 37
CONOR,
  Mary, 79
CONTEE,
  Jane, 87
COOK,
  Henry, 37
COOKE,
  Henry, 68

COOLEY,
  Thomas, 37
  William, 37
COOPER,
  Araminta
   Warfield, 209
  Cecil, 37
  Edward, 37
  George, 37
  Thomas, 37
COPE,
  John, 37
COPPUCK,
  Samuel, 27
CORD,
  Ann, 37
  Catherine, 37
  George, 37
  Hellen, 37
  Henry, 37
  James, 37
  Jesse, 37
  John, 37
  Rebecca, 37
  Roger, 196
  Sarah, 37
  Sophia, 37
CORNELIUS,
  John, 37
CORNWALL,
  William, 27
COSIVE,
  John, 37
COTTER,
  Sarah, 76
COUDEN,
  Mary, 192
COUGHLAN,
  Edward, 38
COUGHLAND,
  Edward, 204
COULSON,
  Robert, 38
COULSTON,
  John, 38
COURSEY,
  Patrick, 38
COURTS,
  William, 64
COWAN,
  Henrietta
   Harwood, 90
COWLEY,
  Edward, 38
  James, 38

Joseph, 44
William, 38
COWMAN,
  John, 38
  Richard, 38
COX,
  John, 38
  Sarah Wood, 228
  William, 38
COYLE,
  Eliza, 34
CRACROFT,
  John, 38
CRAGG,
  Robert, 38
CRAGON,
  Lawrence, 38
CRAIG,
  John, 196
CRAIGE,
  Alexander, 38
  John, 68
CRAMBLICK,
  Jacob, 38, 39
CRAMLICK,
  Andrew, 38
  Elizabeth, 38, 39
  Frederick, 38
  Jacob, 38, 39
  John, 38
  Michael, 38
  Stephen, 38
  Thomas, 39
CRAMPTON,
  James, 196
CRAN,
  Lydia, 168
CRANDAL,
  William, 136
CRANDALL,
  Elizabeth
   Caroline, 39
  Francis, 39
  George, 39
  Hester, 39
  John, 39
  Priscilla, 79
  William, 39
CRANDEL,
  Ann, 81
CRANDELL,
  Adam, 39
  Francis, 39
  Joseph, 39
  Thomas, 39.

INDEX

William, 39
CRANDLE,
  Joseph, 39
CRANE,
  John, 139
  Reuben, 139
CRASBY,
  Joseph, 39
CREGAN,
  Lawrence, 196
CRESAP,
  Capt., 161
CROCKETT,
  Hannah, 47
  Mary, 49
CROK,
  George, 39
CROMWELL,
  Anne, 39
  Elizabeth, 39
  Elizabeth Jacob Roles, 107
  Francis, 39, 136
  John, 39
  Joshua, 39, 135
  Margaret Anne, 87
  Mary, 39
  Richard, 40, 113, 135, 136
  Sarah, 39
  William, 39
  Zachariah, 39
CROOK,
  Charlotte Sellman, 177
CROSBEY,
  Joseph, 64
CROSBY,
  Elizabeth, 28
CROSS,
  Elizabeth, 40
  Harriet Howard, 98
  Jemima, 40
  John, 40
  Mary Ann, 40
  Rebecca, 40
  Robert, 40
CROW,
  Edward, 40
CROWE,
  Samuel, 40
CROXALL,
  Charles, 40

CROZIER,
  James, 64
CRUCHLEY,
  Richard, 40
CRUTCHLEY,
  Joseph, 40
  Leggy, 195
  Richard, 40
  Thomas, 40
CULBERTSON,
  William, 40
CUMMING,
  David, 40
  James, 40
CUMMINGS,
  Mary, 51
CUMMINS,
  Ruth H., 168
CUNNINGHAM,
  Martha, 104
CUPIT,
  John, 68
CURRAY,
  James, 40
CURTIS,
  John, 40
  Thomas, 41
CUTLER,
  Jacob, 41
CUTONG,
  Peter, 41

-D-

DABBS,
  John, 41
DACE,
  Michael, 41
DADS,
  John, 41
DAFFIN,
  James, 68
DAILY,
  John, 68
DALEY,
  Mathew, 41
DANIELSON,
  Moses, 41
DANNISON,
  Ann, 152
DARBY,
  Anna, 41
  Anne, 41
  Asa, 41
  Elizabeth, 41
  George, 41

  James, 41
  John, 41
  Lydia, 41
  Mary, 41
  Nancy, 41
  Thomas, 41
  William Jefferson, 41
DARE,
  Elizabeth Ridgely, 167
  Gideon, 41, 135, 136
  Joseph, 41
DARLING,
  Robert, 68
DARNALL,
  Bennit, 41
  Henry, 42
  Mary, 28, 29
  Philip, 42
DASHIELL,
  Ann Ridgely, 167
  Robert, 158
DAVENPORT,
  William, 42
DAVEY,
  Ruth Dorsey, 49
DAVID,
  John, 42, 120
  Valentine, 42
DAVIDGE,
  Azel, 42
  Dinah, 207, 208, 211
  Elizabeth, 208
  Robert, 42
DAVIDSON,
  Ann Janette, 42
  Eleanor, 42
  James, 42
  John, 42, 135, 157
  John Thomas, 42
  Margaret, 42
  Matilda, 42
  Nelson, 42
  Pamela, 42
  Pinkney, 42
  Priscilla, 42
  Thomas, 42
DAVIES,
  Thomas, 43
DAVINSON,
  James, 43

INDEX

DAVIS,
  Amos, 43, 191
  Barbara, 151
  Daniel, 43
  Ichabod, 43
  Ignatius, 43
  Jesse 43
  John, 43
  Joseph, 43
  Luke, 43
  Margaret, 214
  Mary, 22
  Mary Beard, 11
  Peter, 27
  Philip, 43
  Robert, 43, 44
  Robert Pain, 44, 136
  Robert Pam, 44
  Ruth, 207, 210
  Thomas, 22, 68
  Walter, 44
  William, 44, 136
DAVY,
  William, 44
DAWES,
  Richard, 44
DAWKINS,
  Thomas, 28
DAWSON,
  Elizabeth, 177
  Henry, 44
DAY,
  Robert, 44
  Sarah Warfield, 210
  Thomas, 44
  William, 204
DDORSEY,
  John, 31
DE VAUBRAN,
  John, 204
DEALE,
  Elizabeth, 45
  Henrietta, 79
  James, 44
  John, 39, 44, 136, 142, 143, 153
  Joseph, 44
  Martin, 45
  Mary Franklin, 70
  Nathan, 44
  Rachel, 79
  Richard, 45
  Samuel, 44
  Thomas, 45
  William, 44, 45
DEAN,
  John, 210
DEANE,
  Francis, 196
DEARDS,
  William, 45
DEASE,
  Michael, 68
DEAVER,
  James, 163
  Joseph, 3, 45
  Samuel, 45
  Stephen, 45
DEAVOUR,
  Misail, 45
DEBOROUGH,
  Mary Hammond, 85
DELANEY,
  William, 204
DELANY,
  William, 45
DELIAZON,
  Peter, 196
DELL,
  James, 45
DEMPSEY,
  John, 45
DENBUGH,
  William, 196
DENISON,
  Richard, 45
DENMASS,
  William, 196
DENNISON,
  Richard, 45
DENT,
  Eleanor, 46
  Elizabeth Maria, 46
  Erasmus, 46
  John, 45, 46
  Richard, 46
  Walter, 46
DENUNE,
  Jeane, 98, 101
DERLING, Robert, 46
DEW,
  Jesse, 28
  Samuel, 28
DICKERSON,
  Susannah, 207
DIFFEY,
  Alexander, 46
DIGGONS,
  Samuel, 46
DILLON,
  William, 64
DISNEY,
  Edward, 46
  James, 6, 8, 9, 32, 43, 46, 84, 96, 98, 110, 111, 112, 115, 118, 123, 142, 151, 162, 165, 166, 170, 178, 189, 195, 197, 210, 215, 216, 217, 225, 226
  John, 46
  Margaret, 46
  Rebecca, 179
  Richard, 46
  Thomas, 46
  William, 46
DITTY,
  Thomas, 46
DIVER,
  Aquilla, 65
DIXON,
  John, 46
  Samuel, 46
  William, 27
DOBSON,
  John, 47
DODSON,
  John, 47
DOHERTY,
  Patrick, 47
DOLTREY,
  Jesse, 47
DONALDSON,
  Caroline Dorsey, 49
DONNELSON,
  Moses, 41
DONNINGHAM,
  James, 47
  John, 47
DONNINGTON,
  James, 47
  John, 47
DONOGUE,
  Daniel, 204
DONOVAN,
  Timothy, 204

INDEX

DORAGHY,
  Arthur, 47
DORAN,
  Barnaba, 196
DORITY,
  Jesse, 47
DORSEY,
  Achsah, 48, 53, 54, 99
  Alexander, 50
  Alfred, 53
  Allen, 49
  Amos, 47, 49, 130
  Andrew, 56
  Ann, 49, 52
  Ann Warfield, 206
  Anne, 50, 54, 56, 85, 166, 167
  Anne Dorsey, 54
  Anne Howard, 98
  Anne Worthington, 53
  Aquila, 47
  Archibald, 55
  Arey, 207
  Basil, 47, 51, 55
  Beale, 46
  Benedict, 55
  Benjamin, 47, 48
  C. A., 47
  Caleb, 48, 49, 50, 51, 54, 55, 118
  Capt., 66
  Caroline, 49, 54, 56
  Catherine, 50, 53, 54, 207, 208
  Cecil, 52
  Charles, 48, 53, 54, 56, 68
  Charles Boone, 50
  Charles Samuel Worthington, 51
  Charles Worthington, 48
  Clarissa, 51, 53
  Clement, 50
  Comfort
    Worthington, 48
  Daniel, 23, 48, 55, 99, 122
  Daniel Horatio, 56
  Darius, 52
  Dathan, 52
  David Alexander, 51
  Deale, 52
  Deborah, 47, 48, 49
  Dennis, 52, 53
  Edward, 48, 49, 50, 51, 52, 53, 54, 55, 133
  Edward Gilliss, 51
  Edward Hill, 48, 49, 54
  Edward John, 54
  Edward Worthington, 51
  Eleanor, 21, 49, 50, 54, 83
  Eleanor Dorsey, 49
  Elenor, 54
  Elias, 49, 50, 55
  Eliza, 54
  Elizabeth, 22, 23, 24, 47, 48, 49, 50, 51, 52, 53, 54, 55, 56, 167, 168, 209, 210
  Elizabeth Dorsey, 48, 50, 51
  Elizabeth Hall, 56
  Elizabeth Hill, 48, 49
  Elizabeth Worthington, 48
  Ely, 25, 47, 48, 49, 147
  Emma Ridgely, 56
  Essex Ridley, 56
  Eudocia, 54
  Evaline Mary, 56
  Evelina, 53
  Ezekiel, 51, 56
  Ezekiel John, 48, 50
  Ezra, 53
  Frances, 53
  Francis, 52
  Frederick, 53
  George, 48, 54
  Gilbert, 50
  Hammond, 49
  Hannah, 7
  Hanson, 54
  Harriet, 50, 51, 55
  Henry, 48, 50, 51, 53, 54, 55
  Henry Gough Kennedy, 54
  Henry Hall, 50, 51
  Hill, 49
  Honor, 6, 48, 49, 50, 52, 55
  Humphrey, 50
  Isaac, 51
  James, 51
  James Ireland, 56
  Jemina, 52
  Jeremiah, 54
  John, 4, 5, 9, 10, 12, 15, 16, 19, 20, 21, 23, 24, 26, 27, 31, 32, 34, 37, 38, 40, 41, 43, 46, 47, 48, 49, 50, 51, 52, 53, 54, 55, 57, 59, 60, 61, 62, 63, 66, 71, 72, 73, 74, 75, 76, 77, 78, 81, 83, 84, 85, 88, 89, 90, 92, 94, 96, 97, 99, 100, 101, 102, 109, 110, 111, 112, 113, 114, 115, 116, 117, 118, 119, 121, 122, 123, 125, 128, 130, 134, 135, 136, 143, 144, 145, 147, 148, 152, 153, 154, 156, 158, 160, 163, 165, 168, 169, 170, 174, 175, 176, 178, 179, 181, 182, 184, 185, 188,

INDEX

189, 191, 193, 194, 195, 196, 197, 199, 200, 205, 206, 208, 211, 216, 221, 222, 223, 232
John Crockett, 49
John E., 50
John Hall, 51
John Ireland, 55
John Lawrence, 48
John Tolley Worthington, 51
John W., 3, 95
John Worthington, 16, 24, 48, 51, 59, 81, 83, 90, 97, 122, 136, 144, 145, 148, 154, 168, 170, 182, 188, 196
Johnsa, 55
Josa., 53
Joseph, 48, 51
Joshua, 50, 51, 52, 53, 56
Joshua W., 53
Josiah, 54
Juliet, 55
Lacon, 52
Lancelot, 52
Larkin, 48, 50, 52, 119
Leakin, 52
Leaven, 48, 55
Lloyd, 52, 53
Louisa, 54, 56
Lucretia, 53
Lydia, 52, 53
Lydia Dorsey, 53
Margaret, 51
Margaret Anne, 50
Maria Cecelia, 56
Mary, 47, 49, 50, 51, 53, 54, 55, 56, 166, 218
Mary Ann, 47
Mary Ann Hammond, 86

Mary Dorsey, 53
Mary Hill, 48, 51
Mary Ridgely, 55
Mary Tolley, 51
Matilda, 51, 53, 55
Michael, 23, 49, 50, 51, 52
Mortimer, 53, 54
Nancy, 48, 51
Nathan, 52, 55
Nichcolas, 48
Nicholas, 53, 54, 55, 113
Nicholas W., 53
Nicholas Worthington, 53
Noah, 53
Orlando, 53
Owen, 52
Patience, 100
Philemon, 50, 52, 54, 113
Philip, 54
Priscilla, 49
Rachel, 48, 53, 56, 208
Rachel Ridgely, 168
Rebecca, 24, 48, 49, 51, 55, 56
Reuben, 53
Reuben Meriweather, 48
Rhesaw, 48
Richard, 1, 7, 9, 12, 15, 16, 19, 25, 27, 30, 32, 34, 35, 36, 37, 38, 40, 45, 48, 50, 54, 57, 63, 66, 67, 79, 87, 93, 99, 108, 110, 112, 113, 114, 120, 127, 128, 130, 131, 138, 140, 141, 142, 144, 149, 154, 157, 163, 164, 165, 170, 183, 185, 187, 193, 198, 202, 204, 206, 222, 224, 225
Robert, 49, 50

Roderick, 53
Ruth, 49, 50, 52, 55, 56
Samuel, 49, 53, 54, 55, 56
Samuel Thomas, 51
Samuel Worthington, 51
Sarah, 21, 22, 48, 49, 53, 54, 99, 100, 118, 212
Sarah Ann, 56
Sarah Anne, 133
Sarah Hammond, 85
Sarah M., 50
Sarah Meriweather, 48
Sarah Warfield, 211
Septimus, 54
Severn John, 51
Sophia, 48
Sophia Dorsey, 48
Stephen Boone, 50
Susannah, 48
Theodore, 55
Thomas, 11, 12, 13, 22, 36, 41, 46, 47, 50, 51, 55, 60, 63, 69, 71, 72, 73, 75, 82, 83, 87, 88, 92, 93, 95, 98, 99, 101, 104, 113, 116, 118, 119, 121, 122, 124, 127, 128, 135, 136, 147, 150, 156, 157, 160, 163, 164, 166, 167, 168, 169, 173, 175, 182, 189, 191, 193, 203, 205, 211, 212, 214, 217, 220, 222, 223, 224, 227, 228, 229
Thomas Beal, 51
Thomas Beale, 48, 51
Vachel, 49, 50, 53, 55, 56
Walter, 50
William, 48, 51,

52
  William Hammond, 50
  William Henry, 51, 56
  Worthington, 12
DOUGLASS,
  William, 196
DOVE,
  Alice, 56
  Elizabeth, 56
  John, 56
  Joseph, 56
  Mark, 56
  Mary, 56
  Sarah, 56
  Thomas, 56
  William, 56
DOWAN,
  Nicholas, 68
DOWELL,
  Ann, 176
  John, 56
  Thomas, 57
DOWLEY,
  Deborah, 181
DOWNES,
  James, 64
  William, 196
DOWNS,
  William, 68
DRANE,
  James, 199
  Thomas, 199
DRAWATER,
  Robert, 57
DRUDGE,
  Thomas, 64
DRUMMOND,
  John, 57
DRURY,
  Ann, 57, 229
  Ann Ijams, 104
  Charles, 57, 136
  Elizabeth, 57
  Elizabeth Ijams, 104
  Henry Childs, 57
  John, 57
  Margaret, 57
  Mary, 57
  Matilda Tillard Simmons, 199
  Plummer, 57
  Ruth, 57

  Samuel, 57
  William, 57
DUBOIS,
  Nancy Dorsey, 51
DUCKETT,
  Elizabeth Howard, 100
  Margaret Howard, 100
  Sophia, 140
DUE,
  Richard, 57
DUFFIELD,
  Richard, 57
DUFFY,
  Michael, 57
DUGAN,
  Elizabeth Chase, 31
DULANEY,
  Daniel, 23
DUMAS,
  William, 68
DUNMORE,
  Lord, 163
DUNN,
  Patrick, 57
DUNNAVIN,
  Timothy, 57
DUNSTER,
  John, 196
DURBIN,
  Cassandra Frances, 174
DURNOR,
  Thomas, 196
DUTTON,
  Notley, 64
DUVALL,
  Amos, 57
  Anne Welsh, 221
  Benjamin, 58
  Cyrus, 58
  Edmund Bryce, 58
  Elizabeth, 71, 73, 134, 210
  Elizabeth Ijams, 103
  Elizabeth Warfield, 211
  Emos, 57
  Gabriel, 57, 58
  Henry, 58
  John, 58
  Joseph, 58

  Lewis, 58, 90
  Louisiana, 58
  Mary, 58
  Miles, 58
  Polly, 58
  Rachel, 214
  Rachel Howard, 101
  Rebecca Ijams, 104
  Rebecca Rawlings, 161
  Sarah Ann Harwood, 90
  Thomas, 58, 157
  Zachariah, 58
DWYER,
  Thomas, 68
DYCUS,
  Isaac, 58
DYER,
  James, 58
  Jonathan, 64

-E-
EADES,
  Thomas, 196
EARL,
  Paul, 58
EARLOUGHER,
  Sarah, 203
EARP,
  Edward, 58
  Joshua, 58
  Petticoat, 59
  Thomas, 59
  William, 59
EASSON,
  John, 59
  William, 59
EASTMAN,
  Joseph, 13
EASTON,
  John, 59, 68
  Richard, 59
EATON,
  William, 59, 196
EDDINGS,
  John, 59
EDGE,
  William, 59
EDGERLY,
  Edward, 137
EDMONDSON,
  James, 114
  Pollard, 59
  Rachel, 114

INDEX

Susanna Howard, 100
EDMONSTON,
　Samuel, 59
EDWARD,
　Margaret Ijams, 104
EDWARDS,
　Anne, 59
　Aquila, 59
　Cadwallader, 59, 60
　Catherine, 59
　Edward, 59, 64
　Elizabeth, 59, 60
　Jemima, 59
　Jonathan, 59, 60
　Margaret, 59, 60
　Mary, 59, 60, 213
　Sarah, 2, 59, 60
　Thomas, 68, 196
　William, 59, 60
ELDER,
　Ann Dorsey, 52
　Ely, 108, 232
　Honor, 52
　Jemina, 100
　Sarah Howard, 99
ELISHA,
　Thomas, 60
ELLICOTT,
　Andrew, 60, 61, 136
　Capt., 135
　David, 60
　Edward, 64
　Jonathan, 60
　Joseph, 60
　Thomas, 64
ELLIOTT,
　Andrew, 60, 164
　Ann, 61
　David, 60
　Edward, 60
　James, 60, 61
　John, 60, 61
　Jonathan, 60
　Joseph, 60
　Matthew, 61
　Richard, 61
　Robert, 61
　Robert Welch, 61
　Samuel, 61, 68,

196
　Sarah, 61
　Sarah Warfield, 213
　Thomas, 61
　William, 61
ELTHAM,
　John, 61
EMANUEL,
　Peter, 196
ENNIS,
　Leonard, 61
　Thomas, 196
ENNISS,
　Thomas, 68
ENSMINGER,
　Katherine, 193
ESSTEP,
　Rezin, 28
ESTEP,
　Richard, 118
　Sarah, 198
ESTES,
　Elizabeth Darby, 41
　Elizabeth Wood, 228
EVANS,
　James, 61
　Jane Norman, 143
　Jemima Edwards, 59, 60
　John, 61
　Joseph, 61, 136
　Lewis, 61
　William, 62
EVERETT,
　John, 62
　William, 62
EVERITT,
　John, 62
EWELL,
　Anne, 219
EWING,
　Col., 221
　James, 158
　Nathaniel, 62
　Thomas, 106
EYEN,
　Frederick, 62
EYER,
　Frederick, 62
EYLES,
　Samuel, 68
EYRE,

Frederick, 62

-F-
FAHEY,
　Patrick, 62
FAIRBROTHER,
　Ann, 62
　Elfrida, 62
　Francis, 62, 64
　Patience, 62
　Thomas, 62
FANNING,
　Thomas, 62
FARIS,
　Priscilla, 63
　William, 62, 63
FARRARA,
　Emanuel, 63
FENLEY,
　Elizabeth Ijams, 103
FENNEL,
　Stephen, 204
FENNELL,
　Caleb, 199
　Eleanor Toft, 199
　Robert, 63
　Stephen, 63
FENTON,
　Charles, 63
FENWICK,
　Richard, 68, 196
FERABY,
　Richard, 196
FERGUSON,
　David, 63
　William, 63
FERNEN,
　Andrew, 64
FERRALD,
　James, 68
FERRALL,
　John, 64
FERRARA,
　Emanuel, 63
FERREL,
　Bryan, 204
FIELDER,
　Jacob, 63
FIELDON,
　Jacob, 63
FIGENCER,
　John, 63
FINLAYSON,
　George, 63

INDEX

FINLEY,
  Coleman, 196
  Ebenezer, 27, 63, 204
FINLEYSON,
  George, 63
FINLISON,
  George, 63
FIPPS,
  Roger, 63
FISH,
  Benjamin, 65, 135, 136
  Rachel Jacob, 107
  Richard, 65
  William, 65
FISHER,
  Basil, 38, 65
  Elizabeth Childs, 33
  Etta, 65
  Hezekih, 65
  John, 65
  John H., 65
  Lewis, 33
  Mary A., 65
  Mary Childs, 33
  Mary Warfield, 206
  Seth, 65
  Susanna, 65
  William, 33, 65, 176
FITGENCY,
  John, 65
FITZGERALD,
  Araminta Warfield Cooper, 209
FITZHUGH,
  Col., 228
  Eleanor, 34
  Elizabeth Chew, 33
FITZJARROLD,
  John, 65
FITZPATRICK,
  John, 204
FLANAGAN,
  William, 68, 196
FLANNEGAN,
  Dennis, 204
FLANNERY,
  Christopher, 68

FLANNIGAN,
  Dennis, 66
FLATTERY,
  John, 66
FLINT,
  Mary Stockett, 192
FLOWERS,
  Ralph, 66
FLUSSER,
  Juliana Waters, 213
FOARD,
  Joseph, 66
FOGGET,
  Richard, 66
FOGGETT,
  Artridge, 66
  Richard, 66
FOLGER,
  Robert, 66
FOLKS,
  Catherine, 154
  John, 66
FOLLITT,
  Joseph, 66
FONDEREN,
  Margaret Edwards, 59
FONERDON,
  John, 60
  Margaret Edwards, 60
FOOKES,
  Jonathan, 66
FOOTEL,
  James, 200
FORBES,
  John, 66
  Will, 66
  William, 204
FORD,
  Archibald, 64
  Joseph, 64, 66
  Polly Warfield, 209
FOREMAN,
  Ann Cavy Fowler, 67
  Eleanor, 67
  Elijah, 67
  Henry, 67
  Leonard, 67, 128
  Mary, 67
  Philip, 67

  Rachel, 67
FORNEY,
  Catherine, 139
FORRESTER,
  Alex, 67
  Cornelius, 67
  John, 67
  William, 67
FORSTER,
  Nathaniel, 67
FORSYTH,
  John, 67
FORSYTHE,
  Polly Warfield, 209
FOSH,
  James, 67
FOSTER,
  William, 67
FOU,
  John, 69
  Thomas, 69
FOUNTAIN,
  Peter, 68
FOWLER,
  Achsah, 69
  Daniel, 68
  Elizabeth, 24
  Hannah, 69
  John, 69
  Jonathan, 64
  Joseph, 69
  Jubb, 69
  Lemuel, 67
  Mary Foreman, 67
  Priscilla, 69
  Samuel, 69
  Sarah, 152
  Thomas, 69
  William, 69
FOX,
  Anthony, 69
  Charles, 60, 69, 135, 168
  Edward, 69
  John, 69
FRANCEWAY,
  John, 70
FRANCIS,
  Alexander, 64
  Lewis, 70
FRANKLIN,
  Ann, 10, 70
  Benjamin, 10, 70
  Elizabeth, 79, 180

Jacob, 70
John, 10, 70
Kitty, 97
Mary, 70
Robert, 79
Samuel, 10, 70
Thomas, 10, 70, 180
William, 64, 70
FRASER,
  James, 70
FRAZIER,
  James, 70
  John, 70, 158
  Joseph, 70
  William, 68, 70
FREELAND,
  James, 70
FRENCH,
  Benjamin, 71
  John, 68
  Otho, 71
  William, 71
FREWEN,
  Richard, 196
FREWN,
  Richard, 68
FRISBY,
  Sarah, 18
FRIVEY,
  Thomas, 195
FROST,
  James, 71
  John, 71
  William, 71
FRY,
  William, 71
FULFORD,
  Capt., 44, 58, 62, 96, 128, 187
  John, 13, 16, 21, 22, 27, 30, 34, 35, 36, 38, 65, 66, 71, 89, 113, 114, 115, 116, 119, 138, 140, 141, 142, 144, 145, 155, 157, 163, 175, 184, 185, 186, 194, 201, 220, 227
FULK,
  Wooldrick C., 71

FULTON,
  William, 71
FUNER,
  Michael, 71
FURGANSON,
  David, 63

-G-
GAINER,
  Hugh, 196
  Robert, 71
GAITHER,
  Actions (Nackey), 73
  Agnes, 72, 74
  Amos, 71
  Anne, 72
  Anne R., 74
  Basil, 72
  Beal, 47
  Beale, 71, 72
  Benjamin, 72, 73, 74
  Catherine Ridgely, 165
  Edward, 60, 71, 72, 74, 127, 136, 151
  Eleanor, 71
  Elijah, 72, 73, 126
  Elizabeth, 22, 73, 74
  Ephraim, 72
  Evan, 72, 74
  Greenbury, 73, 74
  Henry, 64, 72
  James, 74
  Jeremiah, 72, 73
  John, 71, 72, 73, 74
  John Howard, 72, 112
  John Marriott, 74
  John Rogers, 72, 73
  Joseph, 72, 73
  Joshua, 73
  Juliette, 74
  Leah, 151
  Lilah, 104
  Lucy, 74
  Margaret Anne Dorsey, 50
  Margarey, 72

Mary, 71, 72, 206, 212, 225
Patience, 106
Rachel, 72, 74
Reason, 72
Rebecca, 73
Rezin, 73
Ruth, 73, 74, 208, 211
Samuel, 72, 73
Sarah, 72, 73, 210
Sarah Ridgely, 168
Sarah Warfield, 209
Seth, 73
Susanna, 214
Susannah, 72, 73
Thomas, 73
Vachel, 2, 9, 10, 40, 69, 72, 74, 136, 146
Vachel Marriott, 74
William, 73, 74
Zachariah, 72, 74
GALE,
  Edward, 74
GALLOWAY,
  Benjamin, 74, 88
  Elizabeth, 189
  Henrietta Maria Chew, 33
  John, 74
  Joseph, 64, 74
  Samuel, 74
GALLWAY,
  John, 74
GALVIN,
  John, 74
GALWITH,
  John, 75
  Jonas, 75
GALWOOD,
  John, 77
GAMBLE,
  William, 196
GAMBRILL,
  Joshua, 75
  Maria, 5, 6
  Mary Gaither, 71
GARDENER,
  William, 75
GARDINER,
  Alexander, 196
  Elizabeth, 75

252 INDEX

George, 75
James, 75
John, 64, 75
Mary, 75
Mary Dorsey, 54
Peter, 75
Richard, 64
Sarah, 75
Sarah Owens, 146
Sophia Gassaway, 76
William, 75
GARDNER,
George, 75
John, 75
Peter, 75
William, 75
GARRISH,
Francis, 196
GARY,
Deborah, 75
Everard, 75
Gideon, 75
Leonard, 75
Lloyd, 75
Mary, 75
GASSAWAY,
Ann, 75, 209
Berry, 76
Brice John, 75
Catherine, 75
Dinah Warfield, 207
Elizabeth, 75, 76
Elizabeth L., 76
George, 75
Hanson, 76
Henry, 64, 68, 75, 76, 196, 226
John, 76
Jon, 64
Louis, 76
Louisa, 76
Louisa Emily, 76
Mary, 75, 76
Mary Quynn, 159
Nicholas, 64, 75, 76, 113, 178, 196
Rachel, 178
Sarah, 75
Sarah Cotter, 76
Sophia, 76

Thomas, 76, 113
Thomas Jefferson, 76
GATES,
William, 64
GATEWOOD,
John, 77
GATWORTH,
Gabriel, 77
GEE,
George, 64
Joseph, 64, 77
GEOGHAN,
George, 135
GEOGHEGAN,
Anthony, 77, 196
Robert, 77
GEOHAGAN,
Denton, 183
GHISELIN,
Ann Robosson, 171
Reverdy, 171
GIBBONS,
Mary Gassaway, 75
GIBBS,
Mary, 34
Thomas, 77
GIBSON,
John, 228
GIDDINGS,
John, 77
GILBERT,
Joseph, 77
GILES,
Hannah Kitty, 31
John, 64
GILL,
Hugh, 68, 196
GILLIS,
Amelia, 50
GILLISS,
Amelia, 51
Betty, 48, 51
Elizabeth, 49
John, 77, 133
GIRD,
Eudocia Dorsey, 54
GIST,
Gen., 216
Mary Dorsey, 54
GIVENS,
John, 77
GLADMAN,
Michael, 77

GLASGOW,
Samuel, 64
GLASSNEY,
Patrick, 68
GLEESON,
Thomas, 27
GLOVER,
John, 77
Rachel Dorsey, 48
Richard, 77
William, 77
GODDARD,
John, 64
GODFREY,
Samuel, 77
GODMAN,
Brutus, 78
Cassius, 78
Francis, 78
John Davidson, 78
Margaret, 78
Robert, 78
Samuel, 78, 113, 196
Stella, 78
Thomas Jefferson, 78
GOFF,
Richard, 196
GOLDER,
Archibald, 78
Elizabeth Howard, 100
George, 78
Henrietta, 78
John, 78
Robert, 78
Sarah, 78
GOLDSBOROUGH,
Achsah Worthington, 230
Henry, 183
John, 68
Susan, 183
GOLDSBURY,
Charles, 64
GOLDSMITH,
William, 78
GOLDWAIT,
Mary Dorsey, 51
GOLLICON,
John, 78
GOLLIER,
John, 196

GOOD,
　John, 78
GOODWIN,
　Richard R., 152
GOORE,
　Dorcas, 41
GORDON,
　Francis, 78
　John, 78
　Thomas, 16, 78,
　　131, 187, 224
　William, 163
GORE,
　George, 78
GOSNELL,
　Samuel, 64
GOSSAGE,
　Thomas, 64
GOTT,
　Elizabeth, 79
　Ezekiel, 79
　Joseph, 79
　Richard, 79
　Rispa, 79
GOVANE,
　Mary, 98
GRABLE,
　Mary, 58
GRAHAM,
　Thomas, 79
GRAHAME,
　James, 79
GRAINGER,
　Thomas, 79, 204
GRAITWOOD,
　John, 79
GRAMES,
　John, 79
GRAMLICK,
　Jacob, 79
GRANT,
　Daniel, 79
　William, 79
GRASON,
　Thomas, 158
GRAVEL,
　Benjamin, 79
GRAVELL,
　Benjamin, 79
GRAVELS,
　Benjamin, 79
GRAVES,
　William, 80
GRAY,
　Benjamin, 64, 79

　Elizabeth, 39, 80
　George, 80
　Hellen, 39
　Jacob, 64
　James, 196
　John, 80, 87, 93,
　　135, 136, 139,
　　169, 177, 227
　John Nelson, 80
　Joseph, 80
　Joshua, 80, 135
　Mary, 80
　Richard, 80
　Robert, 68, 196
　Zachariah, 80
GREEN,
　Amos, 64
　Elijah, 80
　Elizabeth, 80
　Jacob, 80
　John, 64, 80
　Lancelot, 80, 177
　Mary Harwood, 90
　Mary Selby, 177
　Michael, 80
　Richard, 64, 80
　Samuel, 157
　Sarah, 80
　William, 64, 80
GREENBURY,
　Randall, 80
GREENUP,
　Samuel, 81
GREENWALT,
　James, 64
GREENWELL,
　John, 81
GREFFIS,
　Hugh, 81
　Littleton, 81
GREGORY,
　Robert, 196
GREYER,
　Lawrence, 81
GRIEST,
　Isaac, 81
GRIFFIN,
　Frederick, 81
　Henry, 81, 135
　John, 64
　Mack, 64
　Nathan, 64, 81
GRIFFIS,
　Elizabeth, 81
　Joseph, 81

　Littleton, 81
　William, 81
GRIFFISH,
　Hugh, 81
GRIFFITH,
　Amelia Ridgely
　　Warfield, 168
　Ann Ridgely, 166
　Anne, 167
　Benjamin, 190
　Catherine, 230,
　　231
　Catherine
　　Warfield, 207
　Charles Greenbury,
　　81
　Dennis, 81
　Dinah, 75
　Elizabeth Ridgely,
　　166, 168
　George, 196
　Henry, 81
　James, 64
　John, 82
　Joshua, 82
　Orlando, 81
　Priscilla Ridgely,
　　168
　Remus, 168
　Sarah, 53, 54,
　　207, 208, 213
　W., 82
GRIFFITHS,
　David, 82
GRIM,
　Francis, 82
GRIMES,
　Nathaniel, 82
　Stephen, 82
　William, 82, 204
GRIMMEL,
　Thomas, 82
GRINALL,
　Thomas, 82
GRINNEL,
　Thomas, 82
GRINNOL,
　Thomas, 82
GUESS,
　Basil, 82
GULDHALL,
　Gilbert, 231
GUMMY,
　Peter, 68

INDEX

GUNDUN,
  Benjamin, 82
GWINN,
  Achsah Dorsey, 48
  John, 196

-H-

HACKETT,
  John, 82
HADD,
  John, 68
HADDER,
  Nehemiah, 64
HADEN,
  George, 82
HAGAN,
  Andrew, 68
HAGAR,
  John, 82
HAGER,
  John, 82
HAISLIP,
  John B., 64
  William, 83, 131
HAISLUP,
  William, 83
HALEY,
  Caleb, 83
  Elizabeth, 83
HALFPENNY,
  Mark, 83
HALL,
  Achsah Warfield, 208
  Ann Anderson, 2
  Col., 3, 134, 216
  Daniel, 106
  Edward, 83, 140
  Elisha, 64, 83
  Eliza, 83
  Elizabeth, 50, 51, 106
  Elizabeth Dorsey, 55
  Elizabeth Lansdale, 117
  Hannah Jacob, 107
  Henrietta Harwood Cowan, 90
  Henry, 25, 83, 135, 140, 211,
  230, 231
  J. Carvil, 24, 79, 82, 213
  Jane, 83
  John, 83, 84, 86, 106
  Joseph, 83
  Josias C., 12, 86, 130, 137, 138, 139, 148, 150, 170, 173, 210
  Josias Carvil, 68, 84, 89, 93, 121, 226
  Margaret, 90
  Margaret Harwood, 90
  Margarey Howard, 100
  Martha, 100
  Mary Dorsey, 50
  Matilda Dorsey, 53
  Nathaniel, 84
  Osborn S., 83
  Rachel S., 83
  Richard, 64, 84, 106
  Richard H., 83
  Sarah, 89, 106
  Thomas H., 83
  Thomas Henry, 84, 113, 140
  Thomas W., 83
  William, 68, 84, 195
HALLER,
  Dorcas Howard, 99
HAMELTON,
  John, 84
HAMILTON,
  George, 196
  Janet, 199
  John, 84
  John G., 84
  Margaret, 174
  Samuel, 64
  William, 64
HAMMNOND,
  Matthias, 169
HAMMOND,
  Andrew, 84
  Ann, 85, 86
  Anne, 85
  Ariana, 85
  Arianna, 86
  Beale, 84
  Capt., 101, 135
  Catherine Gassaway, 75
  Charles, 84, 85, 86, 126, 135
  Denton, 86, 138
  Edward, 64
  Elizabeth, 85, 86
  George, 85, 86, 135, 136
  George Washington, 86
  Greenbury, 85
  Hannah, 85, 98, 221
  Harriet, 86
  Harriet Dorsey, 50
  Henry, 86
  James, 27
  John, 80, 85, 86, 135, 177
  Lawrence, 85, 86
  Lloyd Thomas, 86
  Mary, 50, 85, 86
  Mary Ann, 86
  Matilda, 86
  Matthias, 85, 86, 177
  Nathan, 85, 86
  Nathaniel, 21
  Nehemiah, 86
  Philip, 21, 84, 85, 86, 200
  Philip Greenbury, 86
  Rachel, 85
  Rebecca, 48, 86
  Rezin, 85, 86, 101, 130, 177
  Sarah, 85
  Thomas, 86, 129, 133
  Thomas Hughes, 86
  Walter Charles, 86
  William, 85, 86, 135
  Worthington, 86
HAMPTON,
  Catherine G., 104
  William, 87
HANASY,
  Edward, 93

INDEX

HANCOCK,
  Absalom, 87
  Anne, 87
  Francis, 87
  John, 65
  Stephen, 87
  William, 87, 135
HAND,
  Jane Ridgely, 168
HANDLEN,
  John, 87
HANDLIN,
  John, 204
HANDS,
  Achsah, 87
  Catherine, 87
  Ephraim, 87
  John, 87
  Lancelot, 87
  Margaret, 87
  Mary, 87
  Nicholas, 87
  Sarah, 87
  William, 87
HANNAH,
  Nicholas, 87
HANNEN,
  Thomas, 87
HANS,
  William, 87
HANSLAP,
  Henry, 87, 230, 231
HANSON,
  Alexander Contee, 87
  Elizabeth Ray, 162
  Isaac, 87
  John, 87
  Priscilla Dorsey, 49
  Rebecca, 171
  Robert, 64
  Samuel, 64
HANSPAN,
  John Codlep, 87
  John Cutlip, 87
HARDE,
  Isaac, 19
HARDEN,
  Nicholas, 88
HARDESTY,
  Agnes, 88

  Eleanor Whittington, 224
  Elias, 88
  Elizabeth, 88
  Harriet, 88
  Henry, 88
  John, 88
  Mary, 88
  Richard, 88
  William, 224
HARDING,
  Daniel, 196
  Robert, 88
HARLEY,
  Jon, 88
HARLING,
  Cornelius, 27
HARN,
  John, 88
HARNSBURY,
  Nathaniel Robert, 88
HARPER,
  Catherine Carroll, 29
  John, 88
  Samuel, 64
HARPHAM,
  Robert, 68, 88
HARRINGTON,
  William, 88
HARRIS,
  Benton, 65
  Isaac, 87, 88
  Nathan, 88
  Richard, 68, 88, 196
  Robert, 89
  Thomas, 89, 196
  William, 89
  Zekiel, 89
HARRISON,
  Ann, 147
  Ann Shipley, 182
  Benjamin, 89, 135, 136, 141
  Clement, 89
  Dorothy, 33
  Eleanor, 89
  George, 89
  Horatio, 89
  John, 44, 89
  Joseph, 89
  Kinsey, 89
  Mary, 89

  Richard, 89, 90, 113, 136
  Samuel, 3, 4, 5, 6, 10, 12, 13, 14, 15, 16, 20, 21, 32, 33, 36, 38, 39, 40, 41, 42, 45, 46, 56, 57, 62, 65, 66, 67, 70, 75, 77, 79, 81, 82, 83, 84, 86, 89, 90, 92, 93, 94, 96, 102, 106, 109, 110, 112, 113, 116, 117, 118, 120, 122, 131, 137, 139, 141, 143, 144, 146, 148, 153, 159, 160, 161, 162, 171, 172, 173, 174, 175, 176, 177, 181, 183, 184, 186, 187, 188, 189, 191, 192, 195, 197, 199, 200, 201, 202, 205, 206, 213, 217, 218, 219, 220, 221, 222, 224, 227, 228, 232
  Walter, 90
HART,
  William, 64
HARTLEY,
  Col., 56
HARTMAN,
  Mary, 157
  Paul, 157
HARVEY,
  Anne, 100
  Carter, 90
  Charles, 90
HARWOOD,
  Ann Elizabeth, 90
  Anne, 90, 91
  Benjamin, 90, 98, 134, 135, 155
  Caroline, 91
  Edward, 91
  Eleanor, 91
  Elizabeth, 91, 177
  Elizabeth Ann, 90

INDEX

Frederick, 91
Henrietta, 90
Henry, 90
Henry Hall, 90
Henry S., 90
James, 90
John Thomas, 91
Joseph, 90
Louisa, 91
Lucinda, 91
Margaret, 90, 91
Maria, 90, 91
Mary, 90, 91, 192
Mary Elizabeth, 90
Nicholas, 90, 151
Osbern, 25
Osborn J., 90
Osborn Sprigg, 90
Priscilla, 90
Rachel Ann, 90
Richard, 2, 3, 4, 6, 8, 9, 10, 11, 14, 17, 18, 19, 20, 24, 26, 30, 32, 34, 36, 40, 43, 44, 46, 58, 60, 61, 66, 69, 71, 77, 79, 80, 83, 84, 90, 91, 92, 96, 98, 102, 103, 104, 105, 106, 107, 110, 111, 112, 113, 114, 115, 116, 118, 119, 120, 121, 123, 129, 131, 135, 136, 141, 142, 149, 151, 152, 153, 155, 157, 158, 159, 160, 161, 162, 163, 165, 169, 170, 173, 174, 175, 176, 177, 178, 183, 185, 186, 187, 188, 189, 190, 191, 192, 194, 195, 197, 202, 203, 204, 206, 214, 215, 216, 217, 218, 219, 221, 222, 223, 225, 226, 231
Richard Hall, 90
Sarah Ann, 90
Thomas, 1, 4, 8, 14, 17, 24, 25, 28, 32, 34, 37, 38, 39, 40, 41, 44, 56, 59, 60, 63, 64, 70, 75, 79, 84, 90, 91, 95, 96, 97, 113, 117, 118, 121, 124, 131, 143, 146, 148, 151, 153, 154, 158, 161, 164, 175, 177, 178, 180, 181, 184, 187, 189, 193, 195, 197, 206, 215, 216, 219, 220, 221, 232
Thomas Richard Sprigg, 90
William, 91, 136, 151
HASLUP,
  Martha Sappington, 174
HATFIELD,
  Edward, 196
HATHARLY,
  Nathan, 92
HATHERLY,
  Benjamin, 91, 92
  John, 91
  Nathan, 92
HATTON,
  James, 27
  William, 92
HAVERS,
  John, 92
HAWARD,
  James, 135
HAWK,
  Machl, 92
HAWKER,
  Robert, 92
HAWKES,
  Robert, 92
HAWKINS,
  Caleb, 92
  Charles, 92
  Elizabeth Dorsey, 54
  John, 92
  Juliet Dorsey, 55
  Martha, 85
  Matthew, 85
  Nicholas, 92
  Priscilla, 92
  Rebecca, 54, 92
  Rezin, 92
  Ruth, 92
  Thomas, 92
  William, 92
HAYCROFT,
  William, 92
HAYNES,
  Richard, 92
HAYS,
  John, 68
  William, 61
HAYWOOD,
  Thomas, 92
HAZEL,
  Caleb, 93
HAZELIP,
  John, 92
  William, 92
HAZEN,
  Col., 126
  Moses, 113
HAZIE,
  Caleb, 136
HAZLE,
  Caleb, 93
HEADWOOD,
  John, 93
HEARN,
  Charles, 93
  Edward, 93
  Michal, 93
HEATH,
  William, 93, 135
HEBB,
  Mary Howard, 99
HEDGE,
  William, 68, 196
HEINS,
  Jacob, 93
HEITLAND,
  Henry, 68
HELLAM,
  Thomas, 196
HELTENHEAD,
  John, 68

INDEX

HENCOCK,
  Stephen, 93
  William, 93
HENDERSON,
  Anne, 78
  Isaac, 65
HENDREN,
  Ariana Ijams, 103
HENDRICKSON,
  James, 93
HENNESSY,
  Edward, 93
  James, 93
HENNIS,
  Joseph, 196
HENRIGHT,
  John, 93
HENRY,
  Adam, 93
  Patrick, 213
HENSHAW,
  Charles, 93, 94
  James, 94
HENSLEY,
  Edward, 93
HENWARD,
  Charles, 94
  William, 94
HENWOOD,
  Charles, 94
  William, 94
HERN,
  Charles, 93
HERNDEN,
  Elizabeth Ijams, 104
HEWITT,
  Thomas, 94
HICKEY,
  Francis, 64
  Leonard, 64
  Thomas, 94, 196
HIGGINBOTHAM,
  Mary, 100
HIGGINS,
  Amelia Warfield, 211
  James, 94
  John, 94
  Joseph, 94
  Patrick, 94
HILGER,
  Sophia Robinson, 170

HILL,
  Abel, 94, 136
  Abell, 135
  George, 94
  Henrietta Margaret, 144
  Henry D., 94
  John, 94
  Joseph, 94
  Priscilla, 49, 54
  Richard, 95
  Thomas, 95
HILLEN,
  William, 27
HILLIARY,
  Thomas, 95
HILLS,
  Eudocia Dorsey Gird, 54
HILLUM,
  Thomas, 95
HILTON,
  John, 83
HIND,
  Isaac, 95
HINDES,
  Jacob, 68
HINER,
  Nichols, 68
HINES,
  Elizabeth Burgess, 24
HINKS,
  Edward, 95
HINTON,
  Lovedy, 95
  Lovely, 95
HIPSLEY,
  Charles, 95
  Joshua, 95
HITCHCOCK,
  Catharine, 232
HITCHOCK,
  Elizabeth, 232
  James C., 232
HOBBS,
  Eliza Dorsey Norris, 54
  Henry Cornelius, 95
  Honor Burgess, 23
  John, 26, 95, 110
  John Henry, 95
  Joseph, 95
  Lydia Warfield, 211

  Mary Warfield, 208
  Nicholas, 95
  Noah, 95
  Peter, 96
  Rachel Warfield, 209
  Susannah, 211
  Thomas, 96
  William, 96
HOBS,
  John, 95
HODGES,
  Elizabeth Jennings, 108
  John, 68, 196
  William, 96
HODGSKIN,
  Thomas Brooke, 113
HOHARO,
  William, 96
HOHNE,
  Christopher, 96
HOLES,
  Thomas, 68
HOLLAND,
  Ann, 173
  Anthony, 96
  Delilah Sands, 173
  Edward, 96
  Isaac, 96, 173
  Mary, 96, 209
  Mary Ann, 170
  Thomas, 96
  William, 96
HOLLIDAY,
  Benoni, 96
  Isaac, 68
  John, 96
  William, 96
HOLLYDYOAK,
  Ann, 97
  John, 97
HOLMES,
  B., 97
  William, 97
HOLSON,
  John, 97
HOOD,
  Benjamin, 97, 135
  Caroline Dorsey Wheeler, 54
  Edward, 97
  Elizabeth, 133
  Henry B., 97

INDEX

James, 97
John, 97, 196
Kitty, 97
Leah, 97
Letitia, 97
Louisa Dorsey, 54
Rachel, 97
Robert, 98
Sarah, 97
Sarah S. Howard, 98
HOOFMAN,
  Andrew, 98
HOOPER,
  Abraham, 98
  John, 56
  Mary, 56
  Mary Ridgely, 165
HOOPMAN,
  Andrew, 98
HOPKINS,
  Anna Maria Snowden, 188
  Elisha, 98
  Gerrard, 195
  Hannah Hammond, 85
  Joseph R., 188
  Margaret Drury, 57
  Philip, 98
  Phillip Hammond, 112
  Rezin, 164
  Richard, 98
  Thomas, 154
HOPPER,
  John, 98
  Susanna, 222
HORN,
  Thomas, 98
HORNE,
  Mary Ridgely, 166
HORRELL,
  Sophie Weems, 219
HOUGHTON,
  John, 98
HOW,
  William, 68
HOWARD,
  Absolum, 99

Achsah, 99
Anna, 101
Anna M., 100
Anne, 98, 99, 100, 204
Anne Slade, 99
Beale, 100
Benjamin, 95, 98, 100
Brice, 23, 98, 99, 101, 113, 135, 144, 182
Brice Worthington, 98
Bruce, 98
Brutus, 99
Charles, 101
Charles Wallace, 98, 135
Cincinnati, 99
Cornelia V., 101
Cornelius, 98, 99, 101
Deborah, 100
Denune, 98, 99, 101
Don, 99
Dorcas, 99
Eleanor, 100
Elisha, 99
Elizabeth, 99, 100, 101, 105
Ephraim, 99, 115, 135
George, 98, 99
Hannah Dorsey, 106, 107
Harriet, 98
Harriet Burgess Watkins, 24
Harvey, 99
Henry, 99, 100, 101
Henry Hall, 100
Honor, 100
Infant boy, 99
J. B., 99
James, 99, 122
James Govane, 98, 99
Jemina, 100
Jeremiah Brice, 98
John, 10, 98, 99, 100, 204

John Beale, 99
Joseph, 99, 100, 101, 186
Joshua, 100
Katherine, 81
Kindsey, 101
Kitty, 100
Louisa Harvey, 100
Margaret, 98, 99, 100
Margarey, 100
Martha, 100
Mary, 42, 99, 100, 101
Mary Howard, 101
Nancy, 39, 101
Patience, 100
Peregrine, 64
Philip, 100
Rachel, 100, 101, 210
Rebbecca Boone, 99
Rebecca, 101
Rebecca Dorcas, 99
Ruth, 100
Ruth Dorsey, 49
Samuel, 100
Samuel Harvey, 100, 135, 140, 144
Sarah, 71, 72, 99, 100, 168
Sarah S., 98
Selby, 101
Susan, 100
Susanna, 100
Thomas Cornelius, 101, 135
Thomas Henry, 101
Thomas Worthington, 98, 101
Vachel, 98, 99, 101
Vachel Denton, 101
William, 99, 100, 101
William Cornelius, 98
HOWELL,
  John, 68
  Mary, 164
HUDDLESTON,
  Thomas, 196

HUDSON,
  Edward, 101
  Robert, 101, 135
HUGH,
  Gabriel, 58
  Miles, 58
HUGHES,
  Frances, 53
  James, 101
  Margaret, 86
  Mary, 98
HUGHS,
  John, 101
  Michael, 101
HULL,
  Nathan, 68
  William, 196
HULMS,
  Susanna, 11
HUMPHREYS,
  William, 101
HUMPHRIES,
  James, 101
  Mary Darby, 41
HUNT,
  Charles, 101
HUNTER,
  James, 102
HUSE,
  Samuel, 102
HUTTON,
  Henry, 102
  James, 102
  Joseph, 102
  Lancelot, 64
  William, 27
HYATT,
  Ely, 102
HYDE,
  Col., 7, 19, 30,
    71, 73, 105,
    107, 109, 118,
    191
  Colonel, 151,
    157, 217, 227
  Elizabeth, 102
  John, 102
  Thomas, 102
  William, 16,
    102, 113
HYNES,
  Isaac, 196
  Jacob, 102

-I-
IGLEHART,
  James, 40, 103,
    159
  Matilda Davidson,
    42
  Rachel Ann
    Harwood, 90
IIAMS,
  John, 103
  Plummer, 104
  Thomas, 104
  William, 104
IJAMS,
  Ann, 104, 192
  Anne, 57, 103,
    104, 105
  Ariana, 103
  Artridge, 103,
    105
  Basil Gaither,
    104
  Beale, 103
  Brice, 103
  Burgess, 104
  Comfort, 105
  Denton, 103
  Elizabeth, 103,
    104, 105
  Frederick, 105
  George, 103, 105
  Isaac, 103, 105
  Jacob, 103
  Jane, 103
  John, 28, 64,
    103, 104, 105,
    136, 153, 190,
    222
  John Frederick,
    103
  John Waters, 103
  Joseph, 104
  Joseph Howard,
    105
  Margaret, 104
  Mary, 103, 104,
    105, 213
  Mary Ijams, 103
  Nancy, 104
  Nicholas W., 103
  Pearson, 104
  Plummer, 57, 103,
    104
  Rachel, 105
  Rebecca, 103,
    104, 105
  Richard, 104
  Richard D., 105
  Ruth, 104
  Sarah, 105
  Thomas, 103, 104,
    105
  Thomas Plummer,
    103
  Vachel, 103, 104
  William, 103, 104,
    105
  William Howard,
    105
  Wilson, 104
INMON,
  Joshua, 105
IRE,
  Frederick, 105
IRELAND,
  Clementine, 55
  Henry, 105
  John, 27
ISAAC,
  James, 105
ISAACS,
  Isaac, 68
ISLECK,
  Pascho, 105
  Pasco, 105
ISRAEL,
  Amelia, 76
  Basil, 105
  Bela, 105
  Elizabeth Burgess,
    23
  Robert, 105
ISREAL,
  Basil, 135
IVERY,
  Charles, 106
IVORY,
  Charles, 106
  Patrick, 64

-J-
JACK,
  James, 204
JACKS,
  Richard, 196
JACKSON,
  Ann, 106
  Anthony, 68, 106
  Elmer M., 164
  Rengard, 106

INDEX

Robert, 106
JACOB,
  Anne, 106, 107
  David Love, 106
  Dorsey, 106, 107
  Elizabeth, 86, 106, 107
  Ezekiel, 106
  Hannah, 107
  John, 106, 107
  Joseph, 106, 107
  Lum, 107
  Priscilla, 106
  Rachel, 72, 107
  Richard, 106, 107
  Samuel, 107, 136, 199
  Sarah, 73, 107
  Shadrach, 107
  Susannah, 107
  William, 107
  Zachariah, 107, 136
  Zachary, 107
JACOBS,
  Joseph, 106, 107
  Robinson, 196
  Samuel, 107
  Zachariah, 64, 107
JALLOME,
  John, 204
JAMES,
  Dinah Warfield, 208
  Francis, 68, 196
  William, 68, 107
JAMESON,
  Adam, 68
JANQUARY,
  Abraham, 107, 195
JARROTT,
  James, 68
JARVIS,
  Jacob, 107
  John, 108
JEAN,
  Thomas, 108
  William, 108
JEE,
  Joseph, 77, 108
JEFFERSON,
  Edward, 108

JENIFER,
  Elizabeth, 192
JENISON,
  John, 109
JENKINS,
  Isaac, 64
  John, 108
  Joseph, 64, 68, 196
  Richard, 108
  Thomas, 108
  William, 108
JENNINGS,
  Ann, 30
  Anne, 108, 110
  Daniel, 108
  Edmond, 108
  Elizabeth, 108
  George, 108
  Horatio, 108
  Horner, 108
  John, 108
  Juliana, 108
  Julianna, 18
  Thomas, 108
  William, 108
JERVIS,
  John, 108
JESSOP,
  Thomas, 68
JESUP,
  Thomas, 108
JIMSON,
  John, 109
JOHNS,
  John, 109
  Kinsey, 109
  Sarah Weems, 218
JOHNSON,
  Abraham, 196
  Archibald, 64
  Benedict, 27, 109
  Catherine Worthington, 230
  Dorcas, 110
  Elijah, 109
  Elizabeth, 110
  Elizabeth Dorsey, 52
  George, 109
  Henry, 109
  Horatio, 109, 113, 135
  James, 109, 110
  John, 109

  Jonathan, 109
  Joseph, 109, 196
  Joshua, 110
  Katherine, 170
  Lancelot, 25
  Mary, 104
  Miles, 68, 196
  Nancy, 25
  O'Neal, 109
  Rebecca, 110
  Rebecca Johnson, 110
  Richard, 109
  Robert, 109
  Sarah Cromwell, 39
  Thomas, 3, 109, 110
  Thomas Jennings, 110
  William, 110
JOHNSTON,
  John, 68
JOICE,
  James, 110
  Richard, 110
  William, 110
JONES,
  Benjamin, 110
  David, 110
  Elizabeth Cromwell, 39
  Emily Pinckney, 153
  Hanbury, 110
  Henry, 111
  Hugh, 111
  Isaac, 64, 111
  Jacob, 111, 115, 116
  Jarson, 111
  Jason, 111
  Jeremiah, 111
  John, 111
  John Paul, 111
  Jonathan, 112
  Joseph, 112
  Morgan, 112
  Nicholas, 112
  Philip, 27, 204
  Rebecca, 103, 105, 170
  Richard, 112
  Samuel, 112, 196
  Sarah, 116
  Thomas, 112

William, 111, 112
JORDAN,
  John, 112, 185
JOYCE,
  Caroline, 18
  Elijah, 110
  James, 110
  Richard, 110
  Sarah, 18
  William, 64, 110
JUDAH,
  William, 112

-K-
KAHOE,
  John, 113
KEATS,
  Thomas, 196
KEEN,
  Sally Lawrence, 118
KEITH,
  Andrew, 113
  Daniel, 113
  Duncan, 196
  John, 114
  Margarey, 100
KELLEY,
  James, 114
KELLIHER,
  Henry, 114
KELLIKER,
  Henry, 204
KELLY,
  James, 114
  Matthew, 68, 114, 204
  Richard, 196
KENDALL,
  John, 114
KENDELL,
  James, 114
KENLY,
  Priscilla Watkins, 215
KENNADY,
  John, 114
KENNEDY,
  Jane, 52
  Timothy, 114
KENNEY,
  Thomas, 196
KENNIDY,
  Peter, 114

KEPLER,
  Pamela Davidson, 42
KERBEY,
  John, 114
KERBY,
  Joshua, 114
KERNAL,
  William, 65
KERR,
  Charles Hammond, 114
  David, 114, 135
  Elfrida, 62
  James, 114
  John, 62
  John Leeds, 114
  Sophia, 114
KILLMAN,
  Lavena, 75
KILTY,
  Augustus, 114
  Catherine Quynn, 159
  Elizabeth, 114
  Ellen, 114
  George, 114
  John, 62, 114, 115, 118, 193
  Mary, 114
  Richard, 114
  William, 114, 115
KING,
  Adam, 64
  Isaac, 196
  John, 68, 115, 196
  Mary, 99, 115
  Michael, 115
  Philip, 64
  Thomas, 64, 115
  William, 68
KIRBEY, James, 115
KIRBY,
  James, 115
  John, 115
  Nathan, 116
  Robert, 116
  Sarah, 116
  William, 115, 116
KIRK,
  Thomas, 116
KIRTON,
  James, 116
KITTIN,

Edward, 116
KNAPP,
  Deborah, 160
KNIGHTON,
  Charity, 178
  Eleanor, 116
  Gassaway, 116
  John, 116
  Nicholas, 116
  Sarah, 226
  Thomas, 116
KNOCK,
  John, 116
KNOLES,
  Edward, 116
KNOX,
  John, 68, 196

-L-
LACKLAND,
  Joshua, 116
LAMB,
  Ann Norman, 143
  John, 116
  Joshua, 64
  Sarah, 231
LAMBETH,
  Henry, 116
  John, 116
  Stephen, 116
  William, 116
LAMBOTH,
  Henry, 116
LAMPLEY,
  Susanna, 18
LANE,
  Benjamin, 117
  Elizabeth, 117, 218
  Gabril, 117
  Harrison, 117
  John, 20, 117
  Joseph, 117
  Rebecca, 20
  Richard, 117
  Samuel, 5, 8, 16, 17, 20, 28, 37, 39, 40, 41, 45, 56, 57, 75, 79, 80, 94, 98, 101, 102, 113, 114, 115, 116, 117, 119, 120, 125, 127, 131, 134, 135, 144, 145,

INDEX

146, 148, 153, 156, 157, 165, 169, 172, 176, 180, 181, 184, 188, 205, 215, 218, 222, 229
  Thomas, 117
  Wilemina, 117
LANGLEY,
  Robert, 123
  William, 117
LANHAM,
  John, 64
  Richard, 64
LANNUM,
  William, 117
LANSDALE,
  Cornelia V. Howard, 101
  Eleanor, 117
  Elizabeth, 117
  Isaac, 117
  Isaac L., 117
  Martha, 117
  Thomas, 117
  Thomas Lancaster, 117
LAPPE,
  John, 118
LARAVIER,
  Jean, 118
LAREY,
  Daniel, 118
LARKIN,
  Thomas, 118
LARKINS,
  William, 118
LARSEN,
  Thomas Copper, 118
LATTIN,
  John, 118
  Mary, 118
  Plummer, 118
  Thomas, 118
LAUGHLIN,
  Thomas, 118
LAURENCE,
  Richard, 118
LAVELY,
  Jacob, 68, 118
LAVEY,
  Mary, 4
LAVY,
  John, 118

LAWELL,
  Abraham, 92
LAWLER,
  David, 196
  John, 196
LAWRENCE,
  Caleb, 118, 119
  Carolina, 118
  Caroline, 119
  Charlotte Warfield, 210
  Hammond, 119
  Hammond Dorsey, 118
  John, 118, 119
  Larkin, 118, 119
  Levin, 118
  Mary, 49
  Mary Dorsey, 49
  Rebecca, 118, 119
  Richard, 119
  Sally, 118
  Sally Ann, 119
  Sarah, 119
  Sarah Dorsey, 48
LAWSON,
  James, 119
  Rebecca, 166
LAWTON,
  John, 119
LEADBOURN,
  George, 119
LEAKE,
  William, 68
LEAMON,
  William, 68
LEARY,
  Daniel, 68, 118, 196
  Michael, 196
  Michall, 68
LEASON,
  John, 119
LEATCH,
  James, 119
LEATHERBURY,
  Abel, 119
LEATHERWOOD,
  Ann, 119
  Mary, 119
  Priscilla, 119
  Samuel, 119
  Thomas, 119
LEAVLEY,
  Jacob, 196

LEDNUM,
  Mary, 226
LEE,
  John, 119
  Joseph, 119
  Lewis, 119
  Mary, 121
  Thomas Sim, 119
  William, 120
LEEK,
  Ann Warfield, 208
LEEKE,
  Anne, 120
  Henry, 64, 120
  Joseph, 120
  Nicholas, 120
LEEKS,
  Avis, 189
LEETH,
  Peter, 120
LEFRANK,
  Cesar, 120
LEGRAND,
  John, 120
LEIPER,
  Andrew, 120
LEMMON,
  Barney, 64
LENNOX,
  John, 196
LESTER,
  John, 196
  Memory A., 41
LETTON,
  Thomas, 120
LETZINGER,
  George, 120
LEVY,
  Samuel, 121
LEWIN,
  Samuel, 120
LEWIS,
  Howel, 204
  Jesse, 120
  Job, 120
  John, 120
  Jonathan, 121
  Keele, 121
  Richard, 27
  Thomas, 121
LICETY,
  John, 121
LIGHT,
  John, 121

INDEX

LIGHTFOOT,
  John, 121
LILLEY,
  William, 64
LILLIE,
  Robert, 121
LILLY,
  Anne, 77
LINCY,
  John, 68
LINDEY,
  John, 68
LINDSAY,
  Rachel Dorsey, 53
LINDSY,
  John, 121
LINSEY,
  John, 121
LINSTEAD,
  Susannah, 121
LINSTED,
  George W., 121
  John, 121
  Susannah, 121
  William, 121
LINTHICUM,
  Ann Robinson, 170
  Anne Edwards, 59
  Burton, 121
  Catherine Warfield, 212
  Elizabeth Beard, 11
  Francis, 121
  John, 60, 121, 136
  Joseph, 121
  Mary, 60
  Rachel, 170
  Richard, 121
  Thomas, 122
  Thomas Tro, 122
  Tro, 121
LITCHFIELD,
  William, 122
LITTELL,
  Joseph, 122
LITTLE,
  James, 122
LITZINGER,
  Henry, 35
LLOYD,
  Edward, 122, 130

Henrietta Maria, 33
  Henry, 122
LOGEY,
  James, 122
LOGIE,
  James, 196
LOLLAR,
  Michael, 64
LORAH,
  John, 122
LOVITT,
  William, 122
LOW,
  Joseph, 122
LOWERY,
  Charles, 122
LOWREY,
  Margaret, 146
LOWRY,
  Margaret Owens, 146
LOWTHER,
  Daniel, 122
LUCAS,
  John, 68, 122, 196
  Rachel, 122, 177
  William, 64
LUCKETT,
  David, 64
  Samuel, 64
LUND,
  William, 123
LUPTON,
  George, 123
LUSBY,
  Ann, 123
  Baldwin, 113, 123
  Catherine, 60, 165
  Catherine Edwards, 59
  Deborah, 123
  Debra, 123
  Edward, 123
  Elizabeth, 123
  Henry, 123
  James, 123
  John, 123
  Mary Rawlings, 160, 161
  Peggy, 123
  Polly, 123
  Rebecca Beard, 11

  Robert, 123
  Samuel, 123
  Susannah, 123
  Vincent, 123
  William, 123
LUTHALL,
  Anne Marie, 42
LUTRELL,
  Anne Marie, 42
LUX,
  Robert, 123
LUZBY,
  Baldwin, 123
  Robert, 123
LYBRANT,
  Christian, 123
LYNCH,
  Robert, 68
  William, 65

-M-

MCADAMS,
  John, 130
MCALLESTER,
  Joel, 196
MCALLISTER,
  Archibald, 64
MCAWAY,
  Stephen, 68
  Thomas, 68
MCCALL,
  William, 130
MACCALLEY,
  Anne, 80
MCCANN,
  Ann Penn, 150
MCCARTIN,
  William, 130
MACCAULEY,
  John, 124
  Nancy, 123
  Thomas, 124
MCCAULEY,
  Thomas, 124
MACCAULEY,
  Zachariah, 124
MCCAULEY,
  Zachariah, 124
MCCAWLEY,
  Thomas, 124
MACCDUBBIN,
  James, 159
MCCENEY,
  Benjamin, 124
  Edward, 124

INDEX

MACCENEY,
  Jacob, 124
MCCENEY,
  Jacob, 124
  Joseph, 88
MACCENEY,
  Zachariah, 124
MCCENEY,
  Zachariah, 124
MCCLAMROCK,
  Nancy Ijams
  Bolton, 104
MCCLANNAUGH,
  Nancy Ijams
  Bolton, 104
MCCLEN,
  Alexander, 130
MCCORMACK,
  Dennis, 27
  Thomas, 68, 130
MCCORMICK,
  Thomas, 196
MACCOY,
  John, 124
MCCOY,
  John, 64
MACCOY,
  William, 125
MACCUBBIN,
  Ann, 30, 167
  Ann Ridgely, 167
  Charles, 124
  Charlotte, 124
  Deborah, 48, 49
  Doris, 124
  Eleanor, 167
  Eleanor Ridgely, 167
  John H., 30
  John Henry, 108
  Joseph, 39, 93, 124, 135, 136, 171
  Mary Clare, 18, 30
  Moses, 124
  Nicholas, 12, 30, 70, 82, 113, 124, 135, 188
  Nicholas Zachariah, 124
  Sarah, 124
  Thomas H., 30

MCCULLOCK,
  Margaret, 19
MACDANIEL,
  Allen, 125
MCDANIEL,
  Ann Owens, 146
  Columbus, 125
  Stephen, 130
MCDARNELL,
  Joseph, 130
MACDONALD,
  Bartholomew, 125
MCDONALD,
  John, 130
  Joseph, 130
MCDOWELL,
  Hugh, 27, 204, 130
MACE,
  Thomas, 125
MCGILL,
  Helen Stockett, 192
MACGILL,
  James, 125
  Patrick, 125
  Sarah, 166
MCGINITY,
  Patrick, 196
MCGINN,
  Bernard, 21
MCGRILL,
  Edward, 130
MCGUIRE,
  Michael, 130
MCHENRY,
  Brice, 68
MCINTIRE,
  Robert, 102
  Robert H., 164
MCINTOSH,
  George, 68, 196, 130
MACKALL,
  John, 228
MACKBEE,
  Stephen, 125
MACKELFRESH,
  Arianna Hammond, 86
  Jane, 22, 23
MCKENNY,
  Lawrence, 197
MACKENZIE,
  Aaron, 125

MCKENZIE,
  Aaron, 125
MACKENZIE,
  Daniel, 125
  Michael, 125
MCKINLEY,
  James, 68, 130
MACKINZIE,
  Aaron, 125
MCKINZIE,
  Barbara, 192
MACKINZIE,
  Daniel, 125
  Michael, 125
MACKUBIN,
  James, 125
  Jo. Creagh, 125
  John Cray, 125
MCKUBIN,
  John Cray, 125
MACKUBIN,
  McCreagh, 125
  Richard, 125
MCLANE,
  John, 130
MCLAUGHLIN,
  Anne Ijams, 103
  Cornelius, 68, 131
MCLEOD,
  Hugh, 131
MCLOCHLIN,
  Cornelius, 64
MCMAHAN,
  Mathew, 204
MCMAHON,
  Elizabeth, 161
MACMANI,
  Nathaniel, 126
MCMEEKEN,
  William, 232
MCMILLAN,
  Hugh, 68
MCMULLAIN,
  Alexander, 131
MCMULLAN,
  Alexander, 204
MCNAMARA,
  Benjamin, 64
MACNAMARA,
  Darby, 126
MCNAMARA,
  Darby, 64, 126
  Nicholas, 131
MCNAUGHTON,
  Peter, 64

INDEX

MCNEALL,
  John, 196
MCNEAR,
  Thomas, 131
MCNEARE,
  Thomas, 131
MCNORTON,
  William, 131
MCPHERSON,
  Mary Weems, 218
MCSENEY,
  Jacob, 124
MADDEN,
  Christopher,
  126, 196
MAGEE,
  Thomas, 126
MAGOWAN,
  Walter, 126
MAGRUDER,
  Ann, 201
  Christina, 230
  Henrietta
    Randall, 160
  Rebecca, 181
  Susanna, 207
MAGUIRE,
  Mary, 130
MALLER,
  Michael, 126
MALLONEE,
  Achsah Sewell,
  179
MALLOWS,
  Robert, 68, 196
MAN,
  James, 126
MANADIER,
  Benjamin, 126
MANNICA,
  Phillip, 126
MANSELL,
  George, 199
  Samuel, 126
MANTLE,
  Michael, 126
MARBURY,
  William, 6, 15,
  19, 31, 34, 44,
  54, 57, 77, 79,
  90, 94, 96,
  107, 109, 110,
  114, 120, 123,
  127, 129, 131,
  141, 148, 158,
  161, 169, 173,
  179, 186, 193,
  194, 196, 198,
  217, 221, 225
MARK,
  Robert, 127
MARKS,
  John, 68, 196
MARONEY,
  David, 204
MARONY,
  David, 127
MARR,
  James, 127
  John, 127
  Orrell, 127
  Orwell, 127
MARRIOTT,
  Anne Ridgely, 167
  Elizabeth, 127
  Henrietta
    Warfield, 213
  John, 127, 205
  Mary Warfield,
  179
  Rachel, 127, 210
  Richard, 127
  Ruth, 74, 127
  Silvanus, 127
  Thomas, 127
MARSH,
  Benjamin, 127
MARSHALL,
  Axey Penn, 150
  Edward, 68, 127
  Eleanor Wood, 228
  John, 127
  Stephen, 127
MARTIN,
  Nicholas, 127,
  158
  Peter, 128
  Sarah, 36
MASH,
  Richard, 128
MASON,
  Ann Maccubbin, 30
  Edward, 128
MASSENBACH,
  Felix Lewis, 128
MASTERSON,
  Philip, 27
MATHEWSON,
  Alexander, 128
MATHIAS,
  James, 128
MATTHEWS,
  John, 128
MATTOCKS,
  Charity, 128
  Charles, 128
  Jacob, 128
  Jonathan, 128
  Susannah, 128
MATTOX,
  Charles, 128
  Cornelius, 128
  Jacob, 128
  Rachael, 67
MAW,
  Edward, 128
  Elizabeth, 128
  William, 129
MAXWELL,
  Lidey Burgess
    Baxter, 23
  Richard, 129
MAY,
  George, 129
  Hannah, 129
  Henry, 129, 188
MAYHEW,
  Samuel, 129
MAYNARD,
  James P., 129
MAYO,
  George, 129
  Henrietta, 129
  Isaac, 129
  John, 129
  Joseph, 129
  Joshua, 129
  Sarah, 129
  Sarah Ann, 129
  Thomas, 17, 20,
  42, 61, 62, 82,
  84, 101, 107,
  108, 117, 127,
  128, 129, 130,
  137, 139, 173,
  181
MEAD,
  Horatio, 131
  Samuel, 131
MEDCALF,
  James, 131
  John, 131
  Richard, 64
  Robert, 64, 131

INDEX

Thomas, 131
William, 131
MEDCALFE,
  Robert, 131
MEDCLEF,
  William, 131
MEED,
  Joshua, 132
MEEK,
  Aron, 132
  James, 132
  John, 132
  Johns, 132
  Joseph, 132
  Wastal, 132
  Westal, 132
MEHENY,
  Florence, 132
MEIXSEL,
  Elizabeth
  Howard, 99
MELSON,
  Daniel, 132
  William, 132
MENCHON,
  Humphry, 132
MERCER,
  Andrew, 92
  Eliza Warfield, 206
  Francis, 132
  John, 22, 92, 132
  Susanna, 22
MERCIER,
  Andrew, 132
  Ruth, 132
  Weldon, 132
MERICAN,
  Edward, 197
MERIWEATHER,
  Eleanor, 133
  Elizabeth, 133
  Louisa, 133
  Nicholas, 133
  Polly, 133
  Reuben, 3, 5, 6, 7, 8, 12, 14, 15, 16, 20, 24, 26, 28, 36, 37, 38, 39, 43, 44, 45, 47, 49, 50, 51, 52, 53, 54, 57, 58, 59, 63, 65, 69, 71, 72,

74, 77, 79, 80, 82, 86, 89, 90, 91, 92, 93, 94, 95, 96, 97, 99, 100, 102, 108, 109, 111, 113, 114, 115, 119, 120, 121, 122, 123, 125, 126, 128, 129, 130, 132, 133, 137, 138, 139, 142, 143, 144, 147, 149, 152, 155, 156, 157, 160, 164, 165, 168, 172, 173, 177, 181, 182, 183, 186, 189, 190, 194, 198, 199, 202, 203, 207, 208, 209, 210, 211, 212, 222, 223, 227, 233
Sally, 133
Sarah, 133
Thomas Beall
  Dorsey, 133
MERRICK,
  Benjamin, 133
  Henry, 133
MERRIKEN,
  Ann, 133
  Elizabeth, 134
  Hugh, 133
  John, 133
  Joseph, 15, 107, 133, 218
  Joshua, 133
  Mary Duvall, 58
  Robert, 133
  Ruth, 106
  Sarah, 133, 134
  Sarah Gaither, 72
  Sarah Jacob, 107
  Sarah Talbott, 194
  Thomas, 133
  William, 134, 194
MERRIKIN,
  Hugh, 133
  Joseph, 133, 136
  Joshua, 133, 135, 136
  William, 134

MERRYMAN,
  Temperance, 194
MIDDLETON,
  Elizabeth, 115
  Gilbert, 1, 6, 13, 18, 26, 31, 33, 34, 35, 44, 57, 68, 69, 70, 78, 80, 83, 86, 87, 99, 101, 118, 121, 123, 124, 128, 129, 130, 134, 136, 137, 143, 148, 149, 160, 163, 164, 165, 174, 176, 183, 188, 195, 198, 201, 204, 220, 221, 227
  Gilberty, 79
  Joseph, 134, 158
  Sarah, 134
  William, 134
MIER,
  John, 134
MILDURPH,
  John, 134
MILES,
  John, 68, 134, 196
  Joshua, 134
  Samuel, 134
  Thomas, 134
  William, 135
MILLAR,
  James, 137
MILLARD,
  Thomas, 137
MILLER,
  Adam, 137
  Benjamin, 137
  John, 13, 137
  Nicholas, 29
  Orpha, 232
  Richard B., 9, 172, 184
  Sarah, 216
  Susanna, 222
  William, 137
MILLIHAN,
  Patrick, 64
MILLS,
  Achsah, 137
  Ann, 137
  Cornelius, 93, 137, 141, 169,

175, 183, 187
  Elizabeth, 137
  Frederick, 137
  John, 64
  Priscilla
    Harwood Weems,
    90
  Thomas, 137
  Zachariah, 137
MINITREE,
  Gifford, 137
MIRE,
  Frederick, 64
MITCHEL,
  Huriah, 137
MITCHELL,
  Capt., 66
  Mary Ann, 159
  Patrick, 137
  Richard, 159
  Robert, 138
MOALE,
  Anne Howard, 100
MOBBERLY,
  Rezin, 138
  Thomas, 138
MOCKABEE,
  Anne Slade
    Howard, 99
  Stephen, 125
MOCKBEE,
  Stephen, 125
MOCKEYBY,
  Stephen, 109
MOFFITT,
  Thomas, 138
MOLONY,
  John, 138
MONKS,
  Michael, 138
MONROE,
  Ann Wells, 220
  Daniel, 11, 64,
    101
MONTGOMERY,
  Alexander, 68
  Jane, 214
  Joan, 214
  Mary Ijams, 103
MOODY,
  Levy, 138
MOORE,
  John, 138
  Mathew, 196
  Peter, 138

Silvanus, 138
MOREE,
  James, 138
  Robert, 138
MORELAND,
  Richard, 138
MOREWARD,
  John, 138
MORFITT,
  George, 138
MORGAN,
  Elizabeth, 152
  John, 139
  Patrick, 139
  William, 27
MORISTON,
  Edward, 68
MORIWARD,
  John, 138
MORLEY,
  Joseph, 139
MORRIS,
  Sarah Howard, 99
  William, 68
MORRISON,
  George, 139
MORTEZ,
  David, 139
MORTON,
  Thomas, 135, 136,
    139
  Vecheld, 68
MOSS,
  Delilah, 139
  Nathan, 136, 139
  Rachel, 139
  Rachel Foreman,
    67
  Richard, 139
  Robert, 136, 139
  Samuel Skidmore,
    139
  Sarah, 139
  Thomas, 139
  Willoby, 139
MOXLEY,
  Ezekiel, 139
  Jacob, 139
  Nehemiah, 139
  William, 139
MOYSTON,
  Edward, 139
MUIR,
  Adam, 140
  John, 16, 140

MULIKIN,
  Thomas, 2
MULLIKEN,
  Ann D., 140
  Barruch, 140
  Basil D., 140
  Belt, 47, 140
  Benjamin Hall, 140
  Jeremiah, 140
  Kitty D., 140
  Margaret, 140
  Mary, 140
  Richard D., 140
  Rignal, 140
  Thomas, 140
MULLIKIN,
  Belt, 140
  Elizabeth Gaither,
    74
  Jeremiah, 140
  Margaret, 231
  Mary, 140
  Thomas, 74, 135,
    140
MUNDUS,
  Machael, 140
MUNRO,
  Daniel, 34, 35,
    108, 140, 159
MUNRO DANIEL,
  William, 108
MUNROE,
  Ann, 220
MURPHEY,
  John, 196
  Michael, 140
  Thomas, 196
MURPHY,
  Anthony, 140
  John, 68, 140
  Patrick, 68, 197
  Thomas, 68
  Timothy, 140
MURRAY,
  Alexander, 64
  Daniel, 141
  Dr., 19, 193
  James, 140, 141,
    195, 200
  Mary Dorsey, 49
  William, 70, 141
MURRY,
  John, 196
MUSE,
  Ann, 228

INDEX

Sophia Kerr, 114
MUSLER,
  Adam, 141
MUSSETTER,
  Ruth Ijams, 104
MUSTON,
  Richard, 68
MYERS,
  Jacob, 141
MYHAN,
  Denniss, 141

-N-

NABB,
  Joseph, 141
NAYLOR,
  Alexander, 64
  Nicholas, 64
NEAL,
  Thomas, 141
NEALE,
  James, 27
  John, 141
  Thomas, 64, 141
NEARY,
  John, 141
NEAVE,
  John, 141
NEIL,
  Daniel, 204
  Thomas, 141
NEILSON,
  Deborah Ridgely, 167
  Thomas, 204
NELSON,
  Richard, 197
  Sarah, 56
  Thomas, 141
NEVIN,
  William, 163
NEWBURN,
  Elizabeth Hammond, 86
NEWCOMB,
  Robert, 197
NEWMAN,
  Freeman, 142, 204
NEWTON,
  John, 142, 144
  Thomas, 197
NICHOLAS,
  Edward, 68

NICHOLASON,
  William, 142
NICHOLS,
  Easy, 142
  Rachel, 125
  Rachel Basford, 10
  William, 142
NICHOLSON,
  Anthony, 197
  Benjamin, 142
  Francis, 142
  Henry, 142
  James, 142
  John, 142
  Joseph, 142
  Mary, 142
  Nicholas, 142
  Stephen, 142
  William, 142
NIXON,
  William, 64
NOBLE,
  Elizabeth, 192
NOCK,
  Thomas, 142
NOLAND,
  Patrick, 64
  Thomas, 197
NORMAN,
  Ann, 143
  Benjamin, 136, 143
  Jane, 143
  John, 143
  Joseph, 143
  Nicholas, 143
  Rispah Randal, 143
  Thomas, 143
NORRIS,
  Eliza Dorsey, 54
  John, 143
  Philip, 197
  Richard, 143
  Thomas, 143
  Zachariah, 143
NORRISS,
  John, 143
NORTH,
  Thomas, 143
NORTHEY,
  Benjamin, 143
NORTON,
  David, 143

NORWOOD,
  Capt., 114
  Edward, 78, 109, 143, 195, 197, 205
  Elizabeth, 139
  Jemina Howard, 100
  Jeremiah, 143
  John, 135, 136, 144
  Mary, 143
  Mary Dorsey, 55
  Patience Howard, 100
  Samuel, 135
  Sarah, 109
NOWELL,
  Richard, 144
  William, 144
NOWLAND,
  James, 197
NOWRY,
  Anthony, 144
NUGENT,
  Patrick, 197
NUTLEY,
  Henry, 144
NUTON,
  John, 142, 144

-O-

O'BRIAN,
  Phillip, 144
O'CONNER,
  Michael, 144
  Patrick, 144
O'CONNOR,
  Dennis, 2, 197
  O'Neal, 2
O'DAVINSON,
  James, 43
ODELL,
  Sarah, 143
ODLE,
  Richard, 47, 144
O'DONALD,
  Robert, 204
O'DONALY,.
  Cornialus, 144
O'FARRELL,
  Michael, 27
OFFUTT,
  Elizabeth Warfield, 210

INDEX

OGDEN,
  James, 144
OGG,
  Rebecca, 7
OGLE,
  Ann, 144
  Benjamin, 144
  John, 145
  Mary, 144
  Samuel, 144
O'HARA,
  Dennis, 145
  James, 145
  John, 122
  William, 45
O'HARIO,
  Dennis, 145
O'HARO,
  William, 96
O'HARRA,
  James, 145
OLDHAM,
  Edward, 197
OLDNEY,
  John, 145
ONANN,
  Betsy Penn, 150
O'NEAL,
  Daniel, 145
O'NEIL,
  Hugh, 197
ONION,
  Charles, 145
  John, 145
O'QUIN,
  Richard, 145
O'QUINN,
  Daniel, 197
ORAM,
  Cooper, 197
  John, 197
  Nancy Ridgely, 168
  Rebecca Burgess, 23
  Samuel, 68, 197
ORBER,
  John, 145
ORME,
  Moses, 145
ORRICK,
  Mary, 167, 168
  Thomas, 136, 145
OSBAN,
  John, 65

OSBAND,
  Samuel, 146
OSBORNE,
  Leonard, 164
OWEN,
  Sarah, 124
OWENS,
  Agnes Gaither, 74
  Ann, 146
  Archibald, 146
  Artridge, 146
  Benjamin, 146
  Capt., 135
  Charles, 146
  Edward, 146
  Eliza, 146
  Elizabeth, 146
  Elizabeth Owens, 146
  Gassaway, 66
  Henry, 146
  Isaac, 146
  James, 146
  Jane, 146
  Jane Owens, 146
  John, 27, 146
  Joseph, 146
  Margaret, 146
  Martha, 146
  Mary, 146
  Nicholas, 146, 207
  Priscilla, 146
  Sarah, 146
  Thomas, 146
  William, 146
OWINGS,
  --, 146
  Caleb, 40, 67, 85, 112, 133, 136, 147, 197
  Carolina Lawrence, 118
  Henry, 147
  John, 64
  Joseph, 64
  Mary Warfield, 212
  Nathaniel, 136, 147
  Rebecca, 100
  Ruth Dorsey, 55
  Samuel, 64
  Sophia, 52, 55
  Sophia Dorsey, 48

OWLEY,
  Bethiah, 107

-P-

PACA,
  Gov., 214
  Henrietta Maria, 147
  Hester, 147
  John, 147
  John Philemon, 147
  William, 147
PAGE,
  John, 147, 197
  Richard, 147
PAINTER,
  Charles, 147
  Daniel, 147
PAISLEY,
  Elizabeth, 4
  Thomas, 148
PALMORNE,
  Benjamin, 147
PALMOUR,
  William, 147
PANACLIFT,
  John, 147
PARKER,
  Edward, 134
  George, 148
  Gerold, 68
  Gerrard, 148
  Jerrold, 197
  Jonathan, 148
  Josiah, 148
  Robert, 148
PARRATT,
  William, 148
PARRETT,
  William, 148
PARRISH,
  Edward, 197
PARRIT,
  Thomas, 148
PARROTT,
  Ann, 228
  John, 148
  Knighton, 148
  Mary, 148
  Thomas, 148
  William, 148
PARSLEY,
  Thomas, 148
PARSON,
  John, 148

INDEX

PARSONS,
  John, 148
  William, 148
PARTRIDGE,
  Samuel, 148
PATTAN,
  Thomas, 148
PATTEN,
  Thomas, 27
PATTERSON,
  Robert, 148, 197
PAYNE,
  Benjamin, 150
  John, 27
PEABODY,
  John, 149
PEACH,
  William, 68, 197
PEACOCK,
  Frances, 221
PEAK,
  Nathan, 149
PEAKE,
  Nathan, 64
PEALE,
  Albert Charles, 149
  Charles, 149
  Charles Willson, 149
  Elizabeth Digby, 149
  James, 64, 149
  Margaret Jane, 149
  St. George, 149
PEARCE,
  Daniel, 149
  Ezekiel, 64
  John, 64
  Joseph, 149
  Joshua, 64
  Walter, 149
  William, 149
PEARSON,
  John, 149
  Thomas, 149
PECKER,
  Capt., 139, 174
  Charles, 136, 150
  George, 136, 150
PEDEN,
  Henry C., 84, 111, 146, 164, 165, 174, 190, 201, 225, 231
PEGEGRAM,
  William, 150
PEIRPOINT,
  Charles, 153
PENDERGAST,
  Julia, 145
PENN,
  Ann, 150
  Axey, 150
  Benjamin, 150
  Betsy, 150
  Charles, 150
  Edward, 150
  Ephraim, 150
  Jacob, 150
  John, 64
  Joseph, 150
  Joshua, 150
  Mary, 150
  Noah, 150
  Peggy, 150
  Polly, 150
  Rachel, 150
  Rebecca, 150
  Richard, 150
  Sarah, 150
  Shadrick, 150
  Stephen, 64
  Zacheus, 150
PENNINGTON,
  Charles, 150
PERKINSON,
  John, 150
PERRY,
  Mary, 73
  Robert, 151
  William, 151
PETCOCK,
  Moses, 154
PETERS,
  William, 64
PETTERFER,
  William, 197
PHELPS,
  Ann Catherine, 152
  Anne, 151
  Archibald, 151
  Basil, 151
  Bazill, 151
  Benjamin, 64, 151
  Catherine, 152
  Edward Gaither, 151
  Elizabeth, 152
  Ezekiel, 151
  Geneva M., 151
  George, 152
  Isaiah, 151
  Isiah, 151
  Jacob, 152
  John, 151, 152
  Joseph, 151
  Joshua, 152
  Josiah, 152
  Julia, 152
  Margaret, 151, 152
  Mary, 152
  Mary Ann, 151
  Middleton, 151
  Nelson, 151
  Richard, 151, 152
  Robert, 152
  Ruth, 152
  Sarah, 151
  Trotter, 152
  Walter, 151, 152
  Walter Watkins, 151
  William, 152
  Wilson, 151
  Zachariah, 152
PHILIPS,
  Paul, 152
  Samuel, 152
PHILLIPS,
  Thomas, 52
PHILPOTT,
  Thomas, 153
PHIPPS,
  Ann, 153
  John Wilson, 153
  Mary Ann, 153
  Nathaniel, 153
  Nicholas, 153
  Randolph, 153
  Roger, 136, 153
  Thomas, 153
PHIPS,
  Benjamin, 153
  John, 153
  Nathaniel, 153
  Roger, 153
  Thomas, 153
PIBUS,
  John, 159
PIERCE,
  Aquila, 153

INDEX

Thomas, 204
PIERPOINT,
  Charles, 153
PIERPONT,
  Rebecca Hawkins, 54
  Sarah, 212
PIERSON,
  John, 204
PIKE,
  James, 68
  Jno., 68
PILLARD,
  William, 153
PINCKENY,
  Betsy, 153
PINCKNEY,
  Charles, 153
  Edward, 153
  Emily, 153
  Frederick, 153
  Henry, 153
  Isabelle, 153
  William, 153
PINDALL,
  Nicholas, 64
PINDEL,
  Samuel, 154
PINDELL,
  Elizabeth, 154
  Gassaway, 153, 154
  John, 153, 154
  Margaret, 154
  Nicholas, 153
  Philip, 154
  Samuel, 154
  Sarah Tillard, 199
  Thomas, 154
PINE,
  Frederick, 154, 204
PINKNEY,
  Mary Gassaway, 76
PINKSTON,
  Thomas, 154
PIPER,
  James, 154
PITCHFORD,
  Edward, 154
PITCOCK,
  Moses, 154
PITSLAND,
  Richard, 154
PITT,
  Ann, 63
PITTS,
  Thomas, 154
PLAIN,
  Jacob, 154
PLAISTER,
  Margaret, 203
PLANE,
  Catherine, 154
  Jacob, 154
PLATER,
  Elizabeth, 200
PLUMMER,
  Cupit, 154
  Elizabeth, 103, 104
  John, 142, 154
  Obed, 155
POFFENBERGER,
  Honor Dorsey, 49
POLAND,
  William, 155
POLK,
  Elizabeth Digby Peale, 149
  Robert, 149
POLTON,
  John, 155
POMAIROL,
  Antoine, 155
POOLE,
  Charles, 155
  James, 155
  Mathew, 155
  Peter, 155
  Richard, 155
  Samuel, 155
  Thomas, 155
POPE,
  James, 155
POPHAM,
  Benjamin, 155
  Capt., 113
  Samuel, 197
PORTER,
  Adam, 156
  Elizabeth Gassaway, 75
  James, 156
  John, 156
  Keziah, 182
  Peter, 156
  Richard, 156
  Thomas, 156
PORTIUS,
  Robert, 156
PORTLAND,
  James, 156
POTEE,
  Silvanus, 156
POTTER,
  William, 156
POTTS,
  Thomas, 197
POULAIN,
  Germain, 156
POULTON,
  Charles, 25
  Sarah, 25
POWELL,
  Edward, 156
  Henry, 156
  James, 156
  John, 157
  Joseph, 157
  Peter, 157
  William, 157
POWER,
  John, 157
POWERS,
  Stephen, 157
PRESTON,
  Francis, 157
PRICE,
  Benjamin, 64
  Daniel, 197
  Edward, 157
  Elizabeth, 76, 157
  Harriet, 157
  James, 227
  Letty, 157
  Mary, 157
  Sophia, 157
  Thomas, 102, 157
  Walter Lane, 157
  William, 157
PRICHARD,
  John, 157
PRIESTLY,
  Mary, 157
PRINTOR,
  Charles, 147
PRIOR,
  Mary, 133
PRITCHARD,
  Ann, 146
PRITCHETT,
  William, 157

INDEX

PROCTER,
  Richard, 64
PROCTOR,
  Joseph, 158
PROUT,
  John, 27
PROVERD,
  William, 158
PRUDDEN,
  Samuel, 158
PRYSE,
  Edward, 158
PRYSS,
  Thomas, 197
PUE,
  Harriet Hammond, 86
  Michael, 34, 158
PUMPHREY,
  Mary Ridgely, 168
  Mary Warfield, 212
  Sophia Ridgely, 168
  Susannah Jacob Bone, 107
PURCELL,
  William, 197
PURDELL,
  Robert, 158
PURDY,
  Alfred, 159
  Anne, 208, 211
  Edmond, 158
  Edward, 159
  Elizabeth, 203
  Henry, 159
  John, 64, 159
  Mary Ann, 159
  Samuel, 159
  Sarah, 159
  William, 159
PURNELL,
  Eleanor, 182
  Stephen, 197
  William, 159
PYBUS,
  John, 159

-Q-

QUANTRELL,
  Alexander, 30
QUANTRILE,
  Prettyman, 159

QUATRELL,
  Alexander, 30
QUAY,
  James, 64, 159
QUEEN,
  John, 197
QUINLAND,
  James, 197
QUINN,
  Allen, 159
  Daniel, 68
  Elizabeth, 159
  Joseph, 159
QUYNN,
  Allen, 76, 113, 114, 159
  Catherine, 114, 159
  Elizabeth, 159
  John, 159
  Joseph, 197
  Mary, 76, 159
  Sophia, 159
  William, 159

-R-

RAITT,
  Barbara, 86
RAMSAY,
  Capt., 145, 172
RAMSEY,
  Henry, 197
  Margaret Jane Peale, 149
  Nathaniuel, 149
RANDAL,
  Ruth, 143
RANDALL,
  Acquila, 160
  Alexander, 160
  Aquilla, 159, 160
  Barton, 160
  Brice, 160
  Christopher, 160
  Henrietta, 160
  John, 160
  Johnsey, 160
  Nathan, 160
  Richard, 160
  Thomas, 27, 204
RANDLE,
  Acquilla, 160
RANER,
  James, 160
  John, 160

RANKIN,
  George, 205
  Mary Bull, 205
RANOLS,
  Christopher, 163
RASH,
  George, 160
RATCLIFF,
  Joseph, 160
RATCLIFT,
  Charles, 160
RAWLINGS,
  Aaron, 136, 160, 161
  Anne, 160
  Eleanor, 123, 161
  Eliza, 161
  Elizabeth, 160
  Elizabeth W., 161
  Francis, 161
  Gassaway, 161
  Isaac, 161
  John, 160, 161
  Jonathan, 161
  Lurana, 161
  Mary, 160, 161
  Moses, 54, 160, 161
  Nathan, 160
  Rebecca, 160, 161
  Richard, 160, 161
  Samuel, 161
  Stephen, 161
  Susanna, 160, 161
  Thomas, 161
  William, 160, 161
RAWLINS,
  Isac, 27
  William, 27
RAY,
  Ann, 162
  Anne, 162
  Elizabeth, 162
  Elizabeth Warfield, 209
  Frances, 162
  Jesse, 161
  John, 135, 161, 162
  Joseph, 162
  Margaret, 162
  Mary, 162
  Matthew, 162
  Nicholas, 162
  Priscilla, 162

INDEX

Rebecca, 162
Richard, 162
Sarah, 162
Susannah, 181
William, 162
RAYLEY,
  Bennet, 27
READ,
  Francis, 162
READING,
  John, 68, 197
READMAN,
  Thomas, 68
REAR,
  William, 162
REB,
  Adam, 186
REDDEN,
  Daniel, 27, 204
REDMAN,
  Alice, 162
  Elisha, 27
  Thomas, 27
REED,
  Amelia, 42
  James, 162
  John, 162
  William, 163, 204
REEVES,
  Patience, 62
REID,
  James, 163
RENCHER,
  John Grant, 163
RENOLS,
  Christopher, 163
RESTON,
  Henry, 163
REWARK,
  James, 163
REYNOLDS,
  Allen, 163
  Benedict, 197
  Charles, 197
  Christopher, 163
  Goven, 163
  James, 64, 163
  John, 64, 163, 164
  Joseph, 164
  Lewis, 163
  Margaret, 164, 201
  Rebecca, 163

Richard, 197
Robert, 163, 164
Sarah, 163
Thomas, 163, 164
Tobias, 163
William, 164, 201
RHODES,
  John, 164
RICE,
  James, 204
RICH,
  Samuel, 164
RICHARDS,
  Anne, 108
  Mary, 25
  Paul, 25
  Peter, 164
  Robert, 164
RICHARDSON,
  Adam, 164
  Edward, 65
  George, 164
  Joseph, 164
  Philip, 165
  Robert, 68, 197
  William, 192, 210, 217
RICKETTS,
  John, 64
  Nicholas, 27, 165, 204
  Richard, 165
  Susanna, 175
  Thomas, 136, 165, 194, 225
  thomas, 225
  Vincent, 64
RICKORDS,
  John, 165
  William, 165
RID,
  James, 165
RIDGELY,
  ---, 165
  Absalom, 165
  Achsah, 167
  Achsah Dorsey, 54
  Actions (Nackey) Gaither, 73
  Amelia, 168
  Ann, 165, 166, 167
  Anne, 53, 98, 166, 167, 168, 174, 229, 230

Archibald, 166
Basil, 165, 168
Bazil, 64, 167
Caroline, 167
Catherine, 52, 54, 165
Charles, 59, 165, 166, 167, 168, 198
Charles Greenbury, 166, 168
Daniel, 167
David, 165
David G., 167
Deborah, 52, 167
Deborah Dorsey, 47
Dorothy, 166
Edward D., 167
Eleanor, 101, 167
Elizabeth, 55, 165, 166, 167, 168, 208, 229, 230
Elizabeth Dorsey, 47, 49
Frances, 165
Frederick, 166
Greenbury, 166, 167, 168
Henrietta, 167
Henry, 12, 24, 55, 79, 82, 83, 89, 113, 121, 130, 137, 138, 139, 148, 150, 165, 166, 167, 168, 170, 173, 213, 226
Jane, 168, 229
John, 165, 166, 167, 168
Joshua, 167
Lloyd, 167
Lydia, 166
Margaret, 165, 168
Mary, 165, 166, 168
Mary Davidge, 166
Matilda, 167
Matilda Chase, 31
Nancy, 168
Nicholas, 55, 135, 165, 166, 167, 168
Philemon Dorsey,

165, 166,
167, 168
Philemon Dorsey,
168
Polly, 167
Priscilla, 168
Rachel, 166,
167, 168
Rebecca, 166,
207, 209, 211,
212
Richard, 165,
166, 167, 168
Robert, 168
Ruth Dorsey, 52
Samuel, 168, 197
Sarah, 73, 166,
167, 168
Sophia, 167, 168
Susanna, 209
William, 165,
166, 167, 168
William Pitt,
168
Zephaniah, 168
RIDGEWAY,
William, 168
RIDOUT,
Ann Weems, 218
RIELY,
John, 197
John A., 148
William, 197
RIFFLE,
Jacob, 168
RIGBY,
Anne Ridgely,
168
James Townly,
168
RIGGS,
Achsah, 20
Achsah Fowler,
69
Elisha, 127,
147, 159, 169,
205
James, 169
Lynon, 169
Ninian, 69
Rachel, 208,
209, 212
Rebbecca Boone
Howard, 99

RIGOREY,
Michell, 68
RILEY,
James, 169
Lawrence, 169
Mark, 169
Thomas, 169
RINGGOLD,
Joseph, 26
RINGROSE,
James, 197
RISTON,
Ann, 109
Henry, 163
RITCHIE,
Benjamin, 169
ROBERTS,
Edwaqrd, 169
Elizabeth, 200
Henry, 169
John, 232
Joseph, 169, 197
Richard, 64, 169
William, 64, 169
Zachariah, 64
ROBERTSON,
Ann, 165
Delilah, 170
Elizabeth, 170
James, 170
Margaret, 170
Matilda, 170
Polly, 210
Pruda, 170
Rachel, 170
Rachel Howard,
100
William, 169
Zachariah, 170
ROBINSON,
Ann, 170
Ann Talbott, 194
Benjamin, 170
Charles, 80, 170
David, 170
Elijah, 194
Elizabeth, 170
George, 170
Hamilton, 170
Hampton, 170
Hugh, 68
James, 170
Jane, 172
John, 172
Lawrence, 170

Patrick, 170
Priscilla, 4
Richard, 170
Samuel, 232
Sarah Jacob, 107
Sophia, 170
Thomas, 170
ROBISON,
John, 171
ROBOSSON,
Ann, 171
Charles, 171
Comfort, 39
Dorsey, 171
Elijah, 5, 9, 12,
15, 16, 17, 18,
25, 30, 37, 43,
63, 65, 67, 71,
74, 80, 81, 85,
92, 93, 94, 96,
106, 107, 109,
113, 116, 119,
121, 122, 124,
125, 126, 127,
128, 129, 131,
132, 133, 135,
136, 138, 139,
141, 144, 147,
157, 159, 160,
165, 166, 171,
172, 177, 180,
187, 190, 194,
199, 200, 205,
206, 211, 213,
217, 231
Elizabeth, 171
George, 171
John, 171
Mary, 171
Obed, 171
Oneil, 171
Polly, 210
Rebecca, 171
Richard, 136, 171
Sarah, 171
Thomas, 171
Vachel, 171
ROBSON,
John, 171
ROBUCK,
William, 171
ROCKHOLD,
Charles, 172
Charlotte, 121
Clark, 172

INDEX

Elizabeth, 172
Jane, 172
John, 172
Mary, 172
Rachel, 172
Sarah, 172
Solorah, 172
Thomas, 172
Thomas Clarke, 172
Thomas Fields, 172
ROGERS,
  Agnes, 72, 73, 74
  Ann, 172
  Ann Marie, 153
  Catherine, 172
  Charles, 172
  Etta, 65
  James W., 73
  John, 172
  Joseph, 197
  Mary, 172
  Mary Ann Truman, 201
  Nicholas G., 172
  Samuel, 172
  William, 172
ROLES,
  Elizabeth Jacob, 107
ROLF,
  Basil, 149
ROSS,
  George, 172
  Robertson, 64
ROURKE,
  Michael, 197
ROUSBATCH,
  Samuel, 172
ROWAN,
  Elizabeth Howard, 101
ROWDON,
  John, 172
ROWE,
  James, 197
  Robert, 64
ROWLAND,
  James, 172
ROWLES,
  William, 172
ROWLEY,
  John, 68, 197

RUKETTS,
  Thomas, 165
RULEY,
  Anne, 72, 73
RUSH,
  Benjamin, 214
RUSSELL,
  Benjamin, 172
  James, 172
  Jane, 172
  Jemima, 173
  John, 197
  Keziah, 172
  Mary, 173
  Providence, 173
  Richard, 173
  Sarah, 173
  William, 173
RUTLAND,
  Margaret Howard, 100
RYAN,
  Charity, 105
  Jacob, 173
  Mary, 212
  Nathan, 173
  Rebecca, 150
  Robert, 173
RYLY,
  Mark, 169
RYOM,
  William, 173

-S-

SAFFELL,
  T. R., 27
  W. T. R., 65, 204
ST. LAURANS,
  William, 173
ST. LAWRENCE,
  Francis, 173
  William, 173
SALLY,
  William, 173
SAND,
  Gabriel, 173
SANDALL,
  John, 27, 204
SANDERS,
  Anne Darby, 41
  Edward, 173
  James, 173
  Lydia Darby, 41
  William, 173

SANDS,
  Delilah, 173
  Eliza, 174
  Jane, 174
  John, 173
  Robert, 174
  Thomas, 174
  Washington, 174
  William, 174
SANK,
  George, 136, 174
SANKS,
  Anne Ijams, 104
SANSBERRY,
  Richard, 174
SAPPINGTON,
  Ann, 174
  Anne Ridgely, 166
  Caleb, 174
  Caroline, 174
  Edward, 174
  Elizabeth, 174
  Francis Brown, 174
  Frederick, 174
  Gerrard, 174
  John, 174
  John K., 174
  Mark B., 40
  Martha, 174
  Mary, 174
  Nathaniel, 174
  Rebecca, 174
  Richard, 174, 175
  Robert, 174
  Thomas, 174, 175, 197
  William, 174
SAUNDERS,
  Elizabeth, 175
  James, 175
  John, 175
SAVAGE,
  William, 175
SAVORY,
  Philip, 175
SAWYER,
  Richard, 175
SCHARF,
  J. Thomas, 158
SCHMID Ann, 52
SCHMUCK,
  Ellen Kilty, 114
SCOOT,
  Richard, 175
  William, 197

INDEX

SCOTT,
  Adam, 175
  Alexander, 175, 197
  Ann Wood, 229
  David, 175
  George, 175
  Henry, 175
  John, 175
  John Day, 76
  Mary, 151
  Mary Ann Phelps, 151
SCREVENER,
  Mary Russell, 173
  Vansant, 173
SCRIVENER,
  Francis, 176
  George, 176
  John, 176
  Mary, 176
  Thomas, 176
SCRIVENOR,
  Francis, 176
  John, 176
  Lewis, 176
  Richard, 176
  Robert, 176
  William, 176
SCRIVNOR,
  Robert, 194
SEALY,
  Nancy Darby, 41
SEARCY,
  Milly, 36
SEARLES,
  Daniel, 176
SEARS,
  John, 136, 141, 176
  Mary, 176
  Noah, 64
SEDGWICK,
  Dorcas, 110
SEFTON,
  Charles, 176
  Edmond, 176
  Edward, 176
  Elizabeth, 176
  James, 176
  John, 176
  Maria, 176
  Mary Harwood, 91
  Richard, 176

Sarah, 176
Thomas, 176
William, 176, 177
SELBY,
  Ann, 177
  Benjamin, 177
  Elizabeth, 177
  Henry, 135, 177
  Jemima, 177
  Jemina, 58
  Jonathan, 177
  Joseph, 177
  Margaret Ijams, 104
  Mary, 177
  Mordecai, 177
  Nicholas, 177
  Polly, 177
  Rebecca, 177
  Sarah, 177
  Susan, 177
SELLMAN,
  Alfred, 177, 178
  Ann, 178
  Ann (Elizabeth), 177
  Ann Elizabeth Harwood, 90
  Charlotte, 177
  Gassaway, 177
  John, 65, 169, 177
  John H., 178
  John Henry, 177
  Jonathan, 64, 68, 177, 178, 197, 216
  Leonard, 75, 178
  Margaret, 75, 177
  Patty, 177
  Richard, 177, 178
  William, 178, 183
SELMAN,
  Leonard, 24
SEPTON,
  John, 176
SEWALL,
  Clement, 64
SEWARD,
  Daniel, 178
SEWELL,
  Achsah, 179
  Augustin, 178
  Augustus, 178
  Benjamin, 178

Charles, 178
Eleanor, 178
Elizabeth Sappington, 174
George, 178
Greenbury, 178
James, 178
John, 179
John M., 178
Joseph, 179
Mary, 179
Philip, 179
Rebecca, 179
Sarah, 179
Vachel, 179
William, 179
SHAAFF,
  Arthur, 179
  John T., 179
  John Thomas, 179
SHADDOWS,
  David, 179
SHADWICK,
  Rebecca Penn, 150
  William, 68
SHANKS,
  Ann, 180
  John, 179
SHANLEY,
  Jacob, 180
SHARPE,
  Capt., 104
SHAW,
  George, 180
  James, 180
  John, 180
  Mary, 180
  Thomas, 180
SHEAN,
  Timothy, 180
SHEARBUT,
  Benjamin Battee, 180
  Richard, 180
  Thomas, 180
SHECKELLS,
  John, 180
  Samuel, 180
SHEDBOLT,
  William, 180
SHEETS,
  Martin, 181
SHEKELL,
  Abraham, 181
  Elizabeth, 181

Francis, 181
John, 181
Mary, 181
Mary Burgess, 22
Richard, 181
Samuel, 181
SHELDA,
 Christopher, 181
SHELLAY,
 Daniel, 68
SHEPARD,
 Henry, 181
SHEPHERD,
 Mary Owens, 146
 Nathaniel, 181
 Nicholas, 136
SHEPPARD,
 Nicholas, 181
SHEPPERD,
 Thomas, 181
SHEREEN,
 William, 90
SHERIDAN,
 Thomas, 64
SHIPLEY,
 Adam, 181, 182
 Ann, 182
 Anna M. Howard, 100
 Benjamin, 47, 181
 Catherine, 7
 Denton, 183
 Elias, 183
 Elizabeth, 119, 182
 Enos, 182
 George, 82, 181
 Greenbury, 182
 Henry, 182
 John, 41, 136, 182
 Joshua, 182, 183
 Ketura, 6
 Larkin, 182
 Patience, 7
 Peggy, 182
 Peter, 182
 Polly, 182
 Rezin, 182
 Richard, 182
 Richardson, 182
 Robert, 130, 182, 183
 Samuel, 182
Sarah, 182
Sarah Warfield, 206
Talbot, 82, 183
Thomas, 183
Vachel, 183
William, 7, 183, 225
SHOBROOK,
 Philip, 183
SHOEBROOK,
 Philip, 183
SHOEMAKER,
 Gideon, 183
SHORT,
 Abraham, 183
SHOUGHNESS,
 Patrick, 204
SHOUGHNESSEY,
 ---, 183
SHRINK,
 Andrew, 27, 183, 204
SHRIVENOR,
 John, 64
SHULES,
 Thomas, 183
SHULMEAR,
 Peter, 197
SIEBERT,
 Justice, 183
SILENCE,
 Susanna Anderson, 2
SIM,
 Patrick, 64
SIMMONS,
 Abraham, 94, 135, 136, 139, 183, 218
 Agnes, 88
 Ann Childs, 33
 David, 183
 Elizabeth, 184
 George, 184
 Isaac, 33, 184
 James, 184
 Jeremiah Chapman, 184
 Jerome Chapman, 184
 John, 68, 184, 197
 Margaret, 184
 Marianna Weems,
219
 Martha, 199
 Matilda Tillard, 199
 Richard, 184
 William, 57, 126, 136, 184, 188, 219
SIMMS,
 Jesse, 64
SIMON,
 Joseph, 184
SIMPSON,
 Amos, 184
 Benjamin, 184
 Charles, 184
 Francis, 184
 Greenbury, 185
 Henrietta Worthington, 229
 Jane Burgess, 23
 Mary, 96
 Matilda Burgess, 22
 Rebecca Warfield, 208
 Sarah Worthington, 229
 William, 185
SIMS,
 Patrick, 165
 Thomas, 68
SKELLE,
 William, 185
SKELLY,
 Daniel, 185
 William, 185
SKIDMORE,
 Sophia, 203
SKIFFINGTON,
 Roger, 64, 185
SKINNER,
 James, 158
 James J., 87
 James John, 185
 John, 185
SLACK,
 John, 64, 185
SLICER,
 Andrew, 231
SLIGH,
 William, 185
SLIGHT,
 John, 185
SLY,

INDEX

John, 185
SLYE,
  John, 185
  William, 185
SMALLWOOD,
  --, 145
  ---, 78
  Col., 149
  Gen., 67, 193
  William, 22,
    143, 186, 196,
    204, 205, 208
SMART,
  Jonas, 185
SMITH,
  Anthony, 185
  Caroline
    Harwood, 91
  Col., 216
  Conrad, 68
  Cosman, 186
  Elizabeth, 147
  George, 186
  Gilbert
    Hamilton, 136,
    186
  Henry, 186
  James, 27, 186,
    197
  John, 27, 64,
    142, 186, 197
  Joseph, 186, 197
  Lab C., 197
  Margaretta Clare
    Brice, 18
  Michael, 187
  Nancy Warfield,
    209
  Nathan, 187, 197
  Nathaniel, 1,
    54, 67
  Philemon, 187
  Reuben, 68
  Rezin, 187
  Richard, 187
  Robert, 136
  Robert John, 187
  Samuel, 187
  Sarah, 186
  Thomas, 68, 187,
    204
  Valentine, 64,
    187
  William, 187,
    197

SMITHE,
  Robert, 187
SMOOT,
  William, 64
SNAIRN,
  Lewis, 188
SNOW,
  Charles, 188
SNOWDEN,
  Anna Maria, 188
  Elizabeth, 33
  Elizabeth
    Warfield, 208
  Gerard A., 188
  Gerard H., 188
  John, 148, 188
  John T., 188
  Laura Victoria
    Warfield, 208
  Margaret H., 188
  Rachel, 188
  Rezin A., 188
  Richard, 33
  Richard P., 188
  Susanna, 49
  Thomas, 147, 188
SOLLARS,
  Jacob, 188
  Robert, 188
SOLLERS,
  Abraham, 188
  Jacob, 188
  Robert, 188
SORRELL,
  John, 188
SOUTH,
  Alexander, 64,
    188
SOUTHER,
  Pheltr, 188
  Valentine, 188
SPARKS,
  Richard, 188
SPARROW,
  Matilda, 22
  Thomas, 188
SPEAKE,
  Francis, 188
SPEDDEN,
  Levin, 78, 145
SPENCE,
  Mary Clare
    Maccubbin, 30
SPENCER,
  Charles, 188

SPICER,
  William, 189
SPICKNELL,
  William, 189
SPINKS,
  Rawleight, 27
SPRIGG,
  Catherine Wallace,
    205
  John, 189
  Lucy, 53
  Margaret, 54
  Rachel, 90, 91
  Richard, 189
  Thomas, 189
SPULMIRE,
  Peter, 68
SPURRIER,
  Aaron, 189
  Deborah Burgess,
    22
  Edward, 4, 12, 13,
    41, 63, 68, 101,
    121, 124, 127,
    147, 163, 164,
    173, 189, 197,
    220, 223
  Green, 189
  Joseph, 189, 227
  Joshua John, 189
  Phoebe Burgess, 22
  Rezin, 22
  Thomas, 189
  William, 35, 136,
    189
STACK,
  Samuel, 189
STALKER,
  George, 189
STALLINGS,
  John, 148
  Lancelot, 189
STALLIONS,
  John, 190
STANLEY,
  John, 27
STANSBURY,
  Eleanor Foreman,
    67
  Elisha, 190
  Patience, 39
STANTON,
  John, 190
STEAD,
  William, 197

INDEX

STEARN,
  John, 223
STEEL,
  Elisha, 64
  John, 190
STELL,
  John, 190
STEPHEN,
  Julianna Brice, 18
STEPHENS,
  Benjamin, 190
  Dennis, 60
STERLING,
  William, 64
STERRETT,
  John, 190
STEUART,
  David, 190
  James, 190
  Robert, 190
STEVEN,
  Vachel, 23
STEVENS,
  Benjamin, 191
  Charles, 190
  Dawson, 190
  John, 190
  Lewis, 190
  Nancy Warfield, 209
  Rezin, 190
  Vachel, 6, 8, 182, 191
  William, 191, 197
STEVENSON,
  Aaron, 191
STEWARD,
  Alice, 56
  James, 56
  Major, 88, 98
  Robert, 136
  Stephen, 191
STEWART,
  Ann Selby, 177
  Caleb, 191
  Charles, 191
  Charles R., 170
  David, 191
  Edward, 177
  Hannah, 170
  Hugh, 54
  James, 193
  John, 36

John N., 191
Louisa Harwood, 91
Maria Harwood, 91
Mary Gassaway, 76
Rebecca Reynolds, 163
Rhody, 87
Richard, 197
Robert, 191
Sarah, 170
Stephen, 141, 191
STOAKS,
  Patrick, 191
STOCKETT,
  Ann, 192
  Anne Ijams, 103
  Eleanor, 192
  Helen, 192
  Henry, 192
  John, 192
  John Shaaf, 192
  Joseph N., 178
  Joseph Noble, 192
  Katharine, 192
  Katherine, 192
  Lewis, 192
  Margaret, 192
  Mary, 192
  Mary Harwood, 192
  Rebecca, 192
  Richard, 192
  Richard G., 83
  Richard Galen, 192
  Thomas, 192
  Thomas Mifflin, 192
  Thomas Noble, 91, 136, 192
  William Ijams, 192
  William Shippen, 192
STOCKSTER,
  John, 192
STOKES,
  Patrick, 197
STONE,
  Anne, 192
  Cassandra Wood, 229
  Col., 19, 25, 26
  Couden, 192
  David, 192

Elizabeth, 192
J. H., 144, 190
John, 192
John Hoskins, 192
Lt. Col., 13
Robert Couden, 192
Thomas, 193
STONER,
  Samuel, 193
STOREY,
  Solomon, 193
STOVER,
  Samuel, 193
STRACHAN,
  Margaret, 91
STREET,
  James, 68
  Samuel, 197
STRINGER,
  Elizabeth Dorsey, 54
  Lucy, 166, 167
  Lydia, 55
  Richard, 12, 113, 135, 136, 167, 189, 193
STRUM,
  Israel, 193
STRUTT,
  George, 68
STUARD,
  Benjamin, 64
STUART,
  James, 68, 193
  Robert, 68
STURT,
  George, 193
SUELL,
  John, 68
SULLIVAN,
  John, 64, 193
  Matilda Dorsey, 55
  Sarah, 228
SUMMERLAND,
  William, 193
SUNDERLAND,
  Benjamin, 228
  Dorothy, 228
  Elizabeth, 228
  Rebecca Ijams, 103
SUNER,
  Matthias, 202
SUTER,
  Sarah Dorsey, 54
SUTHERLAND,

INDEX

SUTHERLAND,
  William, 64, 193
SUTTON,
  Thomas, 193
  William, 194
SWAIN,
  Isaac, 194
SWAN,
  John, 194
  William, 64
SWANARD,
  John, 194
SWANN,
  Barton, 64
  John Thomas, 194
SWENNEY,
  Dennis, 68
SWIVNOR,
  Robert, 194
SYBLE,
  Henry, 194
SYKES,
  William, 194
SYNG,
  Deborah, 164

-T-

TAGUE,
  Richard, 68
TALBOT,
  Benjamin, 136
  Coxon, 64
  Richard, 12, 15, 31, 43, 67, 71, 77, 110, 112, 125, 128, 152, 175, 178, 221
  Sarah Dorsey, 48
TALBOTT,
  Ann, 194
  Benjamin, 194
  Edward, 194
  Elisha, 194
  James, 194
  Richard, 194, 195
  Sarah, 194
  Temperance Merryman, 194
  Thomas, 194
TALOR,
  Samuel, 195
TAME,
  Edward, 195
TANGUARY,
  Abraham, 195
TARVEY,
  Thomas, 195
TASKER,
  Anne, 144
TAYLARD,
  William, 199
TAYLOE,
  Ann Ogle, 144
TAYLOR,
  Aquila, 64
  Edward, 195
  Elizabeth, 228
  Griffith, 197
  James, 195
  John, 64, 195, 197, 204
  Joseph, 103
  Ludowick, 64
  Robert, 64
  Samuel, 195
  Samuel Caleb, 195
  Sega, 195
  Snowden, 195, 197
  Solomon, 195
  sophia, 151
  Susanna, 103
  Sydney, 195
  Thomas, 195
  William, 64, 195, 196
TEARN,
  Joseph, 196
TELLOTT,
  Sarah, 220
TERRENCE,
  William, 196
THACKARD,
  Rezin, 196
THACKREL,
  Nicholas, 196
THOMAS,
  Anne Warfield, 208
  Ebenezer, 67
  Ellis, 197
  Evan, 197
  James, 65, 197
  Jeremiah, 197
  Jerre, 197
  John, 16, 197
  Mary Anne, 87
  Mary Howard, 100
  Otho, 198
  Philip, 164, 197, 225
  Thomas, 64, 197
THOMPSON,
  Alexander, 198
  Catherine, 151
  Elizabeth, 111
  Francis, 198
  Jesse, 27
  John, 198
  Joseph, 64
  Laurance, 68
  Richard, 198
  Robert, 198, 204
  Samuel, 204
  Thomas, 64
  William, 198
THOMSON,
  Samuel, 198
THORNTON,
  Joseph, 198
  Samuel, 198
  Sarah Ann, 213
  William, 198
THORPE,
  John, 198
TIDINGS,
  Caleb, 203
  Calib, 68
TILDEN,
  Louisa Harvey Howard, 100
TILGHMAN,
  Margaret, 28
TILLARD,
  Ann, 199
  Edward, 2, 10, 12, 17, 33, 36, 38, 43, 44, 45, 56, 70, 77, 108, 111, 117, 124, 134, 135, 148, 156, 174, 184, 185, 188, 192, 195, 198, 202, 215, 221, 223
  Elizabeth, 198
  John Hamilton, 199
  Matilda, 199
  Sarah, 199
  Thomas, 199
  Thomas Hamilton, 199
  William, 199
  William Smallwood, 199

INDEX

TIMMONS,
  William, 64
TIMS,
  John, 199
TINDALE,
  Samuel, 199
TINDALL,
  Samuel, 199
TIPPET,
  Notley, 64
TISER,
  James, 197, 199
TODD,
  Alexander, 199
  Caroline
    Ridgely, 167
  John, 199
  Lancelot, 199
  Mary, 199
  Nicholas Dorsey,
    53
  Rezin, 199
  Rhesa, 199
  Richard, 199
  Ruth, 23, 52, 54
  Sarah, 48, 49,
    50, 52, 54, 172
  Thomas, 199
TODDD,
  Ruth, 50
TOFT,
  Eleanor, 199
  John, 199
  Mary, 199
  Thomas, 199
TONER,
  J. M., 192
TONGUE,
  Elizabeth, 200
  Thomas, 113,
    135, 136, 200
TOOTEL,
  Dr., 193
  James, 136
TOOTELL,
  Ann, 200
  Dr., 191
  Hellen, 200
  James, 133, 135,
    175, 187, 200,
    210, 211, 212,
    232
  Richard, 200
  Rosanna, 200
TOPHOUSE,

Thomas, 200
TOPPING,
  John, 200
  Peter, 197, 200
TOWBAIRN,
  Benjamin, 138
TOWNSEND,
  William, 200
TOWNSHEND,
  William, 197
TRACEY,
  Robert, 200
TRIG,
  Samuel, 65
TRIGG,
  Charles, 200
TRIGGS,
  Margaret, 149
TROTT,
  Allison, 201
  Elizabeth, 201
  Ester, 201
  James, 201
  John, 200
  Nancy, 201
  Rebecca, 201
  Sabret, 200
  Sarah, 201
  Thomas, 201
TROY,
  John, 197
TRUEMAN,
  John, 201
TRUMAN,
  Alexander, 3, 35,
    43, 66, 101,
    112, 140, 142,
    156, 162, 164,
    187, 201, 206,
    221, 225
  Alexander M., 201
  Henry, 201
  James, 206
  John, 197, 201
  Margaret
    Reynolds, 164
  Mary Ann, 201
  Thomas, 201
TUCK,
  William, 201
TUCKER,
  Abel, 202
  Ann, 45, 201
  Eleanor Rawlings,
    161

Isaac, 201
James, 45, 201
Jane, 202
John, 64, 201
Joseph, 201
Mary Ann, 202
Nancy, 202
Rachel, 202
Sarah, 26, 201,
  202
Seaborn, 201
Susannah, 163
Thomas, 201, 202
William, 64, 201,
  202
Zachariah, 161,
  202
TUMBLERT,
  Eleanor Davidson,
    42
TUNER,
  Matthias, 202
  Michael, 71
TURNER,
  Abraham, 202
  Abram, 202
  Anne Stone, 192
  Johanna, 202
  John, 202, 204
  Joseph, 202
  Richard, 202
  Thomas, 68, 197,
    202
  William, 202
  Zachariah, 202
  Zephaniah, 202
TWINER,
  John, 203
TWINING,
  Nathaniel, 197
TYDIE,
  William, 203
TYDINGS,
  Ann, 203
  Caleb, 197, 203
  Catherine, 203
  Cele, 203
  Ferdinando, 203
  Horatio, 203
  John, 203
  Kealey, 203
  Mary Mullikin, 140
  Richard, 203
  Samuel, 203
  Sarah, 186

INDEX

TYLER,
  Jervis, 203
  Susanna, 58
-U-
UNCLES,
  Benjamin, 203
  Rebecca, 203
-V-
VALLETTE,
  Elie, 203
VALLIANT,
  Nicholas, 204
VAN BEBBER,
  Elizabeth Hill
  Dorsey, 48
VANSANT,
  John, 204
VAUBRAN,
  John, 204
VENNOM,
  Ray, 204
VERNON,
  Belinda, 77
VINALL,
  Richard, 204
VINEM,
  Ray, 204

-W-
WAASHOLE,
  John, 209
  Zion, 209
WADE,
  Nancy Howard,
  101
  William, 204
WAIGHT,
  Thomas, 205
WAINWRIGHT,
  Jacob, 153
WALDRON,
  Joseph, 197
WALDRUM,
  Joseph, 205
WALKER,
  Ariana Hammond,
  85
  Gideon, 205
  James, 135, 205
  John, 180, 205
  Joseph, 205
  Matilda, 31
  Thomas, 158

WALLACE,
  Anne, 205
  Catherine, 205
  Charles, 26, 128,
  205
  George, 205
  Hugh, 64
  John, 205
  Michael, 205
WALLER,
  Susan, 170
WALLINGSFORD,
  James, 68, 197
WALLINGSFORT,
  James, 206
WALSH,
  David, 204, 206
  Edmond, 206
  Robert, 158
WALSTON,
  Boaz, 206
WARD,
  Benjamin, 130,
  206
  Elizabeth, 206
  Elizabeth
  Whittington, 224
  Igantius, 64
  Ignatius, 64
  John, 206, 224
  Samuel, 206
  Sarah, 176, 206
  Sarah E., 206
  Thomas, 64, 206
  West, 206
  William, 206
  Yate, 206
WARDEN,
  Jacob, 206
WARFIELD,
  Absolom, 208
  Achsah, 208
  Achsah Dorsey, 53
  Aldred, 207
  Alexander, 22,
  207, 208, 209,
  211, 212
  Alfred, 207
  Allen, 210, 211,
  212, 213
  Amelia, 208, 211
  Amelia Ridgely,
  168
  Amos, 212
  Ann, 13, 22, 206,
  208
  Ann Gassaway, 75
  Ann Rogers, 172
  Ann Stockett, 192
  Anne, 207, 208
  Anne Warfield, 208
  Araminta, 209
  Arnold, 209
  Asel, 207
  Azel, 206, 207,
  208, 212, 213
  Bani, 207
  Basil, 208
  Beale, 207
  Bela, 212
  Beni, 207, 212
  Benjamin, 5, 135,
  136, 148, 207,
  208, 209, 210,
  211, 212
  Brice, 207, 209
  Caleb, 207, 210
  Calife, 208
  Catherine, 207,
  209, 212
  Catherine Burgess,
  22
  Catherine D., 168
  Catherine Dorsey,
  50
  Charles, 136, 208,
  210, 211, 213,
  226
  Charles A., 206
  Charles Alexander,
  113, 207, 208
  Charles Dorsey,
  207
  Charles M., 209
  Charlotte, 210
  Daniel, 207
  Davidge, 23, 208
  Deborah, 22
  Dinah, 48, 207,
  208
  Edmond, 208, 211
  Edward, 208, 209,
  212
  Eleanor, 207, 208,
  210
  Eleanor (Nelly),
  209
  Eli, 212
  Elisha, 209
  Eliza, 206

INDEX

Elizabeth, 29, 100, 109, 166, 206, 207, 208, 209, 210, 211, 212
Elizabeth (Betsy), 209
Elizabeth Dorsey, 53, 55, 210
Elizabeth Ridgely, 166
Ephraim, 208, 209, 211
Evan, 210
Fielder, 208
Frances Dorsey Chapman, 53
George Fraser, 207
George Hanson, 209
George W., 168, 206
Gerard, 212
Greenbury Ridgely, 212
Gustavus, 208
Harriet, 210
Henrietta, 213
Henry, 206, 208, 209, 210
Henry Ridgely, 208
James, 208, 209
James Henry, 209
Jemina Dorsey, 52
John, 208, 209, 210, 211, 212
John W., 209, 210
John Worthington, 209
John X., 209
Joseph, 135, 136, 164, 210
Joshua, 207, 210, 212
Juliet, 210
Kitty, 208
Laban, 209
Lancelot, 135, 136, 210, 211

Larkin, 212
Laura Victoria, 208
Lemuel, 210, 211
Leven, 208
Lloyd, 212
Luke, 211
Luther, 209
Lydia, 211
Margaret, 207
Margarey Gaither Brown, 72
Marion, 207
Mary, 206, 208, 210, 211, 212, 213
Mary Ann, 55, 208, 212
Mary Ann Warfield, 212
Matilda, 206, 208
Nancy, 209
Nicholas, 209, 212
Nicholas Dorsey, 207, 210
Nicholas Ridgely, 23, 105, 211
Peregrine, 208
Philemon, 69, 135, 136, 210, 211, 212, 229
Philemon Dorsey, 207, 212
Philip, 127, 208, 211
Polly, 208, 209, 211
Polly Penn, 150
Polly Warfield, 208
Prestley, 208
Rachel, 53, 207, 208, 209, 210, 211
Rebecca, 208, 212
Rebecca Burgess, 24
Richard, 206, 209, 210, 211, 212
Ridgely, 212
Robert, 95, 136, 189, 208, 209, 212

Ruth, 209, 211
Ruth Burgess, 23
Ruth Welsh, 221
Sally, 209
Samuel, 136, 209, 212
Sarah, 23, 52, 61, 74, 80, 206, 207, 208, 209, 210, 211, 213
Sarah (Susanna), 207
Seth, 200, 206, 207, 208, 212
Silvanus, 116
Singleton, 208
Surrat Dickerson, 207
Susanna, 207
Thomas, 135, 136, 207, 208, 210, 212, 221
Thomas J., 183
Tilghman, 208
Vachel, 212, 213
Walter, 64, 135, 207, 213
Welsh, 212
William, 206, 211, 213
William R., 168
Zachariah, 207
Zadock, 207
WARING,
 Sarah M. Dorsey, 48
WARNER,
 Joseph, 213
WARREN,
 Basil, 83
WARRICK,
 James, 68
 William, 68
WARWICK,
 James, 197, 213
 William, 197
WASHINGTON,
 George, 63, 115, 128, 145, 163, 164, 180, 201
WASHSINGTON,
 George, 68
WASON,
 John, 213

INDEX

WATERMAN,
  Phyllis, 213
WATERS,
  Ann Janette
    Davidson, 42
  Anne, 2
  Anne Warfield,
    207
  Aquilla, 213
  Asenah
    (Asseneth), 211
  Cephas, 60
  Clarissa Dorsey,
    53
  Edward, 213
  Elizabeth, 214
  Elizabeth
    Warfield, 209
  Elizabeth Wells,
    220
  Ezekiel, 213
  Henry, 213
  James L., 213
  John, 213
  John Wilson, 214
  Jonathan, 213,
    214
  Joseph, 213, 214
  Josephus, 213
  Juliana, 213
  Margaret, 214
  Maria Louisa,
    214
  Martha, 140, 214
  Mary, 103, 213,
    214
  Mary Edwards,
    59, 60
  Nancy, 207
  Nathan, 213, 214
  Nicholas B., 213
  Ramsay, 214
  Rebecca
    Lawrence, 118
  Richard, 64
  Robert, 214
  Sally, 207
  Sarah (Susanna)
    Warfield, 207
  Sarah Ann Mayo,
    129
  Susannah
    Gaither, 72
  Thomas Gassaway,
    213
  William, 214
  William
    Montgomery, 214
  William Thornton,
    213
  Wilson, 33, 214
WATKIN,
  Thomas, 46
WATKINS,
  Aaron, 214
  Ann, 215
  Anne, 90, 91
  Anne Harwood, 91
  Ariana, 103
  Arthur, 216
  Benjamin, 215
  Capt., 5, 9, 19,
    25, 26, 83, 88,
    89, 92, 101,
    104, 217
  Charles, 215
  Eleanor, 215
  Eleanor Harwood,
    91
  Eleanor Stockett,
    192
  Elizabeth, 83,
    215
  Frances, 216
  Gassaway, 215,
    216
  Gassaway
    Chambers, 215
  Hannah, 216
  Harriet, 216
  Harriet Ann, 216
  Harriet Burgess,
    24
  James, 197, 216
  Jeremiah, 215
  John, 49, 215,
    216
  Joseph, 216
  Julianna, 215
  Lafayette, 216
  Leonard, 64
  Manelia, 216
  Margaret, 151,
    203
  Margaret Harwood,
    91
  Nicholas, 103,
    135, 215, 216
  Olive P., 216
  Priscilla, 215
  Rachel, 215
  Rachel Sprigg, 215
  Richard, 216
  Ruth, 11
  Ruth Dorsey, 50
  Samuel, 136, 216
  Sarah, 216
  Stephen, 68, 106,
    215, 216
  Susanna, 103
  Thomas, 17, 19,
    30, 31, 34, 37,
    40, 44, 47, 50,
    58, 60, 61, 70,
    71, 74, 75, 78,
    79, 80, 84, 90,
    91, 93, 103, 108,
    113, 116, 118,
    119, 121, 122,
    126, 127, 129,
    135, 136, 142,
    143, 144, 145,
    147, 150, 153,
    156, 162, 163,
    164, 169, 171,
    182, 184, 185,
    186, 187, 191,
    192, 194, 197,
    199, 203, 204,
    209, 214, 215,
    216, 217, 223,
    225, 226, 230
  Thomas W., 216
  William, 197, 215
  William P., 216
  William Pitt, 216
  William T., 216
WATSON,
  Charles, 217
  David, 217
  Mary, 217
  Samuel, 217
  William, 217
WATTS,
  George, 39, 113,
    114, 124, 135,
    217, 231
  John, 217
  Rebecca, 11
  Richard, 217
  Samuel, 217
WATTSON,
  Joseph, 217
WAUGH,
  Elizabeth, 215

INDEX

WAYMAN,
  Ann, 54
  Edmond, 217
  Hezekiah, 217
WAYSON,
  Mary, 143
WEAKLE,
  Thomas, 217
WEBB,
  Joseph, 197, 217
WEBSTER,
  John, 197
WEDON,
  Joseph, 218
WEEDON,
  Joseph, 218
  Oliver, 218, 221
  Richard, 218
WEEMS,
  Ann, 218
  Anne, 219
  David, 218
  Eleanor, 218
  Elijah, 219
  Elizabeth
    Ridgely, 165
  James, 218
  James Ewell, 219
  John, 13, 14,
    15, 19, 44, 65,
    71, 82, 91,
    102, 107, 110,
    112, 113, 117,
    118, 120, 136,
    160, 176, 183,
    185, 186, 189,
    190, 192, 197,
    198, 199, 200,
    201, 202, 206,
    217, 218, 223,
    224, 228, 232
  John Beale, 218
  Marianna, 219
  Mary, 218
  Priscilla
    Harwood, 90
  Richard, 2, 3,
    4, 5, 10, 32,
    41, 44, 69, 70,
    79, 89, 94,
    102, 110, 117,
    118, 125, 131,
    135, 136, 139,
    141, 159, 178,
    180, 202, 206,
    218, 220, 221,
    226, 227
  Richard Dorsey,
    218
  Sarah, 218
  Sophie, 219
  Thomas, 218
  Thomas Lane, 218
  William, 218, 219
  William Morris,
    219
WEIR,
  Andrew, 219
WELCH,
  Aaron, 219
  Ann (Elizabeth)
    Sellman, 177
  Benjamin, 219
  Catharine, 219
  Elizabeth, 219
  Henry O'Neal, 219
  Jacob, 219
  John, 68, 219
  Mary Anne, 137
  Patrick, 197
  Patty Sellman,
    177
  Priscilla Owens,
    146
  Rachel, 219
  Richard, 219
  Robert, 219
  Sarah, 209, 212
  Thomas, 178
  Upton D., 183
  Zachariah, 219
WELLING,
  Elizabeth, 206
  Henry, 168
  Sarah Ridgely,
    168
  William, 220
WELLS,
  Ann, 220
  Benjamin, 220
  Daniel, 220
  Elizabeth, 220
  Elizabeth
    Warfield, 210
  Floyd, 220
  Frederick, 220
  George, 220
  James, 220
  John, 197, 220
  Matilda, 220
  Nathan, 220
  Nathaniel, 220
  Richard, 220
  Susan, 220
  Susanna, 220
  William, 220, 221
WELSH,
  Aaron, 136, 219
  Ann, 86, 221
  Ann May, 85
  Anne, 221
  Benjamin, 221
  Catherine, 221
  Charles, 221
  Damaris, 192
  Eleanor Warfield,
    210
  Hamutal, 221
  Henry, 221
  Jacob, 219, 221
  Jemima, 59, 104
  John, 197, 221
  Lucretia Dorsey,
    53
  Mary, 221
  Philip, 221
  Rachel, 221
  Razia, 221
  Rispah Randal
    Norman, 143
  Robert, 136, 219,
    221
  Ruth, 221
  Samuel, 221
  Sarah, 209, 212,
    221
WENTWORTH,
  Isaac, 221
WEST,
  Alexander, 64
  Clarissa Dorsey,
    51
  Frederick, 197
  James, 196, 221
  John, 64
WESTALL,
  Jane, 168
WESTEMEY,
  John, 221
WESTENEYS,
  John, 221
WESTLEY,
  Eleanor (Nelly)
    Warfield, 209
  William, 221

INDEX

WESTON,
  Thomas, 221
WHALE,
  Samuel Byer, 232
WHEDON,
  Oliver, 221
WHEELER,
  Caroline Dorsey, 54
  Charles, 222
  Henry, 222
  John, 204
  Luke, 222
WHELAN,
  George, 68
WHETERCROFT,
  William, 223
WHIDDON,
  Oliver, 218
WHIPS,
  Benjamin, 222
  John, 222
  Samuel, 222
WHITCHOASE,
  Joseph, 223
WHITCOMB,
  Robert, 223
WHITE,
  Absolom, 222
  Alfred, 223
  Andrew, 222
  Caleb, 222
  Charles, 35, 222
  David, 204, 222
  Edward, 222
  Elisha, 222
  Elizabeth, 222, 223
  Frances, 223
  Frances Freeland, 223
  Francis, 222
  George, 223
  Gideon, 222
  Horatio, 223
  Isaac, 222
  Isabelle Pinckney, 153
  James, 223
  Jennie, 36
  John, 119, 223
  Jonathan, 64, 223
  Joseph, 25, 223
  Margaret, 223
  Mary Ann, 223
  Nackey, 222
  Polly, 222
  Regancy, 222
  Reuben, 222
  Robert, 223
  Roena, 223
  Samuel, 223
  Sarah, 222
  Sarah Cotter Gassaway, 76
  Thomas, 223
  Vachel, 223
WHITECROFT,
  William, 223
WHITEHOUSE,
  Joseph, 197, 223
WHITHIM,
  William, 223
WHITTINGTON,
  Eleanor, 224
  Elizabeth, 176, 224
  Francis, 223, 224
  James, 224
  John, 224
  Joseph, 173
  Mary, 3, 224, 228
  Sarah Russell, 173
  Susanna, 228
  Thomas, 224
  William, 224
WHITTLE,
  John, 224
WHITTOM,
  William, 224
WHYTE,
  Anne, 91
WIESENTHAL,
  Charles, 12
WIGGINS,
  Jemima Cross, 40
WIGHT,
  Margery, 189
WILBEY,
  John, 224
WILDERMAN,
  Jacob, 197
WILKERSON,
  Richard, 224
  Young, 225
WILKINS,
  Elizabeth Hill Dorsey, 49
  John, 204, 224
  Joseph, 170, 224
  William, 113, 224, 225
WILKINSON,
  Richard, 204, 224
  Young, 27, 204, 225
WILKS,
  Joseph, 225
WILLIAMS,
  Agnes Rogers, 72
  Andrew, 225
  Ann, 87
  Anna, 26
  Anne, 105
  Benjamin, 225
  Betsy Pinckney, 153
  Capt., 36
  Chaney, 225
  Charles, 225
  Col., 178
  Elizabeth, 140
  Isaiah, 225
  Jarvis, 68, 197, 225
  Jeremiah, 225
  John, 64, 68, 72, 98, 197, 225, 226
  Joseph, 226
  Juliet Warfield, 210
  Margaret, 100
  Mary, 2
  Mary Elizabeth, 91
  Moses, 226
  Rachel Foreman Moss, 67
  Richard, 105, 226
  Sally, 87
  Samuel, 226
  Thomas, 27, 68, 226
  William, 68, 226
WILLILAMS,
  Lilburn, 42
WILLIS,
  Daniel, 226
  John, 227
WILLISS,
  John, 68
WILLSHIRE,
  Samuel, 64
WILLSON,

INDEX

Edward, 227
James, 227
Samuel, 227
WILMOTT,
  Frederick, 65
  Robert, 27, 204
WILSON,
  Barney, 64
  Catherine, 213, 214
  Deborah Dorsey, 48
  Edward, 227
  Elizabeth Kilty, 114
  Harriet Dorsey, 51
  Henry, 227
  James, 227
  John, 64, 227
  Mary Hill Dorsey, 51
  Math, 227
  Richard, 227
  Samuel, 227
  Sarah, 162
  William, 197, 227
WILTSHIRE,
  Jonathan, 227
WINCHESTER,
  Sarah Howard, 100
WINDHAM,
  Sarah Lamb, 231
WINSER,
  Samuel Q., 227
WINSTANLY,
  Francis, 197
WINTERBURN,
  John, 227
WOAKLIN,
  Charles, 227
  William, 227
WOLFE,
  Letitia Hood, 97
  Rachel Hood, 97
WOOD,
  Ann, 229
  Anne Hammond, 85
  Benjamin, 228
  Cassandra, 229
  Catherine Dorsey, 53
  Dorsey, 197, 227

Eleanor, 228
Elizabeth, 228
Henry, 228
Hopewell, 228, 229
Isaac, 228
James, 228
Jesse, 228
John, 148, 197, 228
Levi, 228
Mary Ann, 229
Morgan, 228
Obadiah, 228
Robert, 228
Samuel, 228
Sarah, 206, 228
Stewart E., 228
Thomas, 197
William, 64, 68, 197, 228
William M., 228
Willis, 228
Zebedee, 228, 229
WOODIN,
  John, 229
WOODWARD,
  Henry, 229
  Priscilla Owens, 146
  Thomas, 229
  William, 229
WOOLF,
  John, 229
WOOLTON,
  Elizabeth, 176
WOOTTON,
  Thomas, 229
WORDEN,
  William, 141
WORKMAN,
  Elizabeth Dorsey, 51
WORTHINGTON,
  Achsah, 230
  Ann, 208, 231
  Ann Gassaway Warfield, 75
  Anna Howard, 101
  Anne, 48, 51
  Anne Worthington Dorsey, 53
  Ariana, 103, 104
  Benjamin, 229
  Brice, 135

Brice B., 229
Brice J. G., 231
Brice John, 230
Brice Thomas Beale, 229, 230
Catherine, 75, 230
Charles, 108, 218, 230
Charles G., 231
Comfort, 51
Deborah Howard, 100
Elizabeth, 48, 51, 53, 55, 56, 229, 230
Henrietta, 229
Henry, 229, 230
John, 135, 166, 167, 185, 229, 230
John G., 231
John Griffith, 230
Julia, 178
Mary Ann Dorsey, 47
Nath, 230
Nicholas, 2, 3, 6, 8, 9, 10, 11, 12, 13, 16, 18, 20, 22, 24, 25, 26, 27, 30, 31, 32, 33, 36, 39, 41, 42, 43, 47, 48, 59, 61, 65, 66, 67, 69, 72, 73, 74, 75, 77, 78, 80, 82, 83, 84, 85, 86, 92, 96, 97, 98, 99, 100, 101, 104, 108, 109, 111, 112, 113, 116, 120, 121, 122, 123, 124, 125, 127, 130, 132, 134, 135, 136, 137, 140, 145, 146, 147, 148, 150, 151, 152, 154, 155, 156, 161, 164, 166, 167, 168, 170, 173, 174, 175, 176, 177, 178, 179, 184, 190, 191,

195, 196, 199,
200, 209, 210,
211, 212, 217,
218, 219, 222,
223, 225, 226,
227, 229, 230,
231, 232
 Polly, 229
 Polly
 Worthington,
 229
 Rachel, 98, 101
 Samuel, 230
 Sarah, 55, 229,
 230
 Thomas, 1, 2, 5,
 8, 11, 12, 17,
 20, 21, 23, 27,
 30, 34, 35, 37,
 38, 43, 44, 45,
 46, 47, 55, 57,
 58, 62, 63, 69,
 72, 73, 75, 77,
 80, 81, 82, 84,
 85, 86, 88, 95,
 96, 97, 98,
 101, 105, 108,
 109, 112, 113,
 114, 116, 117,
 118, 120, 121,
 124, 125, 126,
 127, 129, 133,
 134, 138, 139,
 140, 145, 150,
 151, 155, 156,
 157, 158, 159,
 160, 162, 163,
 165, 166, 167,
 168, 169, 172,
 173, 175, 181,
 184, 185, 188,
 189, 192, 193,
 198, 203, 206,
 207, 208, 209,
 210, 211, 212,
 213, 214, 217,
 220, 221, 222,
 223, 224, 227,
 229, 230, 231,
 232
 Thomasine, 22,
 209
 Vachel, 231
WRIGHT,
 Benjamin, 231

 Elizabeth, 86
 Mary, 50
 Mary Norwood, 143
 Rebecca, 84
 Thomas, 231
 Thomas H., 143
WYLLBE,
 William, 231
WYNDHAM,
 Sarah, 231
 Thomas, 64, 231
WYVILL,
 William, 231

-Y-

YARNALL,
 Benjamin, 197
YATES,
 Joshua, 231
YEALDHALL,
 Aaron, 231
 Aquila, 232
 Benjamin, 231
 Elijah, 232
 Elizabeth, 232
 Frances, 232
 Frederick, 232
 Gilbert, 231
 Harriet, 231
 Henry, 232
 Joshua, 232
 Robert, 232
 Samuel, 232
 Susanna, 231
 Thomas, 232
 William, 232
YIELDHALL,
 Gilbert, 135, 231
 Rebecca, 73
 Sarah, 73
 William, 232
YOUNG,
 Benjamin, 197,
 233
 Caroline
 Sappington, 174
 Comfort, 233
 Elizabeth
 Ridgely, 166
 James, 106
 Jason, 232
 John, 197, 232
 Joshua, 232, 233
 Lurana, 233
 Mary, 233

 Nathan, 233
 Orpha, 232
 Rachel, 233
 Rebecca Howard,
 101
 Richard, 232, 233
 Robert, 232
 William, 232, 233

Other books by the author:

A Closer Look at St. John's Parish Registers [Baltimore County, Maryland], 1701-1801

A Collection of Maryland Church Records

A Guide to Genealogical Research in Maryland: 5th Edition, Revised and Enlarged

Abstracts of the Ledgers and Accounts of the Bush Store and Rock Run Store, 1759-1771

Abstracts of the Orphans Court Proceedings of Harford County, 1778-1800

Abstracts of Wills, Harford County, Maryland, 1800-1805

Baltimore City [Maryland] Deaths and Burials, 1834-1840

Baltimore County, Maryland, Overseers of Roads, 1693-1793

Bastardy Cases in Baltimore County, Maryland, 1673-1783

Bastardy Cases in Harford County, Maryland, 1774-1844

Bible and Family Records of Harford County, Maryland Families: Volume V

Children of Harford County: Indentures and Guardianships, 1801-1830

Colonial Delaware Soldiers and Sailors, 1638-1776

*Colonial Families of the Eastern Shore of Maryland
Volumes 5, 6, 7, 8, 9, 11, 12, 13, 14, and 16*

Colonial Maryland Soldiers and Sailors, 1634-1734

Dr. John Archer's First Medical Ledger, 1767-1769, Annotated Abstracts

Early Anglican Records of Cecil County

*Early Harford Countians, Individuals Living in Harford County, Maryland in Its Formative Years
Volume 1: A to K, Volume 2: L to Z, and Volume 3: Supplement*

Harford County Taxpayers in 1870, 1872 and 1883

Harford County, Maryland Divorce Cases, 1827-1912: An Annotated Index

Heirs and Legatees of Harford County, Maryland, 1774-1802

Heirs and Legatees of Harford County, Maryland, 1802-1846

Inhabitants of Baltimore County, Maryland, 1763-1774

Inhabitants of Cecil County, Maryland, 1649-1774

Inhabitants of Harford County, Maryland, 1791-1800

Inhabitants of Kent County, Maryland, 1637-1787

*Joseph A. Pennington & Co., Havre De Grace, Maryland Funeral Home Records:
Volume II, 1877-1882, 1893-1900*

Maryland Bible Records, Volume 1: Baltimore and Harford Counties

Maryland Bible Records, Volume 2: Baltimore and Harford Counties

Maryland Bible Records, Volume 3: Carroll County

Maryland Bible Records, Volume 4: Eastern Shore

Maryland Deponents, 1634-1799

Maryland Deponents: Volume 3, 1634-1776

*Maryland Public Service Records, 1775-1783: A Compendium of Men and Women of
Maryland Who Rendered Aid in Support of the American Cause against
Great Britain during the Revolutionary War*

*Marylanders to Carolina: Migration of Marylanders to
North Carolina and South Carolina prior to 1800*

Marylanders to Kentucky, 1775-1825

Methodist Records of Baltimore City, Maryland: Volume 1, 1799-1829

Methodist Records of Baltimore City, Maryland: Volume 2, 1830-1839

Methodist Records of Baltimore City, Maryland: Volume 3, 1840-1850 (East City Station)

More Maryland Deponents, 1716-1799

More Marylanders to Carolina: Migration of Marylanders to North Carolina and South Carolina prior to 1800

More Marylanders to Kentucky, 1778-1828

Outpensioners of Harford County, Maryland, 1856-1896

Presbyterian Records of Baltimore City, Maryland, 1765-1840

Quaker Records of Baltimore and Harford Counties, Maryland, 1801-1825

Quaker Records of Northern Maryland, 1716-1800

Quaker Records of Southern Maryland, 1658-1800

Revolutionary Patriots of Anne Arundel County, Maryland

Revolutionary Patriots of Baltimore Town and Baltimore County, 1775-1783

Revolutionary Patriots of Calvert and St. Mary's Counties, Maryland, 1775-1783

Revolutionary Patriots of Caroline County, Maryland, 1775-1783

Revolutionary Patriots of Cecil County, Maryland

Revolutionary Patriots of Delaware, 1775-1783

Revolutionary Patriots of Dorchester County, Maryland, 1775-1783

Revolutionary Patriots of Frederick County, Maryland, 1775-1783

Revolutionary Patriots of Harford County, Maryland, 1775-1783

Revolutionary Patriots of Kent and Queen Anne's Counties

Revolutionary Patriots of Lancaster County, Pennsylvania

Revolutionary Patriots of Maryland, 1775-1783: A Supplement

Revolutionary Patriots of Maryland, 1775-1783: Second Supplement

Revolutionary Patriots of Montgomery County, Maryland, 1776-1783

Revolutionary Patriots of Prince George's County, Maryland, 1775-1783

Revolutionary Patriots of Talbot County, Maryland, 1775-1783

Revolutionary Patriots of Worcester and Somerset Counties, Maryland, 1775-1783

Revolutionary Patriots of Washington County, Maryland, 1776-1783

St. George's (Old Spesutia) Parish, Harford County, Maryland: Church and Cemetery Records, 1820-1920

St. John's and St. George's Parish Registers, 1696-1851

Survey Field Book of David and William Clark in Harford County, Maryland, 1770-1812

The Crenshaws of Kentucky, 1800-1995

The Delaware Militia in the War of 1812

Union Chapel United Methodist Church Cemetery Tombstone Inscriptions, Wilna, Harford County, Maryland

www.ingramcontent.com/pod-product-compliance
Lightning Source LLC
Chambersburg PA
CBHW071658160426
43195CB00012B/1506